To Linda,

Happy Birthday 199

Love from

Ann

An Isle called Hirte

History and Culture
of the St Kildans to 1930

An Isle called Hirte

History and Culture of the St Kildans to 1930

MARY HARMAN

MACLEAN PRESS

Published with financial assistance of
The National Trust for Scotland

First published 1997 by Maclean Press,
10 Lusta, Waternish, Isle of Skye IV55 8GD

© 1997 Mary Harman

ISBN 1 899272 08 9

Typeset in 11½/14pt Berkeley

Printed and bound by Cromwell Press Limited

Contents

List of Tables

List of Figures

List of Plates

Acknowledgements

Many people have helped with this work in a number of ways, and it would not be possible to mention everybody here.

I was fortunate in having been accepted by the University of Edinburgh as a postgraduate student in the School of Scottish Studies, and in being awarded a studentship by the Faculty of Arts. While all the staff of the School were very helpful, I wish to mention particularly Ian Fraser, Donald Archie MacDonald, Morag MacLeod and Angela West, and especially Margaret Mackay and John MacInnes, who supervised my research. I am also grateful to the staff of the Celtic Department for welcoming me in the first year Gaelic class. Jill Evans in the Main Library, a St Kilda enthusiast herself, has been particularly helpful.

The pursuit of this work as a postgraduate research project was the idea of Meg Buchanan, formerly of Glasgow Museums and Art Galleries; both she and Iain Buchanan have helped in many other ways, including access to the outstanding collection of material from St Kilda in the museum. Other curators who have kindly allowed me to study material in their care are: J Edwards, City of Aberdeen Museums; Winifred Glover, Ulster Museum, Belfast; David Phillipson, University Museum of Archaeology and Anthropology, Cambridge; D J Robinson, Grosvenor Museum, Chester; in Edinburgh, at the Royal Museum of Scotland: Alison Sheridan and Trevor Cowie, Department of Archaeology, Irene MacKay and David Caldwell, Department of History and Applied Art, Jerry Herman and Bob McGowan, Department of Natural History, David Bryden and Gavin Sprott, Department of Science, Technology and Working Life, and Dorothy Kidd, Scottish Ethnological Archive; Fiona Marwick, West Highland Museum, Fort William; in addition to Meg Buchanan, Richard Sutcliffe at Glasgow Art Gallery and Museum; Donald Bateson and Euan MacKie, Hunterian Museum, Glasgow; all the staff, especially Janet Watson and Steve Moran, in Inverness Museum and Art Gallery; Ross Noble and Janette French, Highland Folk Museum, Kingussie; Tommy Watt, Shetland Museum, Lerwick; Jane Kimber, Bruce Castle Museum, Tottenham, London; K Baker, Oban Library; Linda Mowat, Pitt Rivers Museum, Oxford and R Palmer, Scarborough Museum. Curators at the following museums responded to let me know they had nothing relevant in their collections: Marischal Museum, Aberdeen; Dingwall Museum; Dundee Art Gallery and Museum; Fleetwood, Lancashire County Museum Service; Ulster Folk and Transport Museum, Holywood; Tankerness House Museum, Kirkwall; Museum of Mankind and the National Postal Museum, London; North-East of Scotland Museums Service; Perth Museum and Art Gallery.

I have made extensive use of several libraries, and would like to thank the staffs of: the National Library of Scotland, particularly the Manuscript and Map departments; the library in the Royal Museum of Scotland in Queen Street, formerly the Library of the Society of Antiquaries of Scotland; the Scottish section of Edinburgh City Library; the Western Isles Library in Stornoway and the library of the Scottish Ornithologists Club. I have also found valuable information in the records and papers held by the Scottish Record Office, papers relating to the Kelsall Fund held by the Royal Highland and Agricultural Society of Scotland, the National Monuments Record, and the Duke of Atholl's collection at Blair Castle.

John MacLeod of MacLeod kindly allowed me to look at and use information from the MacLeod of MacLeod Muniments and objects from St Kilda at Dunvegan Castle, and I am grateful to John Lambert, and particularly to Donald Stewart, at the Castle, for their help.

The National Trust for Scotland has a good collection of papers, and I am grateful for access freely given to these and to the collection of artefacts found on the island. Staff in the factorial department have been extremely helpful in giving me access to these and to the islands: Donald Erskine, David MacLehose, Alexander Bennett, Philip Schreiber, John Williamson and Susan Adair.

I am grateful to the following for permission to reproduce material: the Trustees of the National Library of Scotland for permission to use quotations from manuscripts in their care and to reproduce maps based on maps in the Library; the Royal Highland and Agricultural Society of Scotland for quotations from papers in their archives and permission to reproduce figures 52 and 90; The National Trust for Scotland for quotations from manuscripts in their archives; Sir Martin Holdgate for permission to use the quotation at the beginning of Chapter 16; MacLeod of MacLeod for quotations from the MacLeod Muniments and permission to reproduce figure 16; The Society of Antiquaries of Scotland and the Trustees of the National Museums of Scotland for permission to reproduce figure 43.

Plates 12 and 13 are reproduced with permission from Sir John Acland, plates 3, 11, 14, 14, 15, 19, 25, 28, 29, 38, 39, 40, 42, 43, 48, 49 and 52 with permission from the School of Scottish Studies; plates 17, 30, 36, 37 and 41 with permission from the George Washington Wilson Collection, Aberdeen University Library; and plate 31 with permission from Glasgow Museums and Art Gallery.

The modern maps are reproduced from Ordnance Survey mapping with the permission of The Controller of HMSO © Crown Copyright, Licence No.MC85777M.

I have reached St Kilda and other islands by many routes and forms of transport, and in connection with this would like to thank Bruce Howard, Kate and Cubby MacKinnon, the crew of the 'Ocean Bounty', the Seabirds at Sea Team, Donald MacSween, Andy Miller Mundy, Donald Wilkie, and the Royal Corps of Transport, with some of whom I travelled under the aegis of the Nature Conservancy Council.

On the islands, successive wardens employed jointly by the National Trust for Scotland and the Nature Conservancy Council (now Scottish Natural Heritage) have facilitated work: Wally Wright, Peter Moore, David Miller, Jim Ramsay, Jim Vaughan, David Buckland and Rhodri and Annette Evans. Many members of the Royal Artillery Detachment have also helped, in particular Mick Bowe. Facilities provided for visitors by the Detachment, in particular power and piped water, have made fieldwork much easier and pleasanter than it might have been, especially in winter.

I have made new friends among members of National Trust for Scotland work parties and other visitors to the islands, and many of them have helped in this work in different ways, especially Harry Dick, Alisdair Fleming, Frances Gulland, Joe Keppie, Kenny MacDonald, John MacLeod, Jean Reinsch, David Rothe, Jane Ryder, Ian Stevenson, Jeff Stone and George Thomson.

Bill Lawson has also generously shared with me his unparalleled knowledge of the island families. Others who have helped in providing information or discussion are: Mairi MacArthur and Calum MacArthur, Jimmy Davidson, formerly of the Ordnance Survey, Arthur O Hazel, Grand Secretary of the Grand Lodge of Scotland, Freemasons Hall and members of staff of the Royal Commission on the Ancient and Historical Monuments of Scotland, including Grahame Ritchie, Jack Stevenson, Lesley Ferguson, Geoffrey Stell, who discussed the cleit recording project with me, Iain Parker, and Sam Scott and Alan Leith, who taught me plane table surveying.

I am particularly grateful to those with strong St Kilda connections, including people who lived on the island before 1930, for sharing much with me: Lachlan and Nancy MacDonald, Flora Craig (nee Gillies), Susan Ogilvie (nee Ferguson) and Elizabeth Ogilvie, Rachel Morrison (nee Ferguson), and Alisdair Fleming.

Others who have been consistently and especially helpful are: Stuart Murray, who has shared his knowledge of the islands and their birds with me and has been very helpful in discussing various points; Isabel Steel who has provided much practical help, especially in Edinburgh, Robert Atkinson, who has recounted his experiences of visiting the island in 1938 and discussed historical matters generally, and my parents, Audrey Harman and the late Edward Harman, who have provided support and encouragement in all my work. While I have gained much from discussion with many of these people, and their advice, I take sole responsibility for the opinions expressed in this work.

1
Introduction

In 1615 when Coll MacDonald raided St Kilda, the proprietor, Sir Rory Mór MacLeod of Dunvegan, wrote to complain of the raid on 'an Isle of mine called Zirta, a day and a night sailing from the rest of the North Isles [Outer Hebrides], far out on the ocean sea'.

In 1969, when working in North Uist, I first saw on the horizon Hirte or St Kilda, 'far out in the ocean sea'. It was not until five years later that I was able to visit it – then a day and a night's sailing (or rather motoring) from Oban.

The place and its history were intriguing, and that was the start of years of work in libraries, archives and in the field, gathering evidence and teasing out connections, to throw more light on the history of the human occupation of St Kilda. Through wider reading and visiting other parts of the Highlands and Islands, I was able to make comparisons with other communities, especially the islands lying far off shore from Lewis, and Mingulay and Berneray off Barra.

The island group known to many as St Kilda was known to its inhabitants and today is known to its Gaelic speaking neighbours as Hirte, though when referring to specific islands individual names are used, Hirte being the largest and the only one to have supported a permanent population. Documentary evidence indicates that Hirte is the older name. In this work St Kilda has generally been used to refer to the archipelago, and Hirte to refer to the main island.

St Kilda is remarkable for a number of things: its outstanding scenery and extensive sea bird colonies, its distinctive subspecies of woodmouse and wren and its unique breed of sheep; the density and character of the buildings left by its departed population.

It is also extraordinary, amongst small Scottish islands, in having attracted the attention of a large number of visitors, from Martin Martin in 1697 to the current travellers visiting the island by yacht, cruise vessel, or in National Trust for Scotland work parties.

These visitors and others interested in the place have produced a vast literature, including no less than twenty books of a general nature, nine devoted to particular aspects of the islands, four novels, innumerable articles in newspapers, in academic and popular journals, and a number of unpublished accounts. In terms of numbers of words per acre of ground, St Kilda is probably rivalled in Britain only by the larger cities, and, among islands, Iona and Rockall, in its wealth of relevant literature.

In addition to material published for general use, there are printed records such as those of some government departments, typescripts and manuscripts, maps, photographs, several films, sound recordings of St Kildans and visitors, and objects brought from the islands, all scattered in a variety of places, some publicly accessible, and some in private hands. As many of these as possible have been traced and recorded by various means.

A considerable amount of information about buildings on all the islands has been gathered during annual visits over fifteen years. Detailed notes, with measurements and plans, have been made of the dwellings, shielings, and bothies, and some 'cleitean' or storehouses.

The St Kildans did not use metric measurements or decimal coinage. To avoid cumbersome notes while retaining a single system for comparison, I have given in imperial measurement and pre-decimal British coinage the equivalents of local and early Scottish measurement and coinage systems. Tables of equivalents to the metric measurement and decimal coinage systems are given in Appendix 1.

This wealth of information has been in need of overall evaluation. Although several books of a general historical nature have been written over the last twenty years, some of the sources of information mentioned above have been neglected. Some subjects have not been considered in detail before, such as the depiction of the islands on maps, the evidence for prehistoric and early mediaeval occupation, analyses of the building types, the whole body of oral literature: songs, stories, beliefs, and customs, and the cultural objects in public museums.

In using earlier literature, it is important to know something of the people who wrote it, and so to make some assessment of their view of the islands. The Gaelic-speaking visitor, for instance, would learn a great deal more than one who did not have the language, and those who stayed for some time, as clergymen or teachers, are likely to produce more reliable accounts than a day visitor on a steamer. An assessment of reliability is particularly important where sources disagree.

There are now few people left who lived on St Kilda before 1930; I have been privileged to meet several of those who in their early lives were part of that community, from whom I have gathered a rare insight into daily life on the island.

2
Geographical Setting

S t Kilda is part of the parish of Harris, in the county of Invernessshire, and
is within the area administered now by Comhairle nan Eilean, the Western
Isles Council. Once the property of the MacLeods of Harris and Skye, it now
belongs to the National Trust for Scotland. A long established human
population left in 1930. Since 1957, when it became a National Nature

Figure 1. *Location of St Kilda*

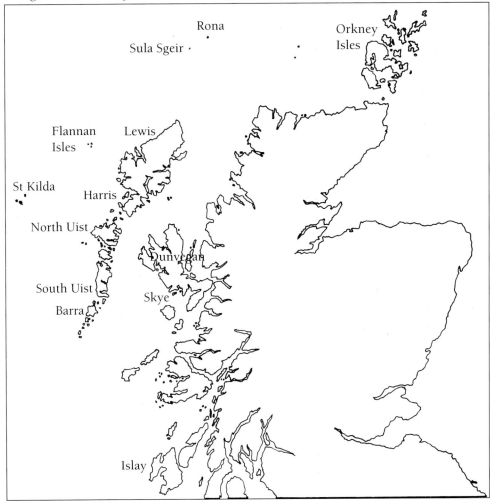

Figure 2. *Map of the archipelago*

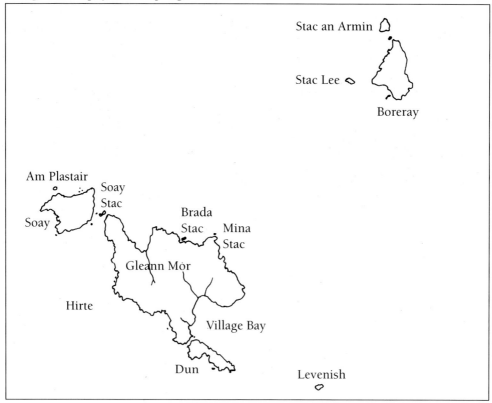

Reserve, a detachment from the Royal Artillery Range in Benbecula has been based on the island.

Location and Topography

The St Kilda archipelago lies in the Atlantic, west of the Outer Hebrides, at 8°33' east, 57°50' north of Greenwich. It is about 66 miles due west of Tarbert, Harris, but the nearest 'mainland', Aird an Runair in North Uist, is about 40 miles away, and the Monach Isles are marginally closer (figures 1 and 2).

The group consists of four islands and two large stacks, with other smaller stacks and rocks. Good topographical maps have been published by the Ordnance Survey (1970, 1973). All the islands include high ground (figure 3) with steep slopes, so that the true surface areas must be considerably more than the areas at sea level.

The largest island is Hirte, just over two miles long east-west and about the same north-south. It has an area at sea level of about 1567 acres. There are two glens each surrounded on three sides by high hills. The village glen, south facing, is a big open bowl, sheltered by hills of over 700', including, to

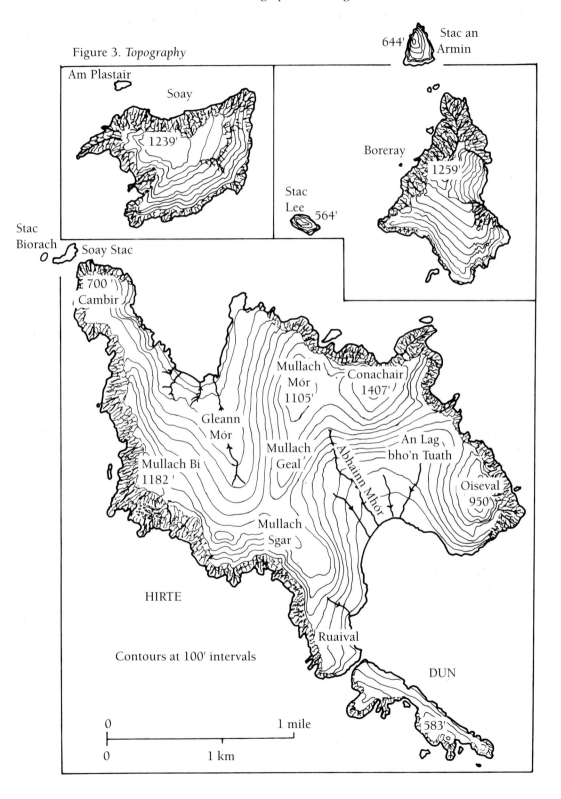

Figure 3. *Topography*

the north, Conachair, the highest hill at 1407'. Between Conachair and Oiseval, to the east, is a hollow: An Lag bho'n Tuath; and between Conachair and Mullach Mór, to the west, is a small high level plateau. Mullach Mór is the summit of a long north-south ridge which drops gently to Mullach Geal, then more steeply to the plateau area of Mullach Sgar, which in turn drops steeply to the south, becoming Ruaival. The north facing glen, Gleann Mór, is long, the low ground widening at its foot around the south side of Loch a'Ghlinne or Glen Bay. It also is sheltered by hills of 700' or more: to the east by the Mullach Mór – Mullach Geal ridge, which at Mullach Sgar merges into another long ridge curving west and then north west where it rises from about 850' to become Mullach Bi and Na Mullichean Móra; to the north west of Gleann Mór this ridge drops to a narrow neck beyond which the land rises again to become the Cambir.

Most of the hill slopes are quite steep, between 1:6 and 1:2; but the coastal aspects which, except around the two bays, range in height from 400' to 1325', are either even steeper slopes, approaching 1:1 and terminating in cliffs, or crags and cliffs, so that for practical purposes, the island is accessible only at the foot of the two glens. In Gleann Mór there is an area of gently sloping rock where it is possible to land; the village glen has a long low shore including a stretch of sand backed by a storm beach, on either side of which are sloping rocks, backed by a very low cliff to the east and rising cliffs to the west. The sand is sometimes swept out into the bay in winter, so that only boulders are visible above low tide mark, but in summer it returns to form a broad beach between the tide levels. According to MacLean (1838, 38) the boulders of this beach were known ironically all over the Highlands as *doirneagan Hirt* or 'St Kilda pebbles', though neither Dwelly nor Carmichael have noted this.

Each glen contains one large water course and several smaller ones. In the village glen, the Abhainn Mhór rises between Conachair and Mullach Mór and flows down through a deep gulley cut in the west side of the glen; a small stream flows from a spring at the foot of Conachair, and two others rising from the slopes of Mullach Mór and An Lag bho'n Tuath are dry for part of the year, particularly in summer. The former of these, Abhainn Riasg, almost certainly once ran into the Abhainn Mhór, but now runs in a canalised course beside the western line of the head dyke. In Gleann Mór, the Abhainn a' Ghlinne Mhóir runs in a gulley through the centre of the glen; it is joined on both sides by small tributary streams which may fail in dry weather; where the glen broadens to the west, there are two other small streams.

The only permanent standing water is a small pool towards the west side of Gleann Mór. Mathieson (1928) marks a 'tarn' between Conachair and

Mullach Mór, and the name 'Loch Sgar' on Mullach Sgar, and it is possible that comparatively recently these were small areas of open water; the 'tarn' may have resulted from peat cutting (p 166), and a shallow hollow on Mullach Sgar is bare of vegetation in dry weather but holds a pool in winter.

Village Bay is sheltered from the south by Dùn, a narrow island nearly a mile long, on the south west side of the bay. Dùn is barely separate from Hirte, being cut off by a narrow strait which is almost dry at very low tides. The north east aspect of the island is a steep slope which rises to a ridge of between 200' and 583'. The south west face of this ridge is either cliff or crag. Landing is possible on the rocks at the foot of the north east slope. There are no water courses.

Soay is just over ¼ mile west of the Cambir. With an area at sea level of about 237 acres it is considerably smaller than Hirte, and more compact. Soay is topped by a gentle slope rising from 850' to 1239'; this is surrounded by steep slopes and cliffs; to the west and south west two craggy ridges drop to the sea. There is no easy access, but a landing is possible near the south east corner. There are no water courses on Soay.

Between Soay and Hirte are two impressive stacks: Soay Stack and Stack Biorach, rising to 200' and 240' respectively. The lesser rocks of Stac Donna and Am Plastair lie to the south east and the north west of the island.

Boreray is 4 miles to the north east of Hirte. It has a slightly smaller area at sea level than Soay, about 217 acres, but it has a more complex surface. The south west aspect consists mainly of a large even slope of 1:2, rising from 300' to 950', bounded by cliff and very steep slope; a narrow area on the north side continues to rise to Mullach an Eilean at 1259'. This point has crags to the west and the steep slope of Sunadal to the east; Mullach an Eilean falls to become the broken ridge running north to Gearrgeo, with a confusion of crag and precipitous slope on either side broken by narrow gulleys. At the low west end of the south west slope, a great pinnacle rises to nearly 800'. The shore is entirely cliff or very steep rock face; landing is possible at the south east corner with access to the slope above. There are no water courses, but it is possible to obtain water in hollows near the foot of the southern slope.

Stac an Armin is the largest of the two great stacks near Boreray. Just under ¼ mile to the north west of Boreray, it rises to 644' on the west side, which is almost entirely sheer cliff. There are steep slopes and cliffs on the other aspects. Landing is possible on the south side. According to Martin (1753, 25) there is a spring on this stack.

The smaller Stac Lee lies just over ¼ mile west of Boreray. It rises almost vertically from the water to about 400', then slopes steeply to 564'. It is

Figure 4. *Geology*

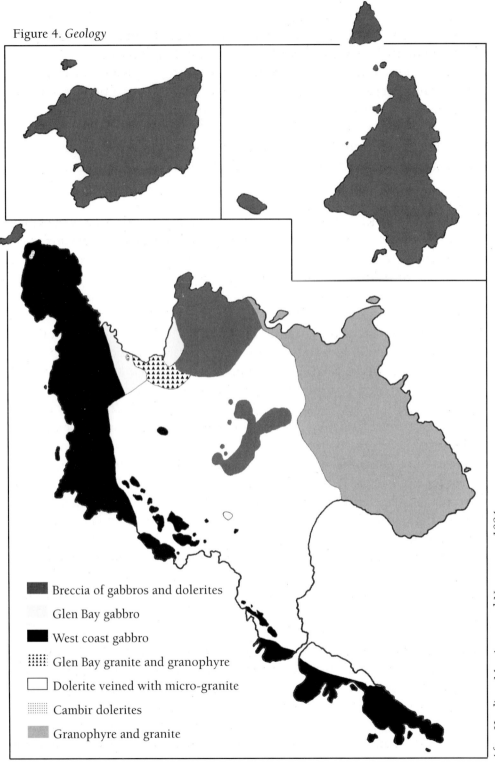

Breccia of gabbros and dolerites

Glen Bay gabbro

West coast gabbro

Glen Bay granite and granophyre

Dolerite veined with micro-granite

Cambir dolerites

Granophyre and granite

After Harding, Merriman and Nancarrow 1984

possible to land on the south side.

Levenish is a compact rock just over ¹/₂ mile east of Dun. It rises to a maximum of 203' towards its northern edge. Landing is possible.

Many authors have written with enthusiasm about the appearance of the islands. Their presence, solitary in the ocean, is striking, but their appearance is even more so; the steep hills, and, viewed from the sea, the dominant features of cliff and crag, dwarf the observer by their grandeur. Neither picture nor film can convey an adequate representation, and even the seasoned traveller, returning to the islands, feels anew a sense of awe.

Geology and Soils

The geology of St Kilda has been studied in detail by Harding, Merriman and Nancarrow (1984), who describe the archipelago as the eroded remains of a Tertiary volcano, the rocks being between 55 and 60 million years old (figure 4). The oldest rocks are gabbros on the west side of Hirte and the south side of Dun. Boreray, Soay and the north-west flank of Mullach Mór and Mullach Geal consist of a breccia composed of gabbros with veins and sheets of dolerites intersecting them. The main north-south ridge of Mullach Mór to Ruaival and the upper part of Gleann Mór is composed of a complex of dolerite with veins and sheets of microgranite and microdiorite, and at the foot of Gleann Mór is a small area of granite. The youngest rock is the Conachair granite which forms that hill, and the area to the east of it. This fractures in a way which makes it more amenable to building than the angular gabbros and dolerites.

There is evidence of two periods of glaciation affecting the island; during the earlier one till was deposited over the village area, and deposits in Gleann Mór may be contemporary. Later deposits of solifluction debris and hill slope deposits in An Lag bho'n Tuath and on the lower slopes of Conachair and Mullach Sgar are deceptively similar to cultivation ridges. A third cold period resulted in frost shattering which created blockfields on Ruaival and the east end of Dun, screes such as Carn Mór and that on the lower slopes of Conachair, and the protalus ridges at the foot of Conachair and on Mullach Sgar.

Differences in rock types are less distinct in the overlying soils because intense leaching resulting from the high rainfall rapidly removes the nutrients derived from the rocks, while nutrients derived from guano, sheep dung and sea spray are contributed in different quantities in different areas (Hornung 1974). In general the soils are acid and peaty, with blanket peat deposits in the area between Mullach Mór and Conachair and on the western slopes of Gleann Mór. There are also small areas of plantago peat on Ruaival and south of the neck of the Cambir.

Hornung considers that the soils in the floor of An Lag bho'n Tuath may have been altered by cultivation and this is borne out by recent excavations (Emery & Morrison 1995, 58). Elsewhere friable and well structured soils are associated with old enclosures. These tend to be popular grazing areas, so are continually enriched by natural manuring. Over much of the village area a long history of cultivation together with intensive manuring has created a dèep man-made soil very favourable to plant growth.

Earthquake

Martin (1753, 24, 77) speaks of an earthquake which occurred in 1686: his account indicates that it was felt on Boreray, and it lasted a few minutes. Campbell (1799, f 71) records that it was still remembered in 1799 and that several of the gannet rocks were split and fell into the sea.

The only other record of an earthquake in that year was in York; probably a minor tremor, as no details were noted. In May 1687 an earthquake was felt in several parts of England (Davison 1924, 15, 349). Earthquakes of varying severity occur occasionally on the lines of the Great Glen and the Highland Boundary Fault, but the only earthquake recorded in the Western Isles was noted by lighthouse keepers on November 28th 1880 (Munro 1982, 27). Although widespread, this must have been very minor, as it does not appear to have been noticed by anyone else.

Clearly earthquakes are unusual in this area, and the tremors felt on Boreray, rather than being the cause of a major rock fall, could have been the result of such a fall; the shock and noise would reverberate through the island. Such falls do occur as a result of natural erosion and splitting: a large area of rock fell from the cliff face at the Gap in the early 1980s, and in the more distant past, similar falls would have created the stacks. It would not be unnatural for Martin to ascribe such a dramatic event to an earthquake.

Climate

There is no good range of meteorological figures for St Kilda, but figures from the weather stations in the Western Isles (O'Dell and Walton 1962, 37–48) can be used with caution and Campbell (1974, 16–18) provides useful local information. Despite its northerly position, St Kilda, together with all the west coast of Britain, enjoys the influence of the warm north Atlantic drift, but it is also exposed to the prevailing south-westerly winds. One of the most notable features is that the weather can deteriorate or improve very rapidly.

At Benbecula, near sea level, the average mean minimum temperature in the coldest month is 34.9°F, while the average mean maximum temperature in the hottest month is 60.6°F. The number of days when frost is experienced at sea level is limited to no more than thirty between early December and late March.

Mean annual rainfall at Stornoway and Lochmaddy are 50.3" and 48.2" respectively; the figures for different years on St Kilda range between 45" and 50" although as Campbell points out, there is likely to be more precipitation on high ground due to hill fog. Rainfall is distributed fairly evenly throughout the year; it often falls as hail in winter, less frequently as snow, and snow rarely lies for long, particularly on the lower ground. St Kilda creates its own cloud masses, and may lie for days beneath a pall of cloud which can drop almost to sea level, while the sun is glinting on the sea around. At times veils of mist rise from the cliffs and flow over the hills. The ground can become very dry in summer, and absorb a considerable rainfall, but after prolonged rain it may become saturated and water flows over the surface, while the streams become white torrents.

Campbell states that St Kilda is probably the windiest place in the British Isles. Over about 900 days from late 1957, there were 212 with winds of gale force (over 42 m.p.h) and gusts of over 120 m.p.h have been recorded. There are rarely days without at least a light breeze, though completely still conditions do occur. Both bays are sheltered from the prevailing wind, but both sometimes have gales blowing straight into them, and even in sheltered conditions, a swell can make landing difficult or impossible. In severe gales, waves can break against the exposed coast to a height of over 100'. Carried by the wind, salt spray can reach everywhere, with effects upon the vegetation. Local topography causes eddies in the wind and whatever the prevailing direction may be, strong updraughts and downdraughts can come from different directions.

The topography also affects the potential hours of sunlight available in the two glens (figure 5, overleaf). Though the pattern of shadow is different in the morning and evening, in early July most of the village area has a maximum potential for direct sunlight of about twelve hours, whereas in Gleann Mór it is closer to fourteen hours, including on the east side the low light at sunset. In late January this area receives no more than three hours of potential sunshine, while the village area has about four and a half hours. This, combined with other features would make the southern glen more attractive for settlement. The maps were drawn on days as close to the equinox and solstices as circumstances permitted; inclement weather and other work commitments prevented their completion. It should be noted that due to the westerly position of St Kilda local time is just over half an hour later than Greenwich Mean Time.

Figure 5. *Seasonal pattern of shadows in the Village Area and Gleann Mór (Time GMT)*

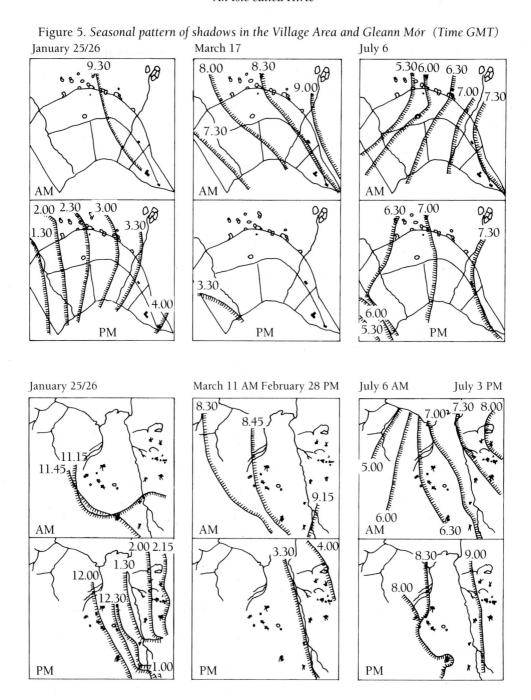

Vegetation

There is only one detailed description of the vegetation written before 1930 (Turrill 1927, 428–444). The cessation of cultivation and of grazing by both sheep and cattle had some effect on the vegetation of Hirte, and from 1932 uncontrolled grazing by sheep has also affected it. The most detailed recent survey of the vegetation distinguishes a number of plant communities distributed over the islands, with lists of the higher plants found in each area. These communities are grouped into broader categories (Gwynne and Milner 1974, 36–70; Milner and Gwynne, 1974, 273–325). Figure 6 (overleaf) shows where they occur. Only the dominant plants are mentioned below.

Wet and dry heaths are composed of heather and grasses, especially bents, fescues, mat grass, hair grass, deer grass and purple moor grass, also tormentil.

Bog areas contain cotton grass, heather, which has increased since the evacuation, and crowberry, with significant amounts of a few grasses and tormentil. There are three bogs, between Mullach Mór and Conachair, the upper part of the west side of Gleann Mór, and on the summit of Soay, though this has more grass and less heather and crowberry.

In the scattered areas of wet grassland the commonest species varies from one area to another, being generally mat grass or purple moor grass. Others which are important are bent grasses, sweet vernal grass, fescues and Yorkshire fog. In some of these areas sphagnum moss, present in other communities also, grows densely. Sedges are common, also heath grass, tormentil and bog asphodel.

Agrostis/Festuca grasslands are drier grasslands, named from two of the dominant species: bent and fescue grasses, the others being sweet vernal grass, Yorkshire fog, purple moor grass, mat grass and heath grass. Certain species dominate in some areas. Other common plants are sedges and tormentil. Heather, thyme, cotton grass, woodrush, bog asphodel, plantains and white clover are also common but do not all occur together. Woodrush dominates this type of grassland on the summits of Conachair, Oiseval and Mullach Bi.

Biotic grasslands are grasslands which are affected by the presence of sheep and birds, in particular by the trampling and grazing of sheep, the faeces of birds and sheep, and the products of decaying sheep carcasses. The commonest species are bent grasses, Yorkshire fog, sweet vernal grass, red fescue, smooth and rough stemmed meadow grasses, and tormentil. Those particularly affected by the fauna are common mouse ear, meadow buttercup, lesser celandine, common sorrel, pearlwort, chickweed and white clover. In areas where sheep lie and shelter the grasses produce a more luxuriant growth, and this 'lair flora' grassland, occurs mostly beside walls, in hollows and on natural sheltering sites, such as beside rock faces. In some areas of steep slopes where there are many nesting fulmars, sorrel is the dominant plant, and chickweed very common. These grasslands occur on the floor of · An Lag bho'n Tuath and on most of the area formerly cultivated within the

Figure 6. *Vegetation*

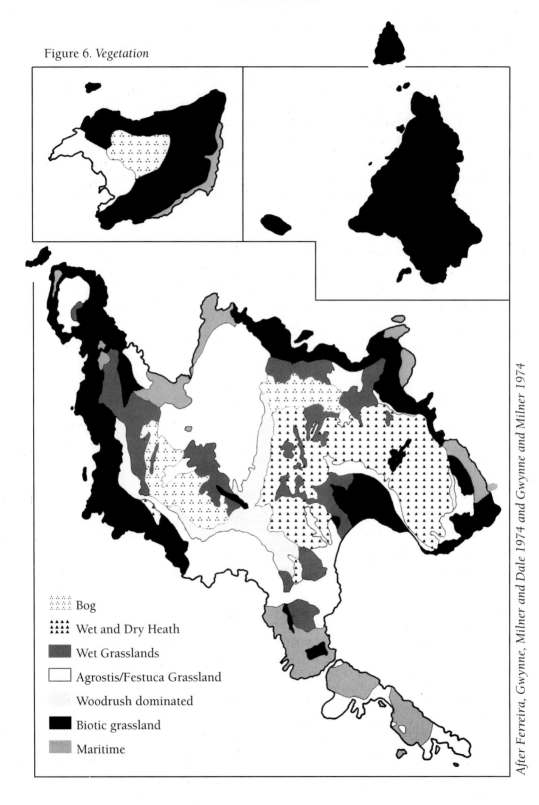

Bog

Wet and Dry Heath

Wet Grasslands

Agrostis/Festuca Grassland

Woodrush dominated

Biotic grassland

Maritime

After Ferreira, Gwynne, Milner and Dale 1974 and Gwynne and Milner 1974

head dyke, also on sea facing slopes particularly on the west side of the island and at the Cambir, on most of Boreray and the east slopes of Soay.

Maritime communities occur in areas affected by sea spray, and in some fulmar and puffin colony areas. These are similar in some ways to the biotic grasslands, but have a wider range of species, and are dominated by red fescue grass, thrift, or plantains. Sedges occur, and smooth hawkbit, meadow buttercup, pearlwort and white clover.

There are no longer any cultivated crops, and weeds associated with cultivation and waste ground have disappeared since the evacuation (Poore and Robertson 1949, 89–90). These include shepherd's purse, corn spurrey, corn marigold, groundsel, common hemp nettle, mugwort, smooth sow thistle and field forget-me-not. Nettles have spread from the burial ground to grow in areas within and beside the houses. Elder bushes noted in the burial ground in 1889 and 1927 (Turrill 1927, 431) no longer exist, nor does the willow planted by MacKay over his sister's grave (Ross 1890, 100). Heathcote (1900a, 98) noticed a man stamping on the roots of a small tree which the minister was trying to grow. He explained that he was anxious lest trees should grow at the expense of pasture.

There are a few tiny willow trees in areas inaccessible to sheep, and creeping willow grows in some areas, but there are no trees or bushes as generally recognised. Several honeysuckle plants grow on crags.

As a simple generalisation, the biotic grasslands and the sorrel maritime sward now provide the best grazing for Soay sheep, the seaward slopes being particularly good, especially in winter, when sheep grazing other areas lose condition noticeably.

Other aspects of immediate relevance to the human population would be the bog areas which could provide supplies of fuel, and the abundance of tormentil, used in tanning leather. Heather was used for making ropes. Parts of dock, silverweed, sorrel and scurvygrass were eaten, as were the seaweeds dulse and sloke, or laver. Crotal, a lichen, was used for dyeing cloth (p 179).

Fauna

There are now only two terrestrial mammals on the islands. All the domestic stock except some sheep were removed at the evacuation in 1930 and the house mouse became extinct within a year or two. A subspecies of woodmouse peculiar to the islands exists on Hirte and Dùn. The St Kildans took care to avoid introducing mice to Boreray and Soay, and on one occasion took down seven cleitean to catch a mouse inadvertently carried in baggage (Sands 1877a, 44). Two different breeds of sheep graze on Hirte, Soay and Boreray. Some of the Soay sheep, a breed of unknown history peculiar to that island, were transferred to Hirte after the evacuation, while most of the islanders' blackface sheep on Boreray were abandoned there. Dùn is not grazed. Grey seals frequent the shores and breed on suitable sites in small numbers, and diminishing numbers of a variety of whales inhabit the surrounding seas.

The birds have been surveyed comprehensively (Harris and Murray 1978). There have undoubtedly been changes in their distribution since 1930, due partly to cessation of human activity in most areas, partly to more general population dynamics. A very limited range of species breeds annually, the list of landbirds being: oystercatcher, snipe, meadow and rock pipits, a subspecies of wren peculiar to the islands, wheatear, starling, raven and hooded crow, of which only the rock pipit and starling are likely to be represented by more than 100 pairs. The sea birds are: fulmar, manx shearwater, storm and Leach's petrel, gannet, shag, eider duck, great skua, herring gull, lesser and great black-back gulls, kittiwake, razorbill, guillemot, puffin and black guillemot. The great skua colonised the islands in 1963. Formerly cormorants and the great auk also bred here. The birds which were mainly exploited for food (Chapter 12) are the fulmar, manx shearwater, gannet, and the auks, all of which breed in very large numbers, except for the black guillemot of which there are less than 100 pairs. Petrels are also present in very large but unknown numbers, and there are normally over 6000 pairs of kittiwakes, but the other sea birds breed in small numbers mostly of less than 100 pairs. Besides the breeding birds, nearly 200 species of migrants and rare vagrants have been recorded, but there is a limited range of regular migrants passing through in spring and autumn. Many species, particularly the rare petrels and the distinctive wren, were exploited within the last sixty or seventy years before the evacuation for their cash value to collectors.

There are no reptiles or amphibians: eels have been found in the Amhuinn Mhór.

Hundreds of invertebrate species have been recorded (e.g. Beare 1908, Evans 1906, Grimshaw 1907, Hamilton 1963, Waterston 1906). Some which would affect the human population directly are midges, clegs, the 'human flea', found in houses and on dogs, and bird ticks, which are common in fulmar and puffin colonies and were abhorred by the St Kildans. Offal provided a breeding ground for bluebottles which, together with several species of dungfly, were common.

The St Kildans and their Environment
Figure 7 shows how the St Kildans used and recycled the natural resources available to them. Some produce was exported, but little was imported until the nineteenth century, when food, clothing, tools, implements and furniture were brought in.

Figure 7. *Relationship between the St Kildans and their environment*

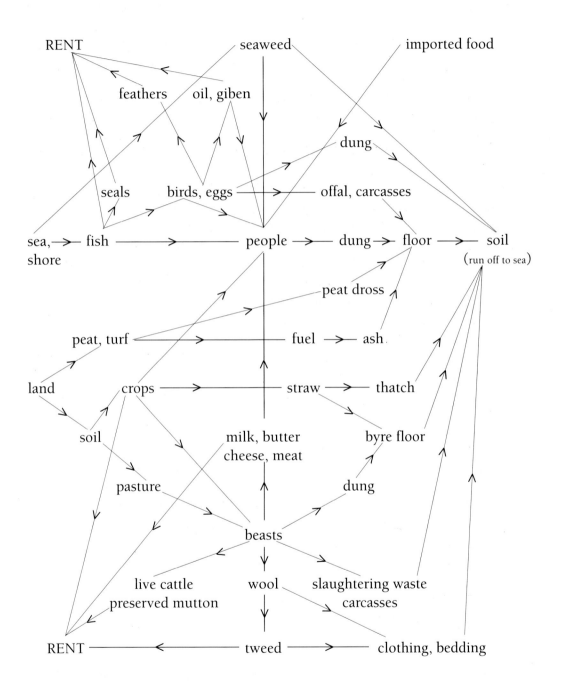

3
Topographical and Historical Maps of St Kilda

Early Maps

An invaluable initial source for any examination of maps of St Kilda is the Royal Scottish Geographical Society's *The Early Maps of Scotland* (Moir et al 1973), which has been used as a source for the historical background, and for locating most of the maps or copies of the maps considered in this chapter.

The earliest known map specifically of St Kilda is Martin Martin's, dating from his visit in 1697. In the following 130 years, several more maps solely of the main island or of the entire archipelago were produced. For earlier representations, and for the supposed position of the islands relative to the rest of the Hebrides and the mainland, smaller scale maps and charts of the whole country or the west coast must be consulted; from these, too, there may be some clarification of the naming of the islands as Hirtha, or St Kilda. Some of the more detailed maps provide information about other names in the island group.

No maps depicting Scotland with any reasonable accuracy seem to have survived from before the sixteenth century. The *Gough* map (*c*.1360) in the Bodleian Library, Oxford, is a good depiction of Southern Britain but the maker had little knowledge of Scotland. A poor map made by Pietro Coppo in Venice about 1520 shows Scotland as an island. An anonymous manuscript map *Anglia Figura*, drawn between 1534 and 1546, has a much better shape. A chart of the Scottish coast and islands, with sailing directions, was prepared by Alexander Lyndsay for James V in connection with his voyage around the northern coasts in 1540. A copy of this was made by Nicolas de Nicolay, cosmographer to the King of France, in 1546, and published by him about 1580, and again in a slightly different version in 1583. In 1546 a map of Britain was published in Rome, probably the work of George Lily; a map of Scotland based on this was published about 1566, and though it contains errors not found in the earlier map, the depiction of the west coast and islands is essentially the same. In 1564 Gerard Mercator published a map of the British Isles; the Scottish portion may well have been based on a lost map drawn by John Elder in or before 1543. The map was copied by Abraham Ortelius in the Netherlands in 1573 when he published an expanded edition of his atlas of 1570, and was copied as well by Nowell, with alterations derived from Nicolay's map, and possibly from another, manuscript map. Mercator revised the map for publication as part of a three volume atlas. The last part, covering the British Isles, appeared in 1595. In 1578, John Leslie, bishop of Ross, in exile in Rome, produced a history of Scotland, accompanied by a map, based on Lily. Later in the same year he produced a better map, based on Ortelius. An anonymous manuscript map, the *Carte of Scotland* dated about 1580, is in the British Museum, and a map was drawn by Robert Adam between 1588 and 1590, showing the route of the Spanish Armada. In 1592 Lucas Jansz Waghenaer, a Dutch chart maker, published a chart of the Hebrides.

In the sixteenth century then, there were eight different maps: those of Coppo (*c*.1520), the anonymous *Anglia Figura* (1534–46), Lyndsay (1540) used by Nicolay (1580 and 1583), Lily (1546), Mercator (1564 and 1595) – possibly based on Elder (1543), and copied by Ortelius (1573), the anonymous *Carte of Scotland* (*c*.1580), Adam (*c*.1588) and Waghenaer (1592). There are some striking differences between these maps, in their depiction of the west coast and the Hebrides.

Coppo's map of Scotland is inaccurate, and he shows only one large and one small island which might represent the Hebrides, but beyond these, to the west, is a circular island called *torta*. It seems reasonable to suggest, both from the location and the name, that this should be identified with 'Hirta', and would thus be the earliest representation on a map of St Kilda. About twenty years later, the anonymous 'Anglia Figura' shows a more recognisable Scotland; several of the Hebrides, including Skye and Lewis, are indicated, and to the north west of Lewis, on the margin of the map, is part of a larger land mass called 'Hirtha'. Lily, with a slightly different but similarly inaccurate pattern of the Hebrides, also shows 'Hirtha', larger than any of them, to the north. Only the name, and the indication of remoteness, permit identification of this vast island with St Kilda. Both Nicolay and Mercator map the Hebrides recognisably; their outlines, of Uist and Skye particularly, are very similar. Nicolay shows no islands north of Rona; neither does Ortelius; in Mercator's earlier version Rona is covered by a scroll. Nicolay shows, not far off the south west coast of Lewis, a small island called 'skilder' in 1580, and 'skilda' in 1583. It does not appear in either of the Mercator maps but is present on Ortelius as 'S. Kylder'. Leslie's second 1578 map, using Ortelius' outline of the Hebrides, including S. Kilder, also shows the large island 'Hirtha', retained from his first map, where it is called 'Hirta'. The *Carte of Scotland* gives a better representation of the relative positions of the islands; Rona is marked, and just to the west of Lewis, is Skaldir; and further west, is an island of modest size, called 'Hyrth'. As Taylor remarks (1961, 41) this is

19

the only map he knows with the Gaelic name correctly applied to the islands referred to by cartographers as 'St Kilda' since the seventeenth century.

The large northern 'Hirta' may reflect its importance rather than its physical size. Cartographers may have been influenced by the historian Boece's reference to the 'last and outmaist isle' (p 80). Other islands are not always depicted to scale: North Rona, another island on the boundary of the British Isles is sometimes very large. Iona, important for other reasons, may be disproportionately large.

Taylor has examined the two names 'Hirta' and 'St Kilda' in great detail (pp 40,43). He notes that 'skilder' in its various versions is an obsolete name derived from the Old Norse 'skildir' meaning 'shields', applied probably to Gaskeir or some other islands just west of Harris. Several sixteenth century cartographers had separated the 'S' from the following part of the word, and in 1592, Waghenaer transferred the name to the St Kilda group of islands. It was still used for an island nearer to Harris in the seventeenth century by people copying from earlier maps, such as Speed copying from Mercator, and rarely the name appears twice on a map as on van Keulen's chart of 1682. He used Waghenaer's representation of the islands and marks them 'I. S. Kilda' at the same time marking 'S. Kilder' much closer to Harris.

The name 'St Kilda' does not appear in travellers accounts until the late seventeenth century. The Sibbald manuscripts collected in the late seventeenth century contain a description of the Western Isles, possibly by Sir George MacKenzie of Tarbat, who says that 'The Isle of Hirta...is calld Saint Kildar island' by some (Adv mss 33.3.20). Martin (1753, 11), writing in 1698, says that the inhabitants of the island and the Western Isles called it 'Hirta' but it was known to sailors as St Kilda; no doubt his own book title *A Voyage to St Kilda* helped to encourage the use of the name, and thereafter it was used in the published literature in preference to Hirta.

Most of the maps published in the seventeenth century are first, second or third generation copies of earlier maps and offer little new information. Among the exceptions are the detailed county maps published by Joan Blaeu in Holland in 1654. These are based on new surveys made by Timothy Pont between the years 1584 and 1596 (Megaw 1969 72–73, Stone 1989). Some of the surveys were revised by Robert Gordon before they were published; he also used them to make a map of the whole kingdom of Scotland. St Kilda is marked on none of the maps, but at the western edge of the Sound of Harris, beyond Pabbay, the sea is marked 'Cheules Yrt' or Sound of Hirte, the last use of 'Hirte' on a map, other than late copies.

There were two important contributions to the mapping of the Western Isles at the turn of the century: Martin Martin's maps of 'St Kilda' in 1698 and the Western Isles in 1703. The map of St Kilda, with an inset showing its position in relation to a short stretch of the Long Island coast, is the first giving any detail. It will be considered below. His map of the Western Isles also marks St Kilda and some of the other islands in the group. His outline is certainly different from Pont's. Moll, who engraved the map for Martin, used it as the basis for the Hebrides in his own maps of Scotland, drawn from an amalgamation of the latest surveys in different areas. Other geographers, such as Kitchin, continued to use Blaeu.

The next major survey was that of Murdo MacKenzie, who in 1750 published a chart of Lewis, and in 1776 large charts of all the Hebrides. These charts are much more accurate than anything earlier, but they do not cover St Kilda, though it is shown in profile in the western margin of his Lewis chart. MacKenzie's nephew explained that he felt it was unsafe to venture to St Kilda when there were privateers in those waters (MacKenzie, 1798). James Dorret must have had access to MacKenzie's drawings before publication as he included the improved shape of Lewis in his new map of Scotland published in 1750, with later editions. St Kilda appears on some of these, and from then on when it appears it is reasonably accurately depicted, at small scales.

Maps of the Islands

Waghenaer's chart is quite detailed and is earlier than any of the maps specifically of St Kilda by over 100 years. Martin Martin made the first detailed map, drawn after his visit in 1697. Kenneth MacAulay, who went there in 1758, included a map in his book, based on Martin's. The next new map is the one made by Robert Campbell of Islay, who visited the island with Lord Brougham in 1799. This was published by Arrowsmith in 1809. The first half of the nineteenth century saw a proliferation of maps of the island. James Wilson, who published an account of his previous year's visit to the island in 1842, included a map prepared from one drawn by Sir George Stuart MacKenzie of Coul during a visit in 1800. John MacCulloch drew one after his visit in 1815. Robert Stevenson drew one in 1826 when he drew up plans for a new church and manse. G.C. Atkinson drew a map after visiting the island in 1831. Another undated manuscript map is in the Dunvegan archive.

From 1846 to 1863 the Admiralty survey vessels were working round the Western Isles and as a result of their work a chart including St Kilda was published in 1865. At the end of the century Norman Heathcote made a survey and published the first reasonably accurate map in 1900. A small detailed chart of the Village Bay was made by the Admiralty in 1909. In 1927, John Mathieson, after retiring from the Ordnance Survey, went out to make a new map of the only inhabited island not mapped by the Ordnance Survey, which published his results in 1928. The island was finally mapped by the Ordnance Survey itself in 1967 as part of a major re-survey programme, and three 'six-inch' (1:10,560) sheets were published in 1970. Most of the maps shown in the following pages have a more spacious design, with the islands

Figure 8. *Waghenaer Chart: 1592*

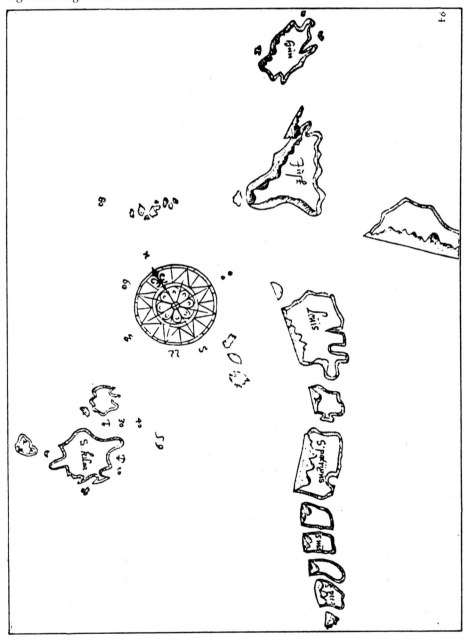

correctly placed in relation to each other. In order to retain legible detail by reproduction at the largest size possible, some alterations have been made, such as putting Boreray in an inset and moving scales and compass points.

Waghenaer's chart (figure 8) gives a rather poor representation of the Hebrides; comparison with contemporary maps suggests that the island marked 'Iust' represents the northern half of Lewis, and should be joined to the island marked 'Leeus' and the smaller one to the south, which would thus be the south end of Harris. The misapplication of 'Iust' to north Lewis supports the idea that 'S. Kilda' has been similarly transferred from some other island closer to the Lewis coast; the islands shown on the map undoubtedly represent those now known as St Kilda and their shape is interesting

Figure 9. *Martin Martin's map: 1697*

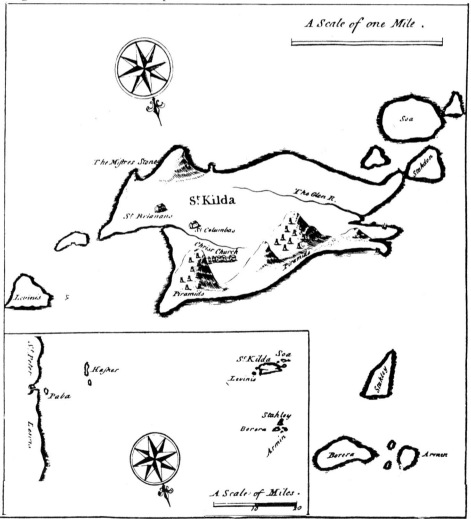

in itself. The main island is, correctly, the largest; two anchorages are shown, probably Village Bay and Glen Bay. The island to the north east must be Boreray with one of the stacs, while that to the north would be Soay, with one of the stacs in Soay Sound. There is nothing which closely resembles Dun, an island which is of major importance in providing shelter for Village Bay.

Martin (figure 9), who spent some time in the islands, shows Dun as quite small and rather insignificant, and he does not name the island. He has an improved shape for the main island and shows the main hills on the eastern part; these may be identified with Oiseval, Conachair, Mullach Mór and Ruaival, but he omits the high ridge to the west of Gleann Mór, and the Cambir is only sketchily indicated. Soay and attendant rocks and stacs are shown, though not to scale. Stack Dona on this map is probably the one now known as Stac Biorach; this would be consistent with Martin's description of Stac Dona, but the situation is confused as Martin marks only two rocks in Soay Sound and there are three major ones. The one now known as Stac Dona is quite small and insignificant compared with the other two, and is some distance from them. It is tempting to identify the two which Martin marks as the ones now known as Stac Biorach and Soay Stac. Though Boreray, Stac Lee, Stac an Armin and attendant rocks are marked about a mile from Hirte on the main map, it is clear from Martin's inset that they are further away to the north east, but he does exaggerate the distance, making it about ten miles rather than the four it is. Levinish is marked, too close to Dun and Hirte, and too large, but Martin's proportions are poor; Soay, Boreray and Dun particularly are much too small. There are interesting details on Martin's map; he marks the Mistress Stone on Ruaival, and explains its significance in his book; two small indentations in the coastline to the east of Glen Bay must represent the natural arch now known as the Tunnel, and the arch on Dun may also be indicated. Finally, he depicts the human settlement with its three chapel sites, and a scattering of 'piramids' or cleitean (small stone storehouses: p 159) on the slopes of Oiseval and Mullach Mor. Though there are still many on both hills, there are also many in other areas, around the village and to the west of St Columba's chapel site, and a good number in Gleann Mór. The fact that Martin does not show these does not necessarily mean there were none in these areas in his time.

On his map of the Western Isles Martin has altered the outline of Hirte so that it is more like an H shape, and he places Stac Lee much closer to Hirte than to Boreray, an error which does not appear on his map of St Kilda.

MacAulay (figure 10) has clearly copied his map from Martin, in outline, but he has added hachures to show the hills and cliffs. He shows how the coast of Hirte consists almost entirely of steep slope or cliff; only in Village

Bay and Glen Bay is the shore readily accessible. He indicates the ridge of Na
Mullichean Móra and that stretching from Mullach Sgar to Mullach Mór and
Conachair, separating the Village Glen from Gleann Mór. There are hachures
all round the other islands and rocks, but these are a standard fringe around
them, with no attempt, for instance, to represent the complexities of the
surface of Boreray. MacAulay adds a few place names: 'Plaste' and the 'Plain of
Spels', and 'Stakbirah' (his version of Stac Biorach) which he gives to the stac
Martin called 'Stakdon', using the latter for the one Martin left unnamed. If
these two stacs are intended to represent the ones now known as Soay Stac
and Stac Biorach, then the relative sizes of the stacs as marked on the map
would suggest that MacAulay's 'Stakbirah' is Soay Stac and his 'Stakdon' is
Stac Biorach, which, as explained, must be the one which Martin calls Stac
Dona. The group of buildings in Gleann Mór might represent shielings,
though together with the group to the north-east of the village, they might
represent the two groups of cleitean marked and identified by Martin. The
village is shown as two rows of houses, and there are sites marked for Christ

Figure 10. *Kenneth MacAulay's map: 1758*

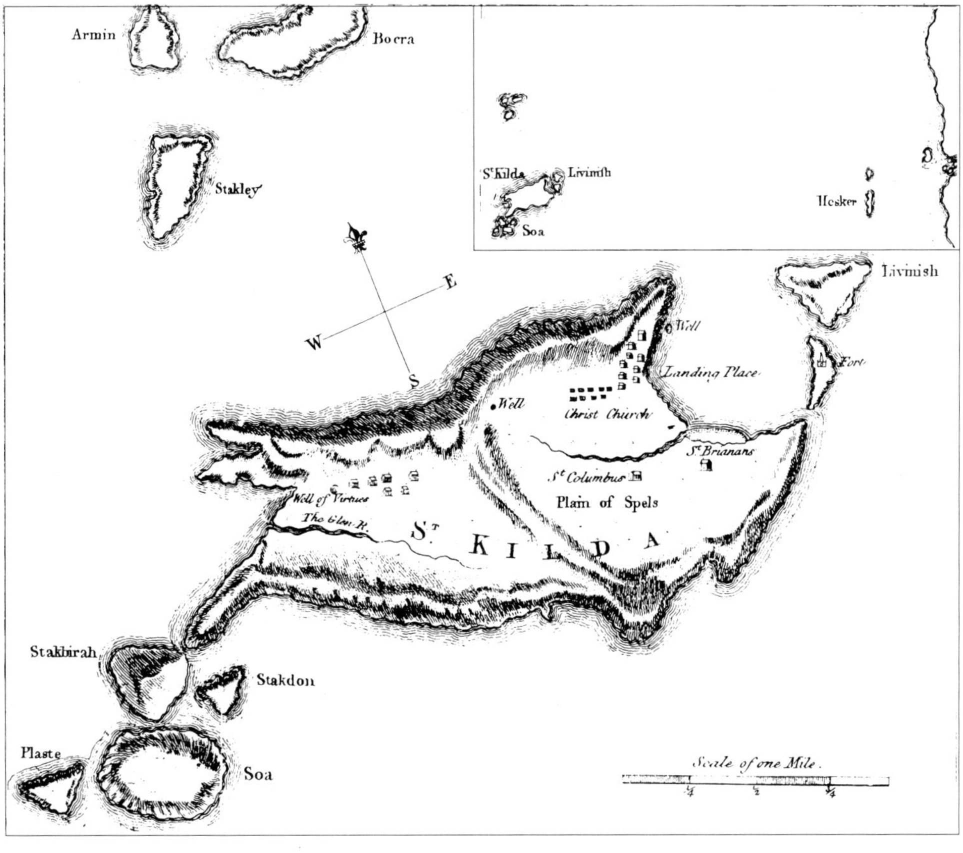

25

Church and the other two chapels; MacAulay also shows three wells, one of which is probably intended as Tobar Childa, another at the foot of Oiseval which is probably Tobar a'Chleirich, and Tobar nam Buaidh. He indicates the landing place and marks a 'Fort' on Dun. Curiously, although he follows Martin in everything else, he does not mark the Mistress Stone, which is not mentioned in his book.

Campbell's map (figure 11) is a great improvement, apart from the shape of Boreray, and the proportions and relative positions of the different islands and stacs are good. He does not give as many names as MacAulay, but some are new: 'Conagra Hill', 'Dun Fir Bholg' where the 'Old' Fort is, and the 'Warrior's House' in Gleann Mór. Campbell shows three rocks in Soay Sound: 'Stack-

Figure 11. *Based on Robert Campbell's map: 1799*

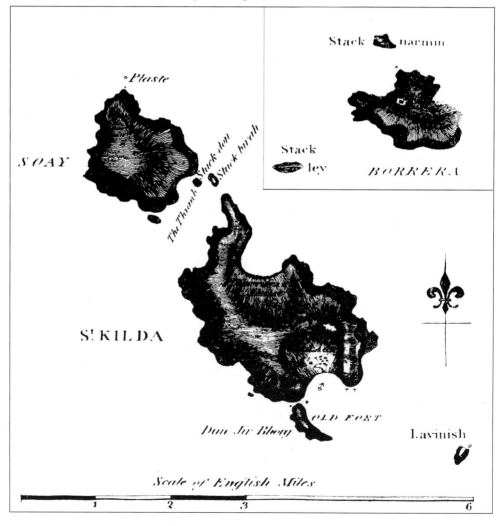

birah', now known as Soay Stac, 'Stack-don', now known as Stac Biorach, and one which is not named but would be the one now known as Stac Dona. The words 'The Thumb' seem to apply to 'Stack-don' and in view of Martin's description of the climb that would be correct. It is suggested that this, the first map on which those stacs are shown accurately enough to be identified correctly 'on the ground', also has them correctly named. Considering that Campbell (1799) had only about twenty four hours ashore, his map is remarkably good.

Sir George Stuart MacKenzie made the survey for his map (figure 12) 'early' in the nineteenth century, probably in 1800 (Laing 1876, 608). It is particularly interesting to the cartographer because he describes the method he used to construct it. It is reassuring to know that he regarded it as 'approximately rather than absolutely correct' as he was a meticulous scientist. His outline of Hirte is close to Martin's, though he does full justice to the length of Dun. He is the first person to name 'Mullach More' and he names the bays simply as 'East or Village Bay' and 'West Bay'.

Figure 12. *Based on George Stewart MacKenzie's map: 1800*

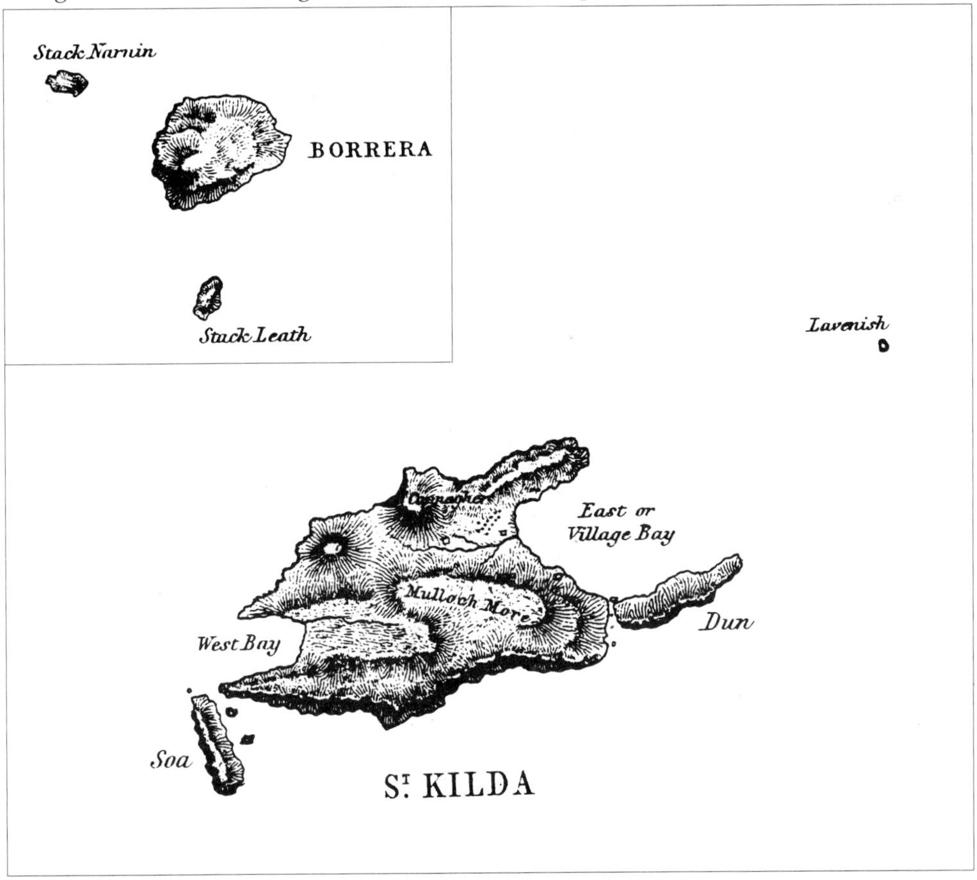

McCulloch's map (figure 13), made some sixteen years later, is chiefly notable for its inaccurate shape, not to be compared with Campbell and not even as good as Martin's. He has made the west end and Glen Bay too big and Conachair and Mullach Mór too small. His indication of cliffs is good and he shows the projection of Aird Uachdarachd. He also shows Dun as two islands, possibly to indicate the tunnel. Both bays are shown as landing places and he shows two streams in each glen. Each one does have a major stream, and there are other minor ones in both, some of them flowing intermittently depending on the weather. McCulloch names very few features.

Figure 13. *John MacCulloch's map: 1815*

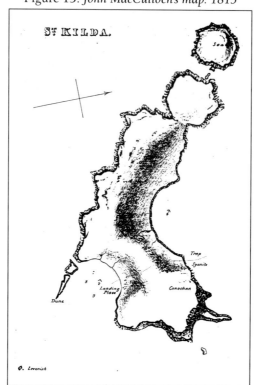

A few years later, in 1826, Robert Stevenson drew a map of St Kilda (figure 14), presumably after a visit. His map is not as good as Campbell's; his Village Bay has too large a curve and Glen Bay is too small; the Cambir is not narrow enough, and Boreray is rather misshapen. He shows the two glens very clearly, the lower ground between Oiseval and Conachair, and the isthmus towards the south east end of Dun. Stevenson, with his exaggerated promontories and his bold hachures, does convey something of the dramatic quality of the scenery. He gives very few place names.

Figure 14. *Based on Robert Stevenson's map: 1827,
original in National Library of Scotland Ms 5862.10*

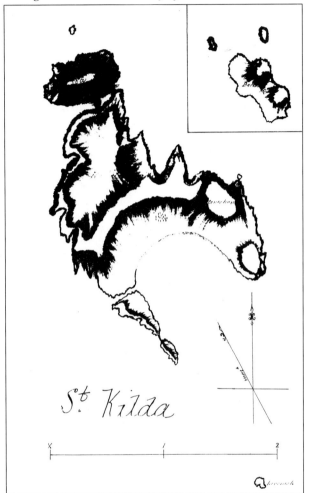

George Clayton Atkinson's map, drawn five years later (figure 15, overleaf), provides a contrast in showing Hirte as a simple oval with minor indentations, with too much space between the Village Glen and Gleann Mór. His shapes for Boreray and Soay would be better if they were transposed, and his 'Down' is too small. His use of the name 'Sulisker' for Levenish is surely the result of confusion, as no one else uses it, and there is no evidence that gannets ever nested on it. Atkinson is the first person to name all three rocks in Soay Sound and his names correspond with those on the Ordnance Survey map.

The anonymous map (figure 16, overleaf) in the Dunvegan archive is difficult to date. It shows the village as a cluster of houses rather than a linear settlement, which suggests that it was drawn before the late 1830s. The

Figure 15. *George Clayton Atkinson's map: 1831*

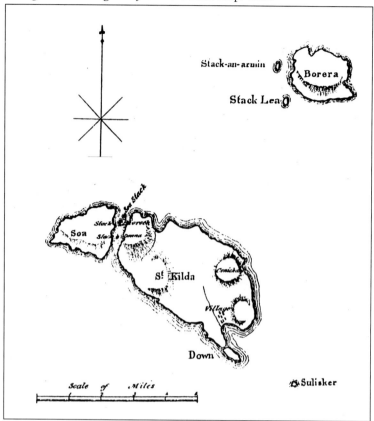

absence of the Church and Manse suggest a date before 1828. Despite this, the style and handwriting suggest a later date, in the mid nineteenth century (Miss Wilkes, Head of Map Library, National Library of Scotland, pers comm). It may be regarded as of a standard similar to Campbell's; although the coast line is inaccurate, it is better than all the others save Campbell's. The shapes of the Cambir, Boreray and Soay are poor, but Dun is better than on any other map. There is no indication of hillslope or cliff; only 'Conagar Hill' is named, and the two main rivulets in Village Glen and Gleann Mór marked. There are more place names than on any of the earlier maps; the stacs in Soay Sound are named as on modern maps. Most of the names given are coastal features; rocks, such as those by 'Stronabec' and 'Levenish' are shown; Village Bay is shown as an anchorage and the landing place or 'Leck' is shown.

Admiralty Chart 2474 (figure 17), first published in 1865 using surveys made in the preceding years, has a poor shape for Hirte, not as good as the anonymous map. Glen Bay is not distinct, the Cambir is too wide, and the south-west coastline too straight. The shapes of Boreray and Soay are not accurate

Figure 16. Based on an anonymous map in Dunvegan archive: ?mid 19th century

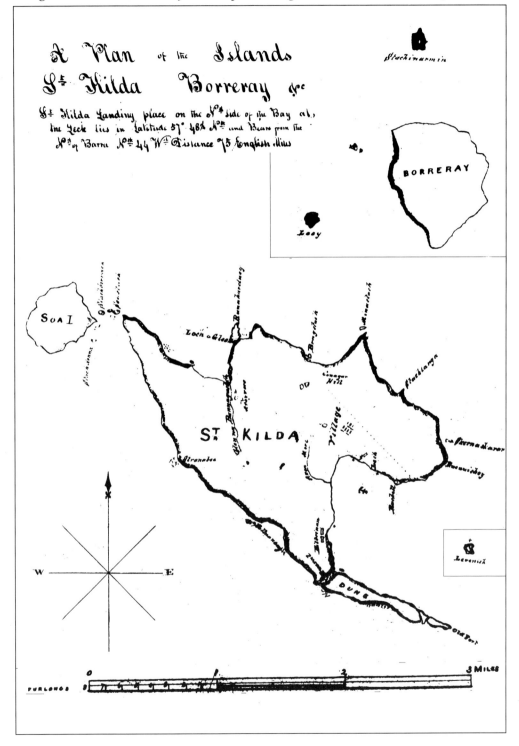

Figure 17. *From Admiralty Chart 2474: 1865*

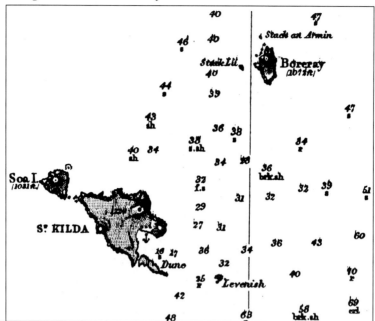

but are an improvement on earlier maps, and their sizes compared with that of Hirte are good. Very few place names are given, but there is some detail of depths in the surrounding waters. Later editions substituted the best available surveys of the islands: first Heathcote's, and now the Ordnance Survey's.

The first reasonably accurate map was that made by Norman Heathcote, published in 1900 (figure 18). He included information from the Admiralty Chart. He indicates slopes by shading and gives a number of spot heights; his figures are close to those of the Ordnance Survey. There are many placenames on his map; he marks the village street and the head dyke, the Factor's House, Church and Burial ground, and in Gleann Mór, the Well of Virtues. He also indicates enclosures in An Lag, and others to the north of the head dyke, and on the western slope of 'Mullach Sgail'. On Boreray he marks the 'Staller's House' and the 'Altar' on Soay. No doubt being a nephew of the proprietor meant that it was easier for Heathcote to gain access to other islands and to circumnavigate all of them, as he probably did if he observed the numerous caves he marks. He would also have been in a good position to gather placenames.

In 1909 the Admiralty made a detailed survey of Village Bay. This appears on Chart 1144, first published in 1911 (figure 19). The greater part of Hirte and all of Dun were incidentally mapped. This is the first map on which contours appear. It is the only record of the name 'Toll sa Duin' for the natural arch on Dun.

Figure 18. *Based on John Norman Heathcote's map: 1900*

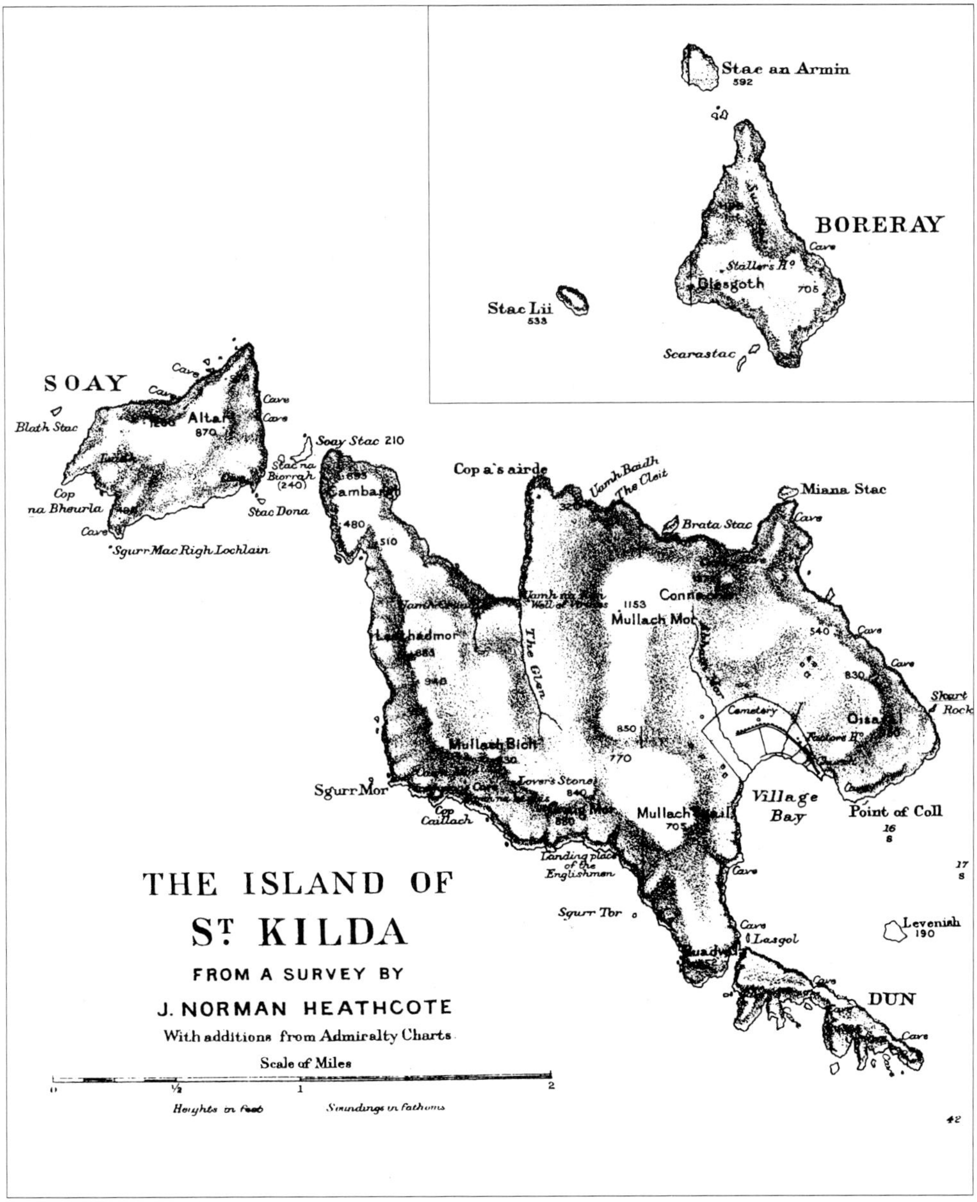

Mathieson's map, made in 1927 and published in 1928, was obviously intended to be definitive (figure 20). It is the first at the large scale of 6 inches to 1 mile. It is an improvement on Heathcote's in its detail and the extra names given, though not in its shape; Boreray and the Stacs and the western coast of Soay are noticeably poor, though better than on most previous maps. On areas of Hirte, Boreray and Soay he shows contour lines at 100' intervals,

Figure 19. *Admiralty Chart 1144: 1911*

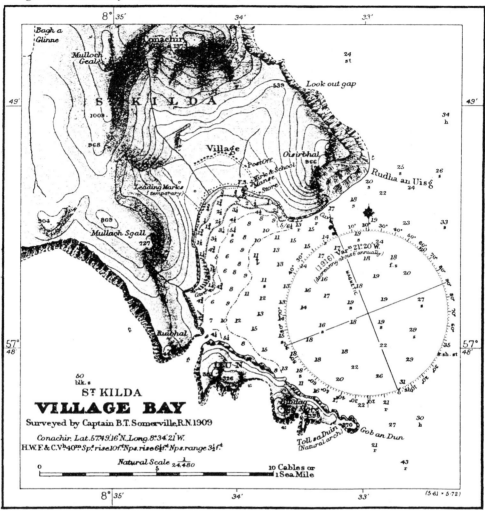

but there are areas of steep slope such as below Claigeann Mór on Hirte, and Sunadal on Boreray, where he does not show these, and there is, reasonably, no attempt to show contours on the very steep and complex slopes. The map includes a detailed inset of the area within the head dyke. This is the first map to show the sites of the three chapels with sufficient accuracy to relocate the spots, though earlier documentary evidence shows that the precise location of Christ Church near the souterrain is wrong as it was clearly within the burial ground. The identification of 'Lady Grange's cleit' (p 144) is questionable, so Mathieson's sites may not always be reliable. It is strange that, having a particular interest in Gaelic place names, he should use the word 'tarn' to describe the two small pools which he marks, but perhaps he was using it deliberately to show that it was not a local name. Mathieson had one great advantage over every subsequent map maker: he was the last person to work on the island while there was still a permanent population living there. Mathieson's version appeared first on the Ordnance Survey 1 inch to 1 mile maps (1:63,360) in the Popular Edition, as an inset on sheet 22, published in 1932.

Though the Admiralty Charts, Heathcote and Mathieson all give latitude and longitude readings in the margins of their maps, it was not until 1957 that the Ordnance Survey finally tied St Kilda in to the national triangulation network (Seymour 1980, 311). The first mapping by the Ordnance Survey and the last mapping of all the islands took place in 1967, and the maps, still at the old 6 inch (1:10,560) scale rather than the 'metricised' 1:10,000 scale, were published in 1970, with the first 2½ inch (1:25,000) map appearing in 1973. This version appears as an inset on the new 'Landranger' (1:50,000) sheet 18, published in 1976.

In the 1970s, new Admiralty surveys took place, and a new Chart, 2524 'Islands of the North West Coast of Scotland' was published in 1977.

St Kilda is a confusing place, with a complicated topography, and it is not surprising that anyone making a short visit, possibly only to Hirte, and working with a limited range of instruments, should produce an inaccurately shaped map. The enthusiasm of the early nineteenth century lapsed; after five maps had been produced between 1799 and 1831, only a few more were made. The islands escaped the attention of the Ordnance Survey itself until the late twentieth century, although, as noted above, it did earlier publish a map made by its retired surveyor.

Area Maps

In 1860, H Sharbau made a plan at a scale of 1 inch to 100 feet (1:1200) of the area within the head dyke, marking dwellings and gardens and some of the cleitean. The names of the tenants of each croft are given (figure 43).

Mathieson's map includes an inset showing the village area at a scale of 25 inches to the mile (1:2500).

In 1957, D R MacGregor mapped the area within the head dyke and a small area just to the north of it in great detail, at a scale of 6 inches to 500 feet (1:100) for the new owners, the National Trust for Scotland. A reduced version was published (MacGregor 1960, 8).

Between 1983 and 1985 A Leith, I Parker, S Scott and G Stell of the Royal Commission for the Ancient and Historical Monuments of Scotland, together with the author, made surveys of the village area, An Lag bho'n Tuath, and a small area on the east side of Gleann Mór (Stell and Harman 1988). This was the first detailed survey of areas outside the village.

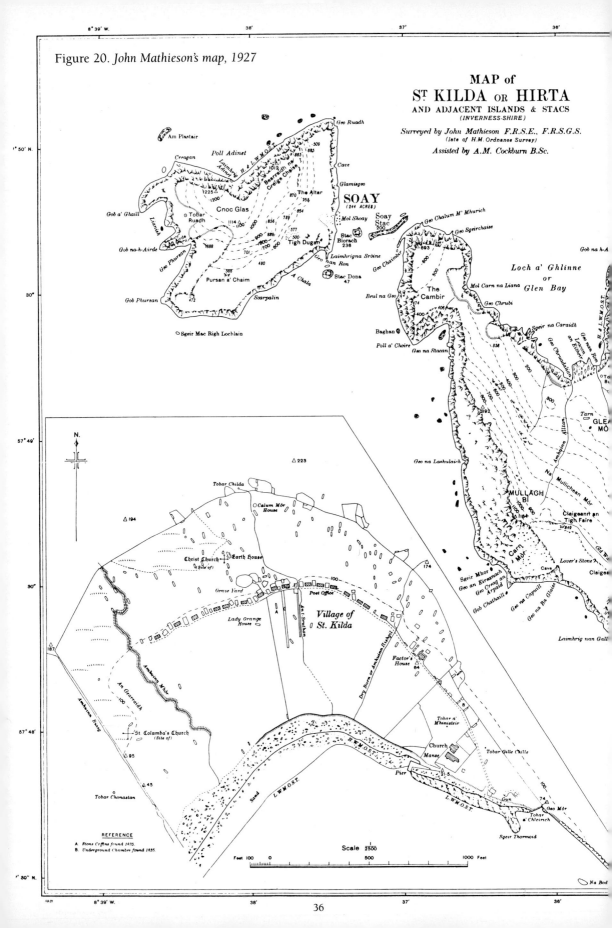

Figure 20. *John Mathieson's map, 1927*

St. KILDA
(1575 ACRES)

BORERAY
(189.7 ACRES)

Stac an Armin
627
Am Biran

Rudh Bhriste

Geargo

Ant-Sail

Geo na Tarnanach

Udraclete

Geo Shunadal

Na Rodchra

Tigh Stallir

Mullach an Tuamail

Clagton

Clagan na Ruskochan

Creagan na
Rubhaig Bana

Geo an Fheachdaire

Geo an Araich

Creagan
Fharspaig

Geo na Leachan Moire

Cleitean
Mc-Phaideim

Geo Sgarbhstac

Coinneag

Sgarbhstac

Rudha Bhrengadal

Gob Scapanish

Laimhail
8° 29′ W.

CONACHAIR

Mina Stac
212

Geo nan Plaidean

Mina Stac

Geo Bhradastac

Na Cleitean

Bradastac
185

Rudh Langa

Geo Lee

Stac Lee
544

1356.8

1044

Tarn

1057

1172
1144
1164

Mullach
Mòr

Mol Ghiasgar

Sgeir Dhomhuill

Stac a' Langa

637

Geo a' Bhroige

Am Broig

Geo na Eaige

The Gap

Rudh Ghill

Glacan
Chonachair

Geo na Muirbhuaile
(Bream)

Lag Aitimir

1397

An Lag
Bho'n Tuath
242

Creagan
Breac

Cnoc na
Gaoithe

OISEVAL

Sgeirnan Sgarbh

Geo nan Sgarbh

Christ Church

Grave Yard

948

Tobar Childa

Glacan
Oiseval

Mullach
Geal

Tigh an Triar

Lady Grange
Ho.

Factor's
Ho.

Creagan
Dubh

Cnoc a' Bheannaichta

St. Columba's Ch.

Church

Manse

Gearraidh
Ard

Tobar a' Chombaiste

Am Blaid

Pier

Rudha an Uisge

Point of Coll or
Rudh Challa

Geo Brababy

Geo d'ha Glann Neill

Loch Sgar
828

Clash na
Bearnaich

Village
Bay

Mullach Sgar

715

or Loch Hirta

Tobar na
Gille

Rudha Mhurch

Na h-Eagan
584

St. Brianan Ch.

Uamh Cailleach Bheag Ruaival

An Torc

Geo Chile Brianan

RUAIVAL
347

Geo Lribli

Ginageir

DÙN
(79.4 ACRES)

Geo na Ruving

Gearr
Sgeir Mhor

Geo Gharran Buidhe

Geo na Seanig

Salg Geo

Altar

An
Fhaing

Bioda

Na Sgarain

Castle

Gob an Duin

Gob na Muce

Sgeir Cul
an Rudha

Hamalan

Scale |1/10560 or Six Inches to One Mile

Heights in feet.
Datum H.W.O.S.T.

Na Bodhan

Levenish
185

Ordnance Survey, 1928.

4
Place names

This survey of place names is based almost entirely on printed sources, mainly maps (figures 9–20), and is limited in two ways. Firstly it is necessary to rely on the recorder having heard and transcribed the names correctly. Mathieson, as a native of Durness, with a particular interest in Gaelic place names and many years of experience in map making, may well be reliable, though he may have been influenced in what he heard by his own local pronunciation (Campbell 1945, 71). Heathcote was not a Gaelic speaker, but as nephew to the proprietor could have called on MacKenzie, the Factor, for advice. Secondly, having no linguistic training, I have relied mainly on Dwelly's *Gaelic-English Dictionary* (1920) to suggest meanings for names which appear to be Gaelic, and largely on Taylor (1967, 124–129) for names which he considered to be Old Norse; I have also considered Watson's (1904) comments on similar place names in Ross and Cromarty, and Coates' (1990) comments on the names of St Kilda, though the catalogue was completed before his book became available. Elsewhere, Coates (1988) has written on the Gaelic dialect of St Kilda, a topic which has also been researched by R D Clement (unpub) and E Hamp (1991, 73–6). I am indebted to Ian Fraser of the School of Scottish Studies Place Name Survey for discussion of this chapter and advice on obscure names. In the following account, only the names and their probable meanings are given, with some discussion; a full list of all versions of names, with sources, and the suggested derivation, is given in Appendix 2. This collection should be of use to others, although I am not competent to comment on the accuracy of the recorders or the derivations suggested by others.

Of 199 place names recorded on Mathieson's (1928) map and copied by the Ordnance Survey (1970), 70% appear for the first time on this map. Eighteen are mentioned by Martin (1753), a native of Skye; only four of these: Hirte, Boreray, Soay and Stac Dona being mentioned by earlier authors. MacAulay (1764), who was from Harris, adds seven more. Both men were Gaelic speakers, and the names they record are important early contributions as are those on the nineteenth century estate map, which provides a further ten names. Eighteen more occur in nineteenth century accounts and thirteen in Heathcote (1900a), some of them in translation. A few names which are quite different from those on the map are given by earlier authors. For instance: MacLean gives Abhainn Bheag for An t-Sruthan; Ross (1890) gives Glen Beag for An Lag bho'n Tuath, and Bid a' Ghaul for Laimhrig nan Gall. These alternatives are not necessarily incorrect. Some names are clearly variations of the ones given by Mathieson, but over twenty names given by others have not been recorded by him; some can be positively located, and others can be located only within a general area (figure 21).

Figure 21. *Place names not marked on Mathieson's map*

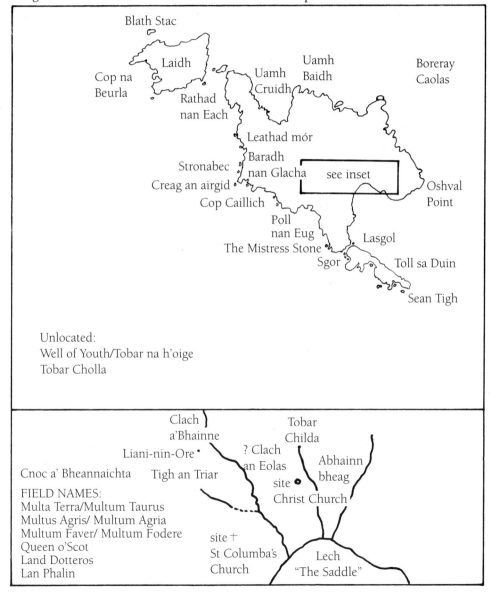

Hirte and St Kilda

The two names of the island group: Hirte and St Kilda, have aroused discussion and controversy for over 200 years, and any consideration of them requires reference to both books and maps; the use of the words in early literature and maps has already been discussed (p 20) and can be summarised briefly: Hirte in various forms was used exclusively in literature until the late seventeenth century; the earliest use of a form of St Kilda appears on Nicolay's maps of 1580 and 1583, copied from a missing map of 1540, but it was used to identify an island close to the west coast of Lewis; not until Waghenaer's chart of 1592 was the name transferred from this to the island group now widely known as St Kilda. MacAulay (1764, 10) said that the true name was 'Hirt' and as far as he could discover, 'St Kilda' was a modern name, scarcely 150 years old. This name superseded Hirte in the published literature after Martin's book of 1698, though Hirte continued to be used in the estate papers early in the eighteenth century; it was the name used by the people of the island for their own home, and it is the name used for preference by Gaelic speakers in the west today. Its precedence is recognised by biologists in the names of the local subspecies of wood mouse (Apodemus sylvaticus hirtensis) and wren (Troglodytes troglodytes hirtensis). Hiort or Hirt (Watson 1926 97–99) or Hirte (MacQueen and MacInnes 1961, 215–219) are spellings in use today: the 'correct' spelling depends ultimately on the derivation, which remains undecided.

Hirte

Boece (1527, fXIIII) wrote in 1527 that the name Hirth 'is given from the sheep, which we call Hierth in the old tongue'.

Buchan (1727, 3) asserts that 'Hirta is taken from the Irish Ier, which in that Language signifies West'. MacAulay (1764, 110–113) derives it fancifully from the exclamation of a storm-driven band of Scandinavian rovers, who might have uttered gratefully 'Hert, Hert' or 'Land, Land' on seeing the island in the midst of the ocean. MacKenzie (1911, 5) derives it from I – island and *ard* – high. Thomas (Kennedy and Thomas 1874, 706) follows Buchan in deriving Hirte from *h–iar–tir* – west land or west country. Watson (1926, 97–99) simply states that Hirte "is identical with Old Irish *hirt, irt* explained by Cormac as *bás*, death" and quotes MacBain's suggestion that it was regarded as the gateway to the Celtic paradise of the Land under the Waves. Watson himself favours the idea that the name was associated with the hazards of living and landing on the islands, and points out that far from being a portal to paradise, the island was regarded in the Hebrides with dislike, verging on fear.

Taylor (1967, 120) consulted with Professor Kenneth Jackson, who felt that the meaning of *irt* or *hirt* was uncertain, being a word which was probably obsolete when Cormac's Irish glossary was compiled about 900 AD. Taylor pointed out that Watson's derivation fails to explain the initial 'h' and he did not believe that an island would be called 'Death', though if the meaning is obscure, that is irrelevant. He expands on a reference noted by Watson to islands called 'Hirtir' mentioned in a thirteenth century Norse saga (p 71). Taylor suggests as Watson did that "the islands that are called Hirtir" can be equated with Hirte, *Hirtir* being the plural of *hjortr* – a stag, so that the islands were called 'Stags', possibly from their jagged outline on the horizon. He quotes Fisher's (1951, 28) comparison of the islands and stacks with "huge and terrible animals, watching each other".

Gauld (1989 43–44) reverts to Boece's derivation. From Fordun, writing about 1380, onwards, early writers associated Hirte with 'wild' sheep (pp 73, 80–81), and Gauld notes that Cody derives 'Hirtha' from Norse *hirth* or *hirt*, meaning a horned animal. He suggests alternatively that it may derive from Old Norse *hjörd*, a flock or herd, as in the Herdwick sheep of the Lake District, so that the Norse might be distinguishing between the 'wild' sheep of Soay and the tended flocks of Hjörd(ay); such a distinction was made by Duke Hakon in a letter about sheep husbandry in the Faeroes in 1298, and there may have been some similar arrangement on Hirte about the same time. In either case, the name would derive from some quality of the sheep population.

Any final decision as to the derivation remains with the etymologists.

There are other place names which apparently include the element *hirt*, but though it might appear to be the same, there could be different derivations in different areas.

For example, Watson points out that *hirt* occurs in *An Duibh-hirteach* which he translates as 'the black deadly one', a small wave-swept rock about sixteen miles west of Colonsay. It was regarded by the people of Colonsay much as Hirte was regarded by the people of Uist: unfavourably. It is certainly very dark in colour, but it is also very low (Munro 1979, 161, 163, 264) so is unlikely to be derived from *ard*; it is in a westerly direction from the southern part of the Inner Hebrides, but Coll and Tiree lie further west; it is undoubtedly a very dangerous rock and must have brought many a seaman to his death before the light began operating in 1872. Only in its dangerous and 'fierce' qualities could it be said to resemble a stag, but these might well be sufficient to warrant the name. It has no association with sheep.

A charter of 1585 (RMS VII 262–5) referring to Orkney and Shetland, begins the detailed list of lands with: lands in the parish of Deerness

41

("Deirnes"), the island of Hirst ("insulam de Hirst"), the lands and the island of Copinsay, and then goes on to list many further properties. The position of the island of "Hirst" in the list suggests that it is geographically close to Deerness and Copinsay but it is not further identifiable at the moment. The name is perhaps unlikely to be derived from a Gaelic or Old Irish word unless it were given by early Irish ecclesiastics. Place names of Celtic origin are very scarce in Orkney, so a Norse derivation is more likely.

Watson also mentions Craighirst in Dumbartonshire (NGR NS 4876) and Ironhirst Moss in Dumfriessshire (NGR NY 0471), the latter, he says, possibly derived from "*earran hirt* or portion of death" referring to the dangers of the morass: but both these names could be derived from 'hurst' (I Fraser pers comm).

Watson and Taylor's identification of "Hirtir" as Hirte/St Kilda is very attractive, and there seems no reason to doubt it, since there is good artefactual evidence for Norse occupation there. If that is the case, then the use of the name "Hirtir" is over a century earlier than the Hert and Heryce/Hyrte of the 1372 charters, or Fordun's Hirth (1380), the earliest known use of the name otherwise. If Hirst in Orkney is another example of the name, then both might well be derived from *hjortr*, or possibly hjörd. Of these, An Duibh-hirteach is more likely to be derived from the former, which might refer to the fearsome character of the rock; just as, perhaps, *An torc* was applied to the small but dangerous rock on the west side of Mullach Sgar. If the Old Irish *irt,* whatever it means, were the origin for Hirte/St Kilda and An Duibh-hirteach it would imply that the name was probably established before Norse occupation, and therefore that there was sufficient continuity of settlement, or reference to the islands, to ensure the survival of the name.

Hirte refers to the main island only. When at sea the islanders did not use the name but referred to it as 'the Country' (Adv Ms 33.3.20) and to Boreray as 'the Northern Country' (Martin 1716, 291).

St Kilda

Scott (1928 193) notes that there is no saint called Kilda though Farmer (1978, 234) has created a 'virtually unknown saint who has given his (or her) name to the remote island to the west of the Outer Hebrides'.

The name St Kilda has been linked with the name of one of the principal wells in the island; Martin (1753, 16) says that it was called "St Kilder's Well" and Buchan (1727, 3) declares that this is "from one Kilder, who lived here". MacAulay (1764, 102–108) dismissed his own suggestions that "St Kilda" could be derived from St Hilda, Abbess of Whitby, or Gildas, the historian, offering instead the idea that Tobar Childa Chalda was derived from "Tober

Ghille Dee Ghaueldie" or the "Well of the stranger Culdee", and that later some one had concluded that the well must be named after a saint, as wells often are, and so produced "St Kilda". MacLean (1838, 4) links the name with "*cill*, a cell or sepulture", but Thomas (Kennedy and Thomas 1874, 706) reverts to MacAulay's idea, deriving it from "Eilean Cheile Dé naomh" or "island of the Holy Culdee".

Watson (1926, 98) also derives St Kilda from the well, the name of which he derived from *Tobar* (Gaelic) a well; *Kelda* (Old Norse) a well; Taylor (1967, 126) adds Norse *Kalda* cold, so that the name would mean Well Cold Well; the repetition of Well and the Gaelic form of *Childa Chalda* implies that the Norse name was taken over by Gaelic speakers who did not understand it. The triple name occurred in a rhyme Watson knew as a child in Easter Ross (p 243).

In another article (1969, 145–158) Taylor dismisses the derivation of "St Kilda" from the well or any other previously mentioned origin, and offers a new and attractive explanation, based on map evidence and summarised in the previous section (p 20). Briefly, the name 'St Kilda' is derived from 'skilder' or 'skalder', a name applied in various forms in early maps to an island near the west coast of Lewis; Leslie (1578) and Ortelius (1573), though copying from earlier maps, inserted a stop after the S. and in 1592 Waghenaer transferred the name from this island to Hirte. 'Skilder' near Lewis disappeared from the maps soon after and can no longer be identified.

However, Heathcote (1900, 12) refers to a Dr MacPhaill who visited Hirte in 1899, and who observed that then the St Kildans
   pronounce r like l, so Hirta becomes Hilta, or almost Kilta, as the H has a somewhat guttural sound. Granted that this peculiarity of pronunciation was in vogue two hundred years ago (a by no means improbable assumption, as Martin mentions that they had a curious lisp in their speech), it is obviously easy to transform Kilta into St Kilda.

Gauld (1985, 3) made the same suggestion independently, and later (1988 32–35) integrated this with Watson's explanation, arguing that 'St Kilda' could be derived from a local pronunciation of Hirte, which would sound to foreign visitors very like the 'Childa' of Tobar Childa, and sailors, knowing that wells were often named for saints, would add the 'Saint' on their own initiative.

Martin (1753, 21, 45–6) mentions visits by sailors in the seventeenth century and Gauld (1989, 48–51) shows that English and continental fishermen were working in the area from at least the sixteenth century.

Names based on physical description
Most of these are self explanatory, and a look at the map shows that they are

reasonable descriptions. Abhainn Mhór may be contrasted with Abhainn Bheag [An t-Sruthan]. The Abhainn Riasg flows through some very soggy areas before dropping to its present canalised course beside the head dyke; it probably once flowed through another wet area to join the Abhainn Mhór. Am Blaid may be 'The Mouth' – or entrance – to Gleann Mór. *Càrn* may refer to an artifical cairn or to a natural boulder field; I have used 'heap of rocks' to avoid any artificial implication of 'cairn'. Watson (1904, 102) notes that *claigionn* is commonly applied to a knob shaped hill and does not have to mean 'skull' literally, so I have used the colloquial 'nob'. *Geo* I have translated as 'cleft', though many people will be familiar with the word, used of the coastal feature of a narrow creek or gulf between rocks. Heathcote's use of *uaimh*, 'cave' instead suggests that sometimes there is an associated cavity; there are many caves round the shoreline. *Mol*, though translated as 'shingle', generally refers to pebble beaches rather than the large boulders found on St Kilda shores, noted ironically by MacLean (1838, 38) as '*doirneagan Hirt*' or 'St Kilda pebbles'; some of them weigh several tons. Mol Carn na Liana is at the foot of the steep boulder field on the north side of level ground at the 'neck' of the Cambir.

Dwelly gives some very precise terms for rocks, particularly in relation to the sea, and there are no brief English equivalents for these. *Bodha* is a rock over which the waves break, but is only visible at low water springs (I. Fraser pers comm); *Sgeir* from the Old Norse *sker* is a 'rock in the sea nearly or not quite covered by neap tides and quite covered by spring tides', while in Lewis *Leac* is 'a ledge of rock jutting out from the foot of a cliff on the foreshore, and covered by the sea at flood tides'.

Names on Hirte: *Abhainn Alltan* Stream of Brooks; *Abhainn Bheag* Little Stream; *Abhainn a' Ghlinne Mhóir* Stream of the Big Glen; *Abhainn Mhór* Big Stream; *Abhainn Riasg* Stream of the marshes or moors; *Aird Uachdarachd* Upper Promontory; *Baghan* Little Bay; *Beul na Geo* Mouth of the Cleft; *Am Blaid* The Mouth – perhaps the mouth of the glen – the way over to Gleann Mór; *Bradastac* Steep Stack; *Cambir* Crest or Ridge; *Carn Mór* Great Cairn or Pile of Rocks; *Clash na Bearnaich* Fissured Gutter; *Claigeann Mór* Big Nob; *Na Cleitean* The Cliffs; *Na h-Eagan* The Ridges; *The Gap* probably originally *Bearraidh na h-Eige* Precipice of the Edge; *Geo na h-Airde* Cleft of the Promontory; *Geo Bhradastac* Cleft of the Steep Stack; *Geo Chaimbir* Cleft of the Cambir; *Geo na Eaige* possibly for Geo na h-eige, Cleft of the Edge/Ridge; *Geo na Mol* Cleft of the Shingle; *Geo Mór* Big Cleft; *Geo Sgeir Chaise* Cleft of the steep rock; *Geo na Stacan* Cleft of the Little Stac; *Giasgeir* Skerry of the Geo or Cleft; *Glacan Mór* Big Gulleys; *Glen Beag* Small Glen [An Lag bho'n Tuath]; *Gleann Mór* Big Glen; *Gob na h-Airde* Point of the Promontory; *Leac*

Mhina Stac Mina Stac Slab; *Leacan an t-Sluic Mhóir* Slabs of the Big Cavern;
Leathad a 'Ghlinne Broad Slope of the Glen; *Loch a' Ghlinne* or Glen Bay; *Mina
Stac* Lesser Stack; *Mol Carn na Liana* Shingle of the Heap of Rocks of the
Plain; *Mol Ghiasgar* Shingle of the Skerry of the Cleft; *Mullach Bi* Pillar or
Post Summit; *Mullach Mór* Big Summit; *Na Mullichean Mór* The Big Summits;
Rubha an Uisge Point of the Water [implying fresh water, is very close to a
trickle of water gathered from the steep slopes above]; *Sgeir Mhór* Big Skerry
[below Carn Mór]; *Sgeir Mhór* Big Skerry [at the end of the Kyles of Dun]; *An
t-Sruthan* The Burn or The Rivulet.

Some of the 'unlocated names' should be included here: *Baradh nan Glacha*
Ridge of the Gulleys; *Lech* Slab used for the landing place [also called The
Saddle]; *Leathadmor* Big Broad Slope; *Sgòr* Rock: a cleft beside the Kyles of
Dun; *Stronabec*? Small Point; *Uamh Baidh* Cave of the Bay.

On Dun: *A' Bhì* The Pillar or Post; *Bioda Mór* Big Peak; *A' Chlaisir* ?The
Cleft; *Cul Cleite* Back of the Cliff or Rock; *Geo Ghiasgeir* Cleft of the Skerry of
the Geo or Cleft; *Na Sgarain* The Fissures; *Sgeir Cul an Rubha* Skerry at the
back of the Point; and for the natural arch: *Toll sa Duin* Hole of Dun.

Beside Levenish are: *Na Bodhan* The Skerries.

On Soay: *An Airde* The Promontory; *Bearraidh na Creige Chaise* Precipice of
the Steep Cliff; *Creagan* Cliffs; *Gob na h-Airde* Point of the Promontory;
Laimhrig na Sròine Landing Place of the Neb; *Scarpalin* Sharp Rock or Sharp
Slope; *Stac Biorach* Pointed Stack; [also given the name 'the Thumb rock'].

On Boreray and its Stacks: *Clesgor* Rift of the Cliff; *Gearrgeo* Short Cleft;
Geo na Leachan Móire Cleft of the Big Slabs (if nan leacan móra); *Mullach an
Eilean* Summit of the Island; *Mullach an Tuamail* Summit abounding in
Hollows or Bumps; *Udraclete* Outer Cliff; on Stac an Armin are: *Am Biran* The
Twig; and *Rubha Bhriste* Broken Point.

Names incorporating direction

The Norse name Oiseval and the Gaelic name An Lag bho'n Tuath suggest
that when these names were first used, the settlement was in approximately
the area where it is now, the most hospitable area. Oiseval could, however,
refer to the geographical position of the hill rather than its relationship to any
settlement. *An Lag bho'n Tuath* The Northward Hollow [Glen Beag]; *North
Glen* [of Gleann Mór]; *Oiseval* Eastern Hill and from this: *Glacan Oiseval*
Oiseval Gulleys; and the 'unlocated' name: *Oshval Point*.

Names incorporating colours or colour qualities

Ruaival is red, or rather pink, for a short time each year when thrift flowers
luxuriantly on its lower slopes. Tobar Ruadh on Soay has no neat well cover

but there is a small trickle of water with iron staining producing a rusty colour. Creag an airgiod, somewhere on the south west side of Hirte, may be associated with mica as MacLean (1838, 3) suggests, but a large expanse of wet rock catching the sunlight can look like a sheet of silver. I have seen this effect on a rock near Carn Mór, and it was startling.

On Hirte: *Abhainn Gleisgil* Shining Stream in the Gully; *Creagan Breac* Speckled Small Crag; *Creagan Dubh* Black or Dark Small Crag; *Mullach Geal* White Summit; *Ruaival* Red Hill; and from this: *Abhainn Ruaival* Stream of Ruaival. An 'unlocated' name is *Creag-an-airgid* Rock of the Silver – the sheep-silver or mica, according to MacLean (1838, 3). Coates (1990, 101) suggests Yellow Point for *Rubha Ghill* though *gile* means 'whiter'.

Levenish possibly Grey Island (Coates 1990, 62).

On Soay: *Cnoc Glas* Grey Hill; *Geo Ruadh* Red Cleft; *Tobar Ruadh* Red Well.

Names incorporating natural aspects and qualities

The top of Mullach Sgar has a thin soil, and is bare of vegetation in places; the loch marked by Mathieson is in a shallow hollow and the small pool is usually dry in summer; however, in local tradition, it was once the home of a water bull (p 235). Updraughts and downdraughts may be responsible for Cnoc na Gaoithe. MacLean (1838, 43) seems to be confused about the location of the name *con'ghair*, which he applies to a stack, or possibly the main cliff of Conachair, deriving it from the noise of the surge at the foot of the cliff. If the name is connected with 'tempest' or 'uproar', which is possible but not certain, then it could be from the noise of the wind blowing down the hill; the inhabitants of a settlement at the foot of the Glacan Conachair, where the pre 1830s village was, would find the noise and buffeting of winter gales roaring down those gulleys memorable.

On Hirte: *Cnoc na Gaoithe* Knoll of the Wind; *Mullach Sgar* Bare Summit and from this: *Loch Sgar* [*Cnoc Sgar* is probably a mistake for Loch Sgar]; and possibly: *Conachair* perhaps Roarer, from the noise of the winds roaring up or down its slopes, and from this: *Glacan Chonachair* Conachair Gulleys. *Na Bodha Sine* may mean Nipple Rock. Another sound name occurs on Boreray: *Geo na Tarnanach* Cleft of the Thunder, and here too is *An t-Sail* probably The Heel. *Rubha Bhrengadal* Point of the Dale of the Breast.

Subjective names

Geo Chruadalian, if it means 'dangerous cleft' and Geo Chrubaidh may refer to difficulties of access to bird colonies.

The name Stac Dona was, in Martin's time, the name of the Stac now known as Stac Biorach, a name which does not occur before MacAulay's account (1764) (pp 24, 25). Martin (1753, 20) explains clearly that it was called the Mischievous Rock, because several people had died in climbing it, and he mentions the part called the *Thumb* where the climber had to support himself only by his thumb in the ascent. There seems no reason to doubt, given this detailed account, that in the seventeenth century the name Stac Dona was used for the stac now called Stac Biorach, and that the latter name came into use some time before MacAulay's visit in 1758; his explanation (MacAulay 1764, 121) that Stack Dona was bad because it was the only rock where there were no breeding birds is perfectly reasonable, but it does not mean that the name cannot have been transferred from a rock which was bad for another reason. It is unlikely that the first name for Stac Biorach would have been forgotten; some of the men who survived the smallpox epidemic in 1727 had probably climbed it, and passed on the route to later generations (p 222).

On Hirte: *Geo Chruadalian* ?Dangerous Cleft possibly the same as Uamh Cruaidh [Hard or Difficult Cave]; *Geo Chrùbaidh* Cleft of the Bending or crouching. I Fraser (pers comm) suggests Point of the Wager for *Rubha Ghill*, commemmorating some lost incident.

On Soay: *A' Chala* The Shore or Port, perhaps to indicate a landing place; and in Soay Sound: *Stac Dona* Bad or Evil Stack.

Names incorporating animals

Few rocks or cliffs are named for birds, although the great bird colonies were so important. Perhaps the number and size of the colonies would render the use of many bird names uninformative. It is difficult to understand why only a few sites should be specially associated with kittiwakes or the great black-backed gull, though the latter occurs in small numbers; gulls were regarded as enemies and these may have been noted nesting or roosting sites. *Skarfr* is usually given as 'cormorant'; these birds bred on the islands in the nineteenth century (Harris and Murray 1978, 14), possibly before, but they are unlikely to have been common and are scarcely ever seen now. Shags, also known colloquially as the green cormorant or the crested cormorant, occur in hundreds, mainly at a few sites. Cormorants and shags are popularly regarded as synonymous, and so *Skarfr* is here translated as 'shag'. Heathcote (1900, 149) says that the place where the great auk used to breed 'is still called "the rock of the garefowl"', though he did not mark it on his map; Elliott (1895a, 30; 1895b, 285) notes that a ledge on Soay where the bird bred was named after it.

A note on Mathieson's map suggests that he translated Geo na Muirbhuaile as Cleft of the Bream; two species of sea bream occur in the area: Sands (1878, 42) noted men fishing for bream from a rock on summer evenings.

Seals occur all round the islands. They haul out on the slabs at Seilg Geo;
and Geo nan Ròn may well be where seals were hunted in the seventeenth
century (p 225). Pigs may have been kept in the remote past, though there is
no record of it (p 187). Gob na Muce may have been named by a native, or
perhaps one of the steward's crew who was more accustomed to pigs. Fraser
(1978, 258–9) has pointed out the common use in Gaelic of animal names for
sea rocks and coastal features and An Torc is probably an example of this: a
feature to steer clear of, quite literally. The unlocated Rathad nan Each may
refer to the grazing of ponies at the Cambir. While the Bó Ghlas and the
Capull may just be coastal features, they could well have been specific
animals who were tempted by rich grazing too far down the steep slopes
above the geos named after them; similarly, the Gearran Buidhe might just be
a rock, or where the animal's body was found.

On Hirte: *Geo na Bà Glaise* Cleft of the grey Cow; *Geo na Capuill* Cleft of
the mare/horse; *Geo Gharran Buidhe* Cleft of the tawny horse; *Geo na
Muirbhuaile* Cleft of the Sea Bream; *Geo nan Ròn* Cleft of the Seals; *Geo nan
Sgarbh* Cleft of the Shags; *Sgeir nan Sgarbh* Rock of the Shags; *An Torc* The
Boar; also the 'unlocated' name: *Rathad nan Each* Track of the Horses or Path
of the Horses, a pass at the Cambir.

On Dun: *Geo na Ruideig* Cleft of the Kittiwake; *Giumachsgor* Lobster skerry;
Gob na Muce Pig's Snout; *Seilg Geo* Geo of Seals.

On Soay: *Soay* or *Soa* Sheep Island and from this: *Mol Shoay* Beach of Soay
and *Soay Stack*; *Geo nan Ròn* Cleft of the Seals.

On Boreray: *Creagan Fharspeig* Crags of the Great Black-backed Gull;
Sgarbhstac Shags' Stack and from this: *Geo Sgarbhstac* Shags' Stack Cleft.

Names incorporating man-made objects

Some of these are probably based on the resemblance, real or fancied, of the
feature to the object for which it is named. However, there is no obvious
association between part of Oiseval and a compass, and the story behind this
name is lost. A small boat could be brought ashore at Leacan an Eithir, in the
same way that several canoes were on one occasion in 1989. Geo na Plaidean
is explained by MacLean (1838, 42): 'where the natives lie the whole night in
narrow cliffs, with blankets to cover them from the sea spray, watching the
arrival of the Fulmer in the morning'. Possibly rooing took place near Clagan
na Rùsgachan.

On Hirte: *Am Broig* The Shoe or Hoof and from this: *Geo a'Bhroige* Shoe
cleft; *Geo nan Plaidean* Cleft of the Blankets; *Gob Chathaill* if it means Chair
Point; *Leacan an Eithir* Slabs of the Boat; *Poll a'Choire* Cauldron Pool; *Tot a*

Chombaiste Knoll of the ?compass and the 'unlocated' name of the landing rock: *The Saddle*.

On Dun: *Hamalan* Anvil Rock?

On Boreray: *Clagan na Rùsgachan* Nob of the Fleeces.

Names incorporating artificial landscape features

Airigh Mhór Big Shieling, refers to the 'Amazon's House' or possibly to the complex of shieling structures in that area (pp 75–78). *Gearraidh* is 'green pasture land about a township; fenced field; enclosed grazing between the arable land and the open moor; common grazing and arable land between the moor and the crofts.' In the Western Isles it is always enclosed (I Fraser pers comm). *An Gearraidh*, west of the Abhainn Mhór is now enclosed by the head dyke; most of it appears only suitable for grazing. If the name is older than the head dyke, it could refer to some sort of enclosure around St Columba's chapel, sited in this area. *An Gearraidh Ard*, on the slope above it, is reasonable grazing land with some shelter; there are several small enclosures which show some evidence of cultivation and there is a hint, in fragments of dyke, that there may once had been a long dyke protecting this area (pp 78–79). *Geo Chille Brianan* Cleft of Brendan's Church is self evident. Wells are considered below.

There are two fortress names. *Dun* Fort or Fastness sometimes with *fir-bholg* – Fort of the ancient Irishmen and from this: *Caolas an Duin* Kyles or Straits of Dun, and *Gob an Dùin* Point of Dun; and *Boreray* Fort Island, and from this *Boreray Caolas*: Sound of Boreray [not on maps]. Neither of these islands is easy to land on or to ascend, particularly Boreray, and thus both give an impression of being naturally fortified. The same is also true of Soay, which of the three is probably the most difficult to land on, but this is not reflected in the name. Dun is sometimes used for a feature which is entirely natural but suited for defence, such as the hill Dun Conuill, Lewis. The name of Dun is generally considered to be based on two fragments of walling at the east end, sometimes named as 'fort', or 'castle' on Mathieson's map, but of no practical defensive value, though beyond them is the *Sean Tigh* Old House (p 66). There is no trace or record of any fortification on Boreray. The Taigh Stallar was clearly not a defensive structure, but if the *Borg* of Boreray refers to a building rather than the natural defences of the island, this is the only known candidate.

Sgeir na Caraidh, skerry of the weir or fish trap may be from its appearance, jutting into Glen Bay like the end of a weir.

An Fhaing on Dun shows no traces of an artificial sheep pen but may have been used as a strategic point in catching sheep on Dun.

Names associated with people

Some of these are people of whom nothing else is known, such as, on Hirte: *Geo Chalum McMhuirich* Malcolm Murchison's Cleft, or Cleft of Malcolm, Murdo's son; *Geodha Clann Neill* The MacNeils' Cleft; *Geo Rubha Mhuirich* Cleft of Murdo's Point; *Rubha Mhuirich* Murdo's Point; *Sgeir Thormoid* Norman's Skerry.

On Boreray: *Cleitean McPhaidein* MacFadyen's Cleitean.

Some are associated with un-named people of whom nothing else is known: On Hirte: *Claigeann an Tigh Faire* Knob of the Watch House and *Tigh an fhir faireadh* The Watchman's House: all the landing places on Hirte were supposed to be visible from here; *Geo na Seanaig* Cleft of the Little Old One (female) Coates (1990, 93) suggests an association with the old woman of the church burning story, who used the cave on Ruaival (p 232); and the 'unlocated' *Cop Caillach* Point of the Old Woman.

On Boreray: *Geo an Fheachdaire* Warrior's Cleft; *Stac an Armuinn* The Warrior's Stack or The Hero's Stack or possibly The Steward's Stack, if the name goes back to the Norse influenced occupation; perhaps at one time the Steward demanded the produce of this stack just as within historic times he demanded a proportion of sheep stock or all the milk. Martin (1753, 19) records that Levenish, or rather its produce, 'by an ancient custom' belonged to the steward's crew.

Names associated with traditional tales or historical incidents

Some names have a particular association with a character who appears only in a traditional tale (Chapter 13), on Hirte: the 'Female Warrior': *Tigh na Banaghaisgeach /Airidh na Banaghaisgeach* House or Shieling of the Female Warrior or Heroine [also Airidh Mhór The Big Shieling and 'Giantess' House'] giving a name to the whole glen: *Gleann na Bana-ghaisgeach* The Glen of the Female Warrior [also Gleann Mór The Big Glen: contrast with Glean Beag for An Lag bho'n Tuath]; *Calum Mór* who built a house: Big Malcolm's House [also The Strong Man's House]; the poor storm-driven Irishman: *Geo an Eireanach* Cleft of the Irishman [also recorded as *Damph-an-Eiranich* and *Uamh an Eireanach*]; and the sole survivor of the church burning incident: *Uamh Cailleach Bheag Ruaival* The Little Old Woman's Cave, Ruaival.

The same incident is remembered on Soay in the name of one of the perpetrators: *Taigh Dugan* Dugan's Home [also Dugan's Cave] together with the unfortunate Scandinavian prince: *Sgeir Mac Righ Lochlainn* Skerry of the Son of the King of Norway [Scandinavia].

On Boreray, much is recorded about the home of an indistinct figure: Stallar or The Stallar: *Tigh Stallar* Stallar's House: for which Taylor (1967, 132) suggests Steward's House from *taigh* G: house; *stallari* ON: king's marshal or similar officer; but alternatively it may be House of the overhanging rock or crag. It had bed spaces called: *Rastalla, Ralighe, Beran, Shimidaran, Leaba nan Con*, or the dog's bed (more properly, the dogs' bed), *Leaba an tealich*, or the Fireside bed; *Bar Righ* was the name of the door (Kennedy and Thomas 1874, 705). Rastalla is obscure; Ralighe might be a crypt, consistent with the subterranean character of the house, but the association with the grave makes this an unlikely name for a bed space and it could be connected with *laighe* lying down; Beran may be related to *beàrn* a cranny; Shimidaran may be related to *similear* a chimney (I. Fraser pers comm.); Leaba nan con and and Leaba an tealich are convincingly translated, and Bar Righ is the top of the Bothy; a reasonable place for the entrance to an underground house.

Poll nan eug, on Hirte, The Pool of Death or Pool of the Spectres, may have its origin in a vision, or perhaps an accident.

Historical incidents are also commemorated. On Hirte, *Laimhrig nan Gall* Landing place of the Strangers [probably the same as Bid a Ghaul and Landing Place of the Englishmen, in the same location] and on Soay, *Gob a' Ghaill* Point of the Stranger [also *Cop na Bheurla* Point of the Englishman] may be associated with particular incidents recorded elsewhere, or with similar occurrences.

The visit of Coll MacDonald to Hirte in 1615 (pp 84–5) may be remembered in *Rubha Challa* or Point of Coll, and in the 'unlocated' *Tobar-Cholla* Coll's Well, though there is an alternative explanation for these names in a traditional story.

Some commemorative names have not stood the test of time; indeed even the pool where peats were cut for Lady Grange (p 90) is no longer readily identifiable, and possibly only the record of its name: *Poll na Ban-tighearna* The Lady's Pool provides evidence of its former existence. It is tempting to identify it with the 'tarn' recorded by Mathieson between Mullach Mór and Conachair. Loch a' Ghlinne was dignified by the name of 'MacLeod's Bay' in 1838 to commemorate the visit of the Rev. Norman Macleod to the island, and at the same time Village Bay was given the name 'Dickson's Bay', after the Rev. Dr. Dickson, controller of the S.S.P.C.K., had fallen into it while getting into a boat. Neither of these names survived for long. *Sgeir Dhomhnuill* Donald's Skerry, according to Lachlan MacDonald (Quine: 1982, 41–2) was named for Donald MacQueen, who was posted there during occasional expeditions to shoot shags near Rubha an Uisge, during the 1920s.

Names associated with Christianity and other beliefs including well names

Visitors in the more distant past (pp 66–9) have left little tangible evidence, but the names of the chapels they founded survive. *Christ's Chapel* or Christ's Church, which stood where the burial ground is, is recorded by MacKenzie as dedicated to Mary, but as almost every other author is agreed that it was Christ's Church, MacKenzie was probably mistaken. A little to the west was *St Columba's chapel*, and further south and west still, *St Brendan's chapel*, referred to by Martin as St Brianan's. The general location of this site is confirmed by the well *Tobar na Cille* Well of the Church, and the adjacent *Geo Chille Brianan* Cleft of Brendan's Church. Although the 'unlocated' names *St Peters*, *St Johns*, and *St Clemens* are recorded by one source (Adv ms 33.3.20), it seems likely that there has been some confusion here with sites in Uist and Harris.

Other wells also have ecclesiastical connections, though perhaps not such a long history: *Tobar a'Chleirich* The Clergyman's Well; *Tobar Gille Cille* Well of the Servant of the Church and *Tobar a' Mhinisteir* The Minister's Well.

The meaning of *Tobar Chonastan* is obscure, but it is probably the same as Martin's *Conirdan*. Martin also mentions the *Well of Youth* which occurs again in some later authors, in some cases incorporated within a tale (pp 236, 243) as Tobir na h'oige.

Martin's *St Kilder's Well/Kilder's Well* or as MacAulay referred to it, *Tober Childa Chalda*, has been considered above.

The islands were famous for another well also: *Tobar nam Buaidh* Well of Virtues or of Excellent Qualities, probably the same as *Tobir na slainnte* referred to by MacGillivray. Here, apparently, the people made small offerings, as they used also to do at several 'altars' in different places: one of these survives on Soay and is marked on the map.

An area on the slopes of Mullach Geal, probably close to the route between the village and Gleann Mór, was clearly held sacred in some way (p 228), and several place names (some 'unlocated') in this area bear this out: here are: *Liani-nin-ore* Plain of spells or Incantations; *Tigh an Triar* House of the Three: possibly Euphemia MacCrimmon had this in mind when she referred to Teampull na Trionaid in her version of the church burning story (Kennedy 1874). Above these is *Cnoc a'Bheannaichta* Hillock of the Blessed; while below is *Clach a' bhainne* The Milk Stone, where milk was offered to a 'Gruagach' – 'Brownie'.

Somewhere is the 'unlocated' *Clach an eòlas* Stone of Knowledge (p 228).

Other supernatural spirits, the *sithichean* or fairies left traces of their occupation; in the low land under cultivation there were *gnocan sithichean* or fairy knolls – 'green mounds looked upon as the abodes of fairies scattered in arable land' (MacKenzie 1911, 6) and the souterrain was known as *Taigh an t-sithiche* the Fairy's House, or more prosaically, *Tigh fo Talamh* House Under the Ground (pp 63–4).

The location of *The Mistress Stone*, first mentioned by Martin, is clearly near the summit of Ruaival (p 229), but in the nineteenth century there was some confusion over its site: it was referred to first as the Lover's Stone in 1861 (Morgan) and was equated by Connell (1887) with Stac Biorach. A completely different stone, no less impressive for the purpose, but not in use, was pointed out to Heathcote, who duly marked it on his map and published an imaginative reconstruction sketch of the test at this site in his book, in which he acknowledges also that this was not the site of Martin's 'Mistress Stone'.

Names of fields

The field names given by Martin (1716) are: *Multa Terra* and *Multus Agris*, and MacAulay (1764) gives: *Multum agria, Multum taurus, Multum favere* or *Multum fodere, Queen o Scot, Land dotteros* or the Doctor's ground, and *Lan-phalin*, or Paul's division. Both authors have probably forced some of these names into a Latin form. Taylor (1967, 127–9) has summarised studies of these names, and Coates (1990, 149–52) has additional comments. Multum Agris/Multum Agria may mean cultivated soil or barren soil; Multum Taurus, probably the same as Multa Terra, may mean 'dry soil' and Multum Favere or Fodere, Fair, in the sense of good, soil. Coates suggests 'turf land' for Multum Taurus. The first part of Queen o Scot probably means enclosure at…, possibly, according to Coates, at the hollow or nook. Land dotteros incorporates land, and may mean Daughter's land, or possibly Land of the Rift, perhaps referring to one of the stream gullies. Lan-Phalin may mean Paul's Land, or slumped, and so, wet land. Both Taylor and Coates agree that these are names of Norse origin rather than Gaelic. I Fraser (pers comm) suggests Lan-phalin may derive from Gaelic *lann*: enclosure, especially a religious enclosure.

Obscure and doubtful names

There is a high proportion of names whose origin is obscure (I. Fraser pers comm). Some names present problems: *Stac a' Langa* on Hirte and *Rubha Langa* on Stac Lee could be 'long' from Old Norse *langa*, or as Coates (1990, 166) suggests they may be 'slim' or even 'treacherous' from Gaelic *langach*. Stac Lee may mean 'Water Stack' (Carmichael 1928b, 318) perhaps because, astonishingly, a spring of fresh water was supposed to exist there (Adv. ms.

33.3.20). Alternatively it may be from *liath* 'grey', which MacLean (1838, 3) gives as 'hoary'. *Geo Lee*, on this stack, presumably has the same derivation.

On Hirte, *Geo na Lashulaich* may have some connection with *lasail*: fiery, inflammable. *Lag Aitimir* may be a Norse Gaelic hybrid name, implying that the name was originally 'Aitimir' which may incorporate *hamarr* hammer or anvil shaped rock (I Fraser, pers comm). *Leathad a' Sgithoil Chaoil* may mean the Broad Slope of the Narrow Bothy, but though there are one or two cleitean on this wide, steep slope, there is now no sign of a bothy, if ever there was one there.

On Boreray *Coinneag* Bay of the Women or Frothy Bay; near Taigh Stallar, *Geo an Araich* might well be the Cleft of the Watchman, if a guard were kept while the house was in use; or it may be the Cleft of the Rearing or Nurturing, or the Cleft of the Apparition; such manifestations were recorded (p 228); *Gob Scapanish* Point Point of Caves or possibly Point Sharp Headland; Coates (1990, 75) rejects Sun Valley as a possible meaning for *Sunadal*, though facing the rising sun, it does not seem unsuitable; he suggests Vertigo Slope, also apt; from this, *Geo Shunadal. Creagan na Rubhaig Bana* may mean Little Rock of the Little White Point if *rubhaig* is a diminutive of *rubha*.

On Soay there are two groups of names incorporating obscure words. *Laimhrig Adinet* and *Poll Adinet*, 'landing place' and 'pool', both use the obscure 'Adinet' which might be derived from *dion aite* 'secure place' (I Fraser pers comm), though the north side of the island is very inhospitable. 'Pursan', possibly from *peursa* 'signal pole' (I Fraser pers comm), appears in *Pursan a'Chaim*? of the Fraud, or Deceit; *Geo Phursan* Cleft of ? ; and *Gob Phursan* Point of ?

Names on Hirte: *Abhainn Ilishgil* Deep Stream of the Spring or Deep Stream of Rage; *Geo Brababy* Cleft ?; *Geo Creag an Arpaid* possibly from Creag an Airgiod, or, Cleft of the rock of the Great Black-backed Gull; *Geo Leibli* Cleft ?; *Geo Oscar* Cleft of the Leap, Cleft of the Ruinous Fall, Cleft of the Champion, possibly Oscar's Cleft; *Geo an t-Samh* Cleft of the Sorrel/Surge/ Stink or possibly Cleft of the Open Sea; *Lasgol*?; *Leathad na Guiltichean* Broad slope of ?.

On Boreray: *Clais na Runaich* Hollow of the Beloved or of the Secret?, Hollow of the Desire or of the Purpose, or Hollow of the Mackerel (I Fraser pers comm); *Laimhil* ? (possibly connected with: *làmh* G: hand, arm; or *laibh* G: clay, mire, dirt); *Na Roàchan*?

On Soay: *Glamisgeo* Noisy Cleft, or, less likely, Glamr's cleft (Taylor 1967, 142), probably refers to sea noise, though Coates (1990, 157) suggests it is Jaws of a Vice Chasm; *Laidh* ?; *Lianish* Ness of the Slope or possibly Grey Ness (Coates 1990, 160): *Am Plastair* ? Smooth Stack or ? The Splashed One.

'Lost' names

Some names not mentioned in literature or on maps are implied by those
which are: for instance, Geo na h'Airde and Gob na h'Airde imply that the
headland at the east side of Gleann Mòr was 'Airde', or 'An Airde' – the
Promontory; and Leacan an t-Sluic Mhóir surely implies that 'The Tunnel': the
vast natural arch through this headland was 'An Sloc Mór' – the Great Hole.

5

St Kilda before the
16th Century

*T*he Edge of the World, the title of Michael Powell's film, based loosely on
the story of the evacuation of St Kilda in 1930, reflects the twentieth
century view of the islands: a place many people have never heard of, where
few have been, remote and not easy to visit (Powell, 1990). While this has not
always been so, it certainly was in the first millennia of man's occupation of
Britain. Indeed, 'the edge of the world' for early European man moved steadily
north and west as he followed the retreating glaciers over dry land into
Britain. Here the first settlers were dependent on hunting and gathering; a
number of occupation sites have been recognised on the west coast of
Scotland, some of them demonstrating the seasonal exploitation of food
resources. Clearly these people had some sort of boat, since they could cross
the difficult waters to the Inner Hebrides. Figure 22 (overleaf) is a time chart
giving approximate dates for some of the chronological phases and types of
structure relevant to the prehistory of St Kilda.

The Neolithic Period
In the Neolithic period, a further migration of people from the south brought
new technologies, notably farming and the manufacture of pottery. The skills
they introduced spread to the very edges of Britain; evidence of their
occupation is known in Orkney and Shetland, and throughout the Hebrides.
Although very few Neolithic habitation sites have been discovered so far in
the Western Isles, the number of megalithic chambered cairns provides
evidence of a sizeable population. On the west coast areas of machair, a light
calcareous sand which was probably more extensive then, would have been
suited to agriculture.

On very clear days St Kilda can be seen from almost the whole length of the
Long Island; it is commonly visible from North Uist and Harris, and is seen
particularly well from the hills. Those who built the chambered tombs on the
hill of Clettraval in North Uist must often have seen St Kilda on the horizon.
They had behind them a long tradition of exploration and expansion and still
maintained contacts across the Minch; it seems likely that they might have

Figure 22. *Chronological chart for St Kilda and Westen Scotland*

BC	St Kilda	West of Scotland
8000		End of last Ice Age
7000–4000		Hunter/gatherers living on Skye, Inner Hebrides and on mainland
3000		First farmers spread quickly through Scotland.
2000		Building of chambered tombs, stone circles and standing stones
1000		First metal working; burial in individual cists
		First use of iron.
		Dun and Broch building
		Flowering of Celtic culture and art
0	Souterrain built	Wheelhouses and souterrains built
500		'Figure of Eight' houses built
	Christianity established?	Christian hermits and missionaries? establish monastic settlements
	Norse burials	Norse raids followed by Norse settlement
1000		Norse Kingdom of Man and the Isles
	Visit by Icelandic bishop?	Lordship of the Isles Castle building
1346	Gift of St Kilda by charter	
1493		Forfeit of Lordship of the Isles Feuds between clans
1615	Raid by Coll MacDonald	
1697	Visit by Martin Martin	
1707		Act of Union
1715		1st Jacobite Rising
1727	Smallpox epidemic	Potato introductions
1745		2nd Jacobite Rising
1779	Sold to MacLeod of Berneray	Gradual collapse of clan system
1804	Sold to MacLeod of Colbost	Kelp industry
1829–43	MacKenzie's ministry: rebuilding of village	Potato blights and famines
1852	36 people emigrated	Clearances of townships in
1871	Sold to MacLeod of Dunvegan	Highlands and Islands - assisted
1877	First visit by steamer	emigration – Crofting Act
1900	Post Office opens	
1901	Jetty built	Land raids
1913	Radio station set up	Mingulay abandoned
1915–18	Naval detachment posted	Great War
1920s	Gradual emigration	Land raids
1930	Evacuation of island	

tried sailing to these islands on the edge of their world, to see if they, too, were worth settling. Though St Kilda would not compare favourably with the larger islands for agricultural work, the bird colonies would have been worth harvesting, and possibly seasonal expeditions were made for this purpose, just as the Ness men still go annually from Lewis across forty miles of ocean to harvest young gannets on Sula Sgeir (pp 300–302).

During the long Neolithic period many changes must have occurred, and it seems reasonable to suggest that St Kilda may have been explored on a number of occasions. There may have been phases when it was inhabited, times when it was visited regularly for the sake of the birds, and times when it lay empty. MacAulay (1764, 265) indulged in the same speculation:

I am apt to suspect, that Hirta was more than once depopulated since its first plantation, and consequently more than once repeopled…if the proprietor should have neglected his vassals, or people there, for a course of years, and if the only boat of the isle should have been destroyed by time, or some unlucky accident, it seems evident, that the inhabitants may have perished totally, or have been reduced to a very small number. Their instruments of agriculture would have been worn out, their fishing hooks lost, the little isles and rocks, which furnish the greatest part of the wild fowl and eggs, would have been inaccessible, and every other resource, excepting that of their cattle, must have failed.

Further technological developments, notably the working of copper and its alloys, were introduced with the Beaker period, and there may be evidence of occupation, or at least of burials implying occupation, on St Kilda at that time.

The Bronze Age

Burials typical of this period involved placing a body or ashes from a cremation in a stone box or cist, usually formed from slabs placed on edge in a pit, with a further horizontal slab making a lid. Several such burials have been found in the Western Isles (Megaw and Simpson 1961, 76–8; Crawford 1986, 7). Little detail has been recorded for most of these, but some were isolated finds, while some were in groups, as at Berneray, Harris; Vallay, Port na Long, Newton, Lochmaddy and Heiskeir, North Uist; and Pollachar, South Uist. A few cists contained pottery, and a few are known to have been covered by small cairns or sand mounds. Three found at Rosinish, Benbecula (Crawford 1977, 94–107), were corbelled constructions rather than rectangular boxes; the largest, a very neatly built chamber, contained the remains of three people, a man and two women, accompanied by two pots and a perforated object, possibly a pendant. Two smaller and simpler cists of similar construction, one containing a pot, were found adjacent to this.

In the late 1830s MacKenzie (1911, 6–7) noted in the village area some archaeological features which were subsequently destroyed (p 105):

> *Scattered about, here and there, and very numerous, were green mounds called* gnocan sithichean, *which were looked upon as the abodes of the fairies. These were all removed in the course of agricultural improvements. They were composed of stones mixed with a little earth to a depth of two or three feet. At some distance below this layer were stone coffins formed in two different ways. At times they were formed of four flat stones set on edge and covered by a fifth. At other times both the sides and roof were formed of several stones set in the same way. These were seemingly of different age from the former. In a few of them bones were found, and in nearly all of them pieces of earthen vessels.*

Figure 23. *Subterranean cell and cists at Rosinish, Benbecula*

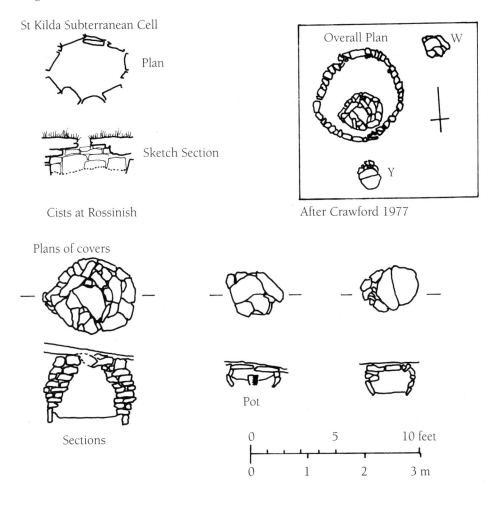

St Kilda Subterranean Cell

Plan

Sketch Section

Cists at Rossinish

Overall Plan   W

Y

After Crawford 1977

Plans of covers

Pot

Sections

0   5   10 feet

0   1   2   3 m

MacKenzie does not say that the bones found were human but it is implied by the use of the word 'coffin'. The description sounds very like that of prehistoric cists covered by small cairns. The name *Cnoc sithean* or simply *sithean*, a 'fairy knoll' often marks a site of earlier occupation.

The 'coffins' made of 'several stones set in the same way', could well be corbelled cists, and a subterranean stone-lined cavity in the village area, not far from the shore, might be one of these. This oval space, 4'2" by 3' by about 1'6" high, is created by a ring of stones, apparently small upright slabs, with two courses of stones oversailing them slightly, the small opening at the top now being covered by three loose stones (figure 23).

MacKenzie's finds, then, might be a mixed group of slab and corbelled cists, the structure in the field being an example of the latter, with Rosinish the best parallel.

Another feature mentioned by MacKenzie may also have been a cist but he apparently regarded it as something different and described it separately:

In clearing for agricultural purposes a small park near the centre of the glebe, and at the foot of Aoismheal, I came upon a flat stone a little under the surface. On the top of it were some ashes. On lifting it up I saw that there was a curiously built space underneath, but as it might be a relic of some ancient place of worship, I did not disturb it but replaced the stone.

Unfortunately this is not adequate to identify the feature; only re-locating it and further investigation could elucidate this reference.

Mathieson (1928) marks sites for 'underground coffins found 1835' and 'underground chamber found 1835' on his map, but his siting of Christ's Church is unreliable and it would be unwise to accept his locations as precise.

A number of small stone 'boat shaped' settings in An Lag bho'n Tuath have been identified as probable Bronze Age graves. Material from within one gave a Carbon14 date of 1833 BC (Cottam 1973 and 1979, 39–45). There is an alternative explanation for these structures. There are more than those noted by Cottam, and they are situated in an area where cleitean are sparse compared with adjacent areas (figure 24). They consist mainly of earth-fast stones, apparently set upright, generally in two parallel lines or a U or V shape. It is possible that these are footings of cleitean which have been robbed, perhaps to build the enclosures in An Lag. Figure 25 shows, for comparison, plans of some cleitean in the area and some of the 'boat-shaped' settings. Without demolishing the former, it is difficult to identify earthfast stones, though a few can be distinguished with some confidence. If the organic material dated to *c.*1833 BC were dross from cut peat or turf stored in the former cleit, the date is readily explained. Recent excavations of two of the settings has revealed them as central features within sub-circular cairns

Figure 24. *An Lag bho'n Tuath: Distribution of Cleitean and Settings*

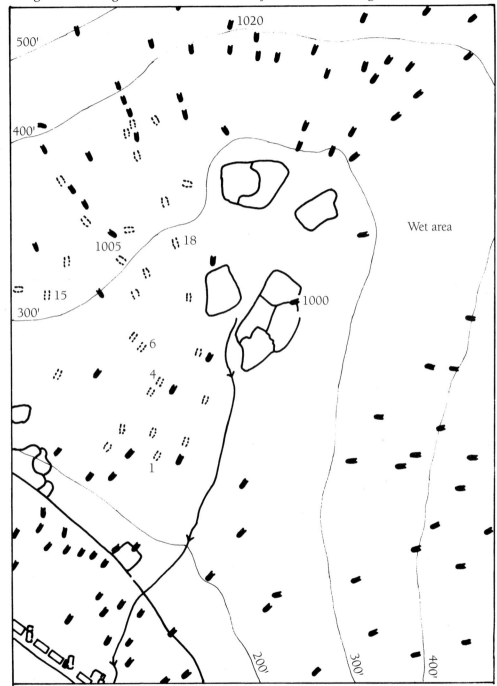

After Cottam 1973 in parts

Figure 25. *An Lag bho'n Tuath: Plans of Cleitean and Settings*

'Boat shaped' settings

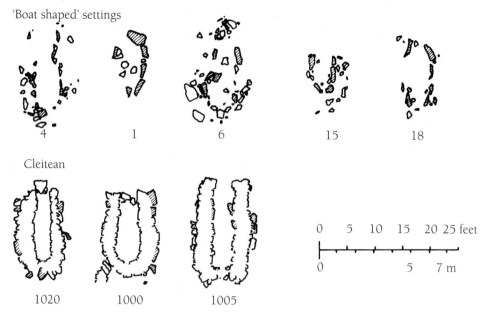

Cleitean

(Emery and Morrison 1995, 54-56). Although these are as yet undated, they are comparable with prehistoric burial cairns.

Heaps of stones identified as possible cairns, near the edge of the steep western slopes on Ruaival and Mullach Sgar, might well be collapsed cleitean, as Cottam suggests for the group on Ruaival.

Pottery found during recent excavations of House 8 has been ascribed, from the form of the sherds, to either the Bronze Age or the Iron Age (Emery and Morrison 1995, 41).

The Iron Age

In the Western Isles structures typical of this period are duns, brochs, circular houses, souterrains and 'ventral' houses. These are all fairly small, and individually are unlikely to have housed more than a few families or an extended family. Duns, or small forts, are generally oval or circular stone-walled structures, often built on islets or promontories in lochs or on coastal promontories. A specialised category of dun is the broch, a circular-based tower with cavity walls providing storage space and access to upper levels. Though they were no longer built after about the second or third centuries AD, some continued in intermittent occupation, with alterations, until mediaeval times. Some circular 'wheelhouses' and 'aisled houses' may have been contemporary with the brochs, though some were built later, within brochs. They are characterised by radial walls, like spokes in a wheel, which do not extend to the centre, and in aisled houses, do not extend quite to the perimeter wall. There is evidence that the radial walls supported a corbelled stone roof, the central area possibly being thatched. The central area provided living space, with a hearth, while the surrounding compartments may have been used for various activities. The 'souterrain', an enigmatic stone-lined subterranean passage, sometimes leading to a chamber, is often associated with circular houses. At the Udal in North Uist (Crawford 1973, Crawford 1986, 12) wheelhouses were followed by smaller dwellings which are variable in plan. They are stone-walled structures partly sunk into the ground, being oval, with a central hearth flanked by one or two low platforms, and one or more cells entered from the main area. These 'ventral' or 'figure of eight' houses continued in use for about five hundred years. Similar buildings were found at Loch na Berie, Lewis (Harding and Armit 1988, 31).

One structure on St Kilda is of this period: the Taigh an t-Sithiche: Fairy House, or souterrain (figure 26). This was found about 1840, and promptly covered up. It was investigated by Sands in 1876, and again by the Keartons in 1896 and Mathieson in 1927.

The main visible feature is an underground passage, stone lined, 25' long, 3'2" to 4'0" wide, and 4'1" to 4'7" high. The walls are built randomly but neatly, of fairly large stones, without mortar, and reaching five to seven courses. They converge towards the top, leaving a gap of 2'0" to 2'6", which is

Figure 26. *Taigh an t-Sithiche or the souterrain: plan and longitudinal section*

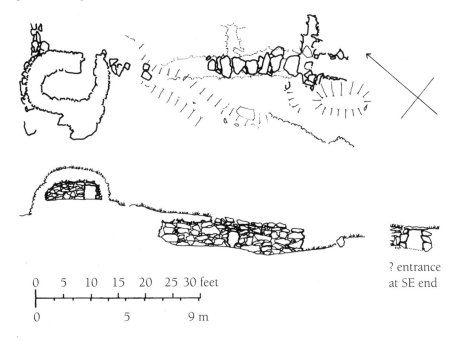

? entrance
at SE end

| 0 | 5 | 10 | 15 | 20 | 25 | 30 feet |

| 0 | | 5 | | 9 m |

spanned by the stone slabs which form the roof. The floor is of earth, with some flat stones in it. The passage is entered at the south east end; the stones to the sides of this opening are all in the same vertical plane and are so similar on either side that their symmetry must be deliberate, indicating that they were meant to be visible. At the north west end, immediately under the field boundary, the roofing slabs end and there is a face of earth and rubble. Sands found that the floor was of flat stones, with a drain beneath; these are not now visible. The plan at the south-east end is not clear.

About half way along the passage on the north east side, there is at right angles a more constricted side passage, 6'0" long. This has much less regular walls than the main passage but ends similarly in a face of earth and stone. The stones on either side at the far end of this passage seem to form corners, as though it might open out, possibly into a chamber.

About 7' to the north-west of the souterrain, and forming part of the field boundary, is Cleit 70, an anomalous cleit, being shorter, wider and much less high than most in the village area (pp 159–161), with its entrance in a curious position in one corner. At its north west end, in the adjacent strip, the outer wall of this cleit is considerably lower than at the entrance, and includes some large stones. The position of this cleit and its peculiarities suggest that it may incorporate a structure related to the souterrain, probably something beneath the present floor level.

Some of the finds from the investigations are in the Royal Museum of Scotland (figure 27). No stratigraphy or contexts were recorded. Some of the pottery fragments are similar to pieces found in brochs, duns, and circular houses in the Western Isles. There are several shaped stones which were probably blades of digging implements, and two hammer stones. Two stones with hollows in them may have been used as lamps. Few of the bones or shells found have been preserved; bones from cattle, sheep and gannets are not necessarily contemporary with the structure.

In 1858 T.S. Muir (Muir and Thomas 1860, 225) found in the floor of the 'Amazon's House' two pebbles, given to the Royal Museum of Scotland. Only one can now be found. This carefully shaped pale pink quartzite pebble is a 'strike-a-light' (figure 28, overleaf), similar to many others found on Iron Age sites in North Uist and Skye. Its occurrence in the 'Amazon's House' does not necessarily imply that that building is itself of pre-Norse date, as the stones could have continued in use, or might even have been regarded as amulets, in which case they could have been moved far from their place of manufacture or use. If they were taken to St Kilda at the time when similar stones were in use elsewhere, they would provide further evidence of Iron Age occupation.

There is no evidence for the existence of any dun or broch on St Kilda. The

Figure 27. *Finds from the souterrain in Royal Museum of Scotland*

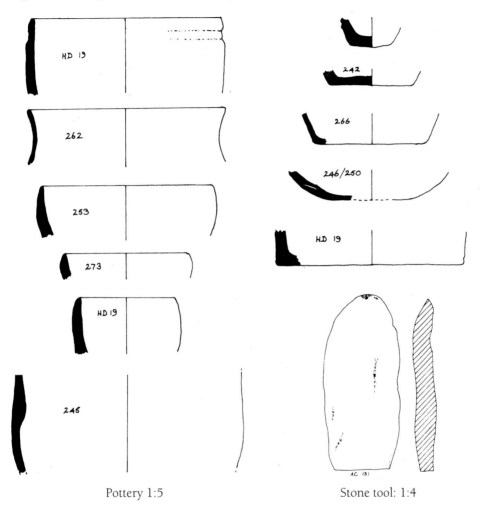

Pottery 1:5   Stone tool: 1:4

Figure 28. *'Strike-a-light' found in Taigh na Banaghaisgeich*

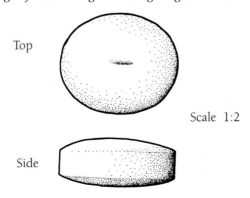

Top

Side

Scale 1:2

name of the island Dun may relate to its natural defensive qualities, or, as
Martin (1753, 13) and MacAulay (1764, 48) note, it may refer to small
sections of wall on the island. At the south-east end of the island, beyond the
narrow isthmus containing the natural arch, a mass of fallen rocks makes
further access difficult. The easiest route is blocked by a small section of well-
built dry-stone wall, which is built on the boulders. There is a second similar
section of wall among the tumbled rocks. At this end of Dun there are three
shelters under very large overhanging rocks. Two have stone walls built
beneath the edge of the overhang, to enclose small low spaces, with traces of
peat or turf ash visible in the floors. One of these is probably the *Sean Taigh* or
Old House mentioned by Sands (1877a, 86). Neither the wall nor the earliest
use of the shelters has been dated.

Early and mediaeval Christian sites

From the late sixth to the eighth centuries monks from Ireland founded
several monasteries in Scotland, particularly on the west coast, notably at
Iona, Eigg and Lismore. Some of these became missionary centres. At the
same time other holy men from these centres and from Ireland were travelling
further north and west, some of them following the urge to establish
hermitages where they could worship alone or in small groups. They went as
far as Faeroe and Iceland, while some found what they were seeking in the
Hebrides, and there is evidence that small islands or places difficult of access
were particularly favoured. Place names including the element *papa* (Watson
1904, 270) and probably *annat* (MacDonald 1973, 135–146) indicate religious
sites of this period.

Many of the early sites and burial grounds in both Ireland and Scotland are
enclosed by a bank or wall. Some of the enclosures are oval: examples on the
west coast are St Ninian's, Bute, possibly Sgor nan Ban-Naomha, Canna, and
the oratory on North Rona (Nisbet and Gailey 1962, 88–115) where the oval
burial ground is slightly larger than that on St Kilda, being 120' x 75'.
Buildings on the Pygmies Isle and possibly the Flannan Isles may also be early
Christian (MacKenzie 1905, 248–258). Dedications to Columba (521–597), a
popular saint whose feast was kept on St Kilda, and Brendan (probably
Brendan the Navigator, *c*.486–575), may be pre-Norse.

In 1697 (Martin 1753, 43–6) there were three chapels on the island, all
orientated east-west with an altar at the east end:

> *The first of these is called Christ Chapel, near the village; it is covered and*
> *thatched after the manner of their houses; there is a brazen crucifix lies upon*
> *the altar, not exceeding a foot in length; the body is completely done, distended,*
> *and has a crown on, all in the crucified posture…The churchyard is about an*

hundred paces in circumference, fenced in with a little stone wall; within which they bury their dead; and take care to keep it perfectly neat, void of any kind of nastiness, nor suffer their cattel to have any access to it.'

The second of these chappels bears the name of St Columba, the third of St Brianan; both being built after the manner of Christ's Chappel; having Church-yards belonging to them.

Christ's Chapel was too small to hold the population of 180, who held their services in the burial ground. The crucifix was 'fixed upon a cross of brass and that to a cross of wood' (Adv ms. 33.3.20) (p 246). It had been removed from the island by 1799 (Campbell 1799, f37).

The chapels had apparently fallen into disrepair by 1758, and Christ's Chapel was no longer used, for MacAulay (1764, 69–72) says

The largest church was dedicated to Christ. It was built of stone, and without any cement: its length is twenty four feet, and its breadth fourteen. This was in former times the principal place of worship in the isle, and here they continue to bury their dead'. St Columba's had 'neither altar, cross nor cell within its precincts', but St Brendan's had 'an altar within, and some monkish cells

Figure 29. *The Burial Ground: plan*

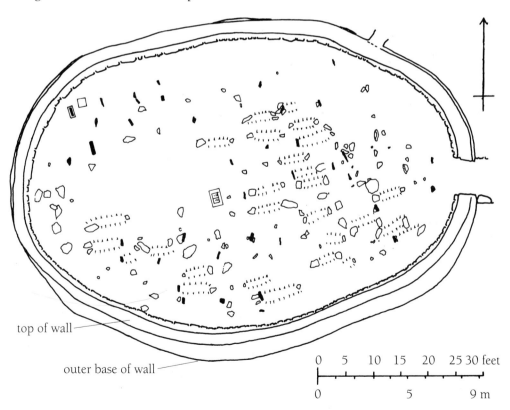

top of wall

outer base of wall

0 5 10 15 20 25 30 feet

0 5 9 m

*without it. These are almost entire and must of consequence be of later date,
than the holy places dedicated to Christ and Columba.*

Traces of these were seen by MacCulloch (1824, 177) in 1815, and
MacKenzie (1911, 6, 23) in the 1830s. Sands (1877a, 82) recorded in 1876
that 'old men remember when the ruins of [a chapel], sixteen feet in height,
stood in the churchyard'. The oldest men then would have been between 65
and 70, so they could have seen as children ruins which had fallen by 1815.

Boece's (1527) chapels dedicated to Clement and Peter probably refer to
Uist and Harris; Sibbald (Adv ms. 33.3.20) seems to have combined these
with those mentioned by Martin and added another dedicated to John, for
which no other authority is known. In the absence of earlier references,
MacKenzie's 'Mary's Chapel' seems unlikely to be accurate, and
MacCrimmon's 'Trinity temple' which she locates on the site of Christ's
Church, may result from confusion with Tigh an Triar (pp 52, 231–2).

Martin's description suggests that the burial ground was roughly circular in
plan, with a circumference approaching 300', rather larger than that of the
present wall, which is about 220', enclosing an oval space 75' x 50' (figure
29). MacKenzie, who built the wall, mentions the difficulty arising from the
difference in ground levels within and without, so probably he retained the
shape and approximate size of the earlier enclosure. There is no trace now of
any burial enclosure at the sites of the other chapels.

Though the chapels and crucifix are gone, there are still visible two stones
with crosses incised on them (figure 30). The complete cross, built into the
wall of House 16, was first noticed by Sands; the other forms part of the
ceiling of Cleit 74: both probably come from Christ's Church. A similar cross
can be seen in the burial ground at Howmore, South Uist, and there are

Figure 30. *Stones with crosses incised on them*

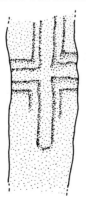

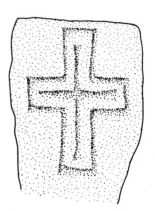

Cleit 74
Scale 1:10

House 16

others: at Kildalton and Trudernish, Islay; St Ninian's Isle, Shetland; Skuö, Faeroe Islands, and several in Wales (Harman 1977, 257). Some of these are dated between the seventh and ninth centuries, and some between the tenth and fourteenth centuries, so it is open to question whether the crosses were the work of a pre-Norse or late Norse/early mediaeval Christian community.

Cumulatively, the evidence suggests that there may well have been early Christian settlers on St Kilda. If all three recorded sites have their origins in this period, it is difficult to explain their scattered location, which is unusual in such a small area. They may have been occupied at different times, or MacAulay's 'monkish cells' might have belonged to a religious community keeping a distance from a civil settlement.

The Norse Period

In the Norse period St Kilda is on the periphery of written history. At the end of the eighth century the first Norse raids on the west coasts of Britain occurred; the Hebrides were plundered in 798, and chronicles record repeated raids on Iona. By the mid ninth century there were Norse settlements in the Hebrides, Ireland and Iceland, with regular communication and movement of people between these areas and Scandinavia. Raiding continued, together with major battles in the struggle for power in the area, nominally under the rule of Norway. The treaty of 1098 between Magnus Barelegs and Malcolm of Scotland was the first formal recognition of Norse supremacy in the Isles.

Despite the evidence of literature and placenames for extensive Norse settlement in the Western Isles, particularly in Lewis and Harris, only a few settlement sites are known. At the Udal in North Uist (Crawford 1971) and at Drimore, South Uist (MacLaren 1974, 9–18) typical Norse long houses with slightly bowed walls and slab-lined hearths have been found. Pagan burials with grave goods demonstrate that Christianity was not universally re-established until the late tenth or eleventh century.

Altogether, there is plenty of evidence for considerable traffic on the west coast during this period, both peaceful and aggressive. St Kilda must have been well known as a landmark, as a place where shelter might be gained in some weather conditions, but a place to avoid in others. It may have attracted the attention of raiders, if only to supplement their supplies. There is evidence that it attracted settlers, though there are no visible structural remains which can be identified as Norse. The possibility that the two crosses are of Norse Christian date rather than of the pre-Norse period has already been considered. Several objects have been found which point to Norse occupation; few of these are extant today.

The *Glasgow Journal* for May 7–14, 1767, reported 'we hear that some fisher-men lately dug up in the island of St Kilda, two antique urns, containing a quantity of Danish silver coin, which by the inscription appears to have lain there upwards of 1800 years'. No further information is available. The inconsistency between the identification of the coins as Danish and the attributed age of 1800 years or more may be explained if the '1' were a printer's error.

Finlay MacQueen (1862–1941) found 'stone bowls and lamps' near Taigh an t-Sithiche (MacInnes and MacQueen SA 1961/19). During recent excavations at House 8 several pieces of carved steatite were found (Emery 1989, 16). This stone was quarried in the Norse period in both Scandinavia and Shetland, and various objects were carved from it, mainly domestic items. Though the stone was also used in prehistory, these fragments are likely to result from Norse rather than prehistoric trade.

MacKenzie (1911, 5) found what were probably grave goods in a burial:
In clearing the glebe I removed a mound in a little field, and found in it a long and narrow whetstone, an iron sword, a spear head, and various other pieces of iron, mostly of irregular shape, and the use of which was not obvious.

In the acid soils the bones might be unrecognisable or entirely decayed. There is no information as to the fate of these finds. Presumably the spearhead is different from the one found by the Keartons in the souterrain (figure 31), which is noted in the catalogue of the Royal Museum of Scotland as 'destroyed June 1910'. Fortunately it was described and drawn on accession (PSAS 1896–7, 154–5).

Taylor (1967, 116–144) has collected and analysed much of the evidence for Norse occupation of St Kilda.

Figure 31. *Viking brooch and spearhead*

Brooch   after Worsaae / not to scale

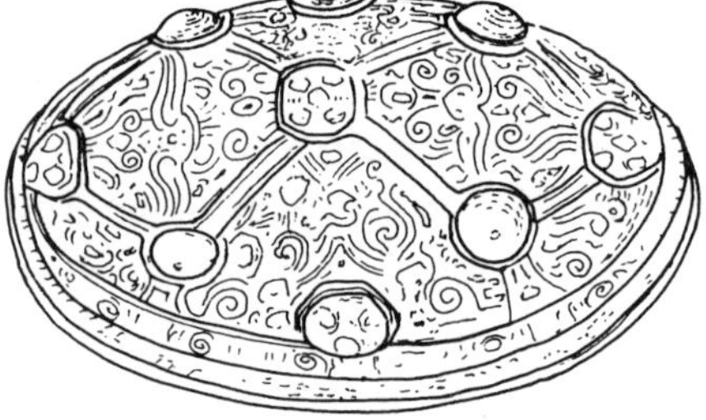

Spearhead   after PSAS 1897 / scale 1:3.5

Some time before 1846, two brooches were found on the island; Worsaae saw one of them during a visit to Scotland in 1846–7, and later published a drawing of it (figure 31). The brooch cannot now be traced, nor is anything known of the second one. Opinion is divided as to whether the brooch is of ninth or tenth century type. The date does not necessarily indicate the date of burial as the brooches may have been heirlooms, but their existence probably indicates a female burial. Such brooches, generally in pairs, have been found in a number of Norse burials in the Hebrides, including several in the Western Isles. If they were found in MacKenzie's time it is curious that he does not mention them.

A reference to 'Hirtir' in an Icelandic saga was noted by Watson (1904, 97) and fully reviewed by Taylor. An Icelander, Gudmundr Arason, sailed for Norway in July 1202 to be consecrated as bishop by the Archbishop of Nidaros. He and his companions were driven south by persistent storms. They recognised the Hebrides, and went 'to the islands that are called Hirtir', perhaps for shelter from the northerly gale. According to one version, they learned there of the death in March of Sverrir, King of Norway. They continued south into the Irish sea before managing to turn and finally reach Norway, where, according to another version, they heard of the King's death. Arason was consecrated in April 1203, and soon after returned to Iceland.

Taylor also distinguished a group of placenames which he regarded as Norse in origin, given on the islands by Norse speakers, rather than names given by Gaelic speakers using Norse elements absorbed into Gaelic. These names were: Ruaival; Oiseval; [Mullach] Sgar; [the] Cambir; Bradastac; Mina Stac; [Tobar] Childa Chalda; [Abhainn] Gleshgil; [Abhainn] Ilishgil; Giasgeir; [Geo] Ghiasgeir; Seilg Geo; Soay; Glamisgeo; Scarpalin; Lianish; Boreray; Scarbhstac; [Gob] Scapanish; [Rubha] Bhrengadal; Coinneag; Sunadal; Udraclete; and Clesgor. Some of the field names may also fall into this category (p 53).

Some of the final versions of the names are tautologous, for instance: Tobar Childa Chalda: Well Cold Well, Abhainn Ilishgil: Stream Stream of the Spring, and Gob Scapanish: Point Point of the Caves or Hollows. This shows that the Norse names were taken over and used by Gaelic speakers who did not understand their meaning; at the same time, the survival of Norse names shows that there was continuity of knowledge of the islands, possibly through continuous settlement. It is significant that the name of the principal well and some field names have survived. Many Norse names must have been wholly replaced.

Figure 32. *Early genealogy of the MacLeods and Lords of the Isles*

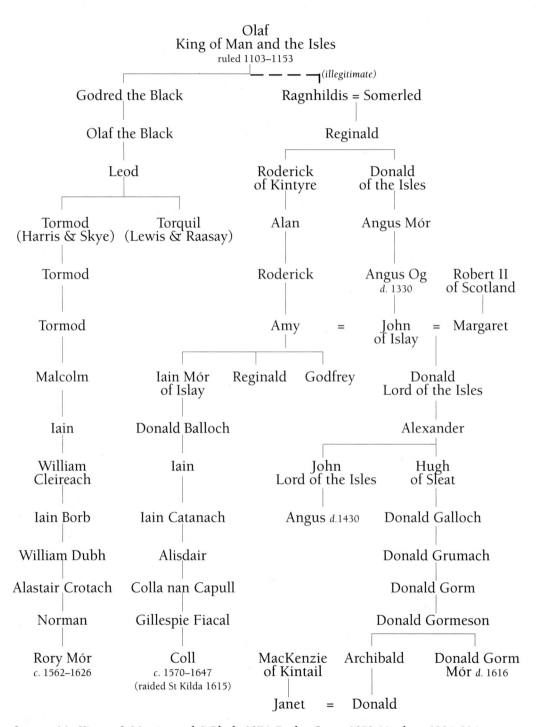

Sources: MacKinnon & Morrison, nd; I. Black, 1974; Burke; Grant, 1959; Nicolson, 1994, 314.

The Lordship of the Isles

After a long period of instability, Godred Crovan emerged as ruler of Man and the Isles in about 1079. About 1156 his grandson, Godfrey, and Somerled, Lord of Argyll, divided the kingdom between them. It was further divided among their sons and grandsons. These formed a confederacy of powerful families, from whom the MacDonalds of Islay emerged pre-eminent as Lords of the Isles early in the fourteenth century. John of Islay received from his wife Amy MacRuari the lands of Garmoran, and in 1346 granted to his son Reginald by charter, parts of these, including the islands of Eigg, Rum, Uist and St Kilda (insula de hert) and areas of the mainland (Munro and Munro, 1986, 10–11, 209).

Lewis, Harris and Raasay traditionally passed to Leod, and were divided between his sons, Torquil receiving Lewis and Raasay, and Tormod Harris and much of Skye; the latter is regarded as the first of the MacLeods of Harris and Dunvegan (figure 32). At some time well before 1549 St Kilda passed into the hands of the MacLeods.

The Lords of the Isles were extremely powerful; though they recognised the superiority of the Scottish king when expedient, they also fought against him and entered into treaties with his enemies. St Kilda lay on the periphery of a kingdom which relied heavily on the sea for communications.

The Lordship of the Isles was forfeit to the Scottish Crown in 1493, though in many repects the control of the Crown was nominal until well into the seventeenth century.

The only documentary reference of this period apart from the charter and its confirmation in 1372/3 is that of John of Fordun who died in 1384 (Fordun 1871, 44; 1872, 40). In his *Chronicle of the Scottish Nation* he refers to:

Hirth, the best stronghold of all the islands. Near this is an island twenty miles long, where wild sheep are said to exist, which can only be caught by hunters.

Any of the larger islands might well be considered a stronghold, though not necessarily a very useful one or easy to defend without a large force. There is no island twenty miles long within forty miles of St Kilda. The particular reference to sheep is followed by many later authors.

Structures and finds of indeterminate date

There are several structures which may, perhaps, date to the mediaeval period.

On the ridge to the south of Gleann Mór, set into a gentle slope, there is a small circular platform about 23' in diameter, with a few stones on the perimeter. This was known as Taigh an Fhir Faireadh or the Watchman's House, and is supposed to be the site where a sea watch was kept for the approach of pirates (MacKenzie 1911, 27). The site commands the approach

Figure 33. *Mullach Sgar 'hiding place':*
plan

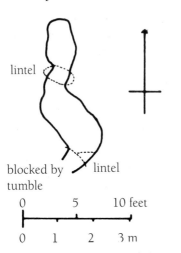

lintel

blocked by   lintel
tumble

0   5   10 feet

0   1   2   3 m

by sea to Gleann Mór, with an easy route to the hill above the village to give warning of any raid. Similar watches for raiders were kept in mediaeval times in Harris (Martin 1716, 35) and in Faroe (Williamson 1970, 22) where villages had hiding places prepared. MacLean (1838, 47) was shown a subterranean hiding place near Uamh Cailleach Bheag Ruaival, and Sands (1878, 188) records that in the scree slope of Mullach Sgar there was a hiding place which he cleared of débris (figure 33).

MacAulay (1764, 83–5) refers to four altars which had been used by the 'ancient St Kildans'. One of these was on Mullach Geal and was dedicated to a god of the weather. Euphemia MacCrimmon (Kennedy and Thomas 1874, 705) said that there was one on Boreray and one on top of Soay. Sands (1878, 189) saw the latter and the site of one on Dun. Mathieson (1928, 130) was also shown the site on Dun. The only identifiable altar now is that on Soay, a dry stone square-based structure about 5'4" square and 3' high, surrounded by a very low bank, roughly circular and about 40' in diameter (figure 34).

In the seventeenth century Gleann Mór was known as Gleann na Bana-

Figure 34. *Altar on Soay: plan*

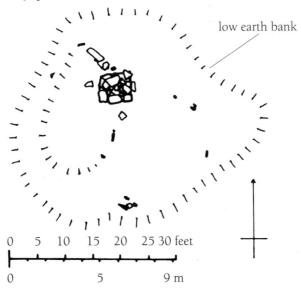

low earth bank

0   5   10   15   20   25 30 feet

0   5   9 m

ghaisgeich or the Female Warrior's Glen (Martin 1753, 15). Martin says of her:

This Amazon is famous in their traditions: her house or dairy of stone is yet extant; some of the inhabitants dwell in it all summer though it be some hundred years old; the whole is built of stones, without any wood, lime, earth or mortar to cement it, and is in the form of a circle pyramid-wise towards the top with a vent in it, the fire being always in the centre of the floor; the stones are long and thin, which supplies the defect of wood: the body of this house contains not above nine persons sitting; there are three beds or low vaults at the side of the wall, which contains five men each, and are separated by a pillar; at the entry to one of these low vaults is a stone standing upon one end; upon this she is reported ordinarily to have laid her helmet; there are two stones on the other side, upon which she is said to have laid her sword.

In the 1830s it was described as a corbelled building covered with turf (MacKenzie 1911, 6). When Muir (1858, 20–21; Muir and Thomas 1860, 225–228) saw it in 1858 it was still complete, and entry was through the vent in the roof. A small square opening at the west end was considered scarcely large enough for a doorway. It was about three feet high. The central chamber was nine by eleven feet and about eight feet high, the smaller chambers being about five feet high. Now the only surviving roofed chamber has a height at the centre of 5'2". Thomas noted that nearby were the ruins of at least two other structures of the same kind; these may well have been the other one in

Figure 35. *Taigh na Banaghaisgeich or 'Amazon's House': plans*

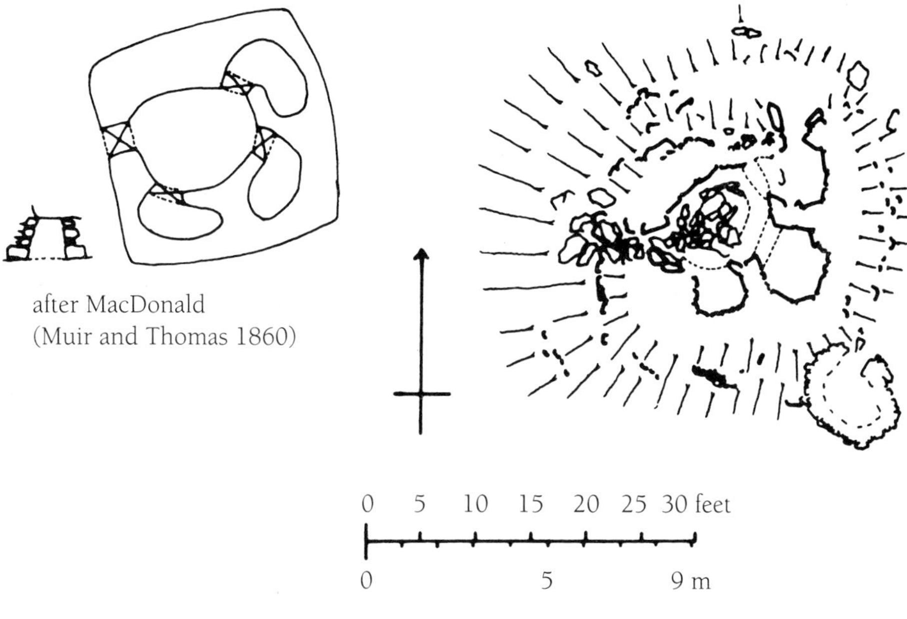

after MacDonald
(Muir and Thomas 1860)

complex F, and G. Thomas provided a plan (figure 35) drawn by Mr MacDonald, minister of Harris.

Sands (1877a, 80) saw the 'Amazon's House' almost complete in 1875, but within two years it was partly demolished by two men who wanted the stones to build cleitean. By 1927 Mathieson found it difficult to interpret.

Martin makes it clear that the 'Amazon's House' was old in 1697: 'some hundred years old'; its association with the 'Female Warrior' implies great antiquity, but he also describes it as her 'dairy', and the people living in it were using it as a shieling. The alternative name of 'Airidh Mhór' or 'Big Shieling' occurs first on the anonymous nineteenth century estate plan. Sands' record of the name is probably independent.

Figure 36. *Gleann Mór: 'Amazon's House' type structures: distribution*

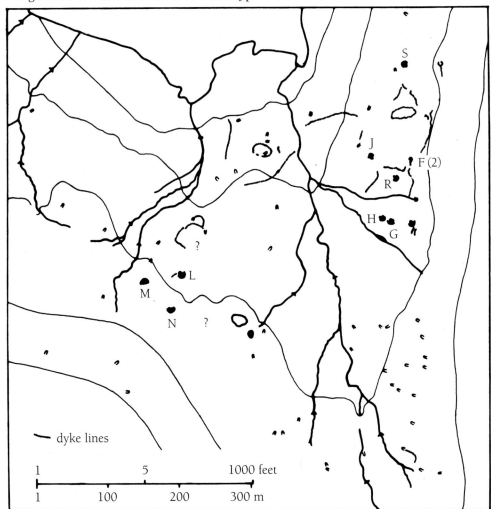

Figure 37. *Gleann Mór: 'Amazon's House' type structures: plans*

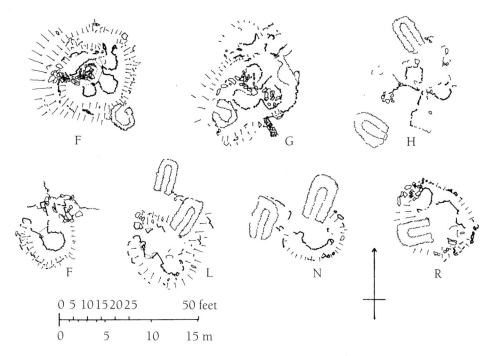

There are in the glen the remains of ten or twelve structures which were probably all similar to the 'Amazon's House' (figures 36 and 37). Some are comparatively well preserved and show very clearly the same plan; others are less complete and only certain features betray their relationship to the Amazon's House: corbelled walling, traces of a turfed mound in which the structure was built, and angular 'corners' between cells. They have been studied in conjunction with the gathering folds by Williamson (1958a, 46–9) and Cottam (1974) (pp 152–5).

Possibly some or all of these were in use in the seventeenth century as shielings, since Martin indicates that some people were staying in Gleann Mór during the summer. If ten were the total number of structures, it would be consistent with the division of lands into ten halfpenny units in the seventeenth century (p 124). Martin's account implies that the shieling system had been in use for some time. Thus that type of structure may well date to the later mediaeval period, and have been used as a seasonal habitation. Traces of enclosures and dykes around the groups of structures on both sides of the burn may indicate small scale cultivation in the summer. A structure of Amazon's House type was found near the foot of Oiseval in the late 1830s (Kennedy and Thomas 1874, 703; pp 233–4).

Another seasonal dwelling, the Taigh Stallair on Boreray, was described in

1697 as similar to Taigh na Banaghaisgeich but larger (Martin 1753, 24). It was a circular subterranean building with a corbelled roof and central hearth and

Round the wall a paved seat, on which sixteen persons may conveniently sit. Here are four beds roofed with strong flag or stone lintels, every one of which is capable enough to receive four men. To each of these beds is a separate entry; the distances between these different openings resembling in some degree so many pillars (MacAulay 1764, 55).

Euphemia MacCrimmon described it as:

Round inside, with the ends of long narrow stones sticking through the walls round about, on which clothes might be hung. There were six croops or beds in the wall.

These were of varying sizes; according to MacCrimmon, four of them would accommodate twelve to twenty men each. There was a passage within the wall allowing access between the bed chambers without entering the central area. The low doorway faced the sea. It was used by fowlers and those working with sheep until the early 1840s, when the roof fell in. Wilson (1842, 57) states that it had fallen out of use by 1841, those who went to Boreray staying in a hut which they had built above ground. Thomas (1868, 174–5) points out that MacCrimmon's perception of the space required for sleeping may have been more economical than MacAulay's. He suggests that the Taigh Stallair was similar to an aisled house. By 1875 it had been demolished and robbed to build cleitean (Sands 1878, 189).

The 'Amazon's House' structures have affinities with dwellings on North Rona (Nisbet and Gailey 1962, 96–101) and with some 'beehive' shielings in Lewis and Harris (Thomas 1860, 127–143: 1868 153–195), and ultimately, perhaps, with the pre-Norse 'ventral' house and early Christian corbelled cells such as those on Eileach an Naoimh and many Irish sites. MacCrimmon's clothes pegs are reminiscent of the 'satchel pegs' at Skellig Michael.

Martin (1753, 15) ascribes the discovery of 'a pair of large deers-horns in the top of Oterveaul hill, almost a foot underground, and a wooden dish full of deer's grease' to the results of the Amazon's favourite pastime: hunting. The deposition of antlers is difficult to explain, but the 'wooden dish full of deer's grease' was probably 'bog butter'. Deposits of butter, often in containers of wood, have been found in various bogs in Scotland and Ireland (MacAdam 1882, 204–223; 1889, 433–4; Anderson 1885, 309–311; Earwood 1991, 231–240) including two in Skye. The date of these deposits is uncertain. The St Kilda example must date from the early seventeenth century or before. MacAdam suggests that burial may have been a means of storage in cool conditions.

The head dyke was built in the late 1830s. There are, outside it, dykes, dyke footings, and other features which together might be the remains of an older head dyke enclosing a larger area, including the area known as Gearraidh Ard (high enclosed area), a name implying that the ground was enclosed (figure 38). To the north of the present dyke some narrow terraces were interpreted by MacGregor (1957) as old paths. A single terrace can be traced for much of the way eastwards towards Geo Mór. These terraces, rather than being constructed as paths, could be the upslope side of former dykes. The present head dyke has, in places, a narrow strip of level ground behind it, while along some stretches the natural slope immediately within it has been quarried, so that if the dyke were removed, a small terrace would result. In places there may have been a secondary use as paths, as the Gleann Mór dyke is today, but the undulating line in the boulder area at the foot of Oiseval is unlikely to have been a path. Dyke footings continue the line westward to the foot of the Conachair talus. Another footing runs west of the Abhainn Mhór, and there are stretches of dyke or dyke footings near the base of the scree areas on Mullach Sgar. The absence of substantial stretches, especially in stone-free areas, may be explained by robbing, or possibly lengths of turf dyke have been entirely destroyed. Though it seems unlikely, it is not impossible that no visible trace would remain in some areas.

Figure 38. *Village area: map showing the line of possible former head dyke*

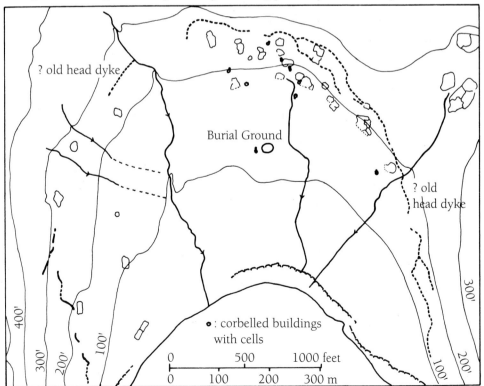

79

6

St Kilda from the 16th Century to 1779

No literary reference to St Kilda between the fourteenth and sixteenth centuries has been found. However, brief accounts written in the sixteenth century mark the beginning of an ever increasing flow of documentation about the island.

Hector Boece, one of the founders and first principal of Aberdeen University, published his *History of Scotland* in 1527, in which he refers to:

> The last and outmaist Ile is namit Hirtha...in this Ile is gret nowmer of scheip...This Ile is circulit on every syd with roche craggis; and na baitis may land at it but allanerly at ane place, in quhilk is ane strait and narowe entres. Sum time thair micht na pepill pas to this Ile bot extreme dangeir of thair livis; and yit thair is na pasage to it bot quhen the seis ar caurme bot any tempest. In the moneth of Juney, ane preist cumis out of the Lewis in ane bait to this Ile, and ministeris the sacrament of baptisme to all the barnis that hes bene borne in the yeir afore. Als sone as this preist has done his office, with certane messis, he ressavis the tindis of all thair commoditeis, and returnis hame the same gait he come (Boece, 1527).

A reference to chapels following this probably refers to Uist, though the next observation, about sheep, probably does refer to St Kilda.

Soon afterwards Donald Monro, Dean of Argyll and the Isles, made an exploratory journey through his diocese in 1549. He is unlikely to have visited St Kilda himself, but he received first hand information from the Steward.

> Out of the mane Ocean seais be 60 mile of sea lyis ane Ile callit Hirta, mane laich sa far as is manurit of it, abundand in corn and girsing, namelie for scheip...The inhabitants thairof are simple creatures, scant learnit in ony Religion: but McCloyd of Haray his Stewart, or quhom he deputtis in sic office, sayles anes in the zeir at midsymmer with sum chaplaine to baptize bairns thair; and gif they want ane chaiplane, thai baptize thair bairns thameselfis. The said Stewart, as himself tald me, usit to tak ane mask of malt thair with ane maskein fat and mask his malt, and or the fat be readie, the commons of the town baith men, women and bairns puttis thair hand in the fat, and finding it sweit greynes eftir the sweitnes thairof, quhill neither wort nor draff are left

unsuppit out thair, quhill baith men, women and bairns were deid drunken, so that thai could nocht stand on thair feit. The saids Stewartis ressaves thair maillis in maill and reistit muttonis, wild reistit foullis and selchis...In thir roch Iles are infinite fair scheippis, with ane falcon nest and wild foullis biggand. But the seais are stark and verie evill entering in ony of the saids Iles. This Ile perteinit to McCloyd of Haray of auld (Monro 1961, 77–8).

An anonymous writer, compiling what may have been an official report to the Crown sometime between 1577 and 1595, provides details not mentioned by Monro:

Irt...is maist fertile of scheip and foullis, quhairof it payis ane great matter yeirlie to...McCloyd and his factors. And albeit thay use na pleuchis, but delvis thair corn land with spaiddis, yet thai pay yeirlie 60 bollis victuall. Thair is na horse nor meiris in this Ile, and but few nolt to the number of 60 or thairby. Thair cummis na men furth of this Ile to oisting or weiris, becaus they are but a poor barbarous people unexpert that dwellis in it, useand na kind of wappinis; but thair daylie exercitation is maist in delving and labouring the ground, taking of foullis and gaddering thair eggis, quhairon thay leif for the maist pairt of thair fude. Thay make na labour to obtene or slay ony fisches, but gadderis sum in the craigis, albeit thai micht have abundance thairof utherwayis gif thai wald ony way make labour thairfore. Anes in the yeir ane Preist or Minister cummis to thame and baptizes all the bairnis born amangis thame sin his last being thair, and celebrattis marriage to the parteis desyrand, and makes sic uther ministration of the sacraments to thame as he thinkis gude, and gifis thame sic directiounis as he wills thame to use and keip for ane yeir thairefter, and gadderis payment of thair teinds (quhilk thai pay maist thankfullie and justlie of ony people), and departs quhill the next yeir agane. In all times thai sustenit ane auld priest or clerk continuallie amangis thame, to shaw and tell to thame the halie dayis to be keipit in the yeir (Anon 1595).

Other sixteenth century authors, George Buchanan (1762 Lib I Cap XLI), an anonymous author (Anon c.1594) and John Leslie (1888, 58–9), all derive their information from those quoted.

These accounts show that the MacLeods had held St Kilda for some time before 1549. There is a traditional account of a boat race between the MacDonalds and the MacLeods, the first to touch the island winning it (p 231). Possession on paper may have been different from possession in practice. In 1610, for instance, James VI granted to Thomas Kerr and his heirs 'the island called Hirt, with the three islands lying close to the same haven, which were appertaining to the said isle, lying about 60 sea miles from the north west part of Uist' (RMS VII, 259); this made no practical difference to the MacLeods' ownership (figure 39, over).

Figure 39. *Genealogy of proprietors and stewards, C17 and C18*

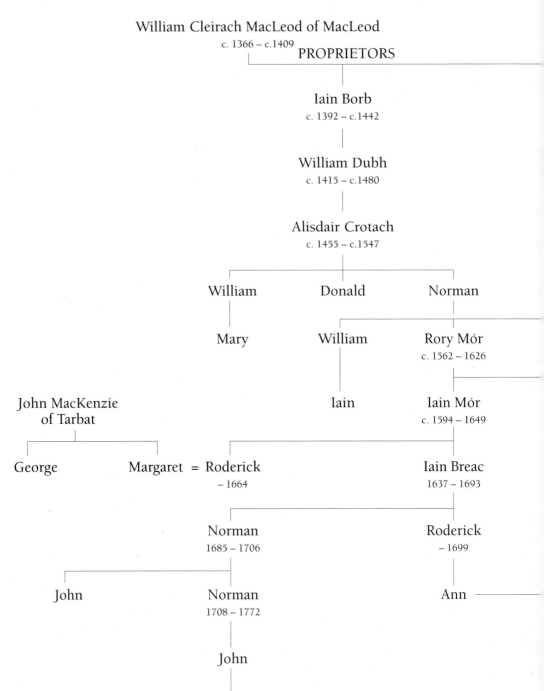

Plate 1. *Stac Lee, Hirte and Soay from the north*

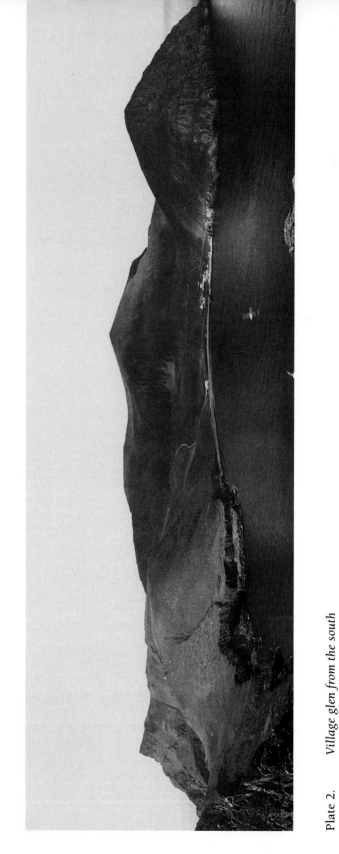

Plate 2. *Village glen from the south*

Plate 3.   *Dun from village (R L Atkinson: School of Scottish Studies collection)*

Plate 4.   *Wind driven spray and waves rolling over jetty: February 1990*

Plate 5.   *Soay from the south*

Plate 6.   *Stac Lee, Stac an Armin and Boreray from the south-west*

Plate 7.   *Boreray and Stac Lee from the west*

Plate 8.   *Stac Lee from the east; Boreray to the right*

Plate 9.   *Stac an Armin from south-east*

Plate 10. Oiseval, 'the Gap' and Conachair from the north

Plate 11. *Abhainn Ilishgil or 'Dry Burn': note stone lining (R L Atkinson: School of Scottish Studies collection)*

Plate 12.   'Town and Harbour of St Kilda' Sir Thomas Dyke Acland, 1812

Plate 13.   'Principal Square in the Capital of St Kilda' Sir Thomas Dyke Acland, 1812

Plate 14.   *Village and bay, 1938 (R L Atkinson: School of Scottish Studies collection)*

Plate 15.   *Packing St Kilda Cloth (R C MacLeod of MacLeod: School of Scottish Studies collection)*

Plate 16.   *Village and Oiseval from the west, under snow*

Plate 17.   *Village from the west*
              (N MacLeod 1886: reproduced with permission from the George Washington
              Wilson Collection, Aberdeen University Library: Ref C7186)

Plate 18.   *House H, and House G behind*

Plate 19.   *'Cleit' 102: note wooden lock. (R C MacLeod of MacLeod: School of Scottish Studies collection)*

Plate 20.   *Gleann Mór from the south-east*

Plate 21.   *'Amazon's House' area from the west*

Plate 22.   *Gleann Mór structure K, from the south-west*

Plate 23.   *Gleann Mór feal dyke, eastern section from the west, under snow*

Plate 24.   *Bothy on Stac an Armin*

Plate 25.   *Interior of bothy, Boreray (A M Cockburn: School of Scottish Studies collection)*

Plate 26. *Cleitean on Oiseval, from the west, under snow*

Plate 27. *Cleitean in old village area, from the south-east*

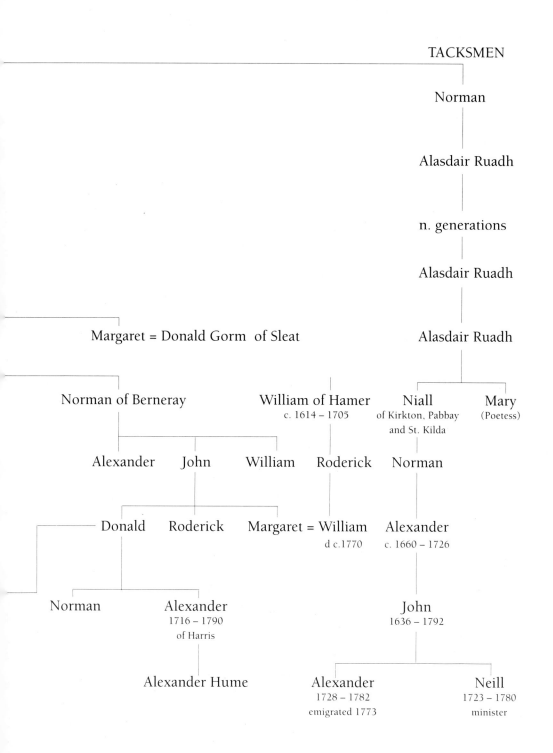

Coll MacDonald's Raid, 1615

In 1615, during a period of piracy after trouble in Islay (Black 1974, 201–243), Coll MacDonald of Colonsay (figure 32) landed on St Kilda and plundered the island. There are three accounts of this episode; a first hand account by one of the participants (Williamson 1615), a report by Sir Rory Mór MacLeod (MacLeod 1615) to Lord Binning of the Privy Council, presumably based on a second hand account by the Steward, and a version collected from descendants of those present by Buchan (1727, 36–7) about a century after the event. About 250 years later, a version conflating Coll's raid and the race for ownership story was collected by Anne Kennedy from Euphemia MacCrimmon (p 231).

Robert Williamson was kidnapped by Coll MacDonald, and accompanied him on his travels for ten weeks, working as a sailor, before he escaped on Rathlin in May. During that time they made their way to Uist, where they were given hospitality. Donald Gorm's wife sent them four horse-loads of meat, including 'two swyne, one salted and one unsalted'. She and others persuaded Coll to go to St Kilda, 'a day and a night sailing from the rest of the north yles, far out in the ocean sea', and provided two Uist men as 'pyllats'. On Hirte, where Williamson says there were only ten men and ten women, they

> Took great store of barley, and some thirty sheep for their provision…There they remained a month. From Art [Hirt] they sailed to another island called Burribaugh [Boreray], which is six miles from Art,…there is no dwelling therein…there Coll had a purpose to keep himself, for it is of such strength as not to be gained but by famine. And from thence they returned back the same way they went thither.

Rory Mór was away on the mainland but on his return to Skye in June he wrote to complain:

> They slew all the bestiall of the ylle, both cowes, and horses, and sheep, and took away all the spoolyee of the yle, onlie reserved the lyves of the enhabitants thereof. And when all was done, they returned to North Wyest againe, where they randered there guyde and pyllats againe, and gave to the enhabitants thereof all and whole the spoyle of my yle.

Coll must have stayed in St Kilda for most of April. The large quantity of barley, part of the previous year's crop, was probably intended mainly for the rent. Williamson's figure of thirty sheep for the stock killed seems more likely; this would provide food during the stay on the island and together with the barley might well fill the boat; 'all the bestiall' must have been exaggeration on Rory Mór's part. Relations between Donald Gorm of Sleat and Rory Mór had been poor for some time.

According to Buchan, when the people saw Coll landing they hid in a cave.

Coll sent men to reassure them and declared his friendly intentions which he reinforced by gestures such as offering snuff. Buchan does not mention the removal of provisions. Part of Coll's time was apparently occupied in revealing the ignorance of the priest who lived with the people and in teaching them correctly the Lord's Prayer, Creed and Ten Commandments (p 245). Buchan is in error in describing Coll as having lost his right hand, and in giving the length of his visit as three quarters of a year.

It is curious that Martin does not mention this incident.

Late Seventeenth Century Accounts

Robert Moray's account (1678, 927–929), probably based on information gathered during a visit to Uist, must have been written before his death in 1673. He gives detailed information about agriculture, boat handling, fowling and religious practices; some of the methods he describes were in use until 1930 (pp 205–6, 267).

George MacKenzie of Tarbat (1630–1725) was connected to the MacLeods through the marriages of several close relatives. It was probably through these alliances that he gathered his brief account, 'from intelligent persons dwelling on the place' (Adv. Ms 33.5.15; MacFarlane 1908, III 28), written between 1681 and 1684 (MacKay 1985, 13–19). It refers to the large numbers of sea birds; the garefowl, the earliest reference to an individual species; one method of fowling; the trade in feathers and 'giben' or bird fat (p 206); the peculiar sheep and the cheese made from their milk; and the manufacture of salt by burning seaweed. MacKenzie had tried the cheese and preferred it to 'Hollands Cheese'.

Martin Martin

Martin (c.1660–1719), a Skye man, graduated in 1681 from Edinburgh University and for a time was tutor to the MacDonald family. Between 1686 and 1692 payments were made to him as tutor to the MacLeods (MacLeod 1938, I 245–251). In 1710 he went to Leyden University and graduated as M.D. He is believed to have lived in London afterwards, until his death in 1719. Buchan says he lived in the Western Isles as a Factor. He was well known to Rory Og MacLeod, 19th of Dunvegan, and attended him at his death in Fortrose in 1699; of him Martin wrote that 'he was the kindest friend I had on earth' (Pennie 1966, 64–73; MacKinnon and Morrison nd I 27).

He had heard about St Kilda locally; he had met the Steward and feeling that earlier second or third hand accounts were not satisfactory, he wished to go there himself. After several unsuccessful attempts, he accompanied the minister of Harris, John Campbell, on his visit in June 1697. In 1698 he published *A Late Voyage to St Kilda, the remotest of all the Hebrides or Western*

Isles of Scotland. A shorter account was included in his volume *A Description of the Western Isles of Scotland* (1703, 280–299). Both these works are invaluable sources of detailed information and have been used extensively throughout this account.

Martin and Mr Campbell left Ensay on May 29th, and after a voyage that was more eventful than comfortable, they landed at St Kilda on June 1st. The Steward and his company were already there. People who were setting snares on Oiseval ran along 'a perilous path' with news of their approach, so that when they reached the landing rock, a group was there to receive them. They stayed for at least three weeks, during which time Martin witnessed from a boat landings on Soay and Stac an Armin, and may well have visited Boreray.

The Steward and his crew were not the only visitors; in 1686 a group of French and Spanish sailors who had been shipwrecked on Rockall arrived in a pinnace. When the sailors began to work on their boat on a Sunday, the people took their tools from them and returned them on Monday. The sailors explained their circumstances to a priest in 'the next island'. The people were also kind to a group of South Uist men whose boat was driven off course, and were well received in that island when the same thing happened to themselves. However, in 1696 the Lowland crew of a ship had behaved badly: they worked on Sunday, gave only a few Irish copper coins for some cattle they took, and made an attempt to rape the women, offering a counterfeit coin as a bribe. No wonder the St Kildans inferred that these men could not be Christians. On another occasion, about 1695, a passing ship sent a small open boat to Soay for water. In the very calm weather some of the sailors landed and collected eggs, one man removing his breeches to hold the eggs. A group of islanders who happened to be on Soay witnessed this theft and dropped some loose stones down upon the men, who left in haste, abandoning both eggs and breeches, which 'were no small ornament in a place where all wore girded plaids'.

After these experiences it is scarcely surprising that the islanders became prejudiced against sailors generally, and resolved that in future if strangers arrived, they would permit only ten people to come ashore, and they must be unarmed. However, if such a small group landed, 'they may expect water and fire gratis, and what else the place affords, on the easiest terms in the world'.

Much of Martin's detailed information about seabirds must have been given to him by the St Kildans. His account of the garefowl is particularly valuable as this bird has been extinct since 1844. The fulmar was a rare bird then, breeding nowhere else in Britain.

Mr Campbell went to St Kilda partly to put an end to the career of 'Roderick the Imposter'. When he was eighteen, this man had asserted that he had met John the Baptist, who had given him some instructions to pass on to the people. These included elements of Christianity and bizarre rites with some biblical influence: for instance, a strict fast to be kept on Fridays, a command that each family should kill a sheep on the threshold, using a spade to cut its neck, and a hymn to be taught to the women on payment of a sheep. This was supposed to protect them from death in childbirth. Roderick taught this to the women individually as an opportunity to seduce them. He pretended to continue to receive instruction from John the Baptist and supervised this contorted form of Christianity for several years, until a man and his son from Harris who were spending a year on the island while working on the boat, informed the Steward of Roderick's behaviour. He was taken to Skye and brought before 'the late MacLeod' (died 1693), who forbade him to preach any more. Evidently he returned to the island, and was still a source of trouble: Campbell and Martin induced him to make a public confession of his errors and took him to Skye, where he remained permanently banished.

A serious disagreement arose in 1697 over the amir, or rather half amir, a measure of volume used in paying the rent (from *amar*: trough or manger). It was made of thin boards and held nearly two pecks (nearly $\frac{1}{2}$ bushel). The measure had worn through use 'these fourscore years', and held less than it did originally. Though the St Kildans admitted this, they felt that the Steward was unfair in the way he compensated for it. The Steward suggested that Mr Campbell and Martin should arbitrate, but the islanders preferred to send their Officer to Skye to state their case before MacLeod. Martin comments that they were 'scrupulously nice and punctilious in maintaining their liberties and properties' and adhered strictly to ancient customs. Another measure of volume was the maile which contained ten pecks ($2\frac{1}{2}$ bushels; probably from *màla*: bag, sack).

Robert Sibbald (1641–1722) was appointed Geographer Royal of Scotland in 1682, with the intention that he should publish a work on the natural history and geography of the country. A first volume was published in 1684 and Sibbald continued to collect material from various informants for a number of years. (Pennie 1964, 159–167; Emery 1958, 3–12). His manuscripts, now in the National Library of Scotland, include four descriptions of St Kilda, mostly based on published accounts. Two accounts (Adv. ms. 33.3.20) are based largely on Martin's books with additional information from earlier accounts, but as MacKay (1985, 13–19) has pointed out there are various minor details found nowhere else (pp 67, 143). He suggests that the source for these may have been notes provided by Martin or possibly a lost earlier account.

Alexander Buchan

Probably as a result of Martin's publications, interest was aroused in the island and the welfare of its inhabitants. The Church of Scotland sent Alexander Buchan, an army veteran, to St Kilda in 1705 as catechist (p 246). In August 1709 he returned to the mainland 'for want of subsistence', but many people gave books and sums of money to support his work, including money to be spent on building a new manse. After he was ordained by the Presbytery of Edinburgh on March 15 1710, the newly-founded Society in Scotland for the Propagating of Christian Knowledge (SSPCK) appointed him schoolmaster on the island, and two weeks later he returned there.

In 1727 he published *A Description of Saint Kilda*. About three quarters of the book is directly copied from Martin, the extracts being re-ordered, but his own contribution provides useful information such as details of burial customs, stock values and compensation schemes (pp 138, 192). It is regrettable that he did not commit more to paper, for during his stay of twenty four years he must have learned much that Martin, despite his enquiring mind, would not have heard or observed in his brief visit, and as an east coast man, there must have been cultural features which were new to him but familiar to Martin.

There is evidence that the people suffered from severe malnutrition, approaching starvation, at this time (pp 126–8).

In 1728 Daniel MacAulay, minister of Bracadale, went to report on Buchan's work. He wrote:

> I have heard Mr Buchan preach, and I found him pretty well read in the Scriptures but otherways of low qualifications. He is fitter for this place than any other person I know…But, it would be a great hardship upon the poor people now in their dismal circumstances to take Mr Buchan from them. The said person is getting very old, and not everyone will go there to succeed him (Svensson 1955, 19–20).

The Smallpox Epidemic, 1727

Daniel MacAulay also recorded a catastrophe:

> I was surprised with the lamentable account of the depopulation of that place by small pox, for of twenty one families that were there, only four remained. Which bore the burden of twenty six orphans, their parents cut off by the foresaid disease.

Some escaped by chance, as in August 1727, three men and eight boys were left 'in a rock' to catch young gannets. The disease took hold in their absence, and the survivors being unable to man a boat, they remained on the rock until the Steward relieved them on May 13th 1728.

The smallpox was carried to St Kilda after a man visiting Harris in 1726 died there of the disease. The following year one of his friends took his clothes back and so introduced the bacillus. According to MacCrimmon (pp 233–4) this man was Donald MacDonald, who earlier in his life had had an encounter with a fairy dairymaid. Only four adults remained to care for the twenty-six orphans (MacAulay 1764, 197–8). As it was some time since the smallpox had visited St Kilda, (pp 126–8, 260), and there is evidence of serious malnutrition, the people would have had little resistance to it, and MacAulay adds that 'the habitual uncleanness of the natives, to which may be added the feculent air pent up within their dirty hovels' probably increased the effects of the disease. A hundred years later, MacKenzie (1904, 399–400) gathered a sad account of the sufferings of the people: the smallpox

> Broke out just after a party had been left on Stac an Armin to collect feathers…Death after death followed. At last there were scarcely sufficient left to bury the dead. As they had then no spades, one man is said to have dug eleven graves with the back board of a wool card…No coffins were attempted…Out of twenty five families only five could keep a fire. There were ninety-four deaths. When the factor came next summer he found those who had been left on Stack-an-armin all well. They lived on fish and fowls, but at times suffered much from cold and hunger. They made fish hooks of a few rusty nails, and also contrived to stitch together their clothing with feathers and patch them with the skins of birds. They returned mostly to empty houses, crops generally never reaped, and the cattle roaming about half wild.

Buchan himself survived the smallpox; most or all of his family were away on the mainland. His presence must have made a considerable difference to the thirty survivors, and his death in February 1729 must have been a severe loss.

The reduction in numbers would have had immediate and severe practical effects. With such an extraordinary imbalance of ages, some of the children must have assumed adult responsibilites earlier than usual. Agriculture was temporarily almost abandoned; activities such as boat journeys to other islands and stacs would be severely restricted until the boys were a little older, and though there would probably be enough eggs and fowls on Hirte and Dun to feed the few people, gannets could only be got by going to Boreray or its stacs, and the men might be anxious to tend the sheep there. The one adult left on Hirte even with the minister's help must have been extremely busy caring for eighteen children through the winter and spring, but the plight of those stranded on Stac an Armin is scarcely imaginable. The single identifiable bothy is in a situation as sheltered as anything can be on a rather bleak stac, but it is only about 300' above sea level, and there must have been many days when the air was full of spray. Water supplies must have been a severe problem, and besides the physical privations, the reasons for their exile and the uncertainty of their fate must have caused these people great mental anguish. Their survival is a tribute to both their physical and emotional strength and resources, and perhaps too to the faith which Buchan had instilled in them.

On some other small and remote islands, disease has been even more devastating. 'The muckle fever' visited Foula about the end of the seventeenth century, and of about 200 people only five or seven survived (Holbourne 1938, 73). The whole of the tiny population of North Rona died in the late seventeenth century; at some time the same thing happened on Mingulay (p 295).

Lady Grange; the search for Charles Edward Stuart

The story of Rachel Erskine, known as Lady Grange, is well known, and several full accounts have been published, including letters written by Erskine herself (MacKenzie 1817, 333–339; Anon 1846, 145–148; Chambers 1874, 449–452; Laing 1876, 597–608, 1878, 312–3; Seton-Watson 1931, 12–24). Briefly, Mrs Erskine and her husband Lord Grange separated in 1730, but she made a nuisance of herself, causing public disturbances and threatening to expose his Jacobite sympathies. In 1732 she was kidnapped in Edinburgh and carried to Heisker, North Uist. Two years later she was taken to St Kilda, where she was kept until her whereabouts became known and an attempt was made to rescue her, so that in 1742 she was removed to Skye where she died three years later. Members of the Berneray family (figure 39) were deeply involved in the kidnapping, but the MacLeods of Dunvegan were involved only latterly, in her removal to Skye. Several points are worth noting. Neither MacLeod (1756–75) nor MacAulay (1764), both of whom must have known of her imprisonment, mention Mrs Erskine. The island was clearly regarded as suitable because it was remote and rarely visited. Erskine refers to it as a 'viled neasty stinking poor Isle' and noted that the 'people is very poor and much oppressed'. The only food provided was milk and barley, and flour sent for her use. One man could speak a little English. By 1734, new immigrants may have been sent to the island, but it would still be hard for a small population, recovering from disaster, to be burdened with the care and concealment of a woman who could not speak their language, did little that was useful, and was probably increasingly disruptive as she gradually became deranged.

The minister Roderick McLennan and his wife, who went to St Kilda in June 1730, had a hard task before them, working with the survivors of the smallpox. It was made no easier by the presence of Mrs Erskine, but she recorded their kindness to her, which 'helped to preserve her life and make it comfortable'. After they left in 1742 or 1743 several catechists by the name of MacLeod followed (p 248).

In 1735 St Kilda was the subject of 'a politicall whim', probably written by Alexander Murray of Stanhope, a staunch Jacobite (Adv ms 29.1.1. Vol VII ff 169–172). Based partly on information gathered from Martin's books, this puts forward a fantastic scheme to increase the population to 5,000 or more, and to form an alliance with the Long Island, providing a power base from which to subdue the mainland.

In 1746, in the search for Charles Edward Stuart, three vessels, the 'Looe', the 'Furnace' and the 'Terror', sailed to St Kilda. On June 20th the last two each landed 50 men, who spent all day on the island. Further landings were made on June 21st and 23rd (PRO ADM 51/379, 538, 1009). Donald MacLeod (Forbes 1895, I, 162) recorded that most of the inhabitants hid in terror, but those who were questioned had never heard of the Prince. 'They said they had heard a report that their laird, MacLeod, had lately had war with a great woman abroad, but that he had got the better of her'.

Neil MacLeod

Neil MacLeod (c.1729–1780), son of John MacLeod the tacksman, must have visited St Kilda a number of times with his father in his youth, and received part of his education there before attending King's College Aberdeen where he graduated MA in 1747. He became minister in Kilfinichen in Mull in 1756. There he married and had a family. In 1773 he entertained Johnson and Boswell (1930, 388; Scott 1926, VI 113).

When Murdoch MacKenzie was working on the west coast of Scotland from 1751 to 1757, making new charts published in 1776 (Moir et al 1973, II 16–17), he was unable to survey St Kilda for fear of privateers. A letter describing the island, found among his papers (MacLeod 1756–1775), was almost certainly written by Neil MacLeod. The writer had not visited the island since 1746, when he had just left grammar school, but his letter indicates that he had been there more than once. Over half of the account is devoted to birds and fowling, but he also describes the houses and how boats were drawn ashore. MacLeod gave MacAulay (1764, 208) information about the 'boat cold'.

Kenneth MacAulay's visit and account

Kenneth MacAulay (1723–1779) succeeded his father Aulay MacAulay as minister of Harris when the latter retired in 1751. In June 1758 he visited St Kilda on behalf of the SSPCK. His book *The History of St Kilda* was first published in 1764. In 1761 he went as minister to Ardnamurchan, and in 1772 to Cawdor, where he died in 1779. Just after his visit to St Kilda, he married Penelope MacLeod; they had five children. Living in Harris, MacAulay would have been in a good position to gather information before his visit. However, neither Boswell nor Johnson (1930, 234), who met MacAulay at Cawdor in 1773, believed that he was capable of writing his book. Boswell had been told that it was written by John MacPherson (1713–1765), minister of Sleat, from material supplied by MacAulay. Some passages imply first hand experience on the part of the author. Powell (1940, 44–53), referring to letters written by MacPherson to Kenneth MacAulay and his brother John (NLS Ms 2958, ff60–75), has argued convincingly that the book is a combination of an account of St Kilda written by MacAulay with discussions of classical parallels written by MacPherson, who was renowned for his literary accomplishments. MacPherson's wife, Janet, was a MacLeod of the Berneray family and his cousin Barbara was married to Alexander MacLeod, catechist on St Kilda, so there were family connections with the island (figure 40). The book has been used extensively in this work.

MacAulay's voyage was not uneventful; the crew of his six-oared boat set off in calm weather, but were overtaken by a violent storm. On their arrival the sea was so rough that they could not land until St Kildans assisted them to do so on the beach.

During his stay, MacAulay was 'towed up against the face of a rock forty feet high' to land on Stac an Armin, but he could not recommend it. He also went to Boreray, where he was conducted to the summit, and wondered at the view and the precipice below. He noted:

The nests of the Solan geese are so close that when one walks between them, the hatching fowls on either side can always take hold of one's cloaths.

A few years before 1758, at the Steward's insistance, the people had cultivated a few plots 'on the north west side of the island' but the grain they sowed grew into very weak plants and the experiment was abandoned. The people had not been in favour of it as they were reluctant to lose good pasture. This may be the area towards the west side of lower Gleann Mór, where two patches of *feannagan* or 'lazybeds' can still be seen.

With little experience or knowledge of the larger world, life on St Kilda was uncomplicated by the trappings of wealth, political intrigue on any scale, complex legal wrangles, or excesses of vice, but perhaps MacAulay paints too rosy a picture when he says

The humble blessings of bread and wild fowl, of peaceful cottages and little flocks, of angling rods and hunting ropes, are all the riches, honours, and profits they aspire after.

Minor References: 1763–1769

William MacLeod of Hamer (figure 39) published in 1763 *A Treatise on Second Sight* under the pseudonym Theophilus Insulanus. Among his examples was one related by Barbara MacPherson (figure 40, p 228), and another by Florence MacLeod 'wife of the present minister' on St Kilda, who, together with her mother, had seen on Pabbay the wraith of a girl brought from St Kilda as a servant, before she died of a fever (MacLeod, 1763, 17–18).

Walker (1980, 59–60) did not manage to visit St Kilda when producing his *Reports on the Hebrides* in 1764 and 1771, and his notes on the island are brief. He records that three vessels had sailed there in 1763 to make a trial of the fishing banks in the area, with little success.

However, in 1765 an advertisement appeared in the *Glasgow Journal* (11.4.1765) for subscriptions towards the cost of fitting out two vessels for fishing round the Western Isles, and it was claimed that forty-three families, with provisions and fishing gear, were to be settled on St Kilda, where 'proper landing stages have already been erected on shore for the cure of cod-fish' (*Scots Mag.* 27 1765, 389). Further advertisements appeared concerning this fishery (*Glasgow Journal* 24.4.1766, *Evening Courant* 14.4.1766) but 'Detector' wrote (*Glasgow Journal* 12.6.1766) that there was no truth in these reports and advertisements, as the subscriptions looked for had been insufficient. Some fishing was taking place in the area, as the following year the *Glasgow Journal* (14.5.1767) reported the discovery of a coin hoard by 'some fishermen' (p 70).

A masonic lodge, St Kilda's Lodge, was formed in Portree, Isle of Skye in November 1769, by petition of Sir Alexander MacDonald of Sleat. It is not known why the Lodge received its name, but MacLeods were among its first members (A O Hazel, Grand Secretary to Grand Lodge of Scotland, pers comm).

Sale of St Kilda, 1779

Donald MacLeod of the Berneray family (figure 39) had the tack of Unish in Skye, and when his uncle, William, gave up the tack of Berneray in 1730 after refusing to pay the increased rents, Donald took it over and continued to hold it until his death in 1781. He was succeeded by his son Norman. His second son, Alexander, became captain of the East Indiaman the 'Lord Mansfield'. According to Morrison (1975, 202–4) he was taken into partnership by the owners of the vessel, and prospered. When Norman, 22nd Chief, was in serious financial difficulties, Alexander MacLeod gave him a loan in return for Norman's granting a feu of Berneray to Donald. At his death in 1772 Norman left the estate burdened by debt, and his heir, his grandson Norman, borrowed again from Captain Alexander, and in an effort to improve matters enrolled for military service in America. Alexander MacLeod had already offered to buy Harris from the 22nd Chief. He renewed his offer but would not increase the original sum of £15,000, and after the property had been on the market for some years it was finally sold to him in 1779. Harris included nearly all the islands in the Sound of Harris, and St Kilda, which Norman had wished to retain 'on account of its curiosity' (Grant 1959, 494–508; MM 1.682/2).

Stewards (Tacksmen) and Rents

The office of Steward is first mentioned in 1549, as the person who made an annual visit to collect the rent, taking a priest with him.

In the late seventeenth century it was customary for the Steward to stay from late May to late August, accompanied by forty to sixty people, including some of the poor of the parish, who benefited from the generous rations provided. Rent was paid in 'down, wool, butter, cheese, cows, horses, fowls, oil and barley' (Martin 1716, 289). The Steward had a resident deputy, the 'Meijre' (*maor*) or Officer (later known as the Ground Officer). At one time he had been chosen, or at least approved of, by the people, but in Martin's time the Steward appointed him without any consultation. He was responsible for the allocation of land, rocks and grazing when these were re-apportioned every three years; he had to make the first attempt at landing on other islands; the day to day organisation was led by him and he generally managed to settle disputes. On the Steward's arrival the Officer fixed the rations to be contributed by each family to support his party, and was himself obliged to give the Steward a large barley loaf at each meal and meat for his Sunday dinners. In addition to this, the Steward's party received a 'treat' on their arrival of the whole island's milk produce, and a second 'treat' on St Columba's day (June 9th).

Any serious dispute between the people or serious offence was referred to the Steward. In any disagreement with the Steward the Officer was the people's champion; he had to argue the case until either he won or the Steward was so provoked that he gave the Officer three blows on the head with his cudgel. If there were any unresolved dispute between the St Kildans and the Steward, the Officer represented the former when the matter was laid before MacLeod, and the whole boat's crew accompanied him to see that he was not cowed by the Steward. This suggests that on such rare occasions, the St Kildans sent their own boat to Skye.

In return for his services, the Officer received from each family an *amir* of barley, and from the Steward some acres of land and the bonnet which the Steward had worn during his visit. Similarly the Officer's wife received from the Steward's wife the kerchief which she had worn, and an ounce of indigo. (Martin 1753, 10, 48–53).

Buchan describes the Steward as living all winter in Pabbay and spending much of the summer on St Kilda. He took with him a large party, all of whom the islanders were expected to sustain. This accounted to some extent for the poverty of many of the people, whom the island might have supported otherwise. Buchan regarded the rent as extortionate. In addition, the Steward had managed to make mandatory a tax formerly paid voluntarily to some of his predecessors, who had received a sheep from each family if they were forced to stay on the island by contrary winds. The Steward had tried to exact this by force before Martin's time, without success, but lately he had exacted one sheep in twenty from each family. Any imported goods, such as salt and tobacco, were brought by the Steward, who fixed his own price (20 pence ($1^2/_3$ d) per peck for each of the above) and placed his own value on the goods offered in exchange, always to his advantage; nor was anyone else allowed to carry goods to the island for barter, so he had a monopoly. The local Officer appointed to look after the Steward's interests held his land free, and in Buchan's time was the richest man on the island, having twenty or more cows and two or three hundred sheep.

MacAulay made observations similar to Buchan's concerning the monopoly of the Steward on trade. Few goods were imported: tobacco, salt, iron, and timber, and he considered that the islanders did not require to purchase anything beyond the necessaries of life; indeed, they were ignorant of most of the luxuries available on the mainland. The Steward had absolute power over them; no mention is made of the right of appeal to MacLeod. In addition to the rent, taxes were still levied on milk production and sheep stock, but MacAulay records that the Steward, and his father before him, had relieved the people of 'many grievous taxes' and he was convinced that the Steward in his own time would not oppress them. There is a hint that some of the men might have left the island to avoid too stern a stewardship, and in explaining the identity of the Staller, he refers to him as 'the rebel (or rather friend of liberty)'. On the other hand, he points out that the Steward had the expense of fitting out a boat to collect his rent, and the voyage was not without danger. He could not pay his own rent to MacLeod until he had collected what was owing to him. However, the Steward was one his parishioners, and MacAulay might well have been unwilling to speak freely about his conduct, even though he had moved to Ardnamurchan by the time his book was published. Possibly MacPherson exerted some restraint.

It is not known who the Steward of St Kilda was in the sixteenth century, but the position may have been in the hands of the Clann Alasdair Ruaidh, a branch of the MacLeod family, for some time before the first record (figure 39). MacAulay (1764, 208, 270) says three generations had had it before 'the present steward' (Alexander MacLeod). Matheson (1952, 12) states that Niall mac Alasdair Ruaidh lived on Pabbay and was Steward of St Kilda. According to tradition, Niall received the tack of St Kilda when his position as MacLeod's business man was taken over by Norman MacLeod of Berneray. Niall's son, Norman, is mentioned in the Harris rent rolls from 1679 to 1685 as occupying land at Baile na Cille, together with other tenants (MacKinnon and Morrison nd, III 202–4). In 1697 his son, Alexander, was Steward. It was he and his crew who survived being wrecked on Rona when storm driven during a return voyage from St Kilda (Martin, 1753, 48, 70), though Morrison (1975, 286–290), writing early in the nineteenth century, transposed the event by a generation. Alexander was succeeded by his son John who was Steward in 1727 (Buchan 1727, 24). John and his brother Norman, tacksman of Northton in Pabbay, were involved in the removal of Lady Grange from Heisker to St Kilda in 1734. In 1735, together with Norman MacLeod of Waterstein, he became a factor on the MacLeod estates in Skye, and within eight years, through his second marriage, was tacksman of Bay, at the foot of the Waternish peninsula, where he took up his residence, and where he died in 1792. He continued to be tacksman of St Kilda for some time after 1735: he is referred to as John MacLeod of St Kilda or John St Kilda as late as 1753, though in 1743 he is also called John MacLeod of Bay; but in 1747 he received reimbursement for payment made to the St Kilda minister, indicating a continued responsibility (Morrison 1968, 72–91). In 1754 both he and his son, Alexander, are mentioned in the St Kilda rental (table 1).

Alexander, together with his father-in-law, Donald Campbell of Scalpay, began a fishing industry in Harris. In 1733 money was paid by the estate for a fishing yole, made by Donald Campbell, who also received money to buy salt, and 'the fishers' in Harris were given butter, cheese, and salt. When the lesser tenants of Pabbay fell into arrears Alexander took over their leases in 1769, but Norman, the 22nd Chief, planned to raise the rents, and in 1773 Alexander gave up his tack and he and several of his subtenants emigrated to North Carolina, where his father-in-law was already settled (MacKinnon and Morrison, nd II 228–9; Morrison 1968, 71). The tack of St Kilda was taken over by William MacNeil of Rodel, Harris (Morrison 1969, 17).

Table 1 shows the more important references to the tack of St Kilda in the eighteenth century. The omission of St Kilda in 1728 and 1729 is hardly surprising after the smallpox epidemic. There is an indication of payment in kind to the tacksman in some entries: in 1750 12 bolls from St Kilda were included in Harry Bain's 'artickle', and in 1753 Harry Bain, who appears in

1732 and 1733 as boatmaster at both Nisabost and Claigin, was to be ordered to 'fetch in his feathers and putt them in new baggs being 17 of them'. Such quantities of feathers are most likely to have come from St Kilda (Morrison 1968, 70, 87, 90).

Table 1
References to Rents in the Eighteenth Century

Year	Notes	Reference
1707–24	Annual rent of Hirt farm: 100 merks (£5.10.6^{2}/$_{3}$)	2/485/11–24
1712	Boat bought for Hirta after remarkable disaster in Boreray 146.6.8 merks (£8.2.9^{1}/$_{3}$). Two years rent remitted because of poverty resulting from disaster	TGSI 44.332
1724	Yearly pay of Isle of Hirt is 16 bolls beare and no more	2/487/19
1727	Received 18 bolls beare from St Kilda	2/487/20
1727–29	No mention made of St Kilda	TGSI 45.66–7
1735	Rent set at 86.13.4 (£7.4.6)	2/487/22
1735	Rents of St Kilda given up to buy boat	TGSI 45.73
1750	Captain John MacLeod younger received tack of St Kilda for 16 years	1/10
1754	Rent of St Kilda (to John and Alexander MacLeod) doubled: 173.6.8 (£14.9.0)	2/487/28,31
1768	Present rent (£11.2.2) changed to £30.2.2. N.B.The whole milk to be abolished	2/486/35
N D	Rent (to Alexander MacLeod) set at £32.0.0. Custom of collecting milk to be abolished, but he could demand butter and cheese instead	2/466/4
1769	Rent of St Kilda to Alexander MacLeod £30	2/485/36
1771	Deduction from rental, reducing St Kilda to £20, to take effect from 1771, only if lessees did not emigrate	2/485/43,44
1773	Settlement of account between Alexander MacLeod and Norman MacLeod of MacLeod. Value of 'effects' left on St Kilda accepted as £48.17.4^{3}/$_{4}$	2/466/28
1776	List of arrears: St Kilda Wm MacNeil £54.10.3	2/485/47
1777	Rent of St Kilda: £20	2/485/50

All MacLeod Muniments except:
TGSI 44 = Morrison 1966, TGSI 45 = Morrison 1968

7

St Kilda from 1779 to 1930

Proprietors and Tacksmen, 1779–1871

Figure 40 shows the relationship between the two MacLeod families who owned St Kilda between 1779 and 1871. No estate records for the period 1779 to 1871 have been located. Scattered through the literature are references indicating that a number of people had some interest in the island; figure 40 shows the relationship of some of these individuals to the proprietors. Table 2 gives some details of rents.

Captain Alexander MacLeod was probably in his sixties when he bought Harris in 1779. He set about improving the estate, building roads, and at Rodel, a harbour, storehouse, boathouse, school, inn, and a spinning house. He made loans to buy boats, provided fishing gear, and allowed fishermen houses rent free, all in an effort to encourage a deep sea fishing industry. In 1785 and 1786 he sent a boat to fish around St Kilda, with great success

Figure 40. *Families associated with St Kilda, 1779–1871*

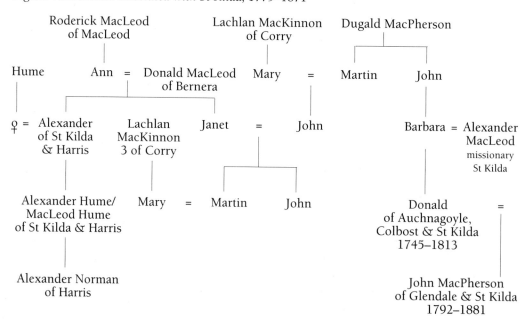

Sources: MacDonald & MacDonald 1904, 494 9; MacInnes 1899, 54; MacKenzie 1881, 262–276; MacKinnon 1954, 26–34; MacKinnon & Morrison nd II 55–58, 75–76; Morrison 1974, 191–5.

(Knox 1787, 158–160). It is possible that the Store on St Kilda was part of this scheme. When Captain Alexander died in 1790 his son, Alexander Hume MacLeod, inherited. He continued working in India for the East India Company (MacLeod, 1792, 365) and his father's schemes were abandoned.

William MacNeil continued as Tacksman under the new ownership; accounts suggest that the islanders were severely oppressed during this time (Buchanan 1793, 136; Clarke 1824, 267; Brougham 1871, I 107; Campbell 1799 f 24–6, 36, 50). The demands on their resources included, as before, all the milk produced between May Day and Michaelmas, made into butter and cheese by one or two dairymaids whom MacNeil sent to the island. Nearly all the barley other than that required for sowing was taken in the rent, and any feathers beyond those taken as rent were to be sold to MacNeil, who paid 3/- per stone for them, selling them at 10/- in the Long Island. He stayed for several weeks on his twice yearly visits, living at the expense of the people, and he kept them in ignorance of external affairs. Campbell implies that the position of Ground Officer no longer existed; it is apparent from different accounts that to some extent the missionary took his place.

In 1804 St Kilda and Pabbay were sold to Lieutenant Colonel Donald MacLeod for £1,350 (Seton 1878, 40). The son of a former missionary, he took an interest in the welfare of the islanders. One of his first actions was to

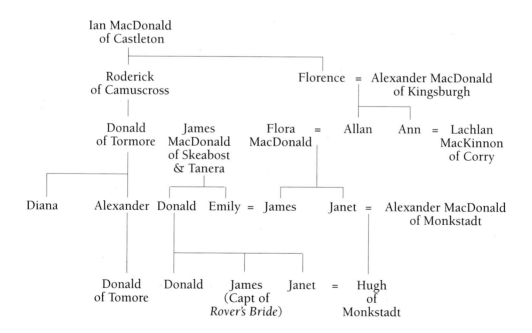

Table 2
Details of Rent at Different Dates

Date	Rent from people and from tacksman	Reference
1790s	50 bolls barley and potatoes, milk, feathers Tacksman: 11 guineas (£11.11.0)	Buchanan 1793, 136
1793	43 bolls barley, 20 stones feathers, dairy produce, salted birds: 2 barrels gannets 4 barrels fulmar. Tacksman: £20	Campbell 1799, f 24-6
1814	140 stone feathers only	MacLeod 1814,912-3
1815	£40 all paid in feathers; export cheese, wool, and feathers	MacCulloch 1819, 26; 1824, 182
1830s	Rent mainly paid in feathers	MacKenzie 1911, 16
1841	240 stone feathers, 23 pecks barley per family (mostly paid in feathers); grazing: 7/- per cow, 1/- per sheep above 10. Feathers valued at 5/- per stone, tacksman sold for 15/-	Wilson 1842, 22, 26, 42, 46
1847	Per family: 7 stone feathers @ 5/- stone; 20 pecks bear @ 1/- peck; grazing: 7/- per cow, 1/- per sheep, 6d per lamb. Send out annually 32 barrels bird oil, selling @ £3 per barrel, also export wool	Milner 1848, 2058
1840s–52	£1.10.0 or more per family for land (= c.£25); grazing: 7/- per cow above one, 1/- per sheep above 10, 6d per yearling; £35 for killing birds; £5 for grazing Boreray. Exports: bird oil 1/- gallon, old fulmar oil 1/- bottle, tweed, feathers, cheese	MacQueen nd, 2, 3, 10
1853	Per family: £1 for arable; grazing 7/- per cow, 1/- per sheep; 7 stone feathers	MacKenzie 1921, 88
c.1863	Per family: £1 for land, £1 for rocks, 5/- for Boreray; complained about rocks, payment removed but added to Boreray	PP 1884, 873
1870s	£2 per croft and static sum of £51.3.0 for grazing	MM 2/629
1883	Same as in 1871; no pressure to pay arrears	PP 1884, 870
1886	Grazing 7/- per cow, young cattle half that; per sheep: Hirte 9d, Boreray 6d, Dun 1/-	MM 2/633 & 635
1900	£1.10.0 per croft; grazing same as before.	MM 2/633 & 635

end the tenancy of MacNeil, who was reluctant to give up St Kilda and was deprived of it only by a court case (Fraser MacIntosh 1897, 299–300). Donald MacLeod's brief *Notices on the present State of St Kilda*, published posthumously (MacLeod 1814, 912–13), were mainly about the potential for exploiting the natural resources. At his death in 1813 he was succeeded by his son, John MacPherson MacLeod (1792–1881), who also purchased Glendale in Skye. He first visited St Kilda in 1804 (RHASS papers). Part of his working life was spent in India; in 1838 he returned to England and retired in 1841. He was knighted in 1866 and made a Privy Councillor in 1871 (DNB Vol 22). He and his wife visited St Kilda about 1840 (MacKenzie 1911, 14). In 1871 he sold the island to Norman MacLeod, 25th of MacLeod, for £3,000 (Seton 1878, 40).

MacDonald (1811, 817–8) noted that the purchase of St Kilda by Donald MacLeod meant that the inhabitants were 'no longer fleeced to the skin or oppressed by starvation, but encouraged to industry'. Two boats were sent to them, and apparently an enterprising young man from Edinburgh had leased part of the island, undertaking to make various improvements. There is no evidence, however, that such a person ever visited the island. In the 1830s MacKenzie (1911, 16–17) regarded the proprietor as 'very kind'.

In 1815 the island was, according to MacCulloch (1824, 185) administered directly by the 'very liberal' proprietor, but by 1821 Murdoch MacLellan was Tacksman (Gaelic School Report 11 1822, 36), continuing in this position until he moved from Scalpay to South Uist in 1827. In that year Lachlan MacKinnon of Corry is recorded as Factor; he intended to visit the island to fix the site for the church and manse, but was not well enough to travel, and MacLellan received part of the rent on his visit in July. MacLellan may have continued as Tacksman, as in 1830 his family tutor, Mr Bethune, acted for the Tacksman (Kennedy 1932, 89, 139–43, 180, 275–277, 287). However, MacKinnon may still have had an interest in the island, as in 1831 Atkinson (1831, 5, 11) secured an introduction to Mrs MacKinnon from her son in Glasgow, and visited the family at Corry on his return from St Kilda.

In the 1830s the Tacksman seems to have been Donald MacDonald of Skeabost, who in 1790 bought the fishing station at Lochinver, and Tanera Island. In 1837 he or his son, Donald, bought the unsuccessful fishing station at Lochbay [Stein] (Dunlop 1978, 96, 172, 182). One of them is known to have rented St Kilda (MacKenzie 1921, 84) and to have been Tacksman in 1841 (Wilson 1842, 46). It was probably he who removed the last ponies from the island (MacDiarmid 1878, 246). Betty Scott from Lochinver probably got the post of servant to the minister's family through MacDonald. Donald MacKinnon was Ground Officer in the 1830s (MacQueen nd, 6; MacLean

1838, 39); after he left in 1840/1, a MacDonald took his place (MacKenzie 1911, 25).

In the 1820s and 1830s the rent was paid almost entirely in feathers, and the Tacksman took any surplus produce, such as barley, cheese, beef, mutton, cloth, oil, and more feathers, and in the following year brought any goods ordered, such as tools, indigo, printed cloth, and hats (Kennedy 1932, 113, 143; MacDonald 1823, 27; MacKenzie 1911, 16–17).

A letter from Norman MacRaild (20.6.1877 RHASS papers; figure 41) implies that he was Tacksman or Factor from 1842 to 1873; he certainly held that position from 1846 to early 1873 (PP 1884, 3157; MM 2/626/1). Donald MacDonald of Tormore may have acted as overseer for his cousin, MacPherson MacLeod, who lived in England. He arranged the purchase of two boats in 1869 (RHASS papers), and in 1872 he advised MacLeod of MacLeod, the new proprietor, on a question of rent (MM 2/637/3).

The Provision of Storage Facilities

The Store may well have been built as part of Captain Alexander MacLeod's fishery development. It has similarities to the larger store at Rodel, and was probably in existence by 1799, when Campbell (1799, f 83) describes how sixty people spent an evening in 'the Steward's house, as being the largest on the island' having sufficient space to hold a dance. A building which is almost certainly the Store appears in a sketch made in 1812 by Thomas Dyke Acland (plate 12). In 1815 (MacCulloch 1819, 24) services were held 'in a house that was erected as a store for the wool and feathers of the natives'. By 1841 it was used only as a store; feathers were stored dirty, damp and unpicked, but the Tacksman still managed to get 15/- per stone for them (Wilson 1842, 10, 46); in 1853 MacKenzie (1921, 89) noted that it was used for storing 'feathers, cloth, wool, etc' and supplies of meal, planks and coals.

The Store is a two storey mortared and slate-roofed building set into sloping ground close to the landing place and facing the sea (figure 41). The generous windows, together with a fireplace in each gable, suggest that the ground floor was intended as a dwelling, though there is no indication or record of any internal partitioning, lining or plastering. The upper floor is part attic, with walls about four feet high. Lit by small openings and without fireplaces, it must have been intended for storage. It is entered from the higher ground on the north-east side. A few internal steps would have been required to reach the floor level. There is no indication as to whether there was ever any internal access between floors.

In 1918 the Store was badly damaged by shells from a German submarine. It was not repaired. The National Trust for Scotland reconstructed it in the 1980s.

Figure 41. *The Store: plans and elevations*

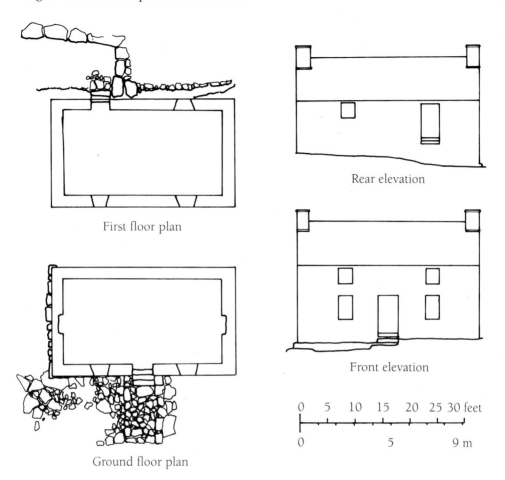

First floor plan

Ground floor plan

Rear elevation

Front elevation

0   5   10   15   20   25 30 feet

0   5   9 m

History 1779–1871

There are few records of visitors before the 1830s, apart from several eminent travellers at the turn of the century. Some of them may have been exploring their own country rather than going on a Continental tour while Britain was at war with France and Spain. Buchanan (1793, 118–146) who copied most of his account from Martin and MacAulay, did not go, but he met a man from St Kilda, and he refers to the men demonstrating their climbing skills by scrambling 'along the ceilings' in a 'gentleman's house'. Possibly he saw this himself during his visit to the Hebrides.

Edward Clarke (1824), later Professor of Mineralogy at Cambridge, accompanied the son of Lord Uxbridge on a tour of the Hebrides in July and August 1797. In 1799 (Brougham 1799) John Joseph Henry, intending to visit Iceland, gathered twelve friends including Charles Stuart, of the Bute family,

Robert Campbell of Islay, and Henry Brougham. One of the favourite late night pastimes of the young Brougham and his friends was to go through the Edinburgh New Town wrenching brass door furniture from its proper place. Brougham (1871, I 88–112) left a brief and flippant account of his visit. Campbell (1799) wrote a more informative account, used throughout this work. He also made a map of the islands (figure 11). Marion Morrison or Gillies recorded his flirtation with her in a song (p 240). Apparently George Stuart MacKenzie of Coul went in 1800 (Laing 1876, 608; MacKenzie 1817, 339; Barron 1912, 27, 33; Wilson 1842, I 3) but the only record he left is a poor map, published by Wilson (figure 12). In 1812 Thomas Dyke Acland (Acland 1981, 50) sailed to St Kilda and made some good sketches, including two of the village (plates 11, 12). In 1815 the geologist MacCulloch (1819, 23) noted that it was more than a year since another visitor had been on the island.

A visitor in 1821 reported to the Society for the Support of Gaelic Schools that St Kilda was in need of a school, and as a result Alexander MacKenzie was stationed there from June 1823 to 1828 or 1829. As well as teaching the children and some adults, he held regular meetings for worship (Gaelic School Reports 11 1822 – 19 1830). He was encouraged in this by John MacDonald (The Apostle of the North), who visited St Kilda in 1822, 1823 and 1827. He travelled with MacLellan, who put himself to considerable inconvenience in 1827, making a special journey to the island. MacDonald was instrumental in the building of a church and manse in 1827, and

Figure 42. *Possible site of early nineteenth century school: plan*

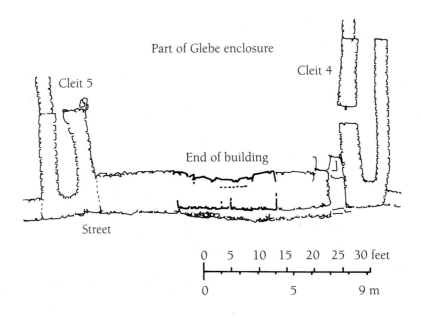

Part of Glebe enclosure

Cleit 4

Cleit 5

End of building

Street

0   5   10   15   20   25   30 feet

0   5   9 m

accompanied Neil MacKenzie, the new minister, to the island in 1830 (Kennedy 1932, 82–99, 106–124, 135–147, 275–292; p 248). Neil MacKenzie also filled the office of teacher. Incorporated within the glebe wall just north of the church are the remains of a building which might be all that survives of the 'new' one-room school in which MacKenzie taught (p.258).

Neil MacKenzie stayed from 1830 to 1844 and wrote a very useful account of the island (1911). He was a man of great energy and initiative, and as well as his care for the spiritual welfare of the islanders, he was responsible for major improvements in agriculture and housing. A catalyst for this was the gift of £20 from Thomas Dyke Acland. He had made many improvements on his own extensive estates in Devon (Acland 1981 45–75) and was disturbed by the squalor of the homes he saw when he visited in 1812 and 1834. Once the people had decided to build new houses, they also wanted to divide the arable land permanently, so that each family could build on its own piece. They felt that the division made by Donald MacDonald of Tanera (MacKenzie 1881, 267) was unfair, so MacKenzie persuaded them to divide the land themselves, as fairly as possible, and then cast lots to apportion the pieces, and with this they were satisfied. New and improved houses were built, and Acland's gift, augmented by others, was used to buy windows and furniture; MacPherson MacLeod sent £20 to cover the carriage.

MacKenzie observed that the people could be led but not directed, and took part himself in clearing and draining the arable land, canalising the streams and building the head dyke. He made improvements to the glebe, and took particular interest in building the great wall around the burial ground, where he buried three of his own children. The pattern of strips within the fan-shaped head dyke, with the long street running across the strips, now so familiar from photographs, is an alien pattern, quite different from the nucleated village and runrig system which preceded it, and was in use for less than a hundred years. The pattern and ownership were first recorded in 1860 by Sharbau (figure 43).

MacKenzie recorded that passing vessels seldom called, unless they needed water or were lost; in this way he heard of the death of William IV in 1837, but not of the succession of a queen rather than a king until the following year. Sometimes ships engaged in smuggling or piracy called in for fresh water and provisions, and the crews got the people to do washing for them. MacKenzie says they never harmed the people and paid them in goods which were useful to them.

G C Atkinson (1831, f 31–2), a naturalist who went in 1831, is the first recorded as chartering a boat from Harris specifically for this trip. Those aboard a visiting yacht, who came ashore with a brass band playing, were,

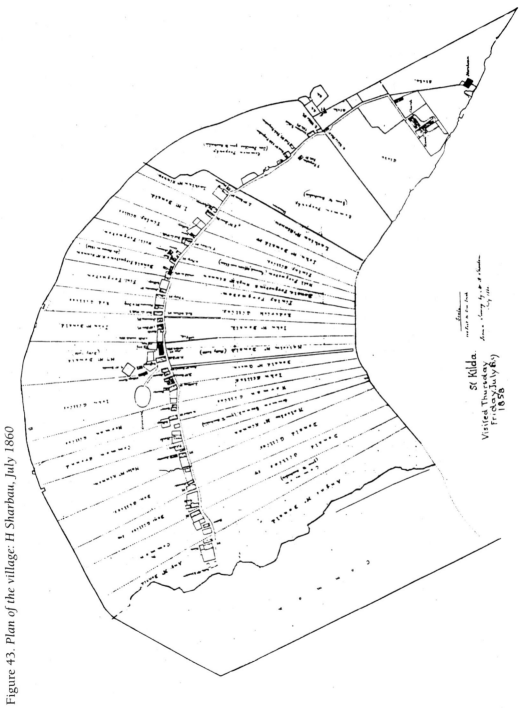

Figure 43. Plan of the village: H Sharbau, July 1860

unintentionally, less considerate than the pirates: both people and stock were terrified of the unaccustomed noise and ran away. Possibly this was the 'Glenalbyn', the first steam vessel to call at the island, in July 1834 (Carruthers 1843, 255–8). Another steam yacht, the 'Vulcan', called in 1838 (MacLean 1838, 25) with over thirty visitors aboard, and Neil MacKenzie returning from a visit to Glasgow with colleagues, and a quantity of furniture and crockery for the new houses.

MacCulloch (1824, 179, 185) noted in 1815 that there was no scarcity of food; indeed, 'want was unknown' and MacKenzie (1911, 15) said in the 1830s that 'I know no place where people can have such a plentiful supply of food with so little exertion', while MacGillivray (1842, 54) wrote in 1842 that: 'the people are now better lodged, clothed, and fed, than are the great mass of the population throughout the Hebrides'. This happy situation was soon to change; St Kilda was affected by the potato blight of 1846 and potatoes, which had been so plentiful that a surplus was fed to the cattle, were scarcer afterwards (MacQueen nd 3). MacPherson MacLeod sent meal for MacRaild to distribute (PP 1884, 3157).

In 1851 the inhabitants of St Kilda were enumerated in the official Census of Great Britain for the first time. The men were all listed as 'Farmer and Birdcatcher' while eight of the women were listed as 'Weaveress', which is curious, as the weaving was normally done by men (PP 1852–3 85, liv–lv).

In 1852 a group of 36 people left St Kilda in the autumn, travelling by Skye and Glasgow to Liverpool, where in January 1853 they boarded the 'Priscilla', bound for Australia (MacQueen nd 13). According to John MacKay (1884, 870), they left on account of poverty, though there may have been some persuasion on the part of MacRaild. McPherson MacLeod instructed MacRaild that no-one was to be sent away from the island. He met the emigrants in Glasgow and accompanied them to Liverpool; he offered to send them back to St Kilda at his own expense, and he paid the fares to Australia of those who could not afford it. In his anxiety to avert further emigration, he bought the Church and Manse from the established Church and presented them to the Free Church (MacQueen nd, 3–4, 8, 13–14). He had already added £100 to the £50 available for a minister's salary, in an attempt to induce someone to take the post (Milner 1848, 2058). No one was found to take the position until Kennedy arrived as catechist in 1859 (p 251).

Several visitors in the 1840s and 1850s produced useful accounts (Wilson 1832, MacGillivray 1842, Milner 1848 and Muir 1858). One of the few accounts by a native was dictated by Malcolm MacQueen (nd) when he was an old man, to his son. MacQueen emigrated in 1852, when he was twenty-four. His recollections of life on St Kilda are of great value.

In 1851 Charles Kelsall of Southampton left £700 to be used to purchase articles of benefit to the inhabitants of St Kilda. After a contest with other legatees, in 1859 £602.2.4 was deposited for this purpose with the Royal Highland and Agricultural Society of Scotland (RHASS), which has the papers concerning the spending of this money, and of additional sums collected from the public in 1860 to assist the St Kildans.

In 1859 MacPherson MacLeod and MacRaild discussed with John Hall Maxwell, the Secretary of the Society, the use of the fund, and reached the conclusion that it could best be spent in providing new houses and a slip or means of hauling up boats, both projects beyond the resources of the people.

From 1846 to 1863 Admiralty ships were sailing in Hebridean waters, making the surveys for the new charts of the area (p 31). Captain H C Otter of the 'Porcupine' was working round St Kilda in 1860 and he befriended the islanders; a number of people visited in that year as passengers on his ship, including Mr Hall Maxwell of the RHASS, the Duke of Atholl, Captain and Mrs Thomas, and Mr H Sharbau, who made a detailed plan of the village (figure 43) (Morgan 1861, 104–6; Murray 1860; Sharbau 1860). Otter became involved in various schemes, the first being a better means of taking boats ashore, using a crane. This was completed in September 1860.

On October 2nd the 'harbour' was badly damaged by a severe storm which tore off house roofs, destroyed a boat and most of the grain crop, and nearly drove the 'Porcupine' to its doom. Otter appealed for help on behalf of the people, and as a result took out in late October a quantity of supplies and household goods. To avoid simply giving these to the islanders as charity, he exchanged them for promises of work, the heads of households putting their names to an agreement to build new houses for the whole community, a wall to shelter their boats, and a building to be used to house a hand mill which would replace the querns. Although MacPherson MacLeod was grateful for the prompt action taken, and the concern for the islanders shown by so many people, he was unwilling to relinquish what he saw as his own responsibilities, and he wished to pay for the provisions sent; nor would he permit the building of any houses other than at his own expense. The first four were built in 1861 (Census 1861; RHASS papers).

In the 1860s visitors were becoming more frequent, some of them on official business. Alexander Gregor went in 1851, 1861 and 1871, to take the census (Mitchell 1901, 441). Morgan wrote a general account (1861) and a more specialist paper dealing with diseases (1862). Thomas published details of some of the buildings in his papers (1862, 1868) and notes on traditions recounted by Euphemia MacCrimmon (Kennedy and Thomas 1874). Mitchell, using information gathered in 1860 from MacRaild, Kennedy and

Thomas, wrote on health (1865). Carmichael collected songs and tradition in 1865 (1928, 1941, 1954).

Two buildings may be associated with this period (figures 44 and 45).

Mill Building, 1861

Otter specified that this building should be near the middle of the village; it was to be 21 feet' long, by 15' wide, with a door 6' square and three windows each 3' square (RHASS papers, Sharbau 1860). The western half, at least, was built, in dry stone walling with two of the three windows, and House 9 was built beside it at about the same time (figure 44). In 1861 Otter purchased in London two mills to be sent to St Kilda. There is no record of their arrival or use.

Figure 44. *Mill Building: plans and sections*

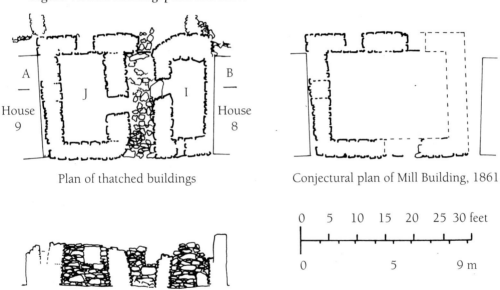

Plan of thatched buildings

Conjectural plan of Mill Building, 1861

Section A - B

The Factor's House

The Factor's House (figure 45) may have been built by MacPherson MacLeod: no records of its building have been located in the MacLeod Muniments. It is not on Sharbau's plan (1860), but it was in existence by 1873 (Smith 1879, frontispiece). It was used by the Factor when he went to collect the rents, but it also housed a succession of schoolteachers and nurses, and some of the more privileged visitors stayed in it.

It is a two storey mortared and slate-roofed building set into sloping ground on the north side of the street. Each storey could function as a separate household. On the ground floor the room at the north-west end had a stove in the gable wall, while that at the south-east end has a fireplace with cast iron surround. The upper floor is part attic, with walls about three feet high. A flight of seven internal stairs is required to reach floor level on the central landing. The two rooms are lit by skylights. The gable at the north-west end had a fireplace with hobs and a grate, while that at the south-east end has a small fireplace with a cast iron surround. A deep stone-lined gulley behind and at both ends of the house carries water from the surrounding ground away from the house. This is the only building with internal partitioning retaining its original plan; much of the timber is probably original.

Figure 45. *The Factor's House: plan and elevations*

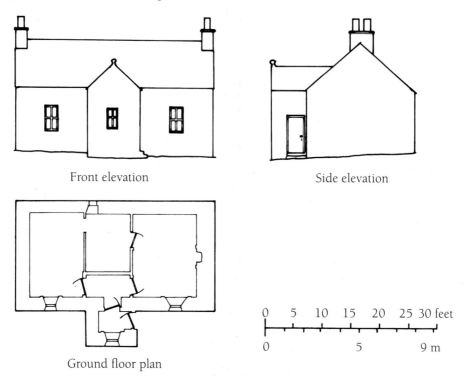

Front elevation

Side elevation

Ground floor plan

0   5   10   15   20   25 30 feet

0   5   9 m

Proprietors and Factors: 1871–1930

In 1871 Norman MacLeod, 25th of MacLeod, purchased St Kilda for £3,000. He spent so much money alleviating distress in Skye during the potato famines of the late 1840s that the estate debts increased. He let Dunvegan Castle and sold some of the contents, and took a job in London in the Civil Service, from which he retired in 1881. His sister, Emily, stayed in Skye and

Figure 46. *Proprietors: MacLeod families 1754–1930*

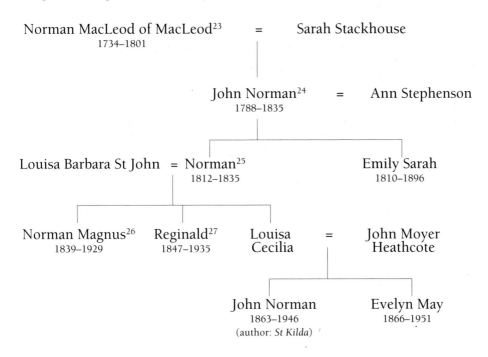

(author: *St Kilda*)

devoted her life to the welfare of the people. She also visited St Kilda, and paid the salary of the first two nurses (p 264) (Grant 1959 582–6). When Norman died in 1895 his son Norman Magnus inherited the estate, and on his death in 1929, it passed to his brother Reginald (figure 46).

In 1873 Norman MacLeod dismissed MacRaild as factor for St Kilda, and thereafter the estate factors, John MacKenzie, father and son (figure 47), continued the system of taking goods from the island and supplying goods ordered. Detailed accounts for each household for most years between 1873 and 1930 provide a wealth of information about the produce leaving the island and the items requested by the islanders, from carding combs to lengths of winding sheet (MM 2/625–635).

Table 2 (p 100) gives details of the rents. MacRaild seems to have been responsible for the payment of a fixed rent for grazing throughout the 1870s; in 1885 the people (MM 2/637/6) wrote to ask if they could return to the former system of a rent per sheep, which they thought was fairer, and this was put into operation. It is not clear whether this rent was charged for sheep above the number 10, as it was in the 1840s, or for all sheep each household had. As calves up to a year or so were ignored for rent purposes, the year's lambs probably were also. It is notable that the rent charged remained the same for almost a century, with a reduction in the charge for land in 1900.

Figure 47. *Factors: MacRaild and MacKenzie families 1840s–1930*

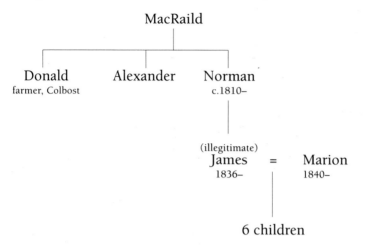

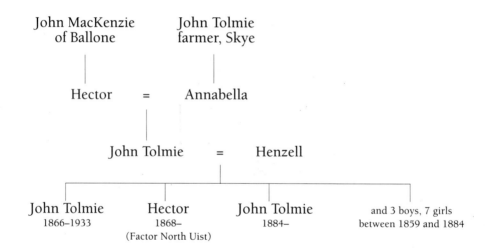

MacRaild also seems to have been involved in some way when the St Kildans sold their cattle to a dealer from Harris in 1872, and there was evidently some idea that the St Kildans might regularly dispose of their produce themselves. In 1875 MacLeod suggested to MacKenzie that he might either send to St Kilda once a year to collect the rents in cash, or let the island to a tenant who would have to deal with the problems of transferring goods to and from the island (MacKenzie mss; MacDiarmid 1878, 244).

Figures 48 to 51, based on the annual summaries for the whole community, show details of rent payments and commodities leaving the island. Very little left the island during the First World War and the figures for grazing were

Figure 48. *Rent: charges, value of goods supplied, payments in cash*

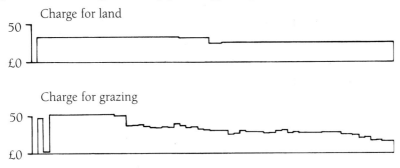

Charge for land

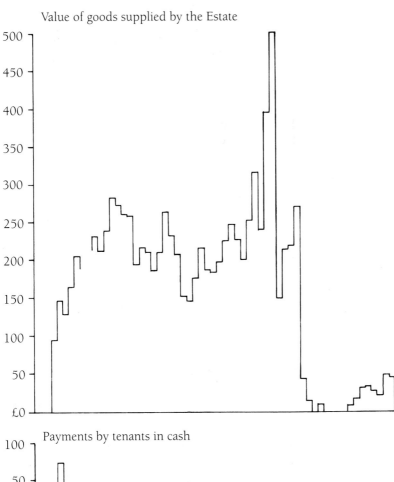

Value of goods supplied by the Estate

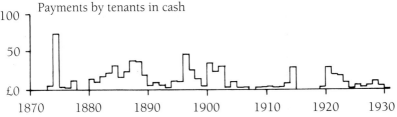

Payments by tenants in cash

static during that period. The demand for feathers, oil and tallow dropped and only a small quantity of feathers was exported after the war, but limited quantities of fish, cattle and tweed continued in part payment of rent. From the late nineteenth century some tweed, and knitwear, was sold directly to visitors on the island, and tweed was also marketed through Alexander Ferguson, who established a business in Glasgow in the 1890s, so the figures for tweed are no guide to the annual production. This was estimated in 1911 as 3,000 yards (Scott 1914, 183) and in 1927 as about 1200 yards (SG 30.9.1927). After the war Ferguson also bought salt fish. The reduction in value of goods supplied after the war reflects the increase in purchases made by St Kildans during visits to Harris, and through Ferguson (MacDonald 1988, 125–8) and catalogue companies such as J D Williams in Manchester. There was no appreciable drop in population until the mid 1920s (p 129).

Generally when people died their arrears were written off. Figure 49 shows that sometimes these amounted to considerable sums; by 1930 the estate had written off £1327 accumulated since 1890, including the £307 owing when the people left. In the nineteenth century a good profit was made when the estate sold on oil, cattle, feathers and tweed, and in most years up to 1888 there was a gain of well over £100 to the estate, but thereafter records up to 1894 show a decline (MM 2/630). The figures for arrears and the value of goods supplied to the islanders indicate that for much of the twentieth century the estate was probably providing a welfare service rather than the island paying its way.

From 1872 the post of Ground Officer was held by the Ferguson family, first by Neil Ferguson, who was credited with the Ground Officer's salary and commission on oil and feathers until his death in 1893, although his son Donald had taken over some of his responsibilites in the 1880s (MacKenzie mss; MM 2.638/3). After Donald's death in 1918 his son Neil took over. In 1872 the salary was £1; from 1873 to at least 1909 it was £3 annually, and by 1921 it was £5 (MM 2.634).

A plan to establish a whaling station was not carried out, though in 1907 Captain Herlofsen, of the Harris whaling station, paid the estate £401, followed by an annual rent of £1 in most years up to 1931 (MM 3/102/2–53). An area of just over 4 acres is noted as 'Norwegian' on a map at Dunvegan (MM drawing 23). The Harris station closed down in 1929.

After the separation of St Kilda from Harris, the owner of South Harris continued to be feudal superior of St Kilda, and in 1877 the Earl of Dunmore was entitled to an annual feu duty of 1/- (Seton 1878, 346). In 1925 40 years of feu duty was paid at this rate, no doubt part of tidying up at the sale of Harris after Leverhulme's death in 1925. A further 6/- was paid in 1931, when the MacLeod association with St Kilda came to an end with the sale of the island to John Crichton Stuart, 10th Earl of Dumfries, for £5,000 (MM 3/102/41 & 53).

Figure 49. *Rent: arrears and arrears cancelled*

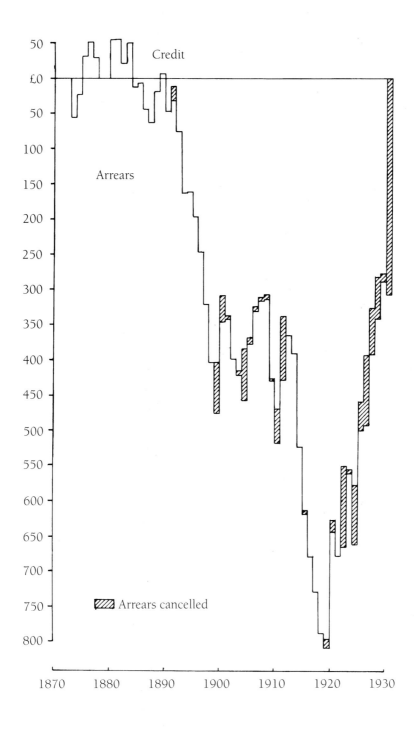

Figure 50. *Rent: values of commodities used for payments in kind*

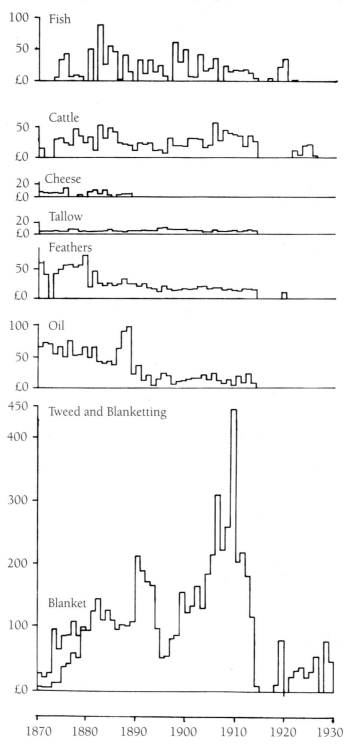

Figure 51. *Rent: quantities of commodities used for payments in kind*

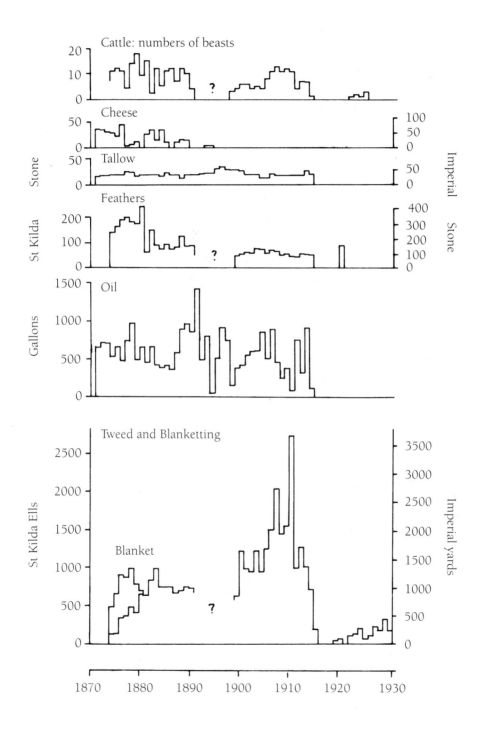

St Kilda and the Government

Sands (1877a, 56) had observed that the Government took little interest in St Kilda. This was generally true until the 1890s, though when an *Act for the Preservation of Sea Birds* was passed in 1869 St Kilda was specifically excluded, as it was from a replacement Act in 1880, presumably in recognition of the islanders' dependence on fowling. In 1904 an Act extended the Act of 1880 to protect birds on St Kilda, except for the gannet, fulmar and auks. From the 1870s MacLeod had an arrangement with Harris Parish Council that no Poor Rate or Education Rate would be paid in respect of the island, the care of paupers and provision of education being managed independently. In 1897 a similar arrangement was agreed with regard to Local Government rates, the Secretary of State for Scotland indicating that if it were not drawn to the attention of the Scottish Office, no action would follow (SRO AF 57/4). The question of constructing a harbour or better landing place was first investigated in 1878, with further reports in 1885, but nothing was done until 1900/1 (p 275).

From the 1890s to the 1930s the St Kildans and their situation took an amount of Government attention disproportionate to the small population. Much time was spent considering the health of the islanders and the provision of a nurse, communications, especially in winter, and, eventually, the removal of the islanders (SRO AF 57/1–37). Throughout these files the prevailing tenor is that improvements were desirable but expense was to be avoided; appeals to the Admiralty, the Fisheries Board and the Northern Lighthouse Commissioners to help over winter communications were consistently refused on grounds of cost and inconvenience. Occasionally there is a sense of weariness as yet again some problem connected with St Kilda is drawn to the attention of the Scottish Office. A press cutting of 1903 describes a schism between the islanders and their former minister, Fiddes, and the reaction noted on file was simple: 'I think they may all stew in their own juice'. However, when emergencies, real or fancied, were reported, such as a shortage of food in May 1912, or the influenza epidemic in June 1913, there was a rapid response with suitable aid, usually conveyed by an Admiralty vessel.

History: 1871–1930

Smith, who visited in 1873 (1879, 25–8, 44), recorded that his party were asked if they could 'do something for the poor people of this island', but he noted that 'amongst all the working people we have seen, we have observed none that looked so sleek and well fed, or more comfortably clad' and he said 'it would be a sad thing to do anything that would make them feel dependent, or to pauperise them'. His party had brought some gifts of food, but noticed that the people seemed to expect more.

In 1875 and 1876 John Sands visited St Kilda. A qualified lawyer, he pursued a career as a journalist, and spent some time on other islands: in Shetland, Tiree, and Faroe (Nicolson 1937). Sands (1877a) went to St Kilda with the Factor in 1875 and six weeks later left by the next boat. He returned in 1876 with a gift of a boat for the islanders, again travelling with the 'Janet' when the Factor went in late June. He planned to leave with the Factor on his second visit in the autumn, but this never took place, and although a steamer was seen in early October, no vessel called until February 1877, and that only as a result of Sands' 'mailboats' (pp 280–2). On January 17th a group of nine Austrian sailors, survivors of the wreck of the 'Peti Dabrovacki', landed and were housed and fed by the St Kildans, who were short of meal and had to grind their seed corn. On February 22nd Sands and the Austrians were taken off by the 'Jackal', which left some supplies, but no more food reached the island until MacLeod's boat went in April. The Admiralty initially refused to carry supplies because MacLeod's boat was going, but later consented to deliver further goods purchased from the Kelsall Fund and a gift of £100 from the Austrian Government. MacDiarmid (1878, 232–253) paid a brief visit to St Kilda accompanying supplies in the 'Flirt' in May 1877, and wrote a very useful account, with particular attention to the agriculture. He did not consider that there had been serious starvation during the previous winter.

Sands apparently formed a relationship with one of the girls which led the people to expect his return in 1877 to marry her (RHASS papers, Seton 1878, 56). He wrote scathingly of the domination of the minister, MacKay, and the oppression, as he saw it, by MacLeod, who had a monopoly over regular trade and communication with the island. He had raised money in 1876 to present the people with a boat suitable for sailing to Harris so that they could trade there themselves. The arrival of his mailboats and the rescue of the Austrians attracted much attention, which gave Sands the opportunity to publicise his campaign for immediate relief of the islanders and, in the long term, improved communications. Correspondence in the *Spectator* in April 1876 and the *Scotsman* in February and March 1877 aroused public interest and controversy, and indirectly helped to achieve some of Sands' aims.

In 1877 Martin Orme announced that the 'Dunara Castle' would call at St Kilda at the end of June (figure 52, overleaf) and Sands (1877a, 136) recorded that five steamers and two other vessels called during that summer, more than in any previous year. The 'Dunara Castle' made another single trip in 1878. This was the start of several visits each summer by the 'Dunara Castle' and, from 1882, McCallum and Company's 'Hebridean', later replaced by the

'Hebrides'. Hutcheson's 'Clydesdale' also called towards the end of the century (Duckworth and Langmuir 1950, 51, 169–170; PP 1884, 865). Although people continued to travel to St Kilda independently, many more were able to visit the island on the steamers, and the number of articles and books appearing reflects this.

Freer (1903, 391) observed, in common with others (Ross 1890, 20–21; Kearton 1897, 49–53), that the visitors were eroding one aspect of the very thing which drew many of them to the island, the culture of the people,

Figure 52. *Martin Orme: Advertisement for tour of St Kilda, 1877*

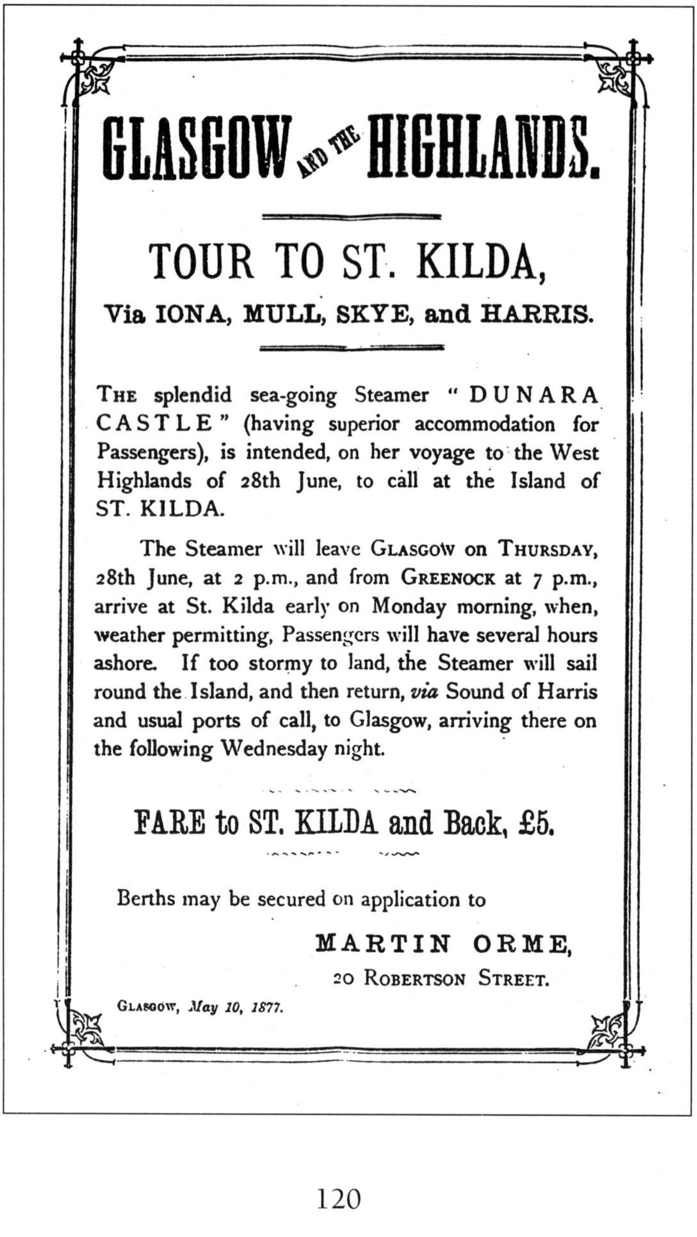

GLASGOW ᴀɴᴅ ᴛʜᴇ HIGHLANDS.

TOUR TO ST. KILDA,

Via IONA, MULL, SKYE, and HARRIS.

THE splendid sea-going Steamer " DUNARA CASTLE " (having superior accommodation for Passengers), is intended, on her voyage to the West Highlands of 28th June, to call at the Island of ST. KILDA.

The Steamer will leave GLASGOW on THURSDAY, 28th June, at 2 p.m., and from GREENOCK at 7 p.m., arrive at St. Kilda early on Monday morning, when, weather permitting, Passengers will have several hours ashore. If too stormy to land, the Steamer will sail round the Island, and then return, *via* Sound of Harris and usual ports of call, to Glasgow, arriving there on the following Wednesday night.

FARE to ST. KILDA and Back, £5.

Berths may be secured on application to

MARTIN ORME,
20 ROBERTSON STREET.

GLASGOW, *May 10, 1877.*

whose values and independence were altered by the behaviour of the visitors and the scale of their gifts and purchases. MacKay (PP 1884, 865) told the Napier Commission that the poor behaviour of visitors who landed on Sundays was often annoying; Heathcote (1900a, 70) saw visitors 'standing at the church door during service, laughing and talking, and staring in as if at an entertainment got up for their amusement'. However, there were visitors, like the Keartons, the Heathcotes, Barrington and Cockburn, who won the respect and friendship of islanders by their considerate behaviour.

In 1878 George Seton, who went on the first excursion by the 'Dunara Castle', published *St Kilda*, a comprehensive history of the island. After visits from Miss MacLeod in 1877 and 1879, the first resident nurse was provided at her expense in 1879/80 (p 264), and in 1884 the first teacher arrived (p 258). Two teachers, Murray (1886–7) and Ross (1890), wrote valuable accounts of the island. In June 1883 the Napier Commission (PP 1884, 864–875) visited St Kilda and questioned John MacKay, Donald MacDonald and Angus Gillies. After a severe storm in September 1885, mailboats were despatched requesting help, and supplies purchased from the Kelsall Fund and private contributions were sent on the 'Hebridean'; Malcom McNeill (1886), from the Board of Supervision, visited a few weeks later on HMS 'Jackal' and found that the islanders had an ample supply of a variety of food, and had been in no real danger of want. Some of the earliest dated photographs were taken in the 1880s, by Whyte (Ross 1884) and MacLeod (Murray 8.1886; Wilson 1886).

Two particularly useful accounts, both illustrated by photographs, result from the visits in the 1890s of Richard and Cherry Kearton (1897) and two relatives of MacLeod, Norman Heathcote (1900) and his sister Evelyn (figure 41). She laid the foundation stone of the schoolroom (p 259). By the late nineteenth century, visitors were occasionally arranging to stay with St Kildan families (Heathcote 1901 146–7; Wiglesworth 1903, 4).

Alice MacLachlan (1906–9), wife of the missionary stationed on the island from 1906 to 1909, kept a diary, chronicling everyday life and exceptional events during those years. It is of especial interest in giving a woman's view, and contains domestic details rarely found in other accounts. It also describes the drowning of three men near Dun when a boat capsized in March 1909. It indicates the extent of the help given by crews of fishing boats and whalers in carrying mail, supplies, and occasionally passengers. Although boats often fished illegally, presents deterred the islanders from reporting them, and the Scottish Office was reluctant to support action against them because of the help they gave (Heathcote 1900 207–8).

After an alarm over the shortage of supplies in 1912, the *Daily Mirror* gave a wireless station to the island (pp 279–280), for use in emergencies. It was taken over by the Admiralty after war broke out in 1914, and from 1915 a small naval detachment was stationed on the island. It employed some of the young men to watch shipping from the hill tops, paying 4/- a day. The detachment was supplied regularly and frequently by vessels from Stornoway. In May 1918 the captain of a German U-boat gave notice that he was about to shell the wireless station, allowing the islanders to take refuge. The Store, Church, Factor's House and two houses were damaged. Wireless communication was restored the same day. A gun was installed in October for the defence of the island (Spackman 1982, 8–9). The estate received from the Admiralty in 1920 £570 in compensation for damage; £595 was spent on repairing the buildings, with the exception of the Store (MM 2.102/33).

Two St Kildans, John MacQueen (Lachlan MacDonald pers comm) and John MacDonald (Gillies 1988, 43) served in the forces during the war. None were called up, though besides those two, between 1914 and 1918 there were thirteen to fifteen men aged between 18 and 40, and eight over 40 years old in a population of seventy-two or seventy-three people. Although the war brought difficulties in, for instance, the transport of cattle from the island (SRO AF 57/19), the St Kildans enjoyed a standard of living and level of communications unknown before it or afterwards, and conversation with those stationed there aroused in some a desire to experience life elsewhere (Gillies 1988, 42; MacDonald 1988, 143).

After the war there were considerable changes on St Kilda. Better communications and comparative affluence during the war resulted in increased expectations. Demand for the island's produce, apart from fish and woollen goods, was decreasing, and some began to look elsewhere to find a better standard of living. Neither of the two men who had served in the forces returned; two girls married navy men and left the island; three young men left in 1919; the whole MacDonald family and two more young men left in 1924. Deaths outnumbered births in the 1920s; by 1925 the population was forty-six (SG 21.5.1925). The land under cultivation had been decreasing for some time (Heathcote 1900a, 215); in 1927 it was less than two acres (SG 28.10.1927).

The Evacuation, 1930

The question of evacuation had been raised as a result of Sands' agitation. In 1878 Trollope (1878, 11) asked: 'who shall say that these people ought to be deported from their homes and placed recklessly upon some point of the mainland?…their existence cannot be good for them, and certainly not for their posterity'. In 1885 McNeill (1886, 8) found that many people wished to emigrate, and suggested that Government assistance in achieving this might 'be wise and in the end economical'. However, this was a passing whim. Heathcote (1900a, 201–228) considered the future of the island in 1898: he found that the people did not wish to emigrate, but he suggested that a system whereby the islanders marketed their own produce through an outlet on the mainland might ultimately be to their advantage, in making them more self-reliant.

In 1923 Rev. Mr. MacInnes, returning from the island, said that 'the opinion is steadily gaining ground that the time is fast approaching when St Kilda will be uninhabited' (SG 16.8.1923). Apparently MacLeod had offered to resettle the people in Skye but this offer was rejected (SG 27.6.1930). A detailed account of events leading up to the evacuation and the departure is given in Government files (SRO AF 57/26–27, 31–37), by Steel (1988) and by MacGregor (1931, 1969; *Times* 8.1930) By 1930 there were just under forty St Kildans on the island, further depleted by the deaths of two young women in the summer. When the MacKinnons decided to leave, with their eight children, it was clear that there would not be sufficient people left to continue the same way of life on the island, and with the encouragement of the nurse, Williamina Barclay, all decided to leave. Dugald Munro, the missionary, drew up a petition, signed by all the adults, requesting the Government to organise the evacuation of the islanders and their resettlement on the mainland. The idea of encouraging suitable immigrants to augment and revitalise the population was never considered. T B Ramsay, M.P. for the Western Isles, and Tom Johnston, Secretary of State for Scotland, visited the island for discussions. Arrangements were made to take off the stock and to transport the people to new houses and work on the mainland. On August 29th thirty-six people, accompanied by the nurse and missionary, left on HMS 'Harebell', and for the first time for centuries there was no human inhabitant on St Kilda.

Throughout the 1930s people visited and stayed on the island, mostly during the summer. The Earl of Dumfries regarded the island as a nature reserve. His family and friends enjoyed visits and scientists studied different aspects of the natural history. The Manse was maintained as accommodation and Neil Gillies was employed as a warden in the summer. During the decade that followed their evacuation, a number of islanders returned in different years for varying lengths of time, to stay in their former homes, and pursue some of their former occupations. Not until the outbreak of war in 1939 did these visits cease.

8

Population and families; birth, marriage and death

Table 3 gives the figures for population (also shown in figure 53) and numbers of families mentioned in different sources. Some of these figures appear to be inconsistent with others and require discussion.

Figure 53. *Total population 1697–1930*

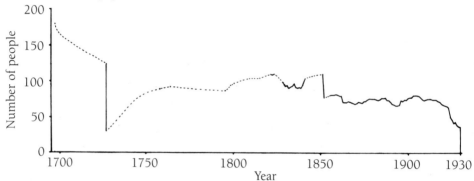

The 'ten men and ten women' noted by Williamson in 1615 implies a small population at that time. In 1697 a figure of 180 is recorded. Campbell (1984, 52) suggests that some people were in hiding during Coll MacDonald's raid (pp 84–5), though it is questionable whether they would remain in hiding for a month.

Moray's 'ten families' must predate his death in 1673. There is cumulative evidence for a division into ten, suggesting that at one time that may have been the number of families: the land was divided into ten halfpenny lands (Moray 1678, 929); the land, fowling rocks and birds were divided into ten shares (Martin 1753, 18, 23); and on each of the two fishing rocks there were ten places from which two men could fish (MacAulay 1764, 256). If Moray's figure was old when he gathered it, it could support Williamson's account, but if it was recent, it could refer to ten extended families, which would be more consistent with Martin's figures in 1697, or, possibly, as MacKay suggests (1985, 18), he confused families with land tenure arrangements.

Martin records 180 people belonging to 27 families. Most had fair

Table 3
Population Figures given by Different Authors

Year	Figures	Authority
1615	10 men, 10 women	Williamson 1615
pre1673	10 families	Moray 1678, 928
1697	180: 27 families	Martin 1753, 51; 1716, 290
1720s	30/33 families	Buchan 1727, 8
1727	124? to 30; 21/24 families to 4	see text pp 153-4
1730/40s	about 20 families	MacLeod *c.*1756–1775
1758	88	MacAulay 1764, 196
1764	92, 10 not native	Walker 1981, 59
1795	87	MacDonald 1811, 817
1797	*c.*100: 22 families (Minister's: 6)	Clarke (1824, 272)
1799?	120 (Mr Campbell of Skipness)	MacDonald 1811, 817
*c.*1800	97 (George Stuart MacKenzie)	Wilson 1842, 104
1809	103	MacDonald, 1811, 817
1815	103: 20 families	MacCulloch 1824, 190
1821	*c.*110	Gaelic Schl Rpt 11 1822, 36
1822	108	Kennedy 1932, 83
1823	110	MacCulloch 1824, 190
1830–43	average 112	MacKenzie 1911, 23
1834	93: 41 males, 52 females	Carruthers 1843, 257
1838	92 excluding minister's family; 26 families incl. 4 poor widows.	MacLean 1838, 24
1840	*c.*120: 23 families	MacGillivray 1842, 53
1841	105	Wilson 1842, 18
1847	below 100; stationary many years	Milner 1848
1851	110	Census
1852	36 left for Australia	
1853	60	MacKenzie 1921, 85
1858	no more than 80	Muir 1858, 13
1860	76: 20 families	Murray 1860
1861	78 including catechist	Census
1863	7 lost at sea	
1871	71 including minister and sister	Census
1875	72: 29 males, 43 females	Sands 1877a, 20
1877	74	MacDiarmid 1878, 238
1881	77 including minister and nurse	Census
1886	76	Connell 1887, 64
1891	71 including minister, servant, nurse	Census
1901	77	Census
1906	78	SRAF 57/9
1911	80 including minister and family (5)	Census
1920	66	SG 4.6.1920
1921	73 including minister and family (4),nurse and sons (3)	Census
1924	61	SG 29.5.1924
1925	46	SG 21.1.1925
1927	43	SG 3.6.1927
1928	36	SG 1.6.1928
1930	36	

complexions; those who had not were 'Natives only for an Age or two' but their children were fairer than themselves. In using 'Age' Martin may have had in mind *linn*: age, century, generation. His statement suggests that some of the people were second or third generation immigrants; some change in the population is suggested by the fact that they had neither the strength nor the longevity of the previous generation. Martin gives no other indication of immigration within the eighty years before his visit; if it had been on a large scale he might have mentioned it, though he does not, for instance, mention Coll MacDonald's raid (pp 84–5).

Possibly Williamson and Moray were correct; ten families could increase to 180 people, especially with some augmentation by immigration. An increase from 50 to 180 was achieved on Tristan da Cunha within fifty years (p 305). If that were so, a further question arises: was an earlier larger population reduced by some unrecorded disaster to ten families? or was there, perhaps, as on Rona, a voluntary limitation on the island population? (p 300).

There is disagreement over the number of families in the early eighteenth century: Buchan refers to 30 or 33; MacAulay (Svensson 1955, 19), writing in 1728 refers to 21 in the previous year and a century later MacKenzie (1904, 400) refers to 25.

There are references to a number of deaths between 1697 and 1727. In 1697 two families were subject to 'leprosy' which had broken out in 1684; Martin relieved one sufferer by his prescription of a change of diet and more exercise, but in 1698 twelve people died of it (Martin 1753, 41–2; 1716, 185). Buchan (1727, 23, 34) refers to a further twenty deaths from 'an unclean disease' resulting from eating 'unclean meats' because of scarcity. He also says that the people believed that if they baptised their children on a Saturday, they would live 'yet they see it has not the wished for effect', which suggests that an unusual number of babies died. There is evidence that the population had fallen to 124 by 1727 (see below).

Furthermore, Buchan (1727, 15–16) records that since Martin's time there had been a reduction in the number of eggs gathered:

Where there were 18 creels of flecked eggs…there is not one creel to be got there now:…and where 16 creels of white eggs were gathered, they gather but 4 now…and the white eggs and little sort of fowls were undervalued [formerly]…because they had no need of them; and now they oftentimes lose their lives pursuing those little fowls, by falling down the rocks into the sea. Yet these poorer sort that take them, must not feed on them, but on sorrel or dockens, when boiled together in summer; whereby strength fails them in steep places, and so many of them are carried home dead, as others fall in the sea, and not found again.

Dr Mike Harris of the Institute of Terrestrial Ecology suggests that the 'flecked eggs' are likely to be guillemot or razorbill eggs, or possibly the smaller kittiwake eggs; 'white eggs' could be gannet, fulmar or puffin eggs. The 'little fowls' might be puffins or kittiwakes; deaths are more likely to result from attempts to take kittiwakes on cliff ledges than from gathering puffins from their burrows on slopes. He points out that if gannets had suffered a major decline it would probably have been noted elsewhere (M Harris pers comm).

If the large population mentioned by Martin had been over-exploiting the seabirds, numbers might have been reduced locally, and as these birds are long lived, it would be some years before the effects of this began to show. Colonies could have recovered after 1727. If there were no significant reduction in seabird numbers, it is possible that the dearth of birds and eggs resulted from inaccessibility through lack of a boat. In 1712 a new boat was purchased by the estate, and the people were excused two years' rent because of the poverty resulting from 'their remarkable disaster in the Island of Borera' (Morrison 1966, 332). This may have been the disaster mentioned by Martin in 1703 (1716 268), which would imply that the people had been without a boat for about ten years; but if it were a second disaster, they would have been without a boat for a year or so on two occasions. Lack of a boat would prevent harvesting of birds from any of the other islands but Dun, and from some colonies on Hirte; no gannets or gannet eggs could be taken, and smaller birds, including, probably, kittiwakes, would assume a much greater importance.

Lamb (1982, 209–214) has shown that a climatic deterioration in Scotland began in the late sixteenth century, and that between 1693 and 1700 the harvest in the Highlands failed in seven years. Martin (1716, 2, 76, 79) mentions no shortage in St Kilda; on the contrary, he gives an impression of a fairly prosperous community in the local context, though in 1703 he does refer to 'late years of scarcity and bad seasons' in Lewis and a climatic deterioration and scarcity of grain in Uist.

In the late sixteenth century the rent included 60 bolls of meal (Skene 1880, III 431). In 1724 it is listed at 16 bolls, and in 1727 18 bolls (p 97). After 1697 the maximum reliably recorded population is an average of 112 in the 1830s, when the islanders had plenty of food 'of a very nutritious kind' and their modest rent was paid mainly in feathers (MacKenzie 1911, 14, 17, 23). It seems possible that in 1697, with a larger population and much of the harvest going as rent or in supporting the Steward's large party, there would be little surplus to feed the St Kildans themselves. This suggestion is supported for later years by Buchan's assertion (1727, 24) that the Steward forced the people to feed his large party 'above their ability' and carried away 'almost, all they should live upon thro' the year'.

It is difficult now to identify the ailments Martin (1753, 39, 41) mentions; some aspects could be consistent with scurvy: the spotted appearance of the 'spotted fever', and in the 'leprosy' the feet beginning to fail (if this were due to leg ulcers), the ulceration of the head, and, notably, the very rapid improvement as a result of exercise and eating sorrel. However, Martin refers elsewhere (1716, 175) to scurvy, which suggests that the St Kildans' ailment was different, and other aspects are inconsistent with scurvy: the redness of the face, limitation to two families, and the absence of any mention of tooth loss and gum deterioration. Possibly the 'leprosy' was a combination of several deficiency diseases, and if scurvy played a part in it, that would help to explain why Campbell (1799, 20, 51) could observe that they no longer suffered from leprosy: scurvygrass was 'a principal part of their food', and potatoes, introduced by 1758 (p 197) also helped to prevent it (Lind and Stewart 1953).

These observations together suggest that there had been a rise in population in the seventeenth century, partly through immigration; that 180 was too great a number for the island to support; that decreasing harvests resulted in a reduction in exported meal, with very little left for the people themselves, so that they had a poorly balanced diet; that for some years they were reliant on small birds and eggs, through lack of access to better colonies because they had no boat, and/or through a local decline in seabirds due to earlier over-exploitation, and that the result of this was a general deterioration in health, with lives lost through debility and deficiency diseases. A high infant mortality may have been caused by poor health in the mothers, or possibly infant tetanus, or both.

If the population were in such straitened circumstances, the death toll from smallpox in 1727 is scarcely surprising. D MacAulay (Svensson 1955, 19) in 1728 said there were four families left, which had to support 26 orphans; in 1758 Kenneth MacAulay (1764, 197–8) records that four adults were left, making a total of 30 people. MacKenzie's five families is inconsistent with this, and throws doubts on his figure of 94 deaths, but if the latter is correct, the total population would have been 124 before the smallpox, and as 11 people escaped it while marooned on Stac an Armin, the mortality would have been 94 deaths in 113 people.

In 1731 the Minutes of the SSPCK mention 'St Kilda, which island, by the yearly transportating of people to it, will shortly become populous again' (Lawson 1981, 38). Immigration, considered below, and natural increase had raised the population figure to 88 by 1758 (MacAulay 1764, 196). The few figures for the later eighteenth century indicate a population of between 87 and 100. For most of the first half of the nineteenth century it was a little over a 100; the emigration of 36 people in 1852 led to a drop in numbers from which the population never recovered; it did not rise again above 80.

Figure 53 shows clearly that the population did not increase by very much between 1758 and 1852. Both this and the failure to recover after the emigration of 1852 can be attributed largely to the effects of infant tetanus and the slight increase in the 1890s may result from the victory over this disease (p 264). Between 1921 and 1930 there was a serious drop in population from 73 to 36; this was due partly to an excess of deaths compared with births, and partly to emigration. The figures given by Campbell for 1799, MacGillivray for 1840, and MacKenzie for 1852 are so different from those of the preceding or following years that they must be regarded as very doubtful, and have been omitted from figure 53.

Figure 54. *Infant Mortality, 1831–1930*

Clegg (1977, 293–307; 1982, 9–14; 1984, 3–11) has considered in detail changes in the population in the nineteenth and twentieth centuries. Besides the reasons already mentioned, he attributes the decline in numbers to a decrease in fertility, which, combined with pre-reproductive deaths, resulted in a failure of successive generations of women to replace themselves as effective reproductive units. He further suggests that a decrease in the marriage rates and the level of emigration in the twentieth century may be partly due to a deliberate attempt to avoid inbreeding. Mitchell (1865, 900) found that in 1860 of thirteen island born couples none were first cousins, but five were second cousins, whereas Clegg found that of the six marriages between 1900 and 1925 between island born couples who produced children, two were between first cousins and one between first cousins once removed, evidence of a decrease in the number of potential partners, thus limiting choice.

Families and Immigrants
A few family names are mentioned before 1727: in 1697 the Ground Officer

was Donald Mack-Gill-Colm (Martin 1753, 51) and in the early 1700s Buchan (1727, 41) was training Murdo Campbell and Finlay MacDonald. According to MacCrimmon, there were MacDonalds and MacQueens on St Kilda before 1727 (Kennedy and Thomas 1874, 702) and MacAulay (1764, 51) records a tradition that the first person to settle there, with some fellow countrymen, was an Irish rover called Macquin. He also noted that those families who were 'true natives of St Kilda' had the surnames Mac Ille Mhoire (Morrison) and Mac Ille Rhiabhich. The former were apparently from Lewis, where the name is still common, and the latter from South Uist: they prided themselves on their connection with Clanranald. This family, probably MacDonalds, may well have been associated with Angus Riabhich (Grizzled Angus) or his descendants; he was a son of Reginald (figure 32) and his family had land in Benbecula until the mid sixteenth century. One of the survivors of the smallpox was Simon MacGillivray, who died in 1767 aged 112 (Lawson 1981, 39). It appears from the above that among the survivors of the smallpox were MacDonalds, MacQueens, Morrisons and MacGillivrays.

People were taken over to augment the survivors. Emily MacLeod in 1877 (RHASS papers) said that her grandfather's ancestors had sent people 'who behaved badly' to St Kilda; this is supported by Heathcote (1900a, 68) and a story of cattle thieves in Skye being transported to St Kilda (MacLeod 1980, 257–9).

Lawson has pointed out that immigrants with different genes probably account for the discrepancy between Martin's description of the men as having little facial hair and the abundant growth seen in some of the photographs (plate 15, 30, 37). Presumably the 'lisp' described by Martin in 1697 (1753, 37) was assumed by the immigrants, as in 1758 MacAulay (1764, 215) found that the whole community 'lisped', and this was also noted by MacKenzie (1911, 5) in the 1830s.

Two names not mentioned after 1802 are MacIver and Campbell (Buchan 1727, 41; *Scots Mag.* 1802, 976–7). By 1822 there were eight family names: Ferguson, Gillies, MacCrimmon, MacDonald, MacKinnon, MacLeod, MacQueen and Morrison. MacQueen (nd, 1) knew that two of his great grandfathers, Finlay Ferguson and Finlay MacQueen, had settled on St Kilda as adults and married there. Lawson (1981, 38–43) has made a study of St Kildan families. He notes that MacQueens in North Uist claim relationship with those in St Kilda, and this, together with MacQueen's evidence, suggests that the nineteenth century MacQueens were an immigrant family rather than descendants of the Irish MacQuin. Possibly MacAulay got a localised version of a Uist tradition. The Fergusons probably came from Berneray, Harris; this is supported by an account of some St Kilda Fergusons visiting Berneray and referring to their namesakes as the lees of the family (J MacInnes pers comm). The Gillieses and MacCrimmons probably came from Skye, though MacCrimmon is recorded in South Harris in 1745; the Christian names used by the MacKinnon family suggest that they also came from Skye, though they could have come from Harris. The MacLeods could have come from Skye or Harris. Roderick the Imposter (pp 86–7) was, traditionally, a Morrison, but as MacAulay recorded in 1758 that of his family only two women survived, the Morrisons must be descendants of another branch, or, possibly, immigrants.

George Stuart MacKenzie met during his visit in 1800 an old woman who claimed relationship with him on the grounds that her mother's aunt had suckled his grandmother's sister (Wilson 1842, 28). As his paternal grandmother was a daughter of Sir James MacDonald of Sleat and Janet MacLeod of the Talisker and Greshornish family, the wet nurse almost certainly came from Skye, and the woman's mother or grandparents were therefore probably emigrants from Skye to St Kilda.

MacKenzie (1911, 30) records two instances of immigration not long before 1830, a MacLeod from Skye who was part of the Factor's crew, and a woman who was one of the Factor's servants; both married St Kildans, and both were murdered (see below).

There were three further instances of immigration: Betty Scott came from Lochinver about 1830, as servant to the MacKenzie family. She married Malcolm MacDonald in 1834. In 1869 their son, Neil, married Isabella Ross Munro from Tain, a relative of John MacKay. In 1912 Ewen Gillies married Annie MacLeod from Kyles Scalpay in Harris; though he died in 1916 she and her daughter stayed on in St Kilda and were among the evacuees in 1930 (Lawson pers comm).

By 1871 there were no MacLeods left on St Kilda, only one Morrison, married to a Gillies, and one MacCrimmon; after 1914 only the names Ferguson, Gillies, MacDonald, MacKinnon and MacQueen continued to 1930.

Emigration

A list of known emigrants is given in table 4.

Despite the small population there may have been emigration by 1758: MacAulay (1764, 211), commenting on the disparity between men and women, remarks obliquely that 'in all countries the males are more ready to run away from out of the reach of tyrants, because more obnoxious to the resentment of such, and better able to shift for themselves'.

According to MacCulloch (1819, 25) and Atkinson (1831, 47), who may be copying him, the St Kildans rarely left their island permanently, but MacKenzie (1911, 23) observed that occasionally they did settle in the Long

Island, and also states that occasionally someone was banished 'as the highest penalty that can be inflicted upon some incorrigible offender'. In the mid-nineteenth century Carmichael (1941, 106) got part of a song from a man in North Uist who had learned it from a servant girl who came from St Kilda, possibly one of the Gillies family. Another song (Carmichael 1954, 46–7) was composed by a St Kilda woman who had married in Lewis, perhaps to one of the Uig men storm-driven to St Kilda (p 276).

Table 4 shows that from 1919 an increasing number of young people left, sapping the strength of the community.

Poverty, Wealth and Social Position

As in any other community there was on St Kilda inequality in many things, such as ability, opportunity, and wealth, measured in goods or cash. These differences, together with differences in age and marital status, led to some differences in social status.

In 1697 (Martin 1753, 44) three people were described as 'poor'; they were assisted by the whole community, 'each particular family contributing according to their ability'. Ability clearly varied: 'the richest man in the Isle has not above eight cows, eighty sheep, and two or three horses' (Martin 1716, 295). Buchan (1727, 20, 25, 33) noted that poor people borrowed querns. The Ground Officer was the richest man on the island, with about twenty cows and two or three hundred sheep. However, when people married, the wealthier families gave a poor couple stock and seed. In 1758 (MacAulay 1764, 125) the wealthiest people had seven or eight cows, some had between one and four cows, and the poorest had none.

MacQueen (nd, 2) born in 1828, recorded that his grandfather, John MacQueen, had more sheep than anyone else on the island, and six or seven horses. MacKenzie (1911, 30) found in the 1830s that the people 'insisted upon an equality which had a deadening influence, and effectually hindered any real progress'. No one was to make improvements which would make him more comfortable than his neighbours. Some neighbours were in poor circumstances: Milner (1842, 2057) notes that providing for widows and old maids was one of the community's first duties, and in 1883 MacKay (1884, 868) said that the elderly were looked after by relatives. There was clearly inequality between families with several able-bodied men who could cultivate the land and catch birds, and those supported by one man, or widows, and elderly people. The system of sharing birds equally among families irrespective of the number of people in each family also resulted at times in want in large families.

The estate records (MM 2.633, 2.635) show that from the 1880s the stock

Table 4
List of Known Emigrants

Year	Person or people	Reference
1726	Donald MacDonald? (poss visiting, died smallpox Harris)	p 89
1760s ?	Girl to Pabbay as servant (died)	MacLeod 1763 17–18
by 1790s	Elderly woman in Uist, former servant to Rachel Erskine	Buchanan 1793, 144;
		MacKenzie 1817, 339; p 110
pre 1822	Woman married in Lewis	Carmichael 1954, 46–7
1810s?	Hector Morrison to Scalpay	Lawson 1981, 40–42
post 1822	John Gillies + family to North Uist	and pers comm
pre 1833	Donald Ferguson to Pabbay then Scalpay	"
early 1830s?	Sloane Ferguson to Lochboisdale	"
1836	Neil MacCrimmon (?visiting) died S Uist	"
1838	Roderick Morrison + family to Obbe	"
1840/1	Donald MacKinnon=Isabella, to Obbe	"
1840s?	Kirsty MacLeod to Harris	"
1852	All to Australia :<u>....</u>=died on voyage or in quarantine	Holohan 1986, 47-8
	Ferguson: Malcolm = <u>Catherine, Mary</u>	
	Ferguson: <u>Hector-</u> = Mary + mother-in-law <u>Mary Morrison</u>	
	Gillies: Ewen = Margaret, Mary	
	MacCrimmon: <u>Donald</u> = <u>Ann, Donald, Marion, Margaret, Christina</u>	
	MacDonald: <u>Roderick</u> = Marion, Neil, Christina	
	MacDonald: Neil + mother <u>Catherine</u>, sister Ann	
	MacQueen: Finlay = Christina, Malcolm, <u>Rachel</u>, John	
	MacQueen: <u>Finlay</u> = <u>Catherine</u>, Donald, Ann, Marion, Catherine, Neil, <u>Finlay, Mary</u>	
1850s?	Christina Gillies to Barra	Census 1861, 1871
1884	Finlay Ferguson to Australia	Lawson pers comm
1889–91	Ann MacDonald + nephew John to Skye	Census 1891
1892	Alexander Ferguson to Glasgow	
1896	Donald Ferguson	
1901–11	Mary Gillies	
	Donald MacDonald	
1913	John MacDonald	
1914	Catherine Gillies to Tiree	
1914–18	John MacQueen joined RNR	
1911–21	Catherine MacDonald to Skye	
1919	Mary MacDonald to Glasgow	
	Neil Gillies	Gillies N 1988, 38
	Donald John Ferguson	
1919–20	Angus MacDonald	MacDonald 1988, 114
1921	Finlay MacDonald	
1923	Annabella MacDonald to Lewis	
1924	William MacDonald = Mary Ann, Mary, Finlay John,	
	Calum, Rachel, Marion, Mary: to Harris, then Lewis	MacDonald, nd
	Donald MacDonald	
	Donald John Gillies	Gillies, 1988, 45
1921–30	Ann MacDonald	
	Elizabeth MacQueen	
	Norman MacQueen	
	Kirsty MacQueen	
	Donald MacQueen	

Table 4 (continued)
List of Known Emigrants: People Evacuated in 1930

(information from W W Lawson, and SRO AF 57/26)

House	Family	Individuals	Destination
1	MacKinnon	Norman 50 = Ann 42, Norman 20, Donald Ewen 19, Finlay 16, Rachel 13, John 10, Kirsty 9, Mary 5, Neil 4	Lochaline, (Achabeg) later to Black Isle
2	MacQueen	Finlay 68 W	Strome Ferry, then Fife
5	Ferguson	Neil 54 = Ann 53,	Culross, Fife
		Neil 31 = Mary Ann 39	Strome Ferry
7	Gillies	Finlay 74 W,	Lochaline
		Catherine 41 W (daughter-in-law), Donald 12, Ewen 9	(Savary)
9	MacDonald	John 59	Inverness
	Gillies	Ann 36 W, Mary Ann 16	Inverness
11	MacQueen	Kirsty 59 W	Lochaline (Larachbeg)
13	Gillies	Donald 39 = Kirsty 35, Catherine 12, Rachel 8	Lochaline (Larachbeg)
14	Gillies	Ann 41 W, Rachel Ann 20, Flora 11	Lochaline (Savary)
15	Gillies	Ann 65 W, John 38 W, Norman 6	Lochaline (Ardness)
16	MacDonald	Rachel 67 W, Ewen 42, Lachlan 24	Lochaline (Savary)

Key: W = Widow/widower

held by different families, particularly numbers of sheep, varied considerably. This would affect the quantity of wool available for weaving and knitting and thus affect both rent payments and sales to visitors.

By the mid-nineteenth century a cash economy existed alongside the barter system. Some of the emigrants of 1852 paid their own passage (MacQueen nd, 14). In 1861 Kennedy told Grigor, the census enumerator, that all the St Kildans had some money (Seton 1878, 102) and in 1885 McNeill (1886, 7) was told that a sum of money said to average no less than £20 per family was hoarded in the island. Figure 43 shows that from at least 1873 some of the rent was paid in cash.

Two families were prominent for a time. From the 1840s until her death in 1863, Betty Scott, for many years the island's midwife, was the only inhabitant with a reasonable command of English, and naturally many visitors sought information from her; the Duke of Atholl and his interpreter were given shelter in her household when stormbound overnight in 1860 (Murray 1860). Morgan (1861, 107) referred to her as 'smart, energetic, talkative and shrewd';

probably her manner was adopted by her two surviving children, described in 1877 by MacDiarmid (1878, 2390 as 'the shrewdest and most managing-like that I came across'. Ann became housekeeper to John MacKay and according to Connell (1887, 36–7, 65) was the 'terror of the island'. It is clear from Murray's diary (1886–7) that her influence was not impartial, and Rachel Gillies referred to her in 1887 as 'that fast woman' (MM 2.638/3). Emily MacLeod in 1877 (RHASS papers) described Malcolm MacDonald as 'one of the richest men on the island'. Neil, his son, followed his father in marrying out of the island.

Members of the Ferguson family are mentioned from early in the nineteenth century. In 1822 John Ferguson was the only person who could read 'to any purpose' (Kennedy 1932, 96) and the only person who spoke any English (Atkinson 1831, 31). He preached in Gaelic and English. In the 1840s his son, Malcolm, was teacher, and in 1852 another son, Neil, took on that position (MacQueen nd 5, 9). Three generations of the family held the post of Ground Officer from 1872 to 1930 (p 114), the last, Neil, being additionally the postmaster from 1906 (pp 278–9). Some of the Fergusons were leaders in the church: John was a preacher while his son Neil and grandson Donald were both elders (RHASS papers; Connell 1887, 52, 87; Murray 2.12.1886). Donald's wife, Rachel, was midwife for a number of years (p 264). One of his sons, Alexander, settled in Glasgow and was importing tweed from St Kilda by 1899. He also imported Harris tweed and continued as a tweed merchant until the mid 1950s. He returned to St Kilda annually for a lengthy visit to his family; by 1925 he was travelling in his own yacht 'Colonsay' (SG 25.6.1925). He bought tweed and fish and latterly much of the islanders' supplies came through him. Donald John Gillies (1988, 45) records that Ferguson was very helpful to other people leaving the island.

It cannot be coincidence that the first two mortared houses built in 1861 (Sharbau 1860) were occupied by Donald Ferguson and Malcolm MacDonald. The Ferguson house is slightly larger than any of the others, being about a foot longer internally (pp 151–2).

Although in 1860 the men undertook in an agreement with Otter to build new houses for everyone, including widows and paupers (RHASS papers), some people continued to live in thatched houses for which no rent was charged. One such was Roderick Gillies, described by Sands (1877a, 23) as an imbecile who was generally peaceable but a terror when enraged, and by MacDiarmid (1878, 238) as 'eccentric'. His behaviour was unusual: Neil Ferguson (Mackenzie ms), referring to him as a 'pauper' asked John MacKenzie to speak to him about his interfering with seaweed collected by other cottars, and concessions were made over his modest rent for grazing, which he paid mostly in feathers and tallow, and also in some years oil, tweed, cash and, several times, wool, which was not accepted from anyone else.

Baptism, Marriage and Death

In the late seventeenth century baptisms were performed by the Ground Officer or a neighbour, who said '[name] I baptize thee to your Father and your Mother, in the name of the Father, Son, and Holy Ghost'; a second neighbour and his wife who acted as godparents then took the child in their arms, thus establishing a bond of friendship between the families that was regarded as inviolable, even if there were enmity between them previously. Marriages were performed by the Ground Officer, who summoned the whole population to Christ's Chapel,

> *Where being assembled, he enquires publickly if there be any lawful impediment why these parties should not be joined in the bond of matrimony? And if there be no objection to the contrary, he then enquires of the parties if they are resolved to live together in weal and woe, etc. After their assent, he declares them married persons, and then desires them to ratify this their solemn promise in the presence of God and the people, in order to which the crucifix is tendered to them, and both put their right hands upon it, as the ceremony by which they swear fidelity one to another during their life-time* (Martin 1753, 46–7).

Sibbald's informant said they married very young, at ten, and cohabited at eleven (Adv ms. 33.3.20), and according to Martin (1753, 41) at the the end of the eighteenth century the St Kildans married 'very young, the women at about thirteen or fourteen'. MacAulay (1764, 221) said they married early, and MacKenzie (1911, 23) considered they married young, but during his stay in the 1830s, of eleven first marriages between islanders, the average age of both men and women was about 24, including one couple aged 20 and 35 respectively. In the period 1860–1868, in seven marriages the average ages for men and women were 26 and 24; between 1870 and 1900 in nine marriages they were 22 and 28, the brides being older than their husbands with one exception; and between 1908 and 1925 in six marriages they were 27 and 25 years (Lawson, pers comm).

In the 1830s MacKenzie (MacLean 1838, 16–18) described a *rèiteach* or betrothal party, and a wedding. The *rèiteach* took place in the evening:

> *On our arrival we found all the men of the island sitting on the ground, or rather reclining close to the walls of the house of the bride's father, on each side feet to feet, so that it was very difficult to get through them. The near female relatives were in the upper apartment with the bride. We were seated on a chest among the men. A glass of spirits was handed round by the bride's father, commencing with us and going round the whole. A short and desultory*

conversation ensued, and then we separated. Not a person mentioned the reason of our coming together, except drinking to the health of the young folk.

On Sabbath-day they were proclaimed three several times, for they were not inclined to wait for three sabbath-days; they were therefore exposed to pay three shillings instead of one, which is thus divided - one shilling to the precentor, sixpence to the person who proclaims them, and the rest to the poor. Early on Monday morning two young men were dispatched to the hill to catch sheep; a certain quantity of barley grain was given to the girls to be ground and baked; two elderly men were appointed to boil the beef, and the rest skulked about the houses, or lent a hand as need required. Having got all things in readiness, in the afternoon, the young people, accompanied by a few of their near relatives, and particularly each of them attended by a young man and woman, dressed in their best clothes, – or rather the best clothes the village could furnish, for they borrow on such occasions from one another, – came to our house to be married. They always come into our kitchen before they enter the church, in order that the bride may get a cap which Mrs M'Kenzie is in the habit of giving them on such occasions…A considerable number of the villagers attended the marriage sermon. As soon as they were married, they went home; and we saw no more of them till after tea, when the governor of the feast, the bride's brother, came, dressed in the uniform (which is a rag of white cotton cloth sewed to each shoulder and the front of his bonnet,) to invite us to the marriage feast. We always go to their feasts to keep them regular, and in case they should think we despise their humble fare. They are not in the habit of asking any person to their feasts till every thing is ready. When we went we found every man in the island seated in the house of the bride's father, with a table of planks before them; the ground served them for seats. One end of the board was raised much higher; this was intended for us, with a chest for a seat, and opposite to us were the bride and bridegroom and their friends. On the board before us were placed three plates, . . . one filled with mutton, one filled with barley bannocks, and the third filled with cheese. The rest had their mutton and bread in wooden dishes made by nailing small boards together. There was neither soup nor drink of any kind on the board, nor used at any of their feasts. After a blessing was pronounced, no conversation for a while interrupted their eating, but afterwards there was some general conversation. When we came out, the women and boys were lounging about the house; the former waiting to get a piece of bread and mutton as a reward for their baking and grinding. Their portion being given out to them, the boys were seated at the table to consume what remained; when these were removed, all went home.

MacCallum (1907, 21; Connell 1887, 73–76) saw the wedding of Finlay Gillies to Catherine Gillies in 1885. A week before, a feast of oatcakes, butter, cheese and mutton, accompanied by bowls of tea and some whisky, was held in the bride's home; men and women were in different parts of the house, and the conversation was of 'the news of the day' and the wedding. Everyone attended the ceremony, dressed in normal clothes, except for the couple to be married who wore their best. Afterwards there was another feast, the couple dining with the minister. Connell adds that the minister, teacher and nurse were not invited to the feast, but the couple took food to the manse, and at the end of the day were 'seen to rest for the night'.

MacLachlan (11.8.1908) witnessed two weddings on the same day in 1908; much of the previous day had been spent baking. The wedding party spent all evening in the manse, where they had tea; then the minister and the MacLachlans accompanied the party to the village where they saw the couples into bed, and kissed them all. The following day the baby of one couple was baptised, and the other couple had a wedding party in the bride's home; the minister and missionary went, and evidently the custom of the women eating after the men continued.

In the early eighteenth century, when anyone died, the news was cried through the island, and all work ceased until after the burial, which took place the following day. Everyone returned home from their work, and food was provided by the relatives of the deceased as their circumstances permitted, particularly to the households of those who watched the corpse and dug the grave.

> At entering the corpse they are so mindful of mortality, judgement and a future life that they all draw to a side, take off their bonnets, and the poor their caps made of cloath, and say prayers; therein humbly craving, that the Lord would prepare them for that state…They esteem the grave, where the corps of the dead is to be interred, so sacred a bed, that they set a person at each end of it, that no dog, cat, or other brute creature, approach to, nor cross over the same. After prayers, a snuff-box or two goes round the best-respected; and the poor gets only a ped-ful [sic] or two in their palms, especially if in haste to be away.

They did not dig a grave or bury anyone on 'the odd day of the year'. A person working on the grave would lift a small quantity of earth out of it on a spade, spit in the grave, and then replace the earth; this was done two or three times, 'for custom's sake'; it is not clear whether this was during the excavation or the infilling (Buchan 1727, 34–5).

In the 1830s MacKenzie (MacLean 1838, 19) found that when a death occurred, there was an extreme but brief demonstration of grief among the relatives, especially the women. All work ceased until after the burial took place, two or three days after the death. A few people who had a skill in joinery made a coffin; as with a marriage, men went to the hill for sheep belonging to the deceased or a near relative, and the women were busy grinding and baking. The food was for

Those that watch the corpse (which they assiduously do till interred,) for a feast of bread and mutton or beef, which they take in the burying ground, and a portion for the women who prepared the meat. The more sheep and cows they kill, and the more barley they use, the more honour do they intend to confer on their deceased friend. Those who have lost many relatives have been much reduced by this foolish custom.

When all things are in readiness for the interment, a few of the young men set off to a distance to get a broad turf for a covering to the grave, while the rest are digging it. They then come to the house and get the coffin well tied on two sticks, and carry it in the course of the sun round the gardens with which the group of houses which form the village are surrounded, though they should go through their corn. As soon as the grave is filled up, they sit down, summer or winter, upon the grass or stones, and eat the bread and beef which has been prepared; and if any of them be detained at home, their portion is sent. If the deceased be an adult, he is interred in the afternoon; and if a child, late in the evening.

Murray (25.7.1886; 27.12.1886 12.3.1887) attended several funerals; the women followed the remains to the burial ground, where they mourned until the body was covered. When a baby was buried he saw the coffins of her baby brothers in the grave opened for her.

Ross (1890, 38) records that when a death occurred, a lament was composed recounting the good deeds of the departed; the body was dressed and a handkerchief wound round the face. It was covered with 'the linen' – probably a winding sheet, and then with a blanket, and was watched over until the burial, which usually took place within two days, a coffin being made expeditiously.

When the sun's shadow has come to a certain place, part of a psalm is sung, a chapter read, another psalm sung and some one engages in prayer. Then the funeral procession starts for the churchyard attended by all the islanders able to turn out.

The women keened while the grave was being filled.

MacLachlan (2.10.1906, 26.4.1907, 2.2.1908, 22.3.1909) records burial within three days; grief was not overwhelming when two elderly women died, but when a boy and three men drowned great sadness pervaded the village. From 1901 onwards entries in the school log book indicate that school was always closed between a death and burial, and that this normally took place within three days. On the occasion of the drowning of the three men in 1909, school was closed for a week.

Morality and Crime

Speaking of 1697, Martin (1753, 46, 66, 68–71; 1716, 288) says: 'there has not been one instance of fornication or adultery for many ages before this time' and described the St Kildans as living in 'innocency and simplicity, purity, mutual love and cordial friendship…free from envy, deceit, and dissimulation'. He goes on to describe the career of Roderick (pp 86–87), who through fraud was guilty of demanding sheep with menaces, sexual assault of married women, and mental and physical abuse (MacAulay 1764, 235–6). He also asserted that 'they never swear, or steal'. MacAulay (1764, 220, 245) noted that there was no adultery, but some were 'rather free of vices than possessed of virtues', and dissimulation and lying were common, particularly over numbers of sheep. Deceit over numbers of sheep, on which tax or rent was paid, is mentioned by several people, and as stealing from the Estate, was probably regarded differently from theft from neighbours, much as stealing from the Government through inexact tax returns is regarded by many today. There may also have been, as elsewhere in the Highlands, a reluctance to count animals in the belief that a true count might attract misfortune (MacKenzie 1793, 561).

Campbell in 1799 (f 26) found that adultery, fornication and pocket picking were very common, and both he and Brougham had their pockets picked, but Brougham (1871, I 107) said that the only adulteress was the Steward's dairymaid, who came from the Long Island, and furthermore, that no murders were ever known.

However, in the 1830s MacKenzie (1911, 29–30, 36–7) found that 'stealing was only limited by their opportunities, and if the thing which it was possible to steal belonged to the proprietor, it was all right'. The Factor rarely discovered the culprits. He was told of two murders: of a MacLeod from Skye, one of the Factor's crew, and at another time of a girl who had come to the island as servant to the Factor; both these people married St Kildans and settled on the island, and both were suspected of giving information to the Factor. The man was thrown off a rock into the sea one winter, while the woman, taken down to the shore by the other women to gather limpets, was strangled there, by all the men pulling at either end of a rope looped around her neck. As all the men were equally guilty, none was likely to inform, and MacKenzie found there was a belief that guilt would be washed away by the sea. These crimes may have been confessed during the great religious revival of the early 1840s; it seems very unlikely that either the people themselves, or MacKenzie, would have fabricated the accounts. After the major revival in 1841–3, he saw a great change in temperament: envy, cunning, theft, Sabbath breaking, gossip and anger were overcome, and the people became diligent, obliging, kind, quiet, and attentive to duty.

Lawson (pers comm) has commented on the rarity of illegitimate births and pregnant brides, evidence of a strong emphasis on sexual morality after MacKenzie's ministry. In the century before the evacuation six live illegitimate births were recorded, and there were two pregnant brides. Four children were legitimised by their parents' subsequent marriage.

There were later incidents of petty theft: in 1897 Fiddes (MacKenzie mss) wrote that thefts were common; hay had been stolen on more than one occasion from Betsy MacDonald, who was too infirm to cut and gather it herself, and it was generally felt necessary to keep a watch over washed wool laid out to dry. When a policeman went to investigate a theft of sheep in the late 1890s, the suspect was surrounded by the community and no action was possible (Heathcote 1900a, 70). Although Lachlan MacDonald (1988, 135, 144) said that there was mutual trust and no necessity for locks, he had made a wooden lock himself, to prevent theft of preserved birds (pers comm).

In 1842 MacGillivray (1842, 56) found that visitors 'created many artificial wants and previously unknown luxuries, as well as encouraged an avaricious spirit'. This comment was echoed by many later visitors (e.g. MacLeod 1877 in RHASS papers; Connell 1887, 164). A Uist man, a member of the steamer crew in the 1900s, was ashamed and angry to see fellow islanders begging (Morrison, pers comm). Shaw (1993, 93) was told in 1930 that if the St Kildans went out in their boats to beg from trawlers anchored in the bay, the trawlermen, weary of their demands, turned the hoses on them.

Though St Kilda clearly suffered the discord and troubles that exist in any community, large or small, at times, there was much of a more positive nature. MacAulay (1764, 220–1) found the people very courteous and respectful, and generously hospitable. In 1853 MacKenzie (1921, 87) found the people 'kind and gentle in speech and obliging and friendly in actions'. Assistance was given to the aged and infirm (Milner 1848, 2057; MacKay 1884, 868; Gillies 1988, 44; MacDonald 1988, 119). Emily MacLeod (RHASS papers) said she had never seen such good people, who were also very industrious, and in 1927 the missionary John MacLeod (SG 20.5.1927) extolled them as hard working, pious, sympathetic and kind.

9

Homes, Shielings, Bothies and Storehouses

Homes

In considering the history of the dwellings on St Kilda there are two major problems: one is the inadequacy of the early documentary sources; the other is the extensive demolition of the village which took place in the 1830s, when there was a major re-organisation of both dwelling types and land tenure, the village being removed to a new site. The extent of the destruction is recorded by MacKenzie (1911, 20): 'when the new houses were built...all [the old houses] except one small one in which dwelt a widow, were removed'.

There is nothing now which is readily recognisable as belonging to the pre-1830s village, but there are numerous vestiges of stone structures, and from these and such accounts of the earlier village as there are, it is possible to make some suggestions concerning the location of the village, and the type of house in use during the late seventeenth century. While the south-facing bay would almost certainly be the preferred site for a settlement, the precise location and form of any earlier village must remain a matter of conjecture.

The village is marked on all the pre-1830 maps (figures 9–15) and described as being near 'St Kilder's well', near Christ Church, and in two regular rows (Martin 1753, 16; Adv ms 33.3.20. f21; MacAulay 1764, 42, 101). Acland's sketch of 1812 (plate 12) shows it huddled below Conachair; an isolated building by the shore is very probably the Store. The general location, below Conachair and near Tobar Childa and the burial ground, is an area which is naturally particularly stony, and would in many ways be a good place to build, having some of the material ready to hand, and preserving the less stony areas for cultivation.

After the smallpox epidemic in 1727 a number of houses would have been abandoned as dwellings, though as the population grew in time by natural increase and immigration, some might have been re-occupied. It seems unlikely, from common features mentioned in accounts written before and after the smallpox epidemic, that the village was moved, though new houses may have been built in the same area.

In the seventeenth century the 'town' was described as having four streets (Adv ms. 33.3.20 f 21), but in 1797 Clarke (1824, 271) described the houses as standing in all directions, and could see no sign of the stone causeway described by MacAulay and MacCulloch (1819, 27). Some of the maps show the village as a cluster of houses and some show it as linear. Acland's sketches suggest a cluster. These are the only extant views of the pre-1830s village, and as a complement to the maps and written descriptions they are invaluable.

Figure 55. *Plan of village area*

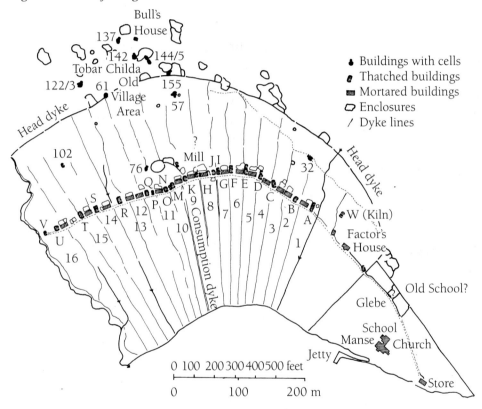

Possibly the seventeenth century village was built in two rough rows, still apparent when MacAulay visited, but towards the end of the eighteenth century some houses may have fallen into disrepair and others were probably built both to replace them and to house the increasing population. This is supported by that fact that the house in which Rachel Erskine had lived was in ruins by 1815 when MacCulloch saw it among the other houses, and MacKenzie's account describes two types of houses, one older than the other.

The identification of cleit 85 as 'Lady Grange's House' (Mathieson 1928, 132), is dubious, although he does say that after the timber roof fell in it was partly rebuilt. Her house was reported by Donald MacLeod of Berneray in 1741 (Anon 1846, 147) to be

A house or cottage of two apartments, tolerably well furnished...Once she was detected in an attempt during the night to obtain a pistol from above the steward's bed in the room next her own...She was well treated...having a house forty feet long, with an inner room and a chimney to it, a curtained bed, armchair, table and other articles.

Although it was in ruins in 1815, in 1838 MacLean (1838, 46) saw it:

The house...is about twenty feet by ten. Like the rest of the houses, it is divided in the centre by a partition of rude loose stone. In one of these apartments sat Finlay MacDonald every night for seven years, and Lady Grange in the other,...thus making the entire of her ladyship's accommodation ten feet semilunar!

According to Sands (1877a, 106) the house in which she lived was demolished a few years before 1876.

Before 1727 the number of families was 27 to 30 (pp 125–6, table 3); between 1797 and 1831 the number of houses was recorded variously as 26, 20 and about 30 (Brougham 1871 I, 104; Kennedy 1932, 294–6; Atkinson 1838, 218), while the number of families is recorded as between 20 and 22 (p 125).

There is considerably more information available about the form of individual houses, much of it repetitive. The essential details are given in table 5. Martin's (1753, 10–11), description is good:

The inhabitants live together in a small village, carrying all the signs of extreme poverty; the houses are of a low form, and the doors are all to the north-east, to secure them from the shocks of the tempestuous south-west winds. The walls of the houses are rudely built of stone, the short couples joining at the ends of the roof, upon whose sides small ribs of wood are laid, and these covered with straw; the whole secured by ropes made of twisted heath, the extremity of which on each side is poised with stone to preserve the thatch from being blown away.

Sibbald (Adv ms. 33.3.20 f 21) describes the houses as cleanly and neat. MacAulay (1764, 43–5) gives more details. The dry stone walls, 'of a rough gritty kind of stones, huddled together in haste, without either lime or mortar' were eight or nine feet high, and the roofs almost flat, to minimise storm damage, while in the thickness of the walls were the bedchambers – large enough to accommodate three people, and entered at the side by a very small opening. The main body of the house was divided into two by a partition wall, the cattle spending the winter in the larger part nearer the door, while the inner area was the living room. It was here that 'compost' was made on the floor, turf or peat ash being carefully spread, then covered with 'a rich friable sort of earth' and peat dust was scattered over; these layers were watered and well trodden until they formed a hard floor, and more fires were lit on top, providing the next ash layer. The process was repeated until they were ready to sow the barley in spring. According to MacAulay 'their method of preparing a sort of manure…proves that they are very indelicate' and it seems that the St Kildans, who valued their compost as a 'commodity inestimably precious' were so reluctant to waste anything which might benefit their poor arable land, that they incorporated their own faeces into their floors. They were living on a deep litter system, so deep, indeed, that by spring sowing time the floor had risen by four or five feet; this was the reason for the unusual wall height and the use of beds made within the thickness of the walls. According to Buchanan (1793, 132), this was also the practice in Harris, where cattle were kept on deep litter.

Clarke (1824, 231, 270) investigated the bed chambers:

Round the walls of their huts, are one or more small arched apertures, according to the number of the family, leading to a vault like an oven, arched with stone, and defended strongly from the inclemency of the weather, in which they sleep. I crawled on all fours, with a lamp, into one of these, and found the bottom covered with heath; in this, I was informed, four persons slept. There is not sufficient space in them for a tall man to sit upright, though the dimensions of these vaulted dormitories varied with every hut, according to the number it was required to contain, or the industry of its owners.

Earlier in his journey Clarke had come across a hut on Mull, in which dry bracken and heather on an earth floor was the bed for a family with nine children, together with one grandmother, an adult female idiot 'harboured in charity', two dogs, a cat, three kittens and a pig: clearly St Kilda was not exceptional in its cramped and uncomfortable sleeping arrangements.

Brougham (1871 I, 104–5) described the roofs as grassy rather than of thatch; his account is particularly disparaging:

Several green tufts of grassy sod, upon heaps of loose stones – these we at last discovered to be the houses, twenty six in number; on the hills, more such molehills, rather smaller, for cutting peats. This is the town, or city of Hirta. The view of this village is truly unique. Nothing in Captain Cook's voyages comes half so low.

Neil MacKenzie (1911, 18–20) is the only person to refer to two different types of pre–1838 houses, one older than the other. He describes the older houses, the dwellings in use at his arrival in 1830, and the reconstruction of the village in the late 1830s.

Of their most ancient houses several still remain entire. They are circular or nearly so, and roughly built. The walls are six or seven feet thick, with spaces for beds left in them. These bed spaces are roofed in with long slabs, and the entrance from the interior of the house is about three feet by two feet. The walls are not arched, but contracted gradually by overlapping of the stones to nearly a point. The entrance is about three feet by two and a half feet. The outside is covered with earth and rubbish and appears like a green hillock. In some places they are almost entirely underground

The houses which they occupied when I came to the island were larger and more oval shaped. The walls were seven or eight feet thick, about six or seven feet high, and the same height all round. The beds were in the thickness of the wall as before. There was also the same absence of a window. The only opening for light was a small circular opening at one end, where the thatch joined the wall, left for the exit of smoke. The door aperture was near the end and faced east. It was higher than that in the former houses, and had a wooden door with wooden hinges and lock. A partition of rough stones about four feet high, called fallan, divided the abode of man and dog from that of the cattle. There was a light wooden roof resting on the inner edge of the wall, covered with a thickness of about eighteen inches of straw; simply laid on, and not in layers as ordinary thatch. When beaten flat and uniform it was secured by numerous straw ropes called siman. The straw used was that of barley. As the wood of the roof was supported not on the outer but on the inner edge of the thick double wall, when the thatching was finished there was left a broad walk along the top of the wall outside of the thatch. The walls were formed of an inner and outer facing of stones about four feet apart, and it was in this space that the beds were left, the remaining space being filled up with earth. On the inside opposite each bed there was left an opening about two feet by three feet. As most of the houses touched each other, there was thus left from house to house a broad grassy walk on the top of the walls...The cattle occupied the half of the house next the door, and the manure was not removed till it was taken to the fields in spring. In the other portion dwelt the family, and there all the ashes, and the dirty water, and many things far worse, were daily spread over the floor. This was covered every few days with a layer of dry peat dust. Before the time for removal to the fields in spring the mixture was often higher than the side walls, so that at times a visit to a parishioner was quite an adventure. Owing to the great thickness of the wall the house door was at the end of a tunnel, and owing to the lowness of the door space one could not stand upright. In front of the doorway, and extending well into the tunnel, was a hollow into which were thrown all the portions of the bird not used for food, the entire carcases of those not edible, and all and every abomination you can think of. Stooping low, you groped your way over this till you reached the door. Inside the door you had to climb over the manure to among the cattle, which, on account of the presence of a stranger, and the barking of dogs, and the shouting of your friends above, soon got very excited. Amidst great confusion and excitement you got helped along and over the dividing fallan. *Here you had to creep along on hands and feet, and it was only near the centre of the space that you could even sit upright. Carefully creeping along in almost total darkness, you made your way to the top of the steep slope which led down to the bed opening. Down this you went head foremost, nothing visible above but your legs, while you spoke and prayed. They wonder themselves why it is that they are not so strong as they believe their forefathers to have been. The wonder rather is that under such conditions of living they survive at all. When new houses were built by them afterwards, all these, except one small one in which dwelt a widow, were removed.*

The houses were thatched with two layers of barley straw. Each spring, the inner layer, impregnated with soot, was removed and spread on the fields and the outer layer replaced; in the autumn, straw from the year's crop was put over this, becoming the new outer layer. Thus each year's straw was on the roof for about eighteen months. Peat dust was spread over the floor at intervals to absorb the moisture and to deodorise it. Half the peat cut was beaten into dust to use in this way. 'A quantity of coarse grass gathered on the hills' (possibly woodrush) was spread on the floor in both human and cattle accommodation (MacKenzie, 1911, 9, 11).

Three buildings conform in some respects to MacKenzie's description of the older houses: Calum Mór's house, and cleitean 122/3 and 142 (figures 55 and 56). The first is not mentioned individually until 1875 (Sands 1877a, 81–2);

Figure 56. *Buildings with cells attached: plans and section*

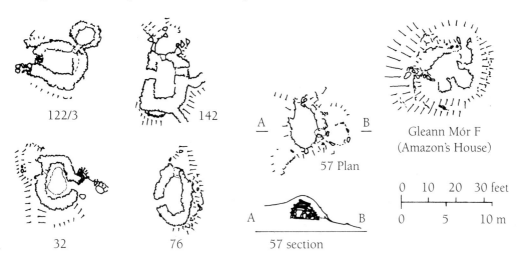

this suggests that only lately had it become remarkable, being regarded earlier as just another of the old houses. All three are within the compass of what is probably the old village area, and here also there are other buildings (figure 57) which have attached to them cells or the remains of cells. Most of these buildings are more like conventional cleitean, and rather than being the remains of old houses, could incorporate fragments of old house walls. Figure 56 shows that there are some similarities between the Amazon's House and some of those in the village area. References to buildings like the Amazon's House in this area (p 234) support the idea that in the mediaeval period or earlier the village may have consisted of dwellings of this type.

Two further buildings may be small houses of MacKenzie's more recent type, and both may have been occupied after his re-organisation of the village. 'Cleitean' 32 and 76 were both thatched late into the nineteenth century; both have blocked entrances to vanished cells (figure 56).

There are two particular problems in identifying these buildings as old houses: firstly, none have very thick walls, though if they were double walled with a core of earth, the outer wall and earth may have been replaced by a thin outer stone wall to allow the buildings to function as cleitean; secondly, in most cases, the entrances to the cells are extremely small, and most would not be negotiable by an adult, so that the cells would be inaccessible to people with the physique compatible with the strength required to build them. Thus none of the anomalous buildings which are not conventional cleitean can be positively identified as pre-1830 houses, but all have some features suggesting that they include elements of old houses.

Figure 57. *Cleitean with traces of cells attached and other unusual cleitean: plan*

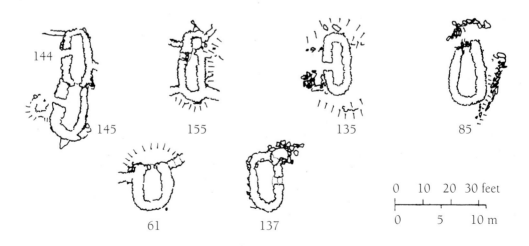

The major relocation and reconstruction of the village which took place in the late 1830s resulted in the building of new thatched houses along the newly laid-out street (figures 43, 55, plate 17). Though the size of the houses was limited by the re-use of the old roofing timbers in the absence of any other, there were several improvements on the old pattern: rubbish was no longer to be accumulated on the floor; each house was to have a window; and the beds were no longer to be in the thickness of the walls, though a few individuals apparently retained this feature (Sharbau 1860; Thomas 1868, 158). MacGillivray, who was from Harris, (1842, 54–55) noted that the houses were built in 'the ordinary way': double stone walls with an earth core, and a thatched roof secured by straw ropes with stones on the ends. The fire was in the centre of the floor. Both MacGillivray and Wilson (1842, 32–34) indicate that there was a single room in each house, though some houses adjoined each other. Neither mention the presence of the cow, though Thomas's plans (figure 68) make it clear that the lower part of the house functioned as a byre.

Figures 58 and 59 show that the 1830s houses were probably all originally similar to those drawn by Thomas. The internal dimensions of unaltered houses range from 18' to 22'7" in length by 9' to 11' in breadth, with wall heights of 5' to 6' in most instances (plate 18). Each house had a door and a window in the same wall, almost always on the east side, away from the

Figure 58. *Plans of thatched buildings and typical 1861/2 house*

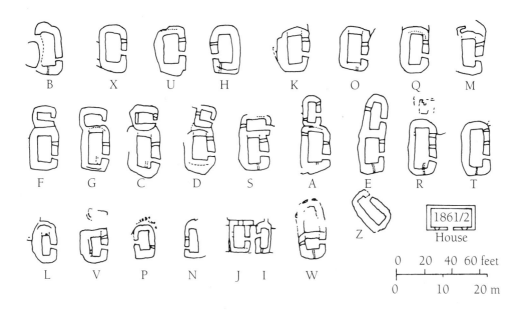

149

prevailing wind. The drains at the south ends of some are still readily visible. There have been a number of alterations to this basic plan. Several houses have a north inner wall face which is not bonded into the side walls, indicating that the wall is a later insertion. In Houses C and G, which are noted on Sharbau's plan as having beds in the wall, this may result from the removal of the beds; traces of a bed entrance were seen when some of the partition wall in G collapsed in 1985. It seems unlikely that all the houses with this feature formerly had beds in the north walls, and in some cases there may have been a desire to reduce the size of the house. This must have been the reason for the insertion of an extra thickness of west wall in House V, which also has a truncated north end and is considerably smaller than it must have been originally. Occasionally a north wall may have been altered when a smaller building was added to the north end of the house, as in Houses A, C, D, F, G, S and possibly R.

House E is exceptional in having been built after 1860, probably as a 'semi-detached'. Houses R and T have probably been lengthened, though it is difficult to discern this in the walls. House L is peculiar, being off the street, and possibly a reconstruction of the 'village barn' marked on the same site by Sharbau. Houses N and P are small, and, like the small secondary building at the end of the kiln, W, may have housed a single widow or elderly spinster. Houses I and J were probably byres or stores rather than dwellings, having been converted from the shell of the 'Mill building' put up in 1861 (p 109). Although MacLeod's photographs (Wilson 1886) (plate 17) show that all these buildings were thatched in 1886, some later had pointed gables added, probably to facilitate the replacement of thatch with tarred felt. Most of these additions are narrower than the main gable walls and some show minimal mortaring.

'Cleitean' 32, 76 and 102 (plate 19) were all thatched in the late nineteenth century, and probably served as dwellings for single people for a time. 102 is probably contemporary with or later than the 1830s houses; its isolated position is difficult to explain.

Most of the 1830s houses were to be used as dwellings for no more than twenty five years. By 1860 they were seen as inadequate by MacPherson MacLeod and MacRaild, and by Otter (p 108). After the hurricane damage in October 1860, arrangements were made for new houses to be built at MacPherson MacLeod's expense. The first four were built in 1861, masons going from Skye to direct the work. Originally, these were to be thatched, but in 1861 Otter purchased 66 sheets of zinc for roofing, and all of the sixteen houses built in 1861 and 1862 were initially roofed with zinc sheets (RHASS papers). These houses were exclusively for human habitation, the cattle being left in possession of the 1830s houses.

Figure 59. *Plans and sections of thatched buildings and elevation of 1861/2 house*

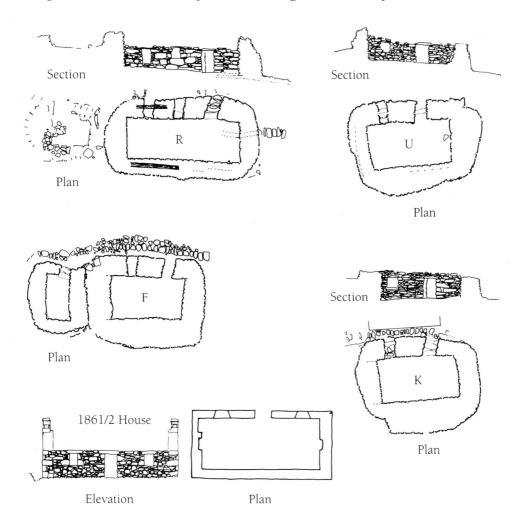

Sharbau noted two houses, besides the Mill, as 'erected 1861', but the 1861 census recorded '4 houses building'. Although Sharbau did not note it, it seems likely that the third house was House 16. The shells of the sixteen mortared houses built in 1861/2 are all very similar (figures 55, 59). A central door flanked by two windows faced the street and the bay. Inside, a small lobby led into a room at each end, and a closet behind the lobby was entered from one of these rooms. There was a fireplace in each gable. Thirteen of the houses are of very similar dimensions: the length being 28'7" to 29'7", while the width is 12'10" to 13'4". Houses 5, 9 and 16 all have widths within this range, but 5 is 30'6" long, while 9 and 16 are 28'0" and 28'3" long respectively. Thirteen houses have a clear floor area of 378 to 389 square feet; 5 has 407, 9 has 364, and 16 has 367 square feet, so 5 is larger and 9 and 16, of similar size, are smaller than the standard thirteen. Houses 5 and 9 both have battered front and back external walls. House 16 is not battered, but is exceptional in having its cupboard space in the west rather than the east gable, and an extra cupboard space in the back wall.

Although ostensibly these houses were an improvement on the previous ones, they had disadvantages. With a larger area than most of the thatched houses, they were more difficult to heat, and the thinner walls and thin roofs provided less insulation. There were problems with draught-proofing and leaking roofs: in 1863 Betty Scott wrote to Otter: 'whenever it rains the rain in is nearly the same as it is out and the wind is blowing in through the wall' (RHASS papers). The pallor of the house roofs in the 1886 photographs suggests the zinc sheeting remained. In 1896 Neil MacDonald and Malcolm MacKinnon both wanted new roofs, the former complaining that the rain poured through the roof and his bed, and in 1897 MacKenzie received a request to send felt and coal tar (MacKenzie mss.). By 1930 most of the 1860s houses and some of the 1830s houses had tarred felt roofs.

Shielings

In the seventeenth century some people stayed in Gleann Mór in the summer, in the 'Amazon's House' and probably in the other similar structures (p 77).

Latterly, although cattle were kept in Gleann Mór in the summer, there is no record of people staying there and the 'Buailtean Chrothaidh' or 'gathering folds', a different type of building, were in use. Some of these were built adjacent to and some on top of 'Amazon's House' type structures, which were almost certainly robbed for building stone, though Cottam (1974) believes that the sequence was reversed and that the Buailtean Chrothaidh were the earlier buildings. If, as the evidence suggests, the use of the two types of building was sequential and not contemporary, it is possible that the smallpox epidemic marked the end of the use of residential shielings on St Kilda.

MacKenzie (1911, 7) says that the lambs were folded at night, allowing the milk to accumulate and keeping the ewes from wandering.

In the morning the ewes were also folded, and the communication between where they were and where the lambs were was through a tunnel in the wall about three feet from the ground, so that only one lamb could come at a time.

The place where the sheep were folded must have been a 'Buaile Chrothaidh'; Thomas (1868, 176) saw examples of these, and drew plans of two:

The cro or fold is hollowed out of a bank, and faced with a wall four or five feet high. From the gate, formed by a straw mat, a wide open fold is made by two enclosing walls. Upon the bank round the inner fold are three beehive huts; and it was their presence that puzzled me, for the entrances to them were too small for a man to enter. The huts or cotanan were for the lambs and kids, from whence they were in sight and smell of their dams, but were prevented from sucking.

There are sixteen 'Buailtean Chrothaidh', one for each family in the later nineteenth century. Thomas's description is good, though not all are set into a slope, some being free-standing. As figures 60 and 61 show, each one has a small fold, with cells attached to it, usually three; a drain from the fold, often a threshold slab at the entrance, and outside, low funnelling walls leading to the fold entrance. Some folds are 'semi-detached' (plates 21, 22).

Figure 60. *Distribution of Buailtean Chrothaidh in Gleann Mór*

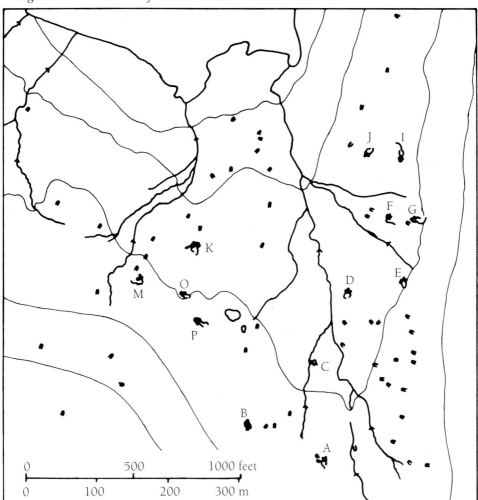

Figure 61. *Plans of Buailtean Chrothaidh*

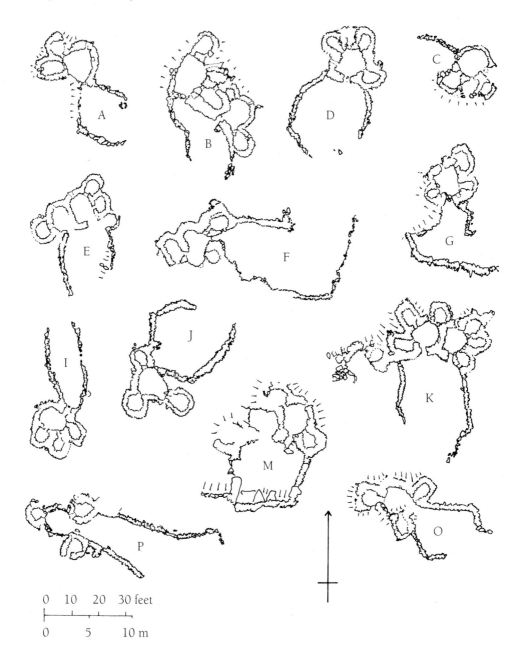

Figure 62. *Map showing Gleann Mór dyke with locations of profiles*

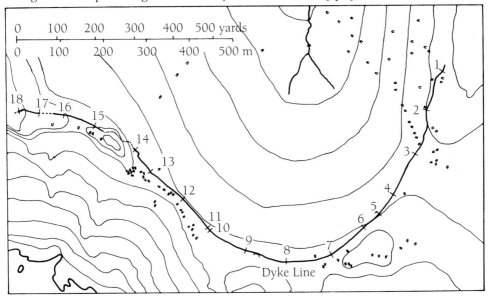

Around the top of Gleann Mór there is a dyke, constructed mainly of turf with some stone, using suitable stone outcrops where available. It is just over three quarters of a mile long (c.1435 yards); the height now varies from a scarcely visible ridge near Mullach Bi to a semi-vertical face about three feet high in various places, where it would still deter a beast on the down hill side (figures 62, 63, plate 23). This dyke was probably intended to prevent cattle leaving the glen, particularly to deter them from wandering down the dangerously steep slopes on the south side of the ridge, where lush grazing might tempt them. Another turf dyke across Ard Uachdarachd may well be for the same purpose. The Gleann Mór dyke has the additional merit of being an easy route to follow round the head of the glen, especially in dim light or mist.

Bothies

There are bothies on all three islands other than Hirte and on both the large stacs. These were used while fowling, and on Boreray and Soay, while working with the sheep (figures 64, 65).

Taigh Stallair (p 78) was the main bothy on Boreray until the early nineteenth century (Kennedy and Thomas 1874, 709). By 1840 it had fallen into disrepair and was used as a quarry for material to build cleitean (Sands 1877a, 75). A bothy had been built above ground (Wilson 1842, 58), and by the 1870s there were three, built in a manner similar to cleitean, and externally

155

Figure 63. *Profiles of the Gleann Mór dyke*

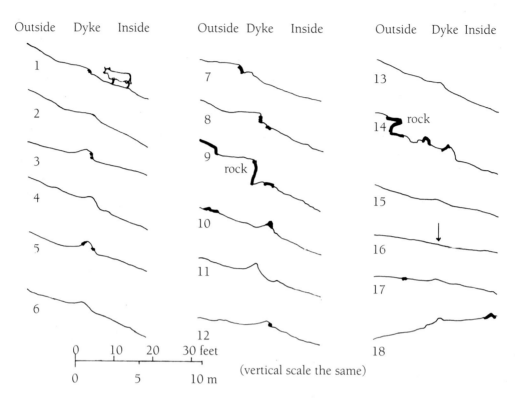

Outside Dyke Inside

Outside Dyke Inside

Outside Dyke Inside

Like little green knolls…The hearth is close to the door. A semicircular seat is close to the hearth, and the space behind is a foot or so higher. This is occupied as a bed…A hole in the roof above the fireplace serves as a vent (Sands 1877a, 52).

In the late nineteenth century a week or more was spent on Boreray in mid June plucking sheep (Murray 6.1887; Ross 1890, 5). Ross says that formerly the men were accompanied by women who plucked birds, though in 1875 and 1876 Sands (1877a, 49, 84) records parties of unaccompanied girls spending several weeks in July on Boreray, plucking puffins, and in 1841 Wilson (1842, 26–7) found that men had stayed for ten days in early August to pluck birds.

Donald Gillies (1930) wrote in his school essays that until a few years previously men would stay on Boreray for up to a fortnight, living in the bothies while plucking the sheep (p 192) or fowling. Turf was cut and stored in cleitean for future use.

Taigh Dugan on Soay is a shelter under a large rock; in the 1870s this and other 'primitive houses' were used by young women who stayed on Soay while plucking birds (Sands 1877b, 188).

Figure 64. *Plans and sections of Bothies*

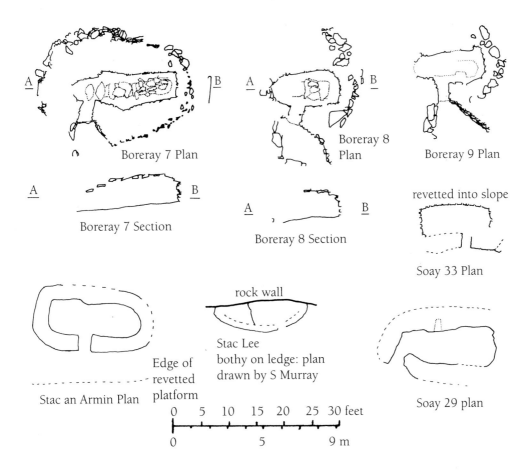

Documentary evidence for the use of the bothies on the other islands is scarce. Waterston (1905, 200) was told that when men slept in a semi-subterranean house on Dun, mice ran over them. About 1840, five men staying for a few days in July in the bothy on Stac an Armin killed the last garefowl on St Kilda (Harvie Brown and Buckley 1888, 159). Martin (1753, 22) refers to the use of a bothy on Stac Lee to be sure of being on the rock before the gannets fledged, though no mention is made of this later, visits to Stac Lee being made overnight.

There are now three bothies on Boreray. They all have a maximum width of about 6', and vary in length from 12' to 19'. There is up to 5' headroom above floors of accumulated sheep droppings and bones, nests and debris. Two bothies on Soay are about 5' wide and 9' and 12' long, and at least 5' high. The bothy on Dun is about 15' long. There are also shelters under overhanging

157

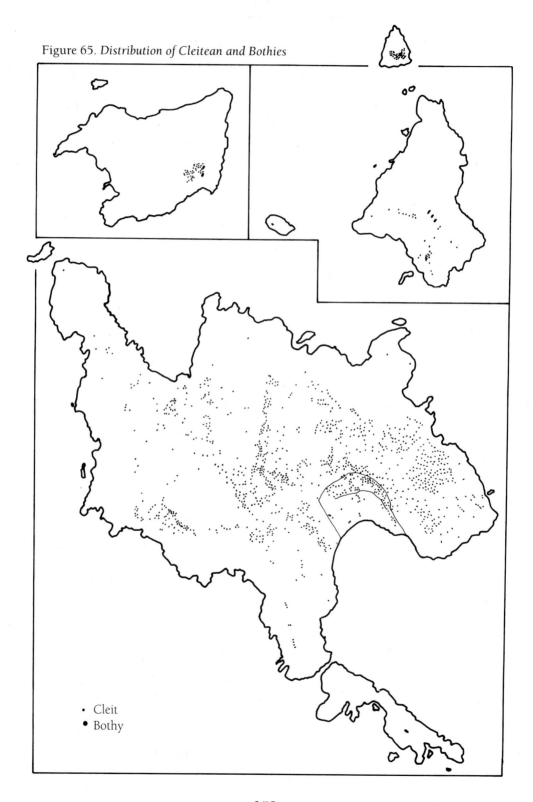

Figure 65. *Distribution of Cleitean and Bothies*

- Cleit
- Bothy

rocks where traces of ash are visible. The bothy on Stac an Armin is about 16' long and up to 6'6" wide, built on a slope with a terrace on the downslope side, where the entrance is. The walls stand to at least 2'6" high, with some corbelling in the upper courses. The Stac Lee bothy is a shelter under an overhang, high up on the south side of the rock. A wall encloses a space about 12' long and up to 6'6" wide (S. Murray, pers comm).

In the nineteenth century if a party on Boreray wanted to be taken off earlier than arranged, an area of ground was dug over as a signal which would be visible from Hirte (MacKenzie 1911, 48). Two cut areas near the top of the slope indicated that one of the party was sick (Sands 1877a, 77); sometimes a fire was lit to convey that something was amiss (Kearton 1897, 84).

Cleitean

The cleit (plural cleitean) is generally regarded as peculiar to St Kilda, though there are a few very similar buildings on Rum, and one on Islay (RCAHMS 1984, 78), but this may be a result of parallel development of a simple building technique.

A typical cleit is a long narrow building, with side walls converging slightly until they are spanned by lintels, which are topped with rubble, soil and turf. The inner wall is often built with an open construction, and the outer wall, built up against the inner wall, consists of smaller stones and is usually slightly battered. The open construction permits the air to pass through the walls, while the turf keeps moisture from penetrating through the roof.

Outside the village area, cleitean on the hills are normally between 6' and 11' in length, and 2'–3' in width internally, within walls about 2' thick. An internal height of more than 4' is unusual, except around An Lag bho'n Tuath and in the Gearraidh Ard area, but height is difficult to measure as in many cleitean there is an accumulation of sheep dung. Within the village area most cleitean are 11'–22' long, 2'6"–4'6" wide and 4'–6'6" high internally. On the hills, most cleitean are entered from one end; normally the side walls simply come to a square end, with no return for the entrance, which is thus as wide as the cleit. The entrance lintel may be some inches lower than the ceiling lintels, and sometimes there is a stone step down into the structure. Almost without exception, end entrances face up the slope, however gentle it may be. Some cleitean have drains or air vents at the base of the rear end wall. Though there are cleitean on the hills with side entrances, they are more common in the village area, where of 155, 85 have end entrances, and 70 have side entrances. One has two entrances on opposite sides, and several others have second, blocked entrances, usually at the side. Occasionally a change in ceiling height or butt joints in the side walls indicate that a cleit has been lengthened. Figure 66 shows examples of the variety of plans of cleitean in the village area.

A diminishing number of village cleitean have timber jambs and occasionally timber lintels in the entrances. One complete door survives (NTS collection 893); it has pintle hinges. Holes in a few timber lintels indicate that other doors had pintle hinges, but there are parts of doors with leather hinges, re-using pieces from boots. On the hills some cleitean have large slabs beside the entrances, probably formerly used to close them; a few still have slabs set across the entrance, effectively closing them.

Figure 66. *Plans of variety of cleitean in village area*

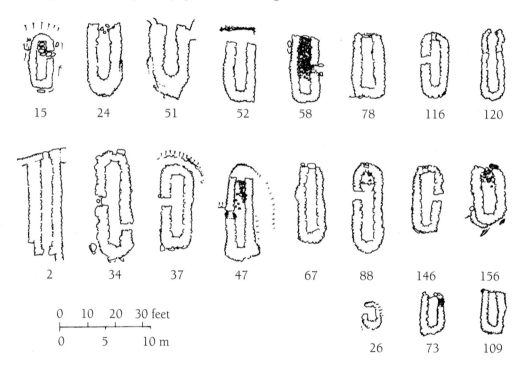

On Hirte there are about 1100 cleitean: many of those outside the village area are roofless and in various stages of collapse, though many are still in good condition. In addition there are about 110 which exist only as foundations or a few courses of walling; some of these are probably the remains of cleitean which have collapsed, the stones being re-used for building a replacement immediately beside the first cleit. There are also about forty shelters under large rocks which have been improved by the addition of walling and in some cases have been used for storing turf. Most of these are among the boulders of Carn Mór.

The distribution of cleitean on Hirte (figure 65) shows a concentration in the village glen, including the slopes of Conachair and Oiseval, with a number in Gleann Mór and on the ridges of Mullach Mór, Mullach Geal and round the south side of Gleann Mór. There are several shelters under rocks on Dun, but no cleitean. On Soay there is a group of about forty cleitean and shelters within a restricted area above the best landing place. On Boreray about thirty cleitean are scattered over the south-western slope, and nearly twenty form a compact group (the Cleitean MacPhaidean) just above the usual landing place. About eighty cleitean are distributed on the steep south side of Stac an Armin.

Cleitean were mentioned by Moray (1678, 929) and Martin (1753, 24–5, 36, 54–5) who said that in 1697 there were over five hundred, including about forty on Boreray, and sufficient on Stac an Armin to contain 800 gannets. Cleitean were used for drying and preserving birds, and preserving eggs in peat ash. They were also used for storing peats (MacAulay 1764, 48). Buchan (1727, 27) adds that there were rules about the doors: if a door were left half-open and stock entered and died in the cleit or one killed another, the owner of the cleit had to pay compensation for the animal. MacAulay (1764, 48) notes that 'every St Kildan had his share of them, in proportion to the extent of land he possesses, or the rent he pays to the Steward'. Latterly crops were stored in cleitean. On Hirte some cleitean on the hills still contain cut turfs, and others have one or two lodged in the walls, evidence of their former use.

Table 5
Details of Pre-1830s Houses

Shape	Roof	Walls	Floor	Compartments	Door	Beds	Reference
Low. Oval/rectangle	Timber rafters Straw thatch Heather ropes	Stone and earth			all to NE		Martin 1716, 1753
	Nearly flat	Stone: 8'–9' high	Manure accumulated to 4' deep	Partition. Inner: people Outer: cattle		In wall, holds 3 people, door very narrow and low	MacAulay 1764
Oblong. Pile of stones	Thatch Ropes of bent	Stone: 3'–4' outside. 2 smokeholes	Peat ash & heath. Fire central		Stoop to enter	1 or more arches lead to vault like oven	Clarke 1824
	To outer wall				Wood lock		McCulloch 1819
All same	Turf and straw	Stone		Inner: people		In walls	MacDonald Kennedy 1932
'Ancient': Circular	Corbelled, earth rubbish and turf	6'–7' thick			c. 3' x 2½'	In walls, slab roof, entrance c. 3' x 2'	MacKenzie 1911
'Old': Larger, oval	Light timber frame to inner wall edge, straw straw ropes	Stone & earth 6'–7' high, 5'–8' thick, smoke hole	Peat dust, ash, grass, deep litter, midden	Rough stone partition; Inner: people Outer: cattle	Near end, to E or NE wood door, hinges, lock	In walls, entrance c. 3' x 2'	MacKenzie 1911
	Rafters to inner wall–Straw				Wood lock	like rabbit holes	Atkinson 1831
Oval c.18' long		Outer c.5' high		Loose stone partition	3' high	cave in wall, below floor level, opposite door	MacLean 1838

10

Domestic Life

Many visitors inspected the homes of the St Kildans; if the people were out, some were thwarted when they found the doors locked.

Wooden Locks

Campbell (1799 f59) is the first to record the use of wooden locks and keys for house doors, and these are also mentioned by MacCulloch (1819, 29) and several other nineteenth century visitors. Muir (1858, 13) was puzzled both by their design and their necessity. The first person to describe the former was Smith (1879, 32), who saw one on an old house in 1873: 'There were three small bolts of wood falling down into notches in the chief bolt. These were lifted up by a key, which was simply a piece of wood with projections corresponding to the falling pieces, and fitted for raising them…Weight is made to do the work now done by our spring, and weight is a constant property which outlasts elasticity.' Sands collected one which he gave to the Society of Antiquaries of Scotland in 1878.

This type of lock had been noticed elsewhere (Romilly Allen 1880, 149–162). Visitors began to make particular enquiry about them. Ross (1884, 83) found them on almost every barn and byre, though the new houses had ordinary rim brass-knobbed locks. Kearton (1897, 12) found them still in use, and observed new ones on the new houses. Lachlan MacDonald (pers comm) remembered making one himself, using an old one as a model. He explained that they were sometimes necessary on cleit doors to prevent petty theft of, for example, hay or salted birds.

The number of wooden locks from St Kilda to be found in museum collections (table 6, figure 67) is an indication of the interest they attracted. Some are more complicated than others, but all are based on the same principle of working by gravity. Hay (1978, 127) has pointed out that these locks might stick in damp weather if the wood swelled, but Lachlan MacDonald said that allowance was made for that. Some are made of hardwood which should swell less, and be more durable than pine. These locks require the use of both hands to open and to lock the doors, and can only be operated on one side of the door. They were used on the outside to secure valuables in a barn or cleit, or to safeguard the house when the occupants were out.

Figure 67. *Examples of wooden locks. Scale 1:10*

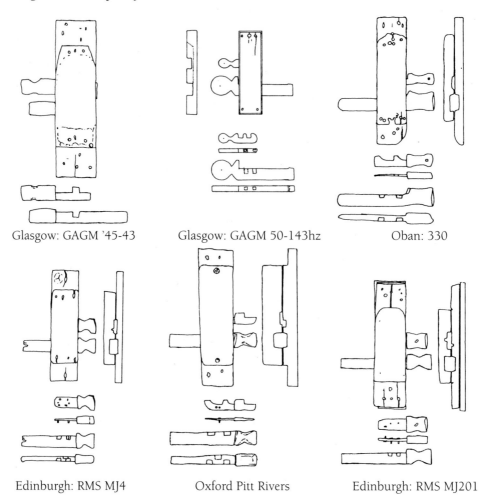

Glasgow: GAGM '45-43	Glasgow: GAGM 50-143hz	Oban: 330
Edinburgh: RMS MJ4	Oxford Pitt Rivers	Edinburgh: RMS MJ201

Of all the locks recorded, one in Glasgow, said in 1901 to be 200 years old, stands out as being particularly finely made, and was probably imported (figure 67). While it may not be as old as claimed, it could have been taken to St Kilda by one of the eighteenth century catechists, and may have served as a model. St Kildans visiting Harris or Skye may have seen other examples, some more intricate, and copied them (Fenton and Hendry 1984).

Fuel

Sibbald (Adv.ms 33.3.20) refers to the cutting of turf to a depth of two or three feet, on the tops of the hills. Possibly it was during such work that antlers were found on Oiseval (Martin 1716, 15).

Table 6
Brief Details of Wooden Locks

No of tumblers	Single/ Double	Date collected	Notes	Location
1	S	1896	Recorded from photograph	Kearton 1897, 12
1	S	1930	Supposed to have been on Lady Grange's house	GAGM '45-43
2	S	1889	Key missing	GAGM '89-74
2	S	1901?	Said to be 200 years old bolt & 1 tumbler replaced	GAGM '50-143hz
2	S	1912		RMS MJ 250
2	S	1912		RMS MJ 251
2	S	00–17		Inverness 00.983
2	S	?		HFM SAH 12
2	S	?		Oban Corran H. 330
2	S	1877	Key has pins	RMS MJ 4
3	D	1896	Key: 2 teeth 1 pin. Said to be last on island	Oxford Pitt Rivers
3	S	1902	Key: 2 teeth 1 pin. Pin and 1 tumbler missing	Aberdeen ABDMS 1113
3	D	?	Key not removeable	Dunvegan Castle
4	D	1883	Key with pins only. 1 pin & 1 tumbler missing	RMS MJ 201
2	S	1966	Key only	NTS (RMS L1967.32)
3?	D?	1877	Key only, 1 tooth 2 pins	GAGM '77-41am

RMS: Edinburgh, Royal Museum of Scotland
GAGM: Glasgow Museums and Art Galleries
HFM: Kingussie, Highland Folk Museum

MacCulloch (1819, 27) speaks of peat from the highest ridge being used for fuel, and MacKenzie (1911, 10–11,16) describes 'moderately good peat' cut 'in the usual way' from hollows among the hills. When the peats were half dry they were gathered into cleitean to finish drying. A family might have as many as twenty cleitean full of peat, 'and perhaps also a score of little stacks outside', but this was never enough, and once the peats were exhausted, the people would cut peaty turf. The peats were carried home by the women in creels as required. Before the nineteenth century ponies were used largely for carrying peat, but few were left by MacKenzie's time and the last ones were removed in the 1840s (p 194).

Possibly this lack of ponies encouraged the St Kildans to give up cutting peat altogether and pare turf, although this resulted in the steady destruction of large areas of pasture. This practice was deplored by many visitors from Wilson (1842, 21) to Heathcote (1900a, 211). The resulting thinness or absence of soil and vegetation is still noticeable in some areas such as the western and southern slopes of Oiseval (Gwynne and Milner 1974, 43). The people said there was no peat, but Heddle (Smith 1879, 65–70) observed peat on the higher slopes of Mullach Mór and Conachair, and Ross (1884, 86) noted a peat moss between Conachair and Mullach Mór. Heddle considered that the peat hags here were natural, though peat was probably cut in this area in former times, and the 'tarn' marked by Mathieson (1928) in this area may well be the pool created by the cutting of fuel for Lady Grange (pp 51, 90).

Murray and MacLachlan (1887, 1907) recorded turf cutting in May. Heddle observed that the hill slopes had been cut up to about 500 feet, and Heathcote noted bare areas in all parts of the island. Kearton (1897, 19) saw women carrying loads of turf back from Gleann Mór besides their pails of milk. Murray (20 & 25.12.1886), out on the hills in December, met men bringing turfs home from Carn Mór, and wrote that 'people in single file carrying home peats over the white hills presents a curious spectacle'. There are still cleitean in various parts of the island with cut turfs in them, or a few turfs lodged in the walls showing a former use of the structure.

MacKenzie (1911, 18) received fuel from the mainland, and no doubt his successors did also; some coal must have been given to the islanders, as Smith (1879, 75) records that they 'expect 36 tons of coals to be sent to them'. The MacLachlans (7.9.1906, 22 & 31.8.1907) got supplies of coal through the whalers from Harris, and various fishing boats gave or sold the islanders coal, though turf was the main source of fuel for most.

Before 1861, the fires were in the centre of the living area. Thomas's plans (figure 68) suggest that the hearth was several flat stones laid in a square, but Wiglesworth (1903, 8–9) saw 'a low stone coping' round Rachel MacCrimmon's hearth. The 1861 houses had fireplaces in the gable ends, but Ross (1890, 151) says no grates were used, the fire burning on a solid hearth raised slightly above floor level.

Domestic Furnishings and Utensils

In 1697 (Martin 1753, 10) the beds were made of straw. There is scarcely any other mention of household furnishings in early accounts, and Campbell (1799, f38) explains why: in the houses he entered, furniture was sparse. The earth or midden floor was covered with dry grass and puffin skins; a few stones served as seats or tables, and a barrel held salted birds. To this inventory MacDonald (1827, 25) adds wooden stools and MacKenzie (1911, 19–20) a wooden chest or two, a straw tub and a few old barrels. There would also be a quern, a hollow stone used as a lamp, or an iron cruisgean, with a cinder of peat for a wick and fulmar oil to burn, a few wooden dishes, a cragan or pot made of poorly fired clay, a water pitcher, a rope, a spinning wheel and a loom. The looms were probably only used in the winter, as they were later in the century, and may well have been put up in outhouses, as they are in Lewis today. The descriptions of the houses before 1838 indicate that there would scarcely have been space to put up and use a loom in winter (pp 176–8).

When the MacKenzies went to a wedding feast they were given a chest to sit on, but the other diners sat on the ground before a table of planks (MacLean 1838, 18). The MacKenzies were given plates but the rest had wooden dishes made by nailing small boards together.

When the new thatched houses were built in the late 1830s, MacKenzie went to the mainland in 1838 and with the money given by Sir Thomas Dyke Acland, augmented by kind friends, he was able to return with '47 bedsteads, making two bedsteads for every house paying rent, and one for each of the poor widows; also 24 chairs, 21 stools, 21 tables, 21 dressers, 21 glass windows, pieces of delf-ware, etc.' (MacLean, 1838, 45). Wilson (1842, 13–14, 36) saw some of these: 'Each house has one or more bedsteads, with a small supply of blankets, a little dresser, a seat or two with wooden legs, and a few kitchen articles' and he also refers to box beds. In contrast, MacGillivray (1842, 55), who may have been accustomed to better things, speaks disparagingly of 'a few articles of the rudest furniture; some agricultural implements, a quern, bundles of ropes…and long strings of the gullets of the Solan goose, filled with fulmar oil, stretched from wall to wall.' Thomas's (1868, 155, 159) plans of two thatched houses showing the disposition of furniture (figure 68) suggest however that MacGillivray's experience was not typical.

By modern standards, these houses would be considered cramped, some of them providing a home for at least half a dozen people, besides the cow in her own portion, but they would probably be fairly warm.

More spacious houses were built in 1861/2, and most of the thatched houses were then used only as byres and barns, though some continued as

Figure 68. *Interior arrangement of 19th century houses*

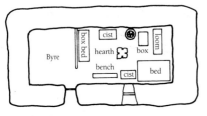

Thatched house K: Malcolm
MacDonald and Betty Scott
after Thomas 1868

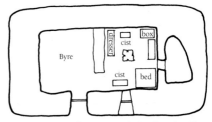

Thatched house with bed in wall
(crub-) after Thomas 1868

0   5   10   15   20   25   30 feet

0   5   9 m

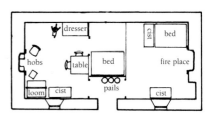

House as in 1920s After Atkinson
1938, MacDonald 1988

homes, the last one being that inhabited by Rachel MacCrimmon until her death in 1914. Some of the furniture was replaced: in 1863/4 purchases from the Kelsall Fund include 18 beds, 16 fir and oak tables, and 36 forms or stools (RHASS papers). In 1877 MacDiarmid (1877, 12, 15) recorded that:

Figure 69. *Examples of furniture*

scale 1:40

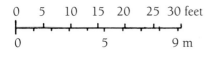

The interior of each house is divided into two apartments by a wooden partition, and in some a bed-closet is opposite the entrance door. Every house I entered contained a fair assortment of domestic utensils and furniture – kitchen dresser, with plates, bowls, etc, pots, kettles, pans, etc, wooden beds, chairs, seats, tables, tin lamps, etc.

Figure 70. *Examples of bed ends in NTS collection*

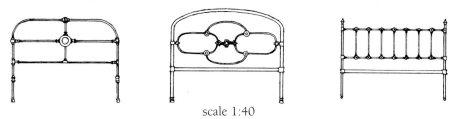

scale 1:40

Many of the kitchen utensils must have been those provided in 1860: Otter (RHASS papers) lists: 18 teapots, 72 tea spoons, 48 tinned table spoons, 48 tin jugs in two different sizes, 24 tin plates in two different sizes, 18 pots and covers, 18 tea kettles, 12 wooden plates, 12 wooden ladles, 30 horn spoons, 2 tall crocks, 22 other crocks of various sizes, 72 handled mugs, 24 brown plates, 36 bowls, 72 breakfast cups and saucers, and 24 black crocks. The total number of islanders in 1861 was 77 in 19 separate households, three of these having single occupants, so nearly everyone was provided for.

Smith (1879, 35–6) noted that the roof was boarded, the pine sarking providing a base for the zinc sheets, but there seem to have been no ceilings below this, as he saw ropes and fishing tackle stored overhead on the rafters. Sands (1877a, 40–41) also mentions the ropes, and bundles of gannet stomachs hanging from the rafters. He says that each house contained two chairs, but few had a table and each family sat around the pot while eating.

Figure 71. *Examples of household crockery*

scale 1:10

169

Stools were made out of straw ropes. Every woman had a chest in which she stored her clothes. Sands and MacDiarmid agree that there was at least one spinning wheel and a loom in every house. Clearly the beds had solid bases, as Sands says that loose straw was used as a mattress, the people having plenty of blankets. Ross (1890, 17–19) comments on the failure to use feathers for a mattress or even for pillows, but this is not uncommon when a product is marketable and may contribute towards income. Sands had an iron lamp in which he burned fulmar oil, but MacDiarmid mentions candles made of sheep tallow. Fulmar oil was still used for lighting late in the nineteenth century, but by the 1920s paraffin lamps were usual, though fulmar oil was still used if this ran out (Cameron 1973, 32, 39).

Both the 1830s houses and the 1861/2 houses had clay floors (Emery 1988, 9; 1990, 19; 1991, 18; McNeill 1886, 9). Ross heard one man express a wish to put in a wooden floor at one end of his house, but others impressed upon him the folly of this plan. Ross mentions box beds and indicates that furniture was sparse, but in describing a sketch he made of a house interior (1890, 132–3), though he lists little furniture, he notes that there is not much 'moving room' in a house and adds 'One can never go wrong in planting a few dogs in every possible corner'.

In the late 1890s several people were lining or part lining their houses: there are orders for 'deals' and 'spars' from the occupants of houses 1, 4, 5, 6 and 7 (MacKenzie ms) and in 1900 further supplies of 'lining boards' and battens were sent out (MM 2.632/3). Today the shells of the houses still provide some evidence of improvements: almost every house but No. 6 has a concrete floor to the lobby area. Seven out of eleven have a concrete floor (part timber in one case) in the west room, which was the living room. Some houses still have areas of plaster on the inner walls and occasionally these bear traces of paint. Atkinson's pictures (S. 262–5, 288, 292–2, 322, 741) show that by 1930 some rooms had plastered walls while some were lined; sometimes both finishes were used in one room, and some rooms were papered. Some rooms had timber floors and most fireplaces had a timber surround.

Atkinson's pictures also give an indication of the position of furniture, and these, together with Lachlan MacDonald's description (1988, 117–8) are the basis of the generalised plan in figure 68.

Remains of iron saucepans, girdles, and kettles, and a quantity of broken crockery, including many fragments of teapots and stoneware preserve jars (figure 71), are now in the collection of the National Trust for Scotland. There are two bone scoops in other collections (figure 73) made from a gannet's breastbone and the lower jaw of a large Pilot Whale. Both bones have been altered by cutting or sawing to make a more useful shape.

Figure 72. *Two bone scoops*

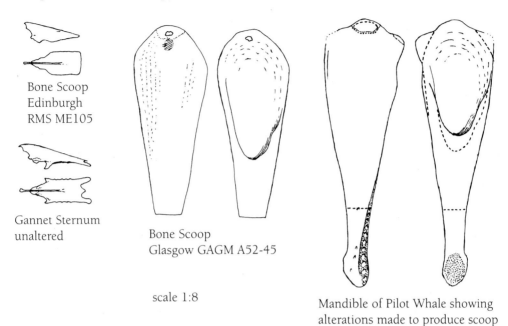

Bone Scoop
Edinburgh
RMS ME105

Gannet Sternum
unaltered

Bone Scoop
Glasgow GAGM A52-45

scale 1:8

Mandible of Pilot Whale showing
alterations made to produce scoop

Cooking and Food

Moray (1678, 928) says "their food is only young fowls and eggs; their drink
whey and water". Martin (1753, 10, 19, 28, 31–6, 39–42, 51, 58–60) enlarges
on this: "Their ordinary food is barley, and some oatbread baked with water".
They also ate seabirds: puffin, guillemot, fulmar and gannet are mentioned,
preserved by drying, without salt, and kept for up to a year; gannets were split
down the back. Fulmar was preferred above all others, both adult and young,
which was 'all fat'. Birds were roasted or boiled. *Giben*, or the fat from birds,
was kept in a gannet stomach and eaten with porridge and as a sauce on other
foods. The eggs of puffin, guillemot, razorbill and gannet were taken, and
were eaten fresh, from the nest, and also preserved in layers in peat ash in
cleitean, for any time up to eight months, by which time the St Kildans might
enjoy them but others found them unappetising. Guillemot eggs were most
highly esteemed. Sometimes raw gannet eggs were drunk, as beneficial for the
lungs and voice. Some fish were caught from the rocks. Although rent was
paid in dried mutton, Martin says that both mutton and beef were eaten fresh.
Few vegetables were eaten: roots of dock and silver weed, boiled scurvy grass
and boiled seaweed: dulse (Rhodymenia palmata) and *slake* or laver
(Porphyra sp); all eaten with giben, as was the fish. The constant use of giben
with their food made it less useful as a medicine. Ashes of seaweed were used
in preserving cheese, giving it a black colour.

There was no set time for meals, which were taken as appetite and work dictated.

By 1758 (MacAulay 1764, 38) cabbages and potatoes had been added to the diet. Buchanan (1793, 129) provides a list of what was in season at different times of the year: guillemot and gannet in late winter and spring, then puffins and a variety of eggs; in late summer fulmar and guga (young gannet), and in winter bread, mutton, potatoes and dried birds. His list, and his suggestion that they had more than they could eat, is contradicted by Clarke (1824, 269–273) who makes the point that all the agricultural produce was taken by the tacksman leaving the people a poor diet of seabirds, eggs, fish and slake. Of these they made two meals a day: dinner at noon; a stew of fulmar and slake, and supper at nine. No salt was used. By 1815 (MacCulloch 1824, 185–6), under a more benevolent proprietor, the people were able to enjoy their own produce again, and MacKenzie (1911, 14–16) says of the 1830s: "I know of no place where people can have such a plentiful supply of food with so little exertion". It consisted of barley, oats and potatoes, fresh birds and eggs in season, and each family had in store two or three barrels of young fulmar and a barrel or a barrel and a half of gugas. At the beginning of winter each family killed a cow, and at intervals thereafter twelve sheep; part was eaten fresh and the remainder salted. This gave each family about six pounds of animal food daily until seabirds again became available. Besides all this there was milk and cheese. Scurvy grass, sorrel and seaweed were used in small quantities. Despite his statement about the abundance of food, MacKenzie had recorded a great scarcity in the winter of 1840/41 and in the following summer (Wilson 1842, 78).

MacKenzie says that the food was very badly cooked. On special occasions the men took over. Some were better cooks than others; one method of cooking meat requiring considerable attention but producing excellent results when well done was hide cooking; the flesh was packed in a raw hide and buried in hot ashes in a large peat fire to bake. A feast consisted of well cooked meat, barley bread and cheese, and if a little whisky were available 'it was perfection'. Burt (1745, II 271–2), writing early in the eighteenth century, had been told that in some of the islands poor people boiled their beef in the hide or with hot stones in a wooden vessel; possibly baking in the hide is a variant of this old method.

Tea was introduced in 1833 (Ross, 1890, 23) but was not in common use until late in the nineteenth century.

MacGillivray (1842, 62) enjoyed a meal consisting of 'fulmar, auk, guillemot, one of each, boiled; two puffins, roasted; barley cakes, ewe-cheese, and milk; and by way of dessert, raw dulse and roasted limpets'.

Puffins were boiled (Wilson 1842, 14), sometimes in the breakfast porridge (Seton, 1878, 103) and split dried puffins were propped before the fire and roasted (Wiglesworth 1903, 20). Giben, still in use in the nineteenth century, is stated by some to have been fat from fulmar, and others, fat from gannets; the thick deposits of fat on the young of both birds was melted and kept in the stomach or crop of adult gannets (MacGillivray 1842, 62; Morgan 1862, 177).

Sands (1878, 33, 39) adds a few cabbages and turnips to the list of vegetables eaten. The people rarely ate fish, believing it caused pimples. They were very partial to sugar but not tea. The three apples which Sands took out were the first the people had seen. By 1877 (MacDiarmid 1878, 20) three meals a day was usual: porridge and milk for breakfast, potatoes and fulmar or mutton for dinner, or occasionally fish, and if there were enough meal, porridge for supper. Milk was scarce at times, usually in spring, before the cows calved. Very little butter was made, both cows' and ewes' milk being used for cheese, which sold better. Connell (1887, 69) adds that sometimes fulmar was eaten at breakfast, being boiled in the porridge. For supper there was tea, and bread and cheese, sometimes fulmar or porridge. Breakfast was taken between 9 and 10, dinner about 4, sometimes later in summer or as late as 11 in winter when they were spinning and weaving late. Cow's milk was the usual drink at meal times, the sheep's milk being reserved for cheese (Elliott 1895, 116).

According to Martin (1753, 53) there was one corn drying kiln, used in turns allocated by lot. Buchan (1727, 19–20) gives more detail about the preparation of grain: it might be kiln dried or dried by 'graddaning', in which the straw of unthreshed oats was burnt, thus drying the grain. Hand mills or querns 'about 2 feet in diameter' were used for making meal; these were put on a piece of cloth or straw matting, or a sheepskin, on the ground. The person milling sat with the quern between his or her legs, and while turning the upper stone fed the grain into the hole in its centre, and the meal trickled out from between the stones onto the mat. 'Every family that is able, provides a pair, and the proper [poorer] sort borrow'. MacCulloch (1824, 185–189) noted that turning the quern was woman's work; it took nearly all day to grind enough to supply a family. He said it was then rarely used elsewhere, as people used water power to turn small horizontal mills. In the 1830s (MacKenzie 1911, 9–10) the grain for food was still dried in the single kiln, each family taking turns. The sheaves were dried and the grain then winnowed. As in keeping it absorbed more moisture, before grinding it was parched again by stirring it with a hot stone in a straw tub. Graddaning was used at harvest time to produce supper for all those helping the family.

Wilson (1842, 38) visited the kiln, a dark building with one 'apartment

…within and of considerably higher level than the other'; the flue ran from the corner of the lower floor under the floor of the kiln platform. The dried grain was threshed on the lower floor. This was almost certainly building W (figure 73). The line of the flue running into the kiln platform at the upper end of the building is visible. After the kiln fell into disuse the upper half of the building was plundered for stone and the lower half turned into a small dwelling by inserting a cross wall. The low level opening opposite the door to create a draught for winnowing was blocked. Excavations in 1989 (Emery 1990, 19–21) proved that the interpretation of this building as a kiln by comparison with other examples in Harris and Uist was correct.

Figure 73. *Building W – kiln and later dwelling, plan and section*

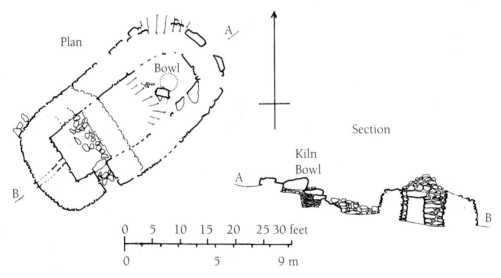

Smith (1879, 35) noted in 1873 that barley was ground with a pestle made of a lump of wood with nails in it, in a stone mortar, but by 1896 (Kearton 1897, 52–3) these were no longer in use. After grinding a sieve of sheepskin was used to separate the meal from the husk (Sands 1877a, 99) (figure 74). The querns were still in use in the 1880s (Connell 1887, 50), though more oatmeal and flour were being imported. J T Mackenzie told Kearton (1897, 9) that each person consumed an average of about 120lb of flour and oatmeal a year, which he considered was 28% more than the ordinary Hebridean crofter.

Monro (1961, 78) learned in 1549, from the Steward, that he used to take malt with him and mash it on the island, but the inhabitants, attracted by the sweet taste of the mash, had consumed all of it, and all, men, women and children, had been incapably drunk. Obviously there was no tradition of brewing on the island at the time. Martin (1753, 58–9) says that 'they brew ale but rarely, using the juice of nettle-roots, which they put in a dish with a little barley-meal dough'; this fermented and made a good ale. By 1799 (Campbell f51) this ale was no longer made, and Campbell's statement that many of the people had never tasted spirits is probably more reliable than Brougham's (1871, I 105) assertion that they had an 'excessive eagerness for them'. MacKenzie implies that rarely whisky might be drunk at feasts, though MacLean (1838, 43) records that the dram he gave to his boatmen was their first taste of whisky. Later, there is general agreement (Sands 1877a, 39; Ross 1890, 38; Kearton 1897, 35) that though most households possessed a bottle of spirits, it was rarely opened, except for medicinal purposes or special occasions, and that drunkenness was unknown.

Figure 74. *Various household items*

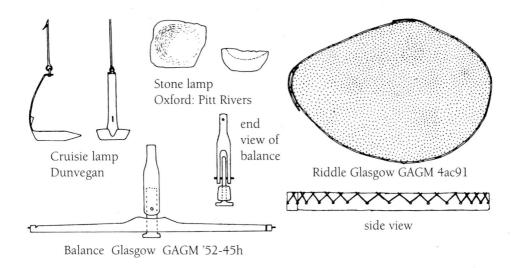

Stone lamp
Oxford: Pitt Rivers

Cruisie lamp
Dunvegan

end
view of
balance

Riddle Glasgow GAGM 4ac91

side view

Balance Glasgow GAGM '52-45h

Housekeeping

The accumulation of midden material inside the houses before the late 1830s has already been described. Wilson (1842, 71) records that dogs, in scavenging bird remains, helped to clear garbage. Although subsequently refuse was kept in cleitean or pits, Milner's impression (1848, 2057) was that most of the houses were very dark and dirty and in 1851 the Registrar General described them as 'dirtier than the dens of wild animals'. Things were no better in the new mortared house of 1861/2. Acheson (MacNeill 1886, 9) and Ross (1890, 17–18, 74) note that they were very dirty, and Ross suggested that 'it would not take long to scrub up everything they possess but they never think of such a thing'. Elsewhere he admits that when doing his own housekeeping he found it difficult to keep the washing up under control. Most of those who remarked on the dirtiness of the houses had probably not considered the labour involved in carrying water for washing and scrubbing and the problem of trying to keep damp at bay in an earthfloored house with inadequate supplies of poor fuel. A trawlerman's children who had a 'trip' to St Kilda in the 1920s on their father's boat stayed overnight with one of the Gillies families and found the bedding 'spotless' (Mitchell 1990, 46). Smith (1879, 33) asks, 'Who can avoid dust with turf fires in the midst of Atlantic winds?'. Sands (1877, 14) and Ross (1889, 18) refer to the use of gannet wings as hearth brushes.

MacLean (1836, 16) makes it clear that human urine contributed to the midden in the pre-1830s houses. After the 1830s in common with most of the houses built in the Hebrides before 1900 and many thereafter, there was no provision of toilets, and most people must have relieved themselves out of doors or in the byre. As in many areas (MacDonald 1982, 21) urine was collected in a large tub in an outhouse in preparation for waulking cloth. In the Western Isles in the 1970s houses with no services other than a cold water tap were not uncommon. For comparison, it is worth noting that, for instance, in the mid 1970s in rural Nottinghamshire there were enough houses with chemical toilets for the County Council to continue a weekly collection of sewage by tanker.

Wool Processing

Cameron (1973, 39) gives a detailed description of wool processing in the 1920s.

The wool was cleaned: men and children picked out pieces of vegetation and lumps, and then worked oil into it to make it easier to handle. The teased wool was carded. About midwinter, most households had a carding party, when a number of people gathered to work together at a first carding. After this the wool was carded a second time, and at this stage different colours would be blended, and the carded wool made into rolls ready for spinning. Most of the carding and spinning was done by the women but weaving was done by the men. Thread for the warp was spun with a tighter twist than the weft thread. The warp threads were wound on a frame so that the full length was ready for threading onto the loom. In winter the looms were brought down from the lofts and put together in the living room. In the spring some of the finished webs were 'waulked': after soaking in the urine tub a web was rhythmically thumped and pounded by a group of women, a short length at a time, until the whole piece was treated, then washed, dried, and rolled up. This shrank and thickened the cloth, raising the nap and making it narrower.

Figure 75. *Example of spinning wheel, Lachlan MacDonald collection*

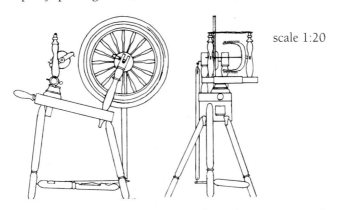

scale 1:20

The same processes must have been in use for a long time, without much variation, as they were in the rest of the Highlands and Islands. There is a general agreement that the wool was plucked from the sheep, a process less painful than it sounds if performed at the right time, when the fleece was about to be shed naturally. Distaffs and spindles were in use in 1697 (Martin 1753, 63) and cloth was finished by waulking on 'mats of hay twisted and woven together in small ropes'. When the arms were tired, the feet were used, and the work lightened by singing, one of the women acting as precentor; latterly singing was given up as too frivolous. Buchan (1727, 19–20) noted that there were two weavers. His wife introduced the use of knitting needles. In 1799 (Campbell 1799, f 58) spinning wheels were unknown, and there were only three looms, of 'the rudest kind' Campbell had ever seen. By the 1830s, spinning wheels had been introduced (MacKenzie 1911, 11–12, 32) and were used in winter evenings, but much of the spinning was still done in the summer using the distaff and spindle, on the way to or from Gleann Mór or when getting turf. The men made their own looms, except for the reed, which was imported. The women also knitted. In 1831 (Atkinson 1831, 31) each man did his own weaving so either they shared looms or there must have been more than three looms. In 1873 Rachel MacCrimmon gave Smith (1879, 33–4) and his friends a demonstration of the use of distaff and spindle; they were impressed by the skill and speed with which she produced the thread. There were thirty six spinning wheels on the island at that time. Sands (1878, 190; 1877a, 62, 101, 109) found that an important distinction was made in spinning; the wheel was used for thread for weaving and knitting, but thread for sewing was spun using the distaff and spindle. He collected examples of the latter, noting that a fragment of sheepskin from a sieve was wound round the distaff. All the woven cloth was twilled, using four headles and treadles on the loom. The women started spinning in the October evenings and in early

December the men started weaving: in winter both men and women worked from dawn (about 8.30 am at midwinter) until 1 or 2 am the following morning. The cloth had a peculiar and strong smell, partly derived from the smell of peat.

Connell (1887, 70–1) remarks that the looms were entirely home made; a goose quill was used for a spindle and a dock stalk for a bobbin. The men were weaving for two months, to the exclusion of almost all else, often sleeping in their clothes.

MacLachlan, over her three years' stay (9.1906 to 5.1909), records carding and spinning going on all autumn from September. 'Carding parties' took place mostly in January, though a few people were still having their 'big cardings' in March. Thread was spun specifically for warp and weft, and the warp thread was spun first. Men were setting up their looms, in 1907 and 1908, from mid February to early March, but in 1909, a month earlier. In 1908 waulking started on April 16th, and took place in a different house every week day until it was finished on May 2nd; in 1909 it started on April 26th and went on every weekday. Lachlan MacDonald (pers comm) said that not all cloth was waulked, and that waulkings followed one another in quick succession partly because the participants' clothing was splashed with the mixture of urine and soap; once all the waulkings were over everyone washed their clothes.

Figure 76. *Implements used in spinning and weaving*

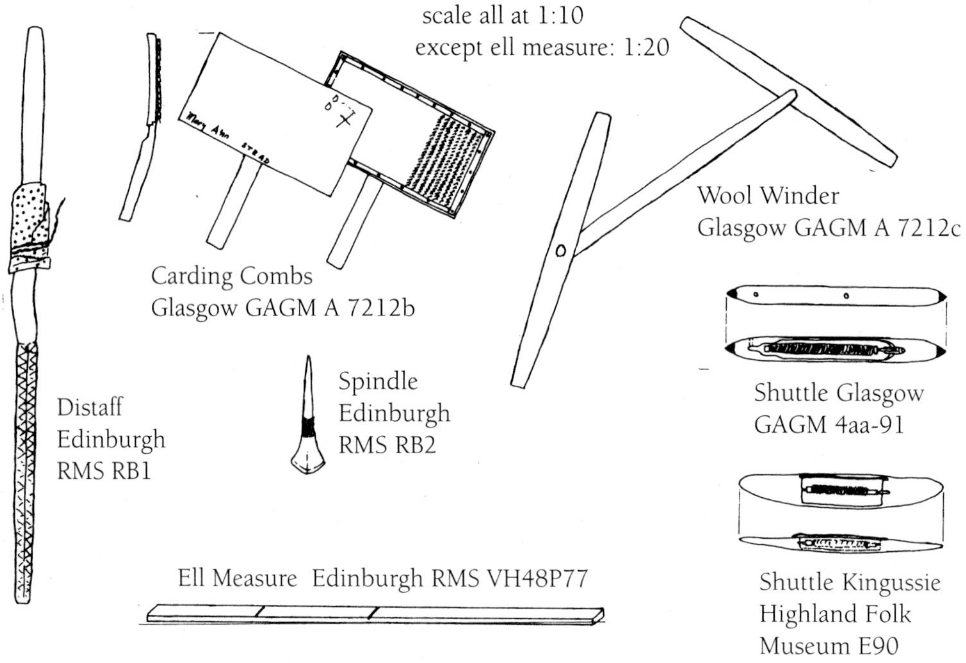

scale all at 1:10
except ell measure: 1:20

Carding Combs
Glasgow GAGM A 7212b

Wool Winder
Glasgow GAGM A 7212c

Shuttle Glasgow
GAGM 4aa-91

Distaff
Edinburgh
RMS RB1

Spindle
Edinburgh
RMS RB2

Ell Measure Edinburgh RMS VH48P77

Shuttle Kingussie
Highland Folk
Museum E90

Plate 28.   *'Parliament' outside House 5 (A M Cockburn 1927: School of Scottish Studies collection)*

Plate 29.   *Bedroom in No. 3 (R L Atkinson 1938: School of Scottish Studies collection)*

Plate 30. *'Parliament' outside House 9 (N MacLeod 1886: reproduced with permission from
the George Washington Wilson Collection, Aberdeen University Library:
Ref C7107)*

Plate 31. *Women and children outside house (N MacLeod 1886: reproduced with
permission from Glasgow Museums and Art Gallery)*

Plate 32. *Example of blanketing in Highland Folk Museum, Kingussie*

Plate 33. *Plaid and three brooches in Highland Folk Museum, Kingussie*

Plate 34.   *Gannets on Boreray*

Plate 35.   *Eggs: centre – great auk; clockwise from top – gannet, guillemot, puffin, razorbill, fulmar; for comparison – domestic hen size 2 (Inverness Museum & Art Gallery Collection)*

Plate 36.   *Fowlers on Stac an Armin (N MacLeod 1886: reproduced with permission from the George Washington Wilson Collection, Aberdeen University Library: Ref C4252)*

Plate 37.   *Sharing fulmar below the Store (N MacLeod 1886: reproduced with permission from the George Washington Wilson Collection, Aberdeen University Library: Ref C7187)*

Plate 38.   *Norman MacQueen snaring fulmar (A MacDonald: School of Scottish Studies collection)*

Plate 39.   *Finlay MacQueen snaring puffins (R L Atkinson: School of Scottish Studies collection)*

Plate 40. *Church interior (R L Atkinson: School of Scottish Studies collection)*

Plate 41. *Schoolchildren and George Murray in 1886 (N MacLeod 1886: reproduced with permission from the George Washington Wilson Collection, Aberdeen University Library: Ref C4251)*

Plate 42. *School interior (R L Atkinson: School of Scottish Studies collection)*

Plate 43.   *Schoolchildren in 1907 (R C MacLeod of MacLeod: School of Scottish Studies collection)*

Plate 44.   *Mingulay: village from the north*

Plate 45.   *Mingulay: village, arable and grazing from the north-east*

Plate 46.   Mingulay: Skipisdale, the shieling area, from the north

Plate 47.   *Shiant Isles: house, old settlement behind, from the north (R L Atkinson: School of Scottish Studies collection)*

Plate 48. *North Rona: village from the north (R L Atkinson: School of Scottish Studies collection)*

Plate 49.   *North Rona: loading sheep into the dinghy, 1936 (R L Atkinson: School of*
            Scottish Studies collection)

Plate 50.   *Bothy on Sula Sgeir*

Plate 51.   *Fowlers returned from Sula Sgeir selling gugas*

Plate 52.   Flannan Isles: fowlers' bothy (R L Atkinson: School of Scottish Studies
            collection)

Table 7
Wool Processing Tools in Various Collections

Implement	Collected	Notes	Location
Carders		Used by Mrs Ferguson	GAGM A 7212b
Distaff	1876		RMS RB 1
Spindle	1876		RMS RB 2
Spinning wheel	c.1912		RMS RC 37
Spinning wheel		Used by Mrs Ferguson	GAGM A 7212a
Spinning wheel		Reputedly oldest in 1930	GAGM '30–51
Spinning wheel		Muckle wheel ?Gillies's	GAGM A 806
Spinning wheel		Mrs MacLachlan's. Bought new 1908, from factor	NTS coll.
Spinning wheel		Used by Mrs MacQueen	Private
Spinning wheel			Private
Wool winder			RMS RD 19
Wool winder		Used by Mrs Ferguson	GAGM 7212d
Wool winder		Used by Mrs Ferguson	GAGM 7212e
Wool winder			CEUT
Hank Unwinder		Used by Mrs Ferguson	GAGM A 7212f&g
Shuttle		? home made	GAGM 4aa–91
Shuttle		? home made	GAGM A 7641b
Shuttle		Factory made	HFM E 90
Bobbin		Dock stalk	HFM E 80
Loom			NMS
Loom Parts		Several shaped parts	NTS coll.
Ellwand	1927		NMS VH 48

RMS: Edinburgh, Royal Museum of Scotland, GAGM: Glasgow Museums and Art Galleries,
HFM: Kingussie, Highland Folk Museum
CEUT: North Uist Historical Society

Martin (1753, 17, 50–1) gives white and philamort or brown as natural wool colours; small quantities of wool must have been dyed blue, as the Steward's wife gave to the Ground Officer's wife an ounce of indigo. MacAulay (1764, 213) mentions black, white, grey and brown as the natural wool colours available, yellow being the only dye used. Campbell (1799, f 58) adds red got from boiling a lichen. Possibly yellow and red are different perceptions of the colour derived from crotal. MacCulloch (1824, 179) speaks of the people's clothing as dingy brown or blue, and Atkinson (1831, 217–8) refers to it as blue. MacKenzie (1911, 11) implies that brown wool was dyed, the white wool being kept for use as it was. When Sands (1876–8, 191) stayed, lichen and indigo were still the only dyes used. Indigo was still being imported in the 1910s (MM 2.632/4, 2.632/7) and Lachlan MacDonald remembers it being used. Mrs Gillies collected crotal during her summer stay in 1938 (Atkinson, 1949, 259).

Examples of the tools used in spinning and weaving and of their products exist in various collections (tables 7–8, figures 76, 77).

Figure 77. *Wooden loom*

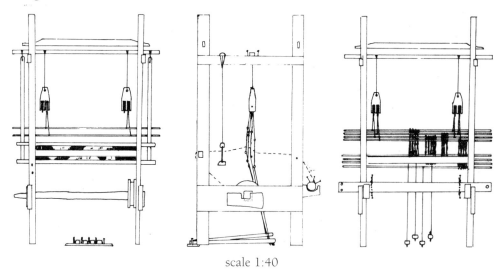

scale 1:40

Almost all of the cloth is woven in a 2 x 2 twill. The width for tweed was generally the same as the standard width for Harris tweed: 27" or a little more. The warp in the known examples is almost always white, and the weft threads often have some dark brown hairs or strands of wool in them (plate 32). Plaids were the same width or a little less, and in most of these the blue or green threads forming part of the check are only in the warp. Plaids were double thickness: some made from a single length of cloth doubled and sewn along one or both selvedges, some from two pieces joined at the edges (plate 33). Blanketing was probably narrower because it was waulked. All known pieces have a border of stripes, generally brown, along one edge. A blanket was made from two lengths sewn together along the plain selvedge. Two examples are double length. Lachlan MacDonald's is of uneven width and has bands which are of a looser weave than the rest, showing that more than one person was working on it.

Leather Processing

Martin (1753, 56) says that leather was tanned with tormentil roots, and MacAulay (1764, 214) gives a recipe. The prepared skin was left for two nights in

Table 8
Pieces of Woven Woollen Fabric in Various Collections
(all 2 x 2 twill unless noted)

Made	Coll.	Width (ins.)	warp	weft	Colour of weft (all warps white unless noted)	Location
	1887		21	20	grey, pale brown, brown flecks	GAGM 87–52
1930	1930	27	18	19	grey, some brown/black threads	NMS NA 517
1925		28½	20	21	pale grey, dark brown and ginger flecks	HFM 38.1959
		29	20	21	medium grey, many brown hairs	HFM no no.
c.1890	1929		22	19	brownish grey (stained?)	NMS NA 508
1930	1930	27½	18	19	reddish brown, dark flecks	NMS NA 518
c.1930		29	18	19	medium brown, brown flecks	WHM 1592
	1880	27	20	18	uneven brown, whitish, dark brown flecks	GAGM 80–65a
			18	18	grey, tinge of green -?age (made into coat – ?mid 1930s)	NTS coll.
		26½			warp and weft very dark blue or black; surface has 'nap'	Private

Blanketing		Width	warp	weft	Length	No. & colour stripes (all thin/thick/thin)	Location
	1984	24–26	25	20	68"	3 brown part reverse twill	GAGM A 8412
1929	1989	25	28	20	150"	3 brown part reverse twill	HFM 1:1989
		23–25	28	19	132"	2 brown, 1 black & brown	Private
		24–25	20	18	64"	3 brown	NTS coll

Plaids		Length	warp	weft		Colours	Location
	1886	27	25	22	125"	folded black, red, blue	GAGM 86-54a
	1972	26½	28	26	120"	folded black, red, green	GAGM A7212-h
		25½	26	22	120"	folded black, red, green	NTS coll
		26	26	23	61"	twice black, red, blue/green	Private
pre 1954		26	28	26	63"	twice black, red, blue/green well worn, patched	HFM J19

Bedspread, formerly skirt

		Width	warp	weft			Location
		30½	22	15		4 pieces 35½ long, sewn to make rectangle. Warp: vermilion cotton yarn Weft: black wool yarn	Private

Fragments, now parts of puffin snares

Made	Coll.						Location
	1972					Now brown. Plain weave, not twill	NMS R177
1927/8?						Black coarse woven cloth	HFM FF85
	1889					? faded plaid. Plain weave, grey/green with 3 buff/brown threads at 1" intervals	Oxford PittRivers

Table 8 (continued)
Pieces of Woven Woollen Fabric in Various Collections

Wool Samples
Small tufts of wool in various colours: grey, dark brown, reddish brown, black and dark blue grey
GAGM A7212c

Sheepskin Hats
Glasgow Museums and Art Galleries have four sheepskin hats, all made in the same way. A strip of skin about 26" by 10" is sewn together at the ends to form a cylinder, woolly side out. One edge is tightly gathered to form the crown, which is almost flat. The other edge is turned in to make an inner woolly band.
GAGM 90–52d; 04ad–91; 4am–94; 4ao–94

RMS: Edinburgh, Royal Museum of Scotland, GAGM: Glasgow Museums and Art Galleries, HFM: Kingussie, Highland Folk Museum, WHM: Fort William, West Highland Museum

a warm infusion of tormentil bark, and then was left, with bruised tormentil root, in a hollow of a rock below high tide mark, until sufficiently tanned. Tormentil, which is very widespread, (p 13) seems to have been used for this purpose until late in the nineteenth century: Sands (1878, 191) sent a sample of sheepskin tanned locally to the National Museum of Antiquities of Scotland.

Clothing
Martin (1753, 9, 50, 56–7) learned in 1697 that within living memory the people had been clad in sheep skins, but when he visited both sexes wore a coarse flannel shirt; over this the men wore a short sleeved waistcoat and a 'double plait of plad': a piece of cloth folded and wound round the body, reaching to the knees; the ends were pinned with a fulmar bone, and the folded cloth held in place by a leather belt. On their heads they wore pointed caps, or bonnets on Sundays. Breeches 'made wide and open at the knees' had lately been introduced. Cloth stockings were worn. The women wore a plaid over the shoulders, fastened at the breast by a large circular brass brooch. On their heads they wore a linen triangle like a head scarf, a long lock of hair being allowed to hang on either side of the face. In the summer they wore no stockings. Shoes were only worn in winter and were made from the skin of gannet necks, which, sewn across at the breast end, fitted the foot nicely, the crown of the head making the heel. They were worn with the feathers inside or out and lasted only a few days, but there was an ample supply. For work on slippery rocks, socks made of old rags pinned together with feathers were worn. Both the Steward and his wife, when they left the island, gave the Ground Officer and his wife their bonnet and kerchief respectively. Formerly the Steward's wife had dressed like the St Kildan women, with a brooch of

silver fastening her plaid, but she no longer used it.

Buchan (1727, 20) says that sometimes the Steward brought a tailor who might be employed by those who could afford it, but later authors agree that all garments were made by the men. According to MacAulay (1764, 214) a very little coarse linen was made, and used for shirts for special ocasions. By the end of the eighteenth century (Clarke 1824, 272, Campbell 1799, f 42–45) the men had adopted trousers, but the women's dress sounds unchanged, apart from the addition of petticoats. The linen kerchief was worn only by married women, young girls going bare-headed, their hair pinned or tied in a knot on the crown of the head. Most of the woollen cloth was 'striped' – probably *drogaid*. Clarke (1824, 272) mentions sheep skin caps, and both he and MacCulloch (1819, 230) comment that the St Kildans were better dressed than some of their neighbours in the Hebrides and Highlands.

Figure 78. *Brooches in different collections*

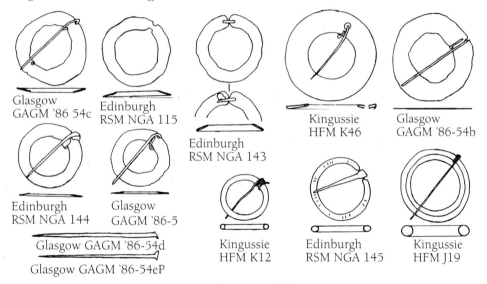

Glasgow
GAGM '86 54c

Edinburgh
RSM NGA 115

Edinburgh
RSM NGA 143

Kingussie
HFM K46

Glasgow
GAGM '86-54b

Edinburgh
RSM NGA 144

Glasgow
GAGM '86-5

Glasgow GAGM '86-54d

Glasgow GAGM '86-54eP

Kingussie
HFM K12

Edinburgh
RSM NGA 145

Kingussie
HFM J19

scale approx 1:3

In the 1830s (MacKenzie 1911, 12–14) womens' shirts and coats, and men's underclothes were made from white cloth. The men were dressed as their neighbours in Harris, but the women's clothes were made after the old patterns: a simple sleeved shift, covered by a gown with sleeves and a plain wide skirt. This was worn with two girdles, one above the breast and the other around the waist; most of the time this dress was worn with a foot or two of the skirt drawn up and folded over the waist girdle, so that the skirt came to the knees, but in church and on other occasions they took off the waist girdle and wore the skirt full length. 'As ordinarily worn', says Neil

MacKenzie,'this dress makes them look like large insects'. The coat was worn over this in cold or wet weather. Some wore a plaid over the shoulders with a brooch. Few people had more than one of any type of garment, so they were rarely washed, and not everyone had new clothes each year, some replacing a shirt or coat alternately. Children were dressed in smaller versions of the women's clothes. Shoes were made of cattle hide sewn with thongs of sheepskin. Cotton for men's shirts, buttons, red cravats for the men and caps for the women were imported. In the late 1830s, MacPherson MacLeod and his wife visited the island; she gave each of the women a shawl (Wilson, 1842, 37).

MacLean (1838, 41, 48) describes the men's clothing: a white woollen shirt, with a sleeved waistcoat and wide legged trousers. The waistcoats were all in tatters at the back due to the men's habit of leaning against walls. He also refers to sheepskin caps.

Morgan (1861, 105) mentions the 'bright dresses of the women and children' which suggests that lighter colours were in use. According to Baillie (1875, 255–7) Isabella Munro (p 131) made the women's dresses, which were simple garments. The women wore red or blue kerchiefs on their heads. MacDiarmid (1878, 6, 24) records the importing of bonnets, caps, cravats, coloured cotton kerchiefs, and Rob Roy plaids. Leather for shoes was also imported, at different prices for uppers and soles. Sands (1878, 191) noted that the women's gowns seemed old-fashioned. The bodice was fastened in front with a large pin made from a fish hook, and the plaid by a brooch made from an old penny. Formerly the bill of an oystercatcher had been used for both garments. Not long before his visit, a shoe made without welts had been in general use, and caps made of lambskin were fashionable, but he saw only one of these. In warm weather both men and women worked clad only in their shirts or shifts. Baillie noted in August 1874 that the men just returned from a fowling expedition were 'scantily clad' and the women helping to haul up the boat as the yacht was leaving were wearing shorter skirts than when the visitors were ashore. Examples of brooches collected in the nineteenth century (table 9) are shown in plates 32 and 33.

Acheson (McNeill 1886, 9) recorded that one day in mid September when the thermometer was 68°F in the shade, he 'found a healthy adult male, wearing a thick tweed waistcoat, with flannel back and sleeves, two thick flannel undervests, a flannel shirt, tweed trousers, flannel drawers, boots and stockings, Tam o'Shanter cap and a thick scarlet worsted muffler around his neck'.

Wilson's photographs (1886; plates 30, 31) show many of the features already mentioned. There are men dressed in white or pale shirts with darker waistcoats; these have pale backs; pockets and buttons at the front. One man has a striped waistcoat. The trousers are dark and baggy, with pockets, and some wear the legs rolled up a little. Some wear shoes and some are barefoot. A group of women and children sitting outside a house shows the 'mutch' visible in front of the kerchief. The dresses are plain. Two checked plaids are displayed on the wall behind the group. The picture of the schoolchildren shows, in front, the three youngest, all boys of 5 and 6, in long skirts and short hair (Plate 41). Some of the older boys have paler trousers than the men; their headgear is different, and they are wearing jackets. Some of the girls' dresses are striped, but they are all dark, and with pale scarfs around their necks the girls might almost be wearing uniform.

Elliott (1895a, 115) refers to blue dresses with thin red stripes, and red shawls.

Cameron's memories of the 1920s (1973, 42) and photographs taken in the late 1920s and in 1930 suggest that there was not a great deal of change in clothing in the intervening years. Women's hemlines crept up to mid calf level, and the skirts of the young girls nearer to the knee. Some wore print dresses and aprons, and there is more variety in the scarves. Some of the men had imported shirts and peaked caps replaced bonnets. More people were wearing shoes for more of the time, though none were worn while climbing and most of the children went barefoot in summer. In common with many other communities in the Highlands and Islands, the people bought clothes though catalogue companies such as J D Williams in Manchester (Lachlan MacDonald, pers comm).

Table 9
Brooches and Pins in Various Collections

All the brooches are annular except one: NMS NGA 143
All have one end of the pin curled round the brooch, except two: HFM K46 and HFM J19, in which the brooch is pierced, the pin passing through the thickness of the ring.

Material	Pin	Date collected	Museum
brass	brass	1877	RMS NGA 144
brass	brass	1877	RMS NGA 145
copper	wire	c.1880	GAGM 80 65b
brass	wire	c.1886	GAGM 86 54c
brass	missing	pre 1892	RMS NGA 115
brass	brass		HFM K46
copper tube	wire	c.1930?	HFM J19
brass	missing	1877	RMS NGA 143
iron	wire	c.1930?	HFM K12
zinc	wire	c.1886	GAGM 86 54b
Pins			
copper		c.1886	GAGM 86 54d
copper		c.1886	GAGM 86 54e

Glasgow Museums and Art Galleries also had on loan in 1894 five brooches, two of brass and one each of silver, copper and zinc, and five copper pins.

RMS: Edinburgh, Royal Museum of Scotland, GAGM: Glasgow Museums and Art Galleries, HFM: Kingussie, Highland Folk Museum

11
Pastoral and Arable Farming

Although seabirds provided a substantial proportion of the diet, the St
Kildans were also heavily dependant on both pastoral and arable
agriculture for food and for contributions to the rent. Table 10 shows the
agricultural calendar. Tables 11 and 12 show the records of crops mentioned
and stock present at different times, with numbers where given.

Table 10
Agricultural Calendar

Month	Cattle and Sheep		Arable
January	Occasional forays to Soay		
February	and Boreray for sheep,		
March	weather permitting		House floors and inner thatch to fields (C18)
April	Lambing		Manuring ground, sowing oats, Inner thatch to barley
May	Last year's lambs off Dun		fields (C19), potatoes
	Cattle & sheep to Glen Mor		Sheep dung on grass
June	Plucking sheep		
July	Occasional catching of sheep on		
August	Soay, cattle return from Glen Mor		Harvest barley
September	Lambs put on Dun.		Harvest barley and oats.
	Catching sheep		Haymaking
October	on islands at	Cattle within	Haymaking, lifting potatoes
	intervals	dyke	thatching
November	for	Rams taken	Lifting potatoes.
	slaughter	off Dun	Grass plucking
December			on cliffs
	Rams returned to Dun		for fodder

Dipping recorded: early September 1907 (MacLachlan)
          August 1920, August 1921 (SRO Ag and Fish 57/23)
          end June 1923 (SG 28.6.1923)

Sources: MacLeod c.1750; MacAulay 1764; Kennedy 1932, 109-122; MacKenzie 1911;
MacDiarmid 1877; Murray 1886-7; Connel 1887, 38; Sands 1878, 49, 76; Ross 1890;
Heathcote 1900; Wiglesworth 1903, 18; MacLachlan 1906–1909; Stornoway Gazette
14.6.1927

Pastoral Farming

The domestic stock recorded are cattle, sheep, horses, dogs, cats, and, for a short time, goats. Hens and ducks, and occasionally pigeons, were kept by some of the clergy and latterly some of the St Kildans. All but the sheep were restricted to Hirte: dogs were taken to other islands for sheep work and fowling. There is no record that pigs were ever kept. Pigs have been uncommon in the Western Isles generally in recent times (p 84; MacDonald 1811, 485).

Cattle

In 1697 the cattle were described as short, smaller than those in the Hebrides, but fat and yielding sweet beef; with black and white foreheads, they were easily seen from a distance. The cows were taken indoors during the winter: some may have been in separate byres as the houses were quite small, and some families had several beasts (the richest man had no more than eight cows). The cattle lost condition over the winter, and though it was usual to kill a cow or a sheep before an interment, this was postponed if the death occurred in spring, when the beast would be too thin (Martin 1753, 18–19, 57; 1716, 295).

In the early eighteenth century the cows gave little milk, the best one giving no more than two pints, but it is not clear if this were per day or at one milking session (Buchan 1727, 9). Probably after the smallpox epidemic some new stock was taken in, as in 1758 MacAulay (1764, 29–30; 123–6) says that the cows, feeding on the rich pastures of Gleann Mór during the summer, yielded more than ordinary quantities of milk, with what he regarded as a high cream content. The total cattle population was only just over 40, but as the Steward owned some and claimed the milk from all the rest, there was scarcely any advantage to the people in keeping them. The number owned by individuals varied, from seven or eight to none at all. They were 'generally red or speckled', 'quite small' and 'very pretty', though Clarke (1824, 282) says that the cows were larger than those he had seen in the Long Island. By this time the Steward was employing a dairy maid on the island to receive all the milk and make butter and cheese (Buchanan 1793, 136; Campbell 1799, 24)

MacKenzie (1911, 7, 14–15) gives only a little information about the cattle in the 1830s. They were kept in Gleann Mór all summer, partly to protect the crops. He implies that most families had two milking cows. Each family killed a cow at the beginning of winter, and made salt beef with what was not eaten fresh. In 1838 MacLean (1838, 44), saw a dozen or so cows in Gleann Mór, 'in excellent condition, and protected by a very fine bull'. Wilson (1842, 43) comments on the small size of the cattle and the fine quality of their milk. A reported tradition that bulls were exchanged annually between St Kilda and Heiskeir in the seventeenth century is probably unreliable (Fergusson et al 1978, 40; Blankenhorn 1979, 53–5; Thomson 1978, 8). In 1815 MacCulloch (1819, 29) specifically noted that no live cattle were exported because of the long sea crossing, but later a regular steamer service or the larger boat used by the factor probably helped to overcome this problem, as from 1871 to 1926 they appear annually as part of the rent payments (figure 50).

In 1877 MacDiarmaid (1878, 244) counted on the island one bull, 21 cows and 27 young cattle, including 12 which should have been sold the previous autumn. In May they were in very good condition, better than in many places on the mainland at the end of the winter. The bull was a brindled beast of the 'West Highland' breed, eight or nine years old, brought from Skye five or six years before, and his progeny were an improvement on the older stock. This was probably the bull purchased in 1869 for £15, paid for from the Kelsall fund (RHASS papers). The cows, MacDiarmaid said, were 'of a degenerate Highland breed, light and hardy-looking; mostly all black in colour'. The young cattle were red and black, some of them good beasts which might have fetched £5 on the mainland; he put an average value of about £3/15/- on the

Figure 79. *Plan of the Bull's House*

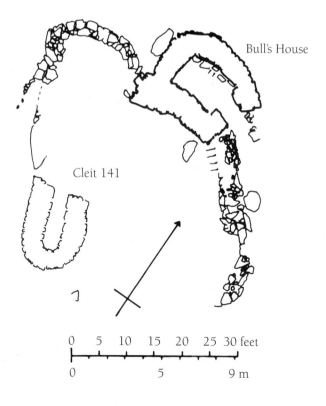

Bull's House

Cleit 141

```
0    5   10   15   20   25  30 feet
├──┴──┼──┴──┼──┴──┼──┴──┼──┴──┼──┤
0              5            9 m
```

young cattle. MacDiarmaid suggested that a Highland bull should be sent out, as, if a family could raise one good beast every year, it would almost pay the rent.

Possibly this was taken up, as in 1879 a bull was purchased by the estate for £16 and sold to the St Kildans for £17/11/4. Bulls were purchased in North Uist in 1890–91, 1896, and 1908, for £15, £10 and £15/16/0 respectively, and in Skye in 1903 for £15. In 1898 or 1899 a bull was shipped off (Heathcote 1900, 203) and in 1901/2 most households were credited with a 'share in the price of the old bull' (MM 2.635, 2.626/2, 626/12, 626/16; 3.102/9, 102/11). In the 1910s St Kilda was included in the Board of Agriculture's peripatetic bull scheme: in 1917 the bull 'supplied some years ago' remained because of transport problems during the war (SRO AF 57/19), and there were problems in removing the incumbent bull in May 1924 when his successor arrived on the steamer; he was shipped off the following month (S.G. 29.5.1924; 29.6.1924). In 1928 winter fodder was so scarce, following a drought, that the bull was sent back to Oban on the last steamer in August (24.8.1928).

A small building was put up outside the head dyke some time before 1886 (Wilson 1886, 6190) to accommodate the bull in winter (L MacDonald pers comm) (figure 79). A space about 9'4" by 6'4" is enclosed by walls 4'0" thick and 4'6" high, with low gables. This was thatched in 1886.

Records by MacLachlan (5.4.1907, 17&20.2.1908, 14.5.1908, 24.8.1907) and the rent returns (MM 2.635) show that in the twentieth century, at least, calving seems to have been spread over the year.

After the people moved into new mortared houses in 1861/62, their old homes continued to function as byres, and there the cows spent the winter (Logie 1889, 28, Ross 1890, 12). The cattle were allowed onto the harvested arable within the head dyke for the winter from October and part of the time were kept in the byres (Murray 12.10.1886; MacLachlan 24.10.1907). In 1909 they were put over into the Glen on May 5th, though they had been grazing outside the head dyke on occasions before that (MacLachlan 5.4.1909). This winter sojourn within byre and dyke was a strain on fodder, even when people had given up growing grain for their own consumption and used it only for cattle feed, and a number of authors record the cutting of grass in places inaccessible to stock. This perilous collection of all the available fodder took place late into the autumn (Sands 1877a, 108; Murray 25 & 28 & 30.10.1886; MacLachlan 25.10.1906, 26 & 28.10.1907, 30.12.1907).

Gleann Mór Shielings
It was common throughout the Highlands and Islands to remove the cattle from the arable areas to more remote pastures in summer, and many authors

refer to the pasturing of cattle in Gleann Mór in summer.

The turf-covered dyke still clearly visible round the head of Gleann Mór is most readily explained as a barrier intended to keep beasts within the glen (p 155).

Martin records that people stayed in the 'Amazon's House', one of a number of structures which were probably seasonally occupied shielings (p 76). In the later eighteenth century when the steward was exacting all the summer's milk as part of the rent, the milk cows were kept in the vicinity of the village, so although some cattle were pastured in Gleann Mór, milking there seems to have been abandoned for a while (Campbell 1799, 6, 24).

By the nineteenth century a slightly different system was in use; cattle and sheep were kept in the glen in summer but the women walked over twice daily to milk them (Kennedy 1932, 290). The time and effort involved in this journey was remarked upon by several people. It is just over a mile from the village to the folds, including an ascent of nearly 700 feet. A single journey carrying a light load takes about 40 minutes walking briskly.

Murray (28.5.1887) recorded that 'the lambs are shut in at night and the ewes milked early in the morning. There is a fold for each family, and it is the women's part to herd them all day keeping them separate'. Ross (1884, 87) refers to 'beehive stone built cow byres', which were 'separated for cows and calves, and are so small that a cow once entering could barely turn round, and would have to back out; smaller compartments are provided for the calves' (pp 152–5).

Ross (1890, 35, 79) recorded that the women went to Gleann Mór at six in the morning and five in the evening. They took great bundles of grass and docks (Kearton 1897, 19) with them to give the cows to keep them quiet during milking. Often they took some turfs back with them as well as the milk. On Sundays the milk was left in cleitean until Monday morning.

The milking of ewes continued until at least the turn of the century (Heathcote 1900a, 76). The milk was used in making cheese (MacKenzie 1681–4; Elliot 1895a, 116). Cheese contributed to the rent payments until 1889, often in considerable quantities (figure 46).

Sheep

Almost from the earliest written records (pp 73, 80–1) St Kilda has been known for its sheep, and the 'Soay' breed is still famous.

In the sixteenth century Boece (1527) and Monro (1961, 77) both described the sheep as large with long tails, and in the late seventeenth century they were described as long legged, long horned, and clad in a 'blewish hair' instead of wool. Soay and Boreray provided very good pasture;

every sheep had twins annually (MacKenzie 1681–4; Moray 1678, 927).

According to Martin (1753, 17, 21, 23) 'generally they are speckled, some white, some philamort (brown) and are of a common size; they do not resemble goats in any respect...except in their horns, which are extraordinary large, particularly those in the lesser isles'. On Soay the sheep generally bore twins or triplets, and ewe lambs regularly bore lambs themselves; this was attributed partly to their not being milked. 'There are none to catch them but the inhabitants, whom I have seen pursue the sheep nimbly down the steep descent'.

The remarkable fecundity of the sheep was supported by MacAulay's (1764, 118) assertion that an old ewe which no longer bore lambs on Hirte would produce them 'for a course of years' if moved to Boreray; Campbell (1799, f59) may simply be following earlier authors when he says that the sheep often have two or three lambs at a time.

Most visitors found it difficult to ascertain the number of sheep, partly because the people were reluctant to reveal figures as they paid rent on sheep, so were not scrupulous about making exact returns (MacAulay 1764, 129; Kearton 1897, 38–9; SRO AF 57/26). In 1758 the steward demanded every second ram lamb, every seventh ewe lamb, and every seventh fleece. In 1799 (Campbell 1799 f 24) he was demanding all the ewes' milk.

There is general agreement from the mid eighteenth to the mid nineteenth century (MacAulay 1764, 129, 213; Clarke 1824, 282; Campbell 1799, f 58; MacCulloch 1819, 29; 1824, 181; MacDonald 1932, 83; Atkinson 1831, f46; MacKenzie 1911, 11; MacGillivray 1842, 56; Milner 1848, 2059) that the sheep were small or even 'tiny'; that they were slim and long legged, with short tails; the contradiction with earlier descriptions may be due partly to an improvement in mainland sheep, thus providing a different comparison. The

Table 11
Approximate Numbers of Sheep Recorded

Date	Hirt	Boreray	Soay	Total	Reference
1697	1100	400	500	2000	Martin 1753
1758	1000	400	500	1900	MacAulay 1764
1815			400–500		MacCulloch 1824, 175
1841				2000	Wilson 1842, 43
1861	700	500	300	1500	Seton 1878, 128
1875	600				Smith 1875, 267
1896			200–300	1200–1300	Kearton 1897, 39
1902	700	300	400	1400+	Wiglesworth 1903, 18, 31
1848	average number per family: 8				Milner 1848, 2058
1876	minimum & maximum per family: 150 and 11:				Sands 1878, 130

wool was white, grey, different shades of brown, or black, and was short and soft, though some hairy fibres, usually left on the sheep in the plucking process, could make it feel coarse. The mutton was good with a fine flavour. Every sheep had two horns; MacAulay, MacCulloch and MacKenzie are agreed that some had four, or more than two. These were considered to be of the 'ancient Highland or Norwegian' breed; some compared them with Icelandic sheep, though MacKenzie says they were peculiar to the island.

By the 1830s (MacKenzie 1911, 15) the sheep on Hirte had been crossed with black-faced sheep, and further black-faced tups were imported about 1871 (MacDiarmid 1878, 245), so that by 1877 (Seton 1878, 130) most of the sheep on Hirte were white and in 1899 could be described as mostly black-faced (Heathcote 1900a, 89), though a few dark animals occurred until 1930 (MacGregor SEA C15527).

Sheep were individually owned, each man having his own ear-mark. Latterly they were marked with keel (MacDiarmid 1878, 245; MacDonald 1988, 123; Gladstone 1988, 234). Buchan (1727, 28) and Ross (1890, 45–7) give detailed information about values and the compensation system by which if a sheep were lost through someone's carelessness or a lamb deserted its mother, the person or persons responsible paid shares to the owner according to the number of sheep they possessed. This applied to sheep falling off cliffs as well as being trapped inadvertently in cleitean, so people moved with care through or near another person's animals. Though MacDiarmid (1878, 245) says that the sheep received very little attention, MacLachlan (25 to 27.12.1906, 12.1.1909) records men going out to look for sheep in bad weather, and sheep were sheltered in cleitean over the winter (Elliott 1895, 118; Wiglesworth 1903, 10; MacLachlan 12.5.1908). Clearly those on Hirte were herded to some extent in the summer, when the ewes were milked.

In 1877 about twelve tups were kept (MacDiarmid 1878, 245–6); presumably this refers to Hirte only. Most of the time they were kept on Dun, being brought over in late November for a few weeks. Ferguson (1885, 25) says that sheep were landed by being slung on ropes and hauled up.

Sheep were always plucked rather than shorn, though latterly it was not always done very thoroughly (Kennedy and Thomas 1875, 705; Elliot 1895, 115; Heathcote 1900a, 216). They were, apparently, free from scab and other skin diseases and in the late nineteenth century were not smeared (MacDiarmid 1878, 245), but those on Hirte were dipped in most years from 1900; dip was purchased in that year and 1903 (MM 2.632/7 and 14) and MacDonald (1988, 132–3) describes the process.

By 1758 (MacAulay 1764, 119) the sheep on Soay were distinguished from the others in belonging to the Steward. MacKenzie (1911, 15) records that in the 1830s, together with the sheep on Dun they belonged to the proprietor. The sheep on Soay continued in the proprietor's possession permanently (Sands, 1877a, 43) though the St Kildans used to take some for eating, passing on some to the Manse, and some being preserved for the proprietor (Murray 10.1.1887, MacDiarmid 1878, 245; MacKenzie mss. MacLachlan 1.2.1906, 29.11.1908). The people were charged 2/6 for each sheep (Kearton 1897, 41; Wiglesworth 1903, 32). Connell (1887, 115) noted that there was a positive attempt to keep the breed pure as the soft wool was worth twice as much as black-faced wool. In the 1820s just over a week was spent on Soay plucking sheep (Kennedy 1932, 122) and latterly the proprietor allowed the St Kildans to keep half the Soay wool crop in return for their plucking them, but they did not always bother to do it (Connell 1887, 114; Heathcote 1900, 222). It is probably impossible now to discover what level of 'management' took place, but by 1896 Kearton (1897, 41) could say that the St Kildans had wanted to cross the Soays with black-faced sheep but MacLeod objected and 'took them over'.

In 1930 virtually all the sheep were removed from Hirte; it proved impossible to take the flock off Boreray, and no attempt was made to take off the Soay sheep, a group of which were transferred to Hirte in 1932.

Goats
Though sheep are compared to goats in some of the early accounts, there is no historical evidence that there were goats on St Kilda apart from brief periods after 1700. Apparently goats imported in the eighteenth century all fell into the sea (Campbell 1799, f 61). The milking goats MacCulloch (1819, 27) saw in 1815 had all been killed by 1831, because they interfered with the seabirds in the breeding season; they could not be prevented from rambling along the ledges where the fulmar bred, being undeterred by the straw ropes stuck with feathers which discouraged the sheep from invading the bird slopes (Atkinson 1831, 46). Possibly they were reintroduced, as in 1840 MacGillivray (1842, 56), a naturalist, says that 'goats are plentiful among the rocks, where they have run wild'. Thomas's reference to kids in the Gleann Mór sheilings, if accurate, indicates domestic milk goats rather than feral animals, but there were none left when MacDiarmid (1878, 246) was making his investigations into the domestic stock in 1877, as he suggested that goats might be a useful addition.

Horses

Horses are specifically mentioned as absent in the late sixteenth century (Anon 1595) though MacLeod lists them in 1615 (p 84). In 1697 (Martin 1753, 17–18; 1716, 295), they were 'all of a red colour, very low, and smooth skinned, and are employed in carrying turf and corn, and at their anniversary cavalcade.' They were not used for ploughing. The richest man might have two or three horses, which were smaller than those in the Western Isles. At Michaelmas (Buchan 1727, 38) the people took it in turns to ride from the shore to the house. They had no saddles or bridles, only a rope (probably a halter) which controlled the horse on one side.

In 1758 (MacAulay 1764, 127–8) describes them as 'of a very diminutive size, but extremely well cast, full of fire and very hardy.' There was not much for them to do, as they did not carry seaweed or manure. MacCulloch (1824, 181) and Atkinson (1831, 46) agree that they were used only for carrying turf. By 1842, only two or three were left, apparently regarded as useless, and no charge was made for their grazing (Wilson 1842, 42).

These last horses must have gone soon after. In 1875 Sands (1877a, 43, 89; 1878, 192) saw ropes forty years old and made from hair cut from native horses (p 214). Middle-aged men remembered horses on the island. MacDiarmid (1878, 246) was told that over 35 years before, the tacksman had shipped off the last ponies on the grounds that they were destructive to the pasture, but in reality because they were fetching a good price elsewhere.

Some time before the 1830s a man had composed a song, now lost, to commemorate the death of a son who was killed by falling from a horse which was frightened by some boys (MacKenzie 1906, 333).

Dogs

Martin (1716, 18, 56) remarks that the dogs were 'speckled' and 'very dexterous in climbing and bringing out from their holes those fowls that build their nests far under ground'. Many others mention the puffin catching dogs (pp 216–7). MacLeod (c.1756–1775) says they were terriers, and Clarke (1824, 270–1, 280) describes them: 'a small rough hardy race, with long back, very short legs, black hair mixed with grey, tan-coloured visages, and erect ears.' Every one (probably every family) had at least one dog, some three or four. He also saw 'Pomeranians or fox-dogs' and others of no particular breed, and was annoyed to be followed by a swarm of miscellaneous dogs as he walked through the fields towards St Brendans. Other authors found them very variable: a cross between collie, terrier, Dutch pug, lurcher, and 'Yellow old wife's dog' (Atkinson 1831, 46), or 'lank long limbed creatures of the terrier kind, with what seemed a dash of shepherd's dog, and exhibiting something of a jackal aspect, though the tail was long' (Wilson (1842, 71). But Sands (1877a, 43) declared that by 1876 'the native breed of dogs', similar to cream coloured collies, were nearly all extinct, and 'a lot of mongrels has been imported from Harris. They are trained to herd sheep and to catch coulternebs'.

MacDonald (Kennedy 1932, 118) in 1823 saw dogs being used to work the sheep on Hirte; they were driven to a particular place beside a cliff and surrounded by men and dogs while their fleeces were removed. Most of the able bodied population was involved in this (Murray 28.5.1887). Murray records that dogs were sometimes taken to Soay to help catch sheep: on one occasion (10.1.1887) he joined a party and saw the dogs re-embarked by throwing them into the sea so that they would swim to the boat. Ross (1890, 8, 45, 90) agrees that the dogs were not necessarily an asset on Hirte, though they might catch individuals on Boreray or Soay. Wiglesworth (1903, 17–18) felt that the dogs were most useful as scavengers;

> Such time as is not taken up with quarrelling among themselves is spent prowling about seeing what they may devour, and in a community where sanitary arrangements are virtually non-existent, and where the refuse of birds and eggs is constantly littering about, a function of this sort is not without its value to the body politic.

He gathered details about the treatment of their teeth, mentioned earlier by Ross (1890, 8):

> Every young dog, when he attains the age of six months, has his canine teeth broken off on a level with his gums with a hammer and chisel, and all the others are blunted by being filed down, which filing process is repeated two or three times a year when the dog is young, the intervals being gradually prolonged up to the age of five years, after which the operation is considered no longer necessary.

Connell (1887, 115–6), like Clarke, found their pack behaviour disturbing and annoying. Later authors (Steele Elliot 1895a, 115; Kearton 1897, 6) refer to the barking of the dogs and their intense interest in any activity on the shore, such as the landing or the launching of boats. Apparently they did not mind the occasional ducking in the cold sea, or they might have avoided boats, but Heathcote (1900a 90–91) gives a graphic account of canine landings and embarkings:

> When the boat comes within ten or twelve yards of the shore, the word of command is given, and a dozen dogs leap into the sea and swim towards the rocks. A few succeed at the first attempt in making good their hold on the steep slope, and scramble up out of reach of the waves, but others are sucked down by the falling waters, vainly pawing at the limpet-covered surface until another

wave hurls them up again, and casts them, panting and bleeding, by the side of their more fortunate fellows. Some of them show extraordinary activity in climbing up the rocks, and will follow their masters unaided up the steepest precipices, but the younger ones have to be assisted by their two-footed friends, and look unutterably miserable as they are hauled up the cliffs dangling at the end of a rope.

They are also wonderfully clever at embarking. I have seen one spring safely into a boat eight or ten feet distant from the steep slippery rock on which the dog was standing.

From the 1880s onwards many of the photographs, and, later, the films, show dogs of a collie type. Generally they are with their owners; one film shows children playing with a puppy, and another a number of dogs rushing excitedly about the jetty as a boat comes in (Pike 1908; Pike c.1917; Low 1929).

In 1930 most of the dogs suffered an unhappy fate. Worried about the cost of the licences which they thought they would have to buy, the people drowned nearly all of them in the bay just before leaving.

Cats

Cats receive less attention in the literature, though one might suspect that there was a continuous cat population at least from Martin's time, particularly as Hirte supported a population of wood mice, and at some stage house mice had also made their way there. Martin (1753, 18) simply tells us that they were 'speckled'.

In the late nineteenth century there was one in almost every house MacDiarmid (1878, 246); Connel (1887, 116) speaks of them as 'plentiful'. Though most households probably had at least one cat, latterly they are mentioned in connection with Rachel MacCrimmon, who continued to live in one of the old thatched houses until 1914. Ross (1890, 133) describes her central hearth 'with probably half a dozen cats lying around, also two dogs'. Kearton (1897, 34) saw her in her box bed 'surrounded by two or three cats', and Mrs Ogilvie (Susan Ferguson, pers comm) remembers as a child going to tea with Miss MacCrimmon and, in the dim interior, seeing the gleam of the cats' eyes as they peered out from their refuge in the box bed.

About a dozen cats were abandoned at the evacuation. The few seen in July 1931 were shot in an attempt to protect the birds and the mice (Harrisson and Moy-Thomas 1933, 109–115).

Poultry

Buchan (1727, 9) tells us that his wife 'carried a cock and some hens there, which was a wonder to the inhabitants, who had never seen any before'. Possibly successive ministers inherited these birds or their progeny, or took their own poultry: Campbell (1799, f 51) observed that the only poultry in the island belonged to the 'parson'. MacDiarmid (1878, 246) saw two hens, but Connell implies (1887, 116) that for some time there had been no chickens when he says 'there are now a few hens…the minister having four' Within a few years they were more common: Kearton (1897, 48) says 'there are a number of domestic fowls…but their owners hold them in no great esteem, as they say the birds eat more than they are worth'. MacLachlan (16.8.1906) records hens among Rachel MacCrimmon's livestock, living in the house.

Alice MacLachlan herself kept several hens, and there are numerous references (18.4.1907, 24.8.1907; 23.4.1908; 6.5.1908; 16.5.1908; 10.4.1909) to the setting of eggs under hens, their success and the numbers of eggs produced; she gave some chickens to Donald Ferguson (12.9.1907). There were also pigeons (24.3.1908), and ducks (15.4.1908, 8.3.1909). Later the Camerons (Cameron 1973, 25, 35) kept hens, and pigeons nested in a loft over the byre.

Arable Farming

As table 12 shows, barley was grown on St Kilda from at least the sixteenth century; oats are not specifically mentioned until 1697. Both crops were probably grown long before. Buchanan (1793, 119) is the only author to mention rye, which was grown in the Hebrides, especially on very poor land. Potatoes were introduced soon after their first appearance in the Hebrides in 1743 (MacDonald 1811, 196, 234). Buchan (1727, 20) says flax was not grown; MacAulay (1764, 214) says they made very little linen, implying that some flax was grown. Vegetables other than cabbages and turnips were grown almost exclusively by the clergy.

In the sixteenth century the 'corn' was grown on fertile land dug with a spade; (Anon 1595). The women harrowed the land while the men were occupied fowling (Moray 1678, 928).

Martin (1753, 11, 17–19, 50, 70; 1716, 286) provides the earliest detailed information:

The soil is very grateful to the labourer, producing ordinarily sixteen, eighteen or twenty fold; their grain is only bear, and some oats; the barley is the largest produced in all the western isles; they use no plough but a kind of crooked spade; their harrows are of wood as are the teeth in the front also, and all the rest supplied only with long tangles of seaware tied to the harrow by the small ends; the roots hanging loose behind, scatter the clods broken by the wooden teeth; this they are forced to use for want of wood. Their arable land is very nicely parted into ten divisions, and these into subdivisions, each distinguished by the name of some deceased man or woman, who were natives of the place; there is one spot called Multa terra, another multis agris. The chief ingredient in their composts is ashes of turf mixed with straw; with these they mix their urine, which by experience they find to have much of the vegetable nitre; they do not preserve it in quantities as elsewhere, but convey it immediately from the fountain to the ashes, which by daily practice they find most advantageous; they join also the bones, wings, and entrails of their sea-fowls to the straw; they sow very thick, and have a proportionable growth; they pluck all their bear by the roots in handfuls, both for the sake of their houses, which they thatch with it, and their cows which they take in, during the winter; the corn produced by this compost is perfectly free of any kind of weed; it produces much sorrel where the compost reaches.

The officer is obliged to adjust the respective proportions of lands, grass, and rocks, and what else could be claimed by virtue of the last tack or lease, which is never longer than for three years.

The re-allocation of land every three years continued until the 1830s (Buchan 1727, 25; MacDonald 1823, 24); while Buchan notes that this kept it all up to a general standard as neglected land came to those more thorough about digging and dunging, MacDonald felt that it was a deterrent to real improvement.

There was a single kiln used by everyone, according to a lotting system. Cloth was waulked on mats woven from hay ropes (Martin, 1753, 53, 11).

The sheep sacrifices demanded by Roderick the Imposter were to be slaughtered using a crooked spade; the edge of the spade being almost half an inch thick. Martin also refers to the 'foot spade', so probably the cas chrom was the implement to be used, but if the cutting edge were half an inch thick, it is unlikely to have had an iron blade, and possibly this was the same as the 'caibe' mentioned by MacKenzie (see below).

Buchan (1727, 19–20) describes the querns used for milling and how oats were sometimes prepared by graddaning rather than using the kiln. In his explanation about sheep values and compensation Buchan says that this was usually assessed and paid in barley, when corn was not scarce, but 'if they want corn, they rather take barley'; 'corn' here referring to oats, as is the common Scottish usage.

MacLeod (*c*.1756–1775) refers to the addition of seaweed to the midden for manuring, and the use of the inner part of the house thatch, removed in March, and not renewed until harvest time. MacDonald (Kennedy 1932, 119) says this took place in late May; he and MacKenzie (below) describe the same process.

In 1758 (MacAulay 1764, 27–39) the reduced population did not cultivate all the land possible, keeping to the eighty odd acres immediately around the settlement. Here there were numerous unequal plots enclosed by stones which had been cleared from the soil; these defined the patches, each of which had a name, so that the individual arable areas could be discussed without being on the spot, and clear boundaries ensured that no one could encroach on his neighbour's ground. The soil was turned with a spade, then raked very carefully, 'removing every small stone, every noxious root or growing weed that falls in their way, and they pound down every stiff clod into dust'. Land intended for barley was fertilised from the midden which had accumulated on the house floor; for oats, ordinary manure was used. The yield from this careful preparation of a small area was greater than that from a larger area treated less intensively as in the rest of the Western Isles, and the people also sowed and harvested earlier, the harvest generally being over by the beginning of September. If it were any later, the whole crop was liable to be lost in storms. MacAulay considered the barley to be of the best quality in the Western Isles.

According to Clarke (1824, 269) the grain paid as rent was the total crop, the people having none left for their own use. While this may not have been altogether true, 50 bolls is a large quantity, and it may well have formed the major portion of the yield; other authors also indicate that the rental left the people in want (pp 99, 126–8).

In the early nineteenth century MacDonald (1811, 817) noted that the oats often suffered from the bad weather, and MacCulloch (1819, 27–28) says that oats were 'scantily cultivated' and were inferior to those in the Western Isles, while the barley was 'by much the finest' and was the chief crop, potatoes not being grown as much as elsewhere. The corn and grass, as soon as they were cut, were thrown loosely into cleitean, and so preserved.

Campbell (1799, f 27–28) indicates the size of the 'miserable patches' of land, which 'seldom exceed forty feet in length by twenty feet in breadth, and some which we measured were even smaller – these are however very highly manured, and promised as plentiful a crop as any we had hitherto seen in the Highlands'.

MacDonald (1823, 24), however, felt that the land was poorly managed, and the grain of inferior quality, seldom yielding more that threefold, and in 1834 Carruthers (1843, 257) agreed, noting that weeds dominated the crops.

MacKenzie had ample opportunity during his stay from 1830 to 1843 to study the agricultural system, and he was responsible for some major changes (p 105). He considered the ground to be of good quality, yielding fair crops, though often there was a lot of storm damage.

Each family possesses from three to four acres of arable land, but on account of the very primitive implements which they use, its cultivation is much more laborious than if they used modern methods. They start cultivation by turning over the sods in a very imperfect way with an implement called a caschrom. *With it one turns over the soil much quicker than with a spade, but the work is very much inferior. It penetrates to no great depth and makes very rough work. In consequence they have to go over the ground a second time using an implement which they call* caibe. *It is hoe-shaped, like a carpenter's adze, but very much heavier. With it they break the clods and improve the seed bed, but when all is done it is very unsatisfactory work. This hoe is not only used for this purpose but for many others. With it they destroy weeds, earth up and dig their potatoes, and do all sorts of odd jobs. The only other implement which they use is a rake with a short handle and wooden teeth, which they call* racan.

The manure is all carried to the fields by the women in ordinary wicker creels, which the men, as their share of the work, fill and put upon their backs. The manure is spread over the fields with their hands, and in this work both men and women take their part.

The barley, which is their principal crop, gets most of the manure. The ground is now ready for the seed, which is sown by the men. While the men are thus engaged the women are employed in throwing soil with their hands from the part which is not sown to that which is. This is done in order that the seed and manure may be better covered with soil than the miserable rake could easily accomplish. If this were not done and there came a gale from the south-east much of the seed would be blown away.

When the blade of the young barley is from one to two inches high, they strip the thatch from the roofs of their houses, and take the half of it which has been next the inside and spread it over the crop as a top dressing. This formed originally the outer half of the former year's thatch, and is now thoroughly impregnated with soot. The half which remains is then roughly replaced and left so till the autumn, when it is covered over with a fresh deep layer of barley straw, and bound down firmly with numerous straw ropes called siman. *Fully half of the straw of this crop is used for thatch.*

When the barley is ripe it is pulled up by the roots and bound into sheaves. These are left lying on the ground for a few days, and if at this time a gale from the north should visit the island much of it may get blown into the sea. After it has dried a little it is built up into small stacks, where it is left till it is quite dry. Then some fine day three or four families combine to take down these little stacks, and with the sickle cut each sheaf in half a little above the band. The grain portion is again built up into a small stack and some of the straw used for finishing the thatching of the house. In this way all the work of one family is finished in a single day. The women of this particular family will not remain long with the workers, but as soon as the ears are cut from a few sheaves they carry them home. There they spread them out and set fire to the straw, which is allowed to burn till the straw is consumed and the grain left, dry and hard enough to grind. It is then freed from dust and rubbish, ground into meal in the quern, and cooked for the supper of the workers...In about two months these ears, except that portion which is reserved for seed, are taken by each family in turn to the kiln, and spread out to dry and harden. When this is done they beat off the grain from the straw, and winnow it from the chaff in the breeze. The grain is now stored, and ground in the quern as required, which is generally only a few days supply at a time. As by keeping, some of the effect of kiln-drying is lost, it is restored by placing a portion of grain in a straw tub, and with it a hot stone, which is moved about among the grain till it is again suitable for grinding. This may have to be done every week or two, with about a bushel each time.

In addition to barley they also grow some oats, chiefly of the black variety, but it does not get much attention.

Their only other crop is a small quantity of potatoes, which does not receive much attention either. They are generally grown year after year in the same place, because it is less trouble. As there is very little frost here at any time, and some years none at all, the potatoes left in the soil come up among those planted; and as they do not take the trouble to destroy them, it often looks as if they had been planted broadcast. Under such conditions the potatoes are small both in size and crop. Further, they are dug up very carelessly, and large numbers are left behind in the ground. If afterwards they require them at any time for food, the ground will be dug over a second or even a third time.

In addition to thatch, straw was used for making baskets, gates for the gathering folds, and thin ropes, used for weaving into sacks and to deter sheep from wandering on fowling ledges (Thomas, 1868, 176; Atkinson 1831, 46).

MacKenzie was largely responsible for the reorganisation of the arable land into the new strip system (p 105). A land drainage system was put in, and the whole surrounded by a head dyke to help protect the crops. The practice of accumulating compost on the house floor was stopped, and instead cleitean were used for establishing a compost heap, and pits for waste from fowling such as heads and feet of birds.

Wilson (1842, 22, 23, 25) says that MacKenzie had effected a change from the use of the caschrom to the English spade, and that the draining of the land had nearly doubled its yield. MacKenzie had tried carrots and onions with some success. 'Turnips seem to thrive well for a time, but are speedily cut off by some kind of destructive insect, and peas and beans blossom, but produce no pods. A little mustard was growing merrily near the manse'. The barley and oats were scarcely sufficient for the people; and although each family was supposed to pay about 23 pecks of barley annually in rent, often extra feathers were substituted.

Sands stayed through the winter of 1875–6 (1877a, 8, 33, 99). The ground was carefully cultivated, the spade being universally used though he noticed a few caschroms put away in the rafters of barns. Wooden rakes were used instead of harrows. He considered that all the crops were planted too thickly. Smith (1875, 266) noted that the potatoes were very small. Sometimes the grain was cut with sickles but generally it was pulled up by the roots. He also noted the drying of grain in a straw tub preparatory to grinding with the quern, mentioned by MacKenzie.

In 1877 supplies were seriously depleted when the people gave shelter to a group of shipwrecked sailors; in April MacLeod sent out 16 bolls of seed oats, together with meal and potatoes, followed in May by further supplies from the Kelsall Fund, including 19 bolls of Sandy oats for seed, and 8 bolls of bere for seed, besides food supplies. MacDiarmid (1878, 242–3) made particular enquiries about the crops:

> I should say that about an acre and a half, or perhaps a little more, of tilled land is held by each family, the most of which lies in strips between the houses and the sea. The soil is a fine black loam resting on granite, and by continued and careful manuring and cleaning, looks quite like a garden. Yet with all this fine fertile appearance, the return it gives is miserable; and this can only be accounted for, I presume, from the land never being allowed any rest under grass. The only crops grown are potatoes and oats, with a little bere. Within the remembrance of some of the older men, the returns were double, or nearly treble, of what they now are. Questioned several of the men upon this point, and got exactly similar answers. From a barrel of potatoes (about 2 cwt.), scarcely 3 barrels will be lifted. They require to sow the oats very thick – at the rate of from 10 to 12 bushels to the acre, and the return is never above three times the quantity of seed sown; formerly it used to be six or seven times. I was shown some of the oats grown there, but they were very small and thin, and thick in the husk. If possible, they avoid sowing home-grown seed, as it never gives a good return.

Turnips had been grown successfully in the past but latterly had not thriven, and there were some cabbages in small enclosures. He gives the same information about the use of the spade rather than the caschrom, the wooden rake, and flails, and says that they had iron graips for spreading manure, which was moved in creels or baskets. He saw no wheel barrows, but there were two hand barrows. Some seaweed was used for manure, but supplies from the shore were limited.

According to Connell (1887, 116, 123) most of the puffins killed were taken for the sake of their feathers, and the carcasses were used as fertiliser. In addition to the area enclosed by the head dyke, there were on the slopes other small areas enclosed for cultivation.

Ross (1890), teacher from 1888–9 described the growing of oats and barley in ground dug over by hand with a spade, harrowing following the sowing, using small wooden rakes. The barley was ripe by about August 25 and was pulled up by the roots; the oats, which ripened later, were cut with scythes or hooks; these crops were considered too poor for human consumption, and were used for overwintering the cattle, together with hay; in early spring this was supplemented by grass hand cut from areas inaccessible to stock. The people grew potatoes, not numerous, but good; no turnips, but some cabbages, 'which are very wild'.

By the time the Heathcotes visited, in 1897 and 1898 (1900a, 215), the area of cultivated ground was limited, the people frankly admitting that when they could import meal it was not worth growing corn or potatoes, but better to concentrate on grass for a hay crop, though the former crops were still grown, as observed by Wiglesworth (1903, 6) and MacLachlan (1906–1909). Some sheep were kept in cleitean during the winter; the dung was dug out in the early summer and spread over the grass crop. Mrs MacLachlan was able to start using the rhubarb from the manse garden in early May.

In 1927 (SG 28.10.1927) the area of cultivated land was reckoned to be about two acres. No crops were sown in 1930.

Table 12

Records of Stock Presence and Numbers, and Crops Grown

Date	Cattle	Sheep	Goats	Horses	Dogs	Cats	Poultry	Barley	Oats	Potatoes	Other	Authority
1595	c. 60	x		0				x				Anon 1595
1615	x	x		x				x				MacLeod 1615
1697	c90	c2000		c18	x	x		x	x			Martin 1753
1710s	10	1000		12	x			x	x			Adv Ms 33320
1720s	x			x	x	x	H	x	x			Buchan 1727
1758	c40	c1900		10	x			x	x	x	c flax?	MacAulay 1764
c1770	x	x	x							x		Carmichael 1941
1793	x	x			x			x	x	x	rye	Buchanan 1793
1797	x	x			x			x	x	x		Kennedy 1824
1799	x	x	f	x	x		H, D	x	x	x		Campbell 1799
1815	x	x	x	x	x			x	x	x		McCulloch 1819
1820s	x	x			x			x	x	x		MacDonald
1831	x	x	f	c20	x			x	x	x		Atkinson 1831
1830s	c42+	x						x	x	x		Mackenzie 1911
1840	x		x	x	x	x		x	x	x	c veg*	McGillivray 1842
1841	c50	c2000	x	2/3	x			x	x	x	veg	Wilson 1842
1830/53	x	x		x				x	x	x		MacQueen nd
1861	43	1500						x	x	x		Seton 1878
1873	32+	x							x	x		Smith 1879
1875–6	x	x		0	x	x		x	x	x	c t	Sands 1877
1877–49	x	x		-	x	x	2H	x	x	x	c r	McDiarmid 1878
1884–5	c32								x	x		MacCallum 1907
1886–7	x				x			x	x	x		Murray 1887
1886	c40	c1000		c40	x		x	x	x	x	c t	Connell 1887
1889	c40	c1000			x			x	x	x		Logie 1889
1890	x	x			x			x	x	x	c	Ross 1890
1894	x	x		24	x		x	x	x	x	p*	Elliot 1895
1896	25-30	c1000		30-40x					x	x	s	Kearton 1897
1902	x	1000		34					x	x		Wigleswth 1903
1906–9	x	x			x	x	H,D	x	x	x	r	McLachlan
1919/27	x	x			x	x	H	x	x	x	veg r	Cameron 1973

Key

x: present, 0: absent, f: formerly; H: hens, D: ducks, c: cabbages, t: turnips, r: rhubarb, s: strawberries, veg: vegetables not specified veg* (1841): carrots, onions, peas, beans, mustard, p* (1894): peas, parsnips

N.B. The more unusual vegetables are recorded in the manse garden.

12

Fowling and Fishing

E vidence from archaeological sites shows that prehistoric and later
communities frequently exploited large seabird colonies in their area.
Those in Orkney are particularly well documented (Smith 1984, 259–264).
Fowling would have been an occupation of Scotland's earliest settlers and
their successors, though the brief notices of St Kilda in the literature before
the mid sixteenth century stress the peculiarity of the sheep and do not refer
to fowling. Monro in 1549 (1961, 77–8) mentions that dried birds were used
to pay the rent. Later in the century (Anon 1595), there is the first description
of the daily work of tilling the ground and 'taking of foullis and gaddering
their eggis, quhairon thay leif for the maist part of their fude', but not until a
hundred years later is more detail available, when Moray (1678, 927–9) wrote
at some length about fowling.

Early Accounts
Moray says that the St Kildan men took birds from Boreray, Soay and the
stacs, which involved difficult landings and climbing. The rocks were divided
so that specific areas went with each of the ten halfpennies of land. The
climbing groups were composed of men of varying ability, to ensure that all
areas were covered.

> The way of their climbing, when they kill their fowls, is thus; they go two and
> two with a long rope, not made of hemp, but of cow-hides salted, and the thongs
> cut round about, and plaited six or nine fold. Each end of the rope is tyed about
> each one of their middle, and he that is foremost goes till he come to a safe
> standing, the other standing firm all that time to keep him up, in case his foot
> should have slip'd: when the foremost is come to a safe standing; then the other
> goes, either below or above him, where his business is; and so they watch time
> about; seldom any of them being lost, when this is observed.

one other way of killing them was:

> Some of these fellows lie beside the door of the little houses they have in their
> islands, flat upon their backs, and open ther breasts. Which, when the fowls
> perceive, they sit upon them, and are presently catched, and their necks broke.
> One fellow has kill'd hundreds of fowls in one night, after this manner.

They would also set strong snares.

The climbing of Stac Dona (now Stac Biorach: p 24) was worth while for the number of seabirds breeding on it:

After they have landed with much difficulty, a man having room for but one of his feet, he must climb up twelve or sixteen fathoms high. Then he comes to a place, where having but room for his left foot and left hand, must leap from thence to another such place before him; which, if he hit right, the rest of the ascent is easie: and with a small cord, which he carries with him, he hales up a rope, whereby all the rest come up. But if he misseth that footstep, (as oftentimes they do) he falls into the sea, and the company takes him in by the small cord, and sits still until he be a little refreshed, and then he tries again; for every one there is not able for that sport.

Apparently they did not always adhere to their safe methods, as Moray says 'the men seldom grow old' most either drowning or breaking their necks.

MacKenzie (1681–4) wrote of the vast number of sea birds, and knew of another way of killing them: 'a man lies upon his back with a long pole in his hand, and knocketh them down, as they fly over him.' The people sold feathers, and bird fat preserved in birds' stomachs, which was a remedy for aches and pains.

Sibbald drew on both these accounts, and another (Adv. ms.33.3.20 f53) which contradicted Moray, saying that the men lived to a great age. Children were trained to climb from an early age by climbing up the house walls, using ropes. Dogs were also trained to climb and to 'creep into the holes of the fowls' to catch them. Snares about a foot long, made of hair, were fixed on the ends of their fishing rods; up to 60 birds per day could be caught with such a noose.

Many visitors, beginning with Martin in 1697, provide a vast body of information about fowling from which a detailed account can be built up, though some of it is contradictory.

Nearly half the survivors of the smallpox epidemic in 1727 were a group engaged in fowling; they would ensure continuity of methods and customs.

Species Exploited

The main prey species were fulmar, gannet, and the auks: guillemot, razorbill, puffin, and, in its day, the garefowl or great auk (Martin 1753 27–36, MacLeod 1756–1775, MacAulay 1764, 133–157). The live weights of different species (figure 80, overleaf) give an indication of dressed carcass weight and demonstrate that, for instance, a single garefowl or gannet would provide considerably more meat than any other bird and might repay the extra effort involved in getting them. It is clear that nestling fulmar and nestling gannets (guga) carry a quantity of fat. All authors who mention a favourite bird are agreed that it was the fulmar, particularly the young bird. MacLeod (1756–1775) says that adult fulmar were not taken. Oil was collected from the fulmar killed, and fat from young fulmar and gugas was added to it. This was 'giben'. Adult gannets were good eating when they were fat, and were at their fattest on their return in the spring (MacKenzie 1911, 47). The harvesting of young fulmar and young gannets in the late summer and early autumn were important events in the St Kildan calendar. Guillemots and razorbills were rarely eaten (Ross 1890, 90), the former being regarded as tough (Connell 1887, 124) and the latter as not very good (MacKenzie 1911, 53), though guillemots were very fat in spring, and were taken in some quantity for eating then, when fewer other birds were available; some carcasses were salted and preserved (Connell 1887, 130, Wiglesworth 1903, 58). Young puffins and shearwaters, also fat birds, were enjoyed (MacKenzie 1911, 44–5, 54). Shearwaters were not collected systematically (MacGillivray 1842, 67). In the nineteenth century kittiwake was eaten very occasionally (MacKenzie 1911, 41) in later years being taken more for its feathers (Elliott 1895a, 128). MacKenzie (1911, 46) says that stormy petrels were caught and MacGillivray (1842, 67) explains that they were released after their oil had been collected.

Figure 80. *Live weights of different species of birds*

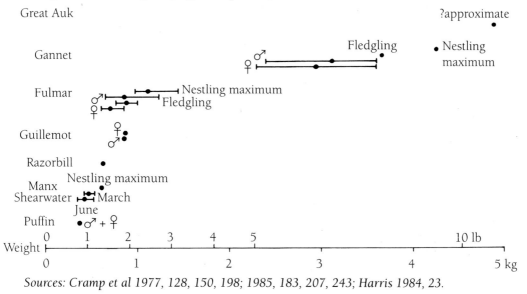

Sources: *Cramp et al 1977, 128, 150, 198; 1985, 183, 207, 243; Harris 1984, 23.*

The garefowl or great auk is not mentioned as uncommon in Martin's day, and his description of the bird and its habits is very useful (1753, 27). It was declining in numbers in the eighteenth century; one of the last seen alive was caught on Stac an Armin in about 1840.

The volumes of eggs from different species (figure 81) shows that while those of guillemot, razorbill, fulmar and gannet are of a very similar size, puffin eggs are much smaller and garefowl eggs much larger. Martin indicates that the eggs of gulls, gannet, manx shearwater, razorbill, puffin and guillemot were taken, the last being favourite. There is disagreement about fulmar eggs; MacLeod (1756–1775) says that these were not taken, as the bird laid no replacement egg, and in this he is supported by MacLean (1838, 9), who relied on MacKenzie for much of his information; but Atkinson (1838, 221) implies that some fulmar eggs were taken, and MacKenzie himself (1911, 43) says that a very few were taken. MacGillivray (1842, 61) and Sands (1877a, 46) say that they were eaten. Kearton (1897, 62) says they were not collected on Hirte. Possibly there was a change over time. MacDonald (Kennedy 1932, 117) found puffin eggs most enjoyable. MacKenzie (1911, 53) notes that both guillemot and razorbill eggs are good when fresh, but apparently the people preferred eggs which were about 10–12 days old, when the young bird was just forming (Wilson 1842, 45). MacAulay (1764, 143) says that eggs were kept for months, and though the St Kildans enjoyed them others found them inedible.

In the seventeenth century, fowls and eggs were used as currency, as, for instance, in the payment which went to the person who risked their cooking pot by taking it on expeditions. When fowling, the men had occasional rests,

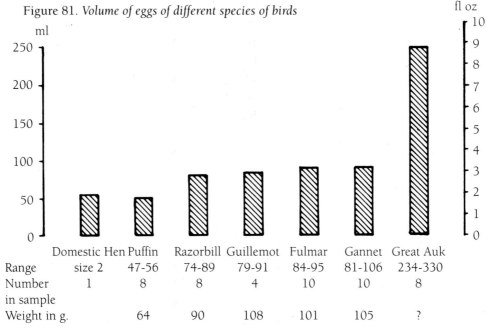

Figure 81. *Volume of eggs of different species of birds*

	Domestic Hen	Puffin	Razorbill	Guillemot	Fulmar	Gannet	Great Auk
Range	size 2	47-56	74-89	79-91	84-95	81-106	234-330
Number in sample	1	8	8	4	10	10	8
Weight in g.		64	90	108	101	105	?

Eggs taken for human consumption: average internal volumes in millilitres with range and number in sample, and weight in grammes for fresh eggs.

and each would pluck the best bird he had as a present for his wife or sweetheart (Martin 1753, 60–1).

The harvesting of both eggs and birds must have been related to their size, the value of the oil and feathers of birds, the accessibility of colonies and the ease with which the birds could be killed.

Allocation of rocks and spoil

MacAulay (1764, 187–8) says that the rocks were divided according to the proportion of land each man had. Like the arable land, they were reallocated every three years. If there were any disagreement over the shares, it was decided by lots, and any encroachment on another's area was regarded as a serious crime. It is implied that each man took the produce of his own share. By the late nineteenth century (Connell 1887, 59–60, 134) this strict division numbered sixteen shares, one for each croft; the divison was made annually and the rocks allocated by lot. Each man was responsible for 'policing' his lot and ensuring that the birds were not disturbed. In the fowling season, each man saw that his area was properly covered, with help, but all the fulmar were shared equally. He says that gannets and fulmar were divided into sixteen equal shares, but all the auks were free for anyone to take and keep for themselves. Feathers and oil, however, used for paying the rent, were also scrupulously divided into sixteen shares. According to him, some fulmar carcasses, stripped of these valuable commodities, were given to those outside the 'syndicate of sixteen'. Ross (1890, 41) supports this, saying that each able bodied man within the sixteen households was expected to do his best to contribute to the total, and after a division of birds, any odd ones over were given to the needy. Any man not able to take part because of sickness, for instance, still received an equal share. An exception to this scrupulous sharing was any young fulmar which had fallen out of its nest, which became the property of anyone who found it. Kearton (1897, 53), however, says that the cliffs of Hirte and Dun were divided into lots which changed hands each year to give everyone a fair share.

Boreray, Soay and the stacs were common property and the proceeds from these were divided. Martin (1753, 22–35) says the birds from Stac Lee were divided proportionately to the land rented, any surplus going to the Ground Officer; but he implies that birds gathered on Stac an Armin were individually owned, each man putting his mark on the birds' feet. In the 1820s gannets were divided equally among families (Kennedy 1932, 286). This system of division took no account of the number of people within each family, and some members of the community did not receive a share by right.

The way in which rocks and different species were shared seems to have changed over time.

The Fowling Calendar

The gathering of eggs, young and adult birds naturally depended on the life cycle of the birds themselves; all the seabirds are migrants and spend a varying length of time away from the breeding site. Egg laying, hatching and fledging are spread over several weeks, and may vary in individual years according to weather. Tables 13 and 14 give an outline of the main events in the year for the most important species, and the human activities associated with them. In the seventeenth century gannet eggs were taken from Boreray and Stac and Armin but not from Stac Lee in order to delay the guga harvest on the first two, where the birds would be the result of a second laying (Martin 1753, 23), and guillemot eggs could be harvested twice, with a gap of about 18 days between raids, as the birds would often lay a third time (Wiglesworth 1903, 58).

Table 13

Simplified Scheme of Main Events in the Avian Calendar

Month	Fulmar	Gannet	Puffin	Guillemot	Razorbill	Manx S.
	return					
February				return	return	
March		return				return
April			return	lay eggs	lay eggs	
May	lay eggs	lay eggs	lay eggs			lay eggs
June	hatch	hatch	hatch	hatch	hatch	
July	hatch					hatch
August	fledge		fledge leave	leave fledge	leave fledge	
September		fledge				fledge leave
October						
November	leave	leave				

Table 14

Main Fowling Activities throughout the Season

Month	Fulmar	Gannet	Puffin	Other
February				Adult guillemots
March		Adults B, SA		Adult Guillemots
		Adults B		Adult Shearwaters
April				Adult Guillemots
May	Eggs & Adults	Eggs B, stacs	Eggs	Guillemot eggs
June			Adults	
July			Adults	
		Gugas B	B and S	
August		Gugas B, SL	Young	Young Shearwaters
	Young	Gugas B, SL		
September		Gugas B, SA		

Key: B: Boreray, SA: Stac an Armin, SL: Stac Lee, S: Soay
Based on: Martin 1753, MacAulay 1764, MacDonald 1823, Kennedy 1932, Wilson 1842, Baillie 1875, Sands 1878, Connell 1887, Murray 1886–7, Logie 1889, Wiglesworth 1903, MacLachlan 1906–9

Climbing cliffs and stacs

The harvesting of both fulmar and gannets required communal effort as climbing was involved. In the fulmar harvest it was necessary to work with ropes all the time on the steep slopes and broken cliffs, but when harvesting gannets they were often only necessary to reach the breeding areas.

No doubt children learned some of the easier and safer ways of fowling at an early age; boys began climbing at 12–14 years (Morgan 1861, 110) though they might accompany their fathers on some occasions when as young as 10 (Ross 1890, 63–4; Cameron 1973, 36).

The fulmar harvest might last from ten days (MacKenzie 1911, 43–4) to three weeks (Sands 1877a, 94–97) while the young birds were at their fattest, just before fledging. The whole population concentrated all their attention on this. In preparation, the women brought back the cattle from Gleann Mór and ground enough meal to last during the fowling. The rocks were prospected and assigned to groups to work them. The areas worked in any one day depended on the weather and the maturity of the birds; those most advanced were taken first if possible (Ross 1890, 56).

Moray's account describes the basic climbing technique used until 1930. Often men worked in groups, and might descend a high cliff by stages, the last pair going furthest (MacLeod 1756–75). Men worked in groups of four or five in MacKenzie's day; the reduction to three or four with a minimum of two recorded by Connell (1887, 126) may reflect the diminishing number of able bodied men (p 129, table 3). Men climbed up the lower sections of cliffs from boats and cleared them, and climbed down or were lowered down to other areas from the top of a cliff or an intermediate stage. The young birds were taken from their nests and swiftly dispatched, their necks twisted round to prevent the oil running out from their stomachs. The catching of the oil in a dish on the end of a rod, as described by Martin (1753, 31), is scarcely credible. On the lower cliffs they might be thrown into the sea for collection by boat (Murray 14.8.1886). Otherwise they were heaped in a convenient cranny or accumulated around the fowler, their heads tucked through his belt, and at length he might tie a group of them to the end of a rope and send them up, or ascend himself. Women went as far down as they might without ropes and relieved the men of their burdens, and women and children on the cliff tops would begin to empty the birds of their oil, which was poured into gannets' stomachs. While the men rested occasionally they would help with this. In the evening the birds were taken home and the people sat up at night plucking them and preparing them for salting. The men worked stripped to their underclothes, but during the fulmar harvest everyone was covered in oil; their clothing was soaked, and there were so many loose feathers that it looked like a snowfall.

Moray did not refer to the more difficult approach to the gannet colonies, located on Boreray and the adjacent stacs. Adult birds were only easily caught on dark nights. The fowlers landed at twilight, and once it was dark crept up to the birds and began to kill them, returning in the early morning (MacKenzie 1911, 49). In the eighteenth century, the Ground Officer was the leader in landing on other islands and in climbing, and he was known as 'Gingach' (MacAulay 1764, 188; p 293). Eggs and young birds could be taken in daylight. Stac Lee was the most difficult to land on: an iron staple above a vertical face up to 20 feet high was lassoed with a rope and the first man 'walked' up the face holding the rope (Wiglesworth 1903, 34–5). In August a small group of men, chosen by lot, landed on Stac Lee before the birds fledged and killed large numbers, which were thrown into the sea and collected by men in a boat below (Martin 1753, 22–3). The teacher told Connell (1887, 131–4) about a trip he made to Boreray with thirteen men for gannets in April. Four men stayed with the boat; the rest landed and waited in one of the bothies until it was dark; they lit a fire and told stories, then had evening prayer, supper and went to work. They divided into three groups to go down the rocks, and continued killing until daylight if the birds were not disturbed. Everyone had cuts on their hands from the sharp beaks. According to Wiglesworth (1903, 50) the autumn raid on the gannets had stopped about the turn of the century, as the price of oil had dropped; adults were still taken in the spring. Gannets were normally brought back from Boreray and the Stacs for processing, though if a party stayed on Boreray for any length of time the birds were plucked and dressed there as Wilson (1842, 27) observed.

Fowling equipment

Clarke (1824, 270) noted the ropes, rods and snares suspended from the hut roofs, together with bunches of bladders full of fulmar oil. Examples of all these survive in museum collections (table 15, figure 82, overleaf).

Martin (1753, 54) refers to three hemp ropes, each 24 fathoms long, protected by salted cow hide cut in a long strip and wound round the rope. These were common property. They might be joined to reach further. MacAulay (1764, 182) speaks of 30 fathom ropes made of plaited cow hide strips and protected by sheepskin. Equal in value to the two best cows on the island, they were the most valuable possession a man could have, inherited by the eldest son, or, failing sons, a daughter. Clarke (1824, 270), saw ropes varying in length from 16 to 30 fathoms, two ply, made of two lengths of sheepskin strips surrounded by plaited cow hide. He acquired one with a circumference of three inches. New ropes could be identified by the hair still adhering to them. The ropes were valued at 13 pence a fathom. The same construction is described by Ross (1890, 57). Here there are different accounts of the materials used for the core and sheath of the ropes; possibly reflecting variation over time. Some of these ropes were older than their owners (MacLean 1838, 9). They were apt to slip in wet weather (Ross 1890, 57). The ropes would probably receive ample dressings of fulmar oil which would keep them supple; Smith (1879, 36) comments on the weight of leather, and suggests that there was a leather sheath to protect the rope where it went over the edge of a cliff, rather than a complete casing of leather.

Table 15
Fowling Equipment in Various Collections

Horse hair ropes

Manufacture	Length and Thickness	Date collected	Collection
3 ply x ?3 ply	150+216" x $^3/_4$" eye one end	pre 1930	Dunvegan Castle
3 ply x 2 ply	over 120" x $^5/_8$" knotted, frayed		HFM FF91
3 ply x 3 ply	540" x $^1/_2$" eye one end 2$^1/_2$ lb.		Private
3 ply x 3 ply	22" x $^5/_8$" sample	1889	OPR (Wallis)
not seen		1877	RMS MP 102
not seen		1931	RMS MP 482
not seen			RMS NT 22

Hide rope

3 ply of 2 strips 12$^1/_2$" x 1$^1/_4$" ?sheepskin		GAGM 4ax–94

Multiple snares

Length	No. nooses	Material in end loops	
501/2"	c 49	grass/rag	HFM FF85
53"	c 41		GAGM 4y-91
60"	33+	grass/grass	Oban
63"	33+ ?	rag	OPR (Wallis)
	c 34	grass	Dunvegan Castle
not seen			RMS
50"		rag/rag	Private

Single snares

Length	
c 16"	GAGM 87-47a
c 19"	OPR
not measured	Dunvegan Castle
not seen	RMS

Gannet stomachs

Length and maximum diameter	
15$^1/_4$ x 2$^1/_4$	GAGM 4af–91
17$^3/_4$ x 3$^1/_4$	GAGM 90-52e
18 x 2$^3/_4$	GAGM 87-47b

Fulmar oil

Phial of oil	OPR

RMS: Edinburgh, Royal Museum of Scotland, GAGM: Glasgow Museums and Art Galleries, HFM: Kingussie, Highland Folk Museum, OPR: Oxford, Pitt Rivers Museum

MacAulay (1764, 185) saw the less valuable horse hair ropes, which were 9 or 10 fathoms long, and were used in easier places than the hide ropes. In 1815 MacCulloch (1824, 173–4) found a man ready to demonstrate his prowess on Conachair cliff with a horse hair rope. Possibly Connell (1887, 127) was confusing the two types when he said that until recently there were ropes of horse hair encased in cow hide as no one else mentions this. A horse hair rope was used for the climb of Stac Biorach in 1883 (Barrington 1913, 199–201). In 1890 there was, apparently, only one left, used only where a rope was not really necessary (Ross 1890, 58). Kearton (1897, 124–6) bought the 'last' old horse hair rope on the island, for 12/6. It was 52 feet long and weighed 3 lb. The hair had cost 5/- per pound. There was apparently no one left who knew how to make one. Heathcote (1900a, 135) however, found that there were still 'one or two' such ropes on the island, still occasionally used.

Figure 82. *Examples of fowling gear*

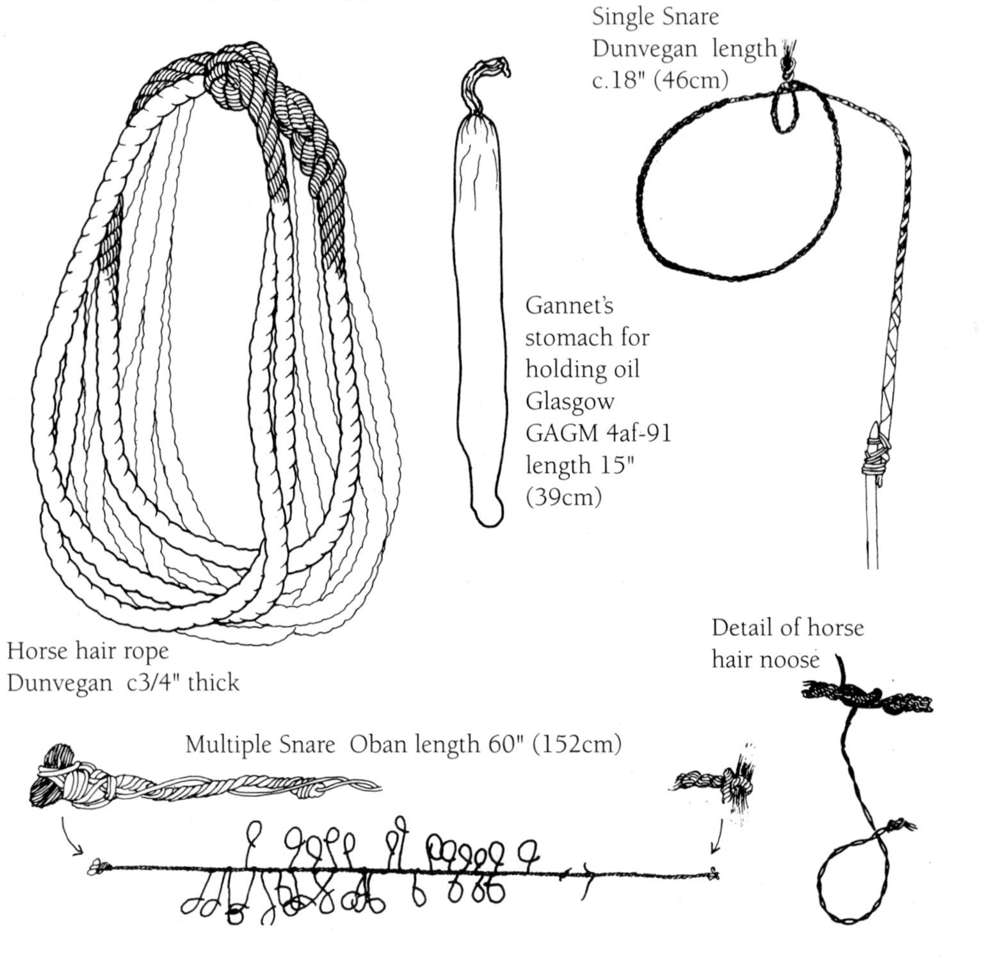

Single Snare
Dunvegan length
c.18" (46cm)

Gannet's stomach for holding oil Glasgow GAGM 4af-91 length 15" (39cm)

Horse hair rope
Dunvegan c3/4" thick

Detail of horse hair noose

Multiple Snare Oban length 60" (152cm)

There are records of horse hair being imported in 1860, 1867, and 1877 (RHASS papers). The surviving ropes are all three strand, each strand in turn made of two or three strands; two of the whole ropes have an eye at one end.

In 1841 (MacGillivray 1842, 62) hemp ropes were being used; Sands (1877a, 89) mentions manilla also. By 1889 (Ross 1890, 58) each man had a hemp rope of 20 to 30 fathoms.

Some later authors such as Wiglesworth (1903, 23) mention the former use of straw ropes; although straw ropes were made for anchoring thatch and making creels, none of the earlier authors mention their use in climbing.

Atkinson (1831, 33), MacKenzie (1911, 43) and Sands (1878, 89) all mention the testing of ropes at the beginning of the fulmar harvest; this was done by three men pulling on each end (Elliott, 1895a 124). In 1927 Cockburn photographed this (SSS BVIII39c 1973) in Gleann Mór.

Barrington (1913, 198) saw fowlers on Conachair working from a rope secured to a stout stick driven into the ground several yards from the cliff edge; Ross (1890, 58) says that they did not secure ropes in this way, but recordings (MacInnes and MacQueen 1961) indicate that they did.

Young birds were caught on the nest. Gugas were either killed by hand or with a stick (MacDonald 1823, 27; Sands 1877a, 55). Adult gannets were killed by dislocating a joint in the neck very near the head (MacAulay 1764, 134).

There were gins or snares made of horse hair; MacAulay says these were fastened to a stake fixed well in the ground, but Martin says the ends were anchored by stones, and probably both methods were used, depending on the terrain. According to Martin, these were used for gannets as well as smaller birds. MacLeod (1756–75) mentions their use for puffins, and by the early nineteenth century (MacKenzie 1911, 55) they were used only for puffins. One woman caught 127 in three hours; another 280 in a day (Kearton 1897, 111–2). Using four or five, a person could catch several hundred on a suitable day. Those surviving have between thirty five and fifty nooses of two ply loosely twisted horsehair twine which is threaded into a two ply cord; the ends often have a loop of cord, which is sometimes round a loop of rag or twisted grass, probably used in anchoring the snare with pegs.

Horse hair nooses were attached to the ends of fishing rods and used to catch birds at a distance; the nooses were stiffened at one end with a gannet feather (Clarke 1824, 284), and the rods were about 13 or 14 feet long (Atkinson 1838, 220). They were used to catch any of the birds, particularly gannets; Campbell (1799, f 75) adds that they were used to catch guillemots on Stac an Armin. Ross' (1890, 65–6) sketch of a snaring rod shows a short curved section between the noose and the main part of the rod; this allowed the operator to slide the rod along the ground, keeping it very steady, and at the same time have the noose at a suitable height for putting over the bird's head. Angus Gillies once took 620 puffins in a day with a fowling rod (Kearton 1897, 81). A few single nooses survive; they are very neatly made. A three strand plait of horse hair diminishes in thickness towards one end, which is knotted to make a small noose. At the other end a strip of quill is incorporated into the plait, and two further strips are woven around the first few inches, to stiffen it. Both Donald and Norman MacQueen described the making of these snares to John MacInnes (1961).

Auks nesting on ledges just below cliff edges might be killed by knocking them down with poles as they were blown upwards by updraughts (MacCulloch 1824, 183). Puffins were also forced out of their burrows using pointed staves (MacLeod 1756–75).

MacLeod gives more detail about another way of catching guillemots. This was regarded as the most difficult feat and was used when the birds first returned, in late February or March; a man was lowered down to a good guillemot ledge, where he stayed overnight with a white cloth on his chest to deceive the birds, which thought they saw a group of white breasted companions, and so alighted beside the man. Large numbers could be killed in this way before it was light enough for the birds to perceive their mistake. This is probably the method briefly noted by Moray. MacKenzie (1911, 51) explains that the white cloth was used until the first bird was killed and could be used as a decoy; but Wiglesworth (1903, 57–8), who spoke to people who had participated, says the men wrapped themselves in white sheets as camouflage on the ledges whitened with droppings. A ledge was raided only once a year, but the men might go on two or three nights in a season, to various ledges. There is considerable variation in the reports of the number of birds which could be killed in this way; from 30 (Connel 1887, 130) or 60–70 (MacKenzie) or 100 an hour (Kearton 1897, 93) to 400 (MacAulay 1764, 152) or 500 (Wiglesworth 1903, 58) in a night.

Many authors mention dogs (p 194): MacAulay (1764, 186–7) gives a good account:

> *Every family in the island is furnished with one or more of those extraordinary dogs. They are a mixture of the tarrier, spaniel, and those that take the water: of their own accord they sally out early enough and soon return, bringing five or six puffins at a time.*
>
> *Sitting on the side of a hill with some of the people, I saw one of these little dogs stealing away from us: the men told me he would soon return with a considerable booty, accordingly he came back in half an hour and laid down his prey at his master's feet; being taught by experience and some friendly stroakings, that his owner had a just sense of the obligation, he went off the second time, and had much the same success.*

In the summer women or children (MacCulloch 1819, 30) took the dogs out and in a short time caught enough puffins to feed the family for the day. The dogs would not part with their captives to anyone but a member of their own family. Clarke (1824, 280) says that they would go to the cliffs with their masters and take to them young fulmars and young gannets. It seems unlikely that many would be capable of carrying a young gannet or would have the opportunity, except perhaps on Boreray. Dogs were taken at night to shearwater breeding sites; they pounced on the birds when they had just landed; a good dog might catch 60 or 70 in one night (MacKenzie 1911, 46). Murray (9.4.1887) saw dogs helping to catch shearwaters by pointing out which burrows were occupied. The use of dogs for catching puffins continued until late in the nineteenth century (Connell 1887, 128; Steele Elliott 1894, 129).

MacLeod (1756–75) says that puffin eggs were collected using a spoon on the end of a stick about three feet long.

Bothies and Cleitean

On Boreray, Soay, Dun, Stac Lee and Stac an Armin there are bothies where people either went to stay deliberately or took shelter if they were stranded by bad weather (pp 155–9). The one on Stac Lee was used as an insurance against unfavourable weather preventing a party landing just before the guga fledged: if they took advantage of an opportunity to land a few days before the critical date, then stayed in the bothy, they were sure of the harvest. On Soay, Boreray and Stac an Armin there were numbers of cleitean for the storage of eggs, birds and turf. When Martin (1753, 22–5) visited Stac an Armin the islanders took home 800 gannets from the preceeding year; these must have been there for at least nine months. The birds were reclaimed by their owners who recognised them by distinguishing marks made on their feet.

Processing

In the seventeenth century birds were preserved by drying in cleitean; no salt was used. By 1758, 'every family has a great number [of fulmar] salted in casks for winter provisions, and the amount of the whole is about twelve barrels' (MacAulay 1764, 149). This became the normal method of preserving the larger birds. Barrel sizes must have varied over time; in the 1830s 80 salted gugas would fill a barrel (MacKenzie 1911, 49).

After plucking fulmar were split lengthways down the back and the giblets removed. If the birds were to be preserved, salt was put in the body cavity, and the birds were pickled in brine like herrings. Before plucking the oil was poured out; the fat from within the body was melted and added to the oil, and sometimes the skins were boiled and the fat skimmed off (Wiglesworth 1903,67).

Some gannets were brought back to the village in the feather, and some were processed on Boreray. If necessary they were dried off before plucking by sticking their long bills into an upper course of walling, allowing the birds to hang (MacLean 1838, 40). For drying, gannets were split down the back. Gugas processed on Boreray were reduced to bundles of feathers and the fleshy joints: the legs and backs (Wilson 1842, 27); this would avoid wasting boat space. Fat from gugas was kept in adult gannets' stomachs (MacAulay 1764, 145). Three of these containers which survive are of a similar size and would hold between two and three imperial pints.

Puffins were plucked, split, cured and hung to dry on strings across the ceiling, providing a 'fast food' facility, as one could be taken down and quickly grilled by the fire (Kearton 1897, 113); they were also salted in tubs for winter (Elliott 1895a, 129).

Feathers and oil

From the late seventeenth century or before (MacKenzie 1681–4) feathers contributed to the rent. MacLeod (1814, 912–3) gives information about the numbers of birds required to produce a stone of feathers. He received 140 stone of feathers annually, each stone containing 24 lb, so that he received 240 imperial stone. These were derived thus (using St Kilda stones):

Species	No. of birds per stone	No. stones	No. birds killed
Gannet	150	70	10,500
Fulmar	160	30	4800
Guillemot	750	5	3750
Razorbill	750	5	3750
Puffin	800	30	24,000

Unfortunately these potentially useful figures are contradicted: according to MacKenzie (1911, 48), 80 adult gannets yielded 1 stone (of 24 lb) of feathers; Milner (1848, 2058) goes further, with 80 fulmar per stone but agrees with the figure of 800 puffins. According to MacAulay (1764, 154) and Sands (1877a, 47, 59) puffins provided best quality feathers; in the late nineteenth century these were worth an extra shilling per stone, which is not consistent with MacKenzie's (1911, 52) assertion that all auk feathers were poor. In the 1890s all the feathers were mixed (Kearton, 1897, 119).

MacCulloch (1824, 195) saw the settlement at plucking time: 'The town is paved with feathers, the very dunghills are made of feathers, the ploughed land seems as if it had been sown with feathers'.

Sands (1877a, 47–9, 84–89) records that in July 1875 and 1876, as in previous years, parties of unmarried women were taken to Soay and to

Boreray, where they stayed for several weeks in bothies and caught puffins almost solely for the sake of their feathers. They took dogs with them and set snares; their fingers were benumbed by the constant plucking and they had to remove the stouter quills with their teeth. Most of the bodies were left on the islands. Occasionally a group of men went over to Boreray for the day and returned with a load of puffins to be plucked at home. At one time the women went at the same time as the men, who were plucking sheep. Even on Hirte, the birds were taken for their feathers, and though some were eaten, many of the bodies were used for manure or thrown away.

By 1889 women were no longer going to Boreray to 'make feathers' (Ross 1890, 6). The price of feathers fell at the end of the century and they became a by-product of harvesting food (Wiglesworth 1903, 19).

According to MacAulay (1764, 148) every fulmar yielded nearly an English pint of oil, but MacKenzie (1911, 44) says it was a gill. A phial of oil collected about 1889 is of a clear yellow colour.

Numbers of birds taken

The numbers of birds taken must be related to the numbers available: that is, the colony sizes. Colonies can disappear, increase or decrease for reasons sometimes apparently unrelated to human activity, so the present pattern is not necessarily a reliable guide to past distribution, nor was there necessarily ever any long-term stability in numbers. Harding et al (1984, 31) suggest that phosphatic cementation of the boulders on Ruaival implies a long history of seabird activity. There are scarcely any reliable figures for the numbers of breeding birds when St Kilda was inhabited, and few until recent counts, which show some variation. Counting birds is not easy, and is often done in terms of nest sites, giving numbers of breeding pairs, rather than counting individuals, but here there are difficulties with birds breeding in burrows or crannies, such as puffins and shearwaters. Thus the results of recent counts (table 16) give figures which are not directly comparable between species.

Table 16
Results from Recent Bird Counts: Main Prey Species

Year	Species and counting unit				
	Fulmar 'apparently occupied sites'	Gannet pairs/ occ. sites	Guillemot counted as individuals	Razorbill counted as individuals	Puffin pairs/occupied burrows (est)
1977	43,977		22,085	3000+?	300,000
1979		c.40,000			
1985		50,050			
1987	62,786		22,705	3814	230,051*

*140701 (Tasker 1995, 62)
Manx Shearwater: impossible to count or estimate, present in 100s, probably not large colonies.
Sources: Harris and Murray 1978; Murray and Wanless 1986; Tasker et al. 1988

Table 17
Notes on Numbers of Birds Reported as being Killed, and Eggs Taken

Year	Location, date, number, comments	Authority
Gannets		
1696	Stac an Armin: 800 (at least)	Martin, 1753, 25
1696	Total: 22,600	Martin, 1753, 59
late C17	Stac Lee, August: 5000–7000	Martin, 1753, 23
late C18	4 men, 1 night: 1200	Buchanan 1793, 122
1823	One expedition: 1600	MacDonald 1823, 27
1827	One expedition July 13: 800	Kennedy 1932, 286
1830–43	Annual total never more than 4000; half adults, half gugas	MacKenzie 1911, 48–9
1840	Adults: 1600	MacKenzie 1911, 48–9
1885/6	Boreray, April, one expedition, 10 men: over 500 (considered poor)	Connell 1887, 131-4
1880s?	Boreray, 20 men, 1 exceptional day: 1000	MacDonald 1886 872
1907	Boreray, April, one expedition: over 100	MacLachlan 9.4.1907
Fulmar		
1830–43	Annual catch of young: c.12,000	MacKenzie 1911, 42
1830s	Annual total: 18,000–20,000 [4–5 barrels per family, 200 per barrel]	MacLean 1838, 9
1885	Preserved: 400–500 per family [x 16 = 6000–9000 plus some eaten fresh]	MacNeill 1885, 7
c.1902	Annual average 7500	Wiglesworth 1903, 67
1902	9600	Wiglesworth 1903, 67
Puffins		
1876	89,600 (calculated)	Sands 1878, 89
Gannet eggs		
1823	Boreray, May 24, one expedition: c.800 plus several hundred left on Boreray	Kennedy 1932, 117
1887	Boreray and stacs, April, one exp. 180	Murray 2.5.1887
1902	Stac Lee summit May 14: 1400	Wiglesworth 1903, 51
Guillemot eggs (eggs from Stac Biorach almost certainly guillemot)		
early C18	Stac Biorach: 288 (24 dozen)	MacAulay 1764
1838/43?	Stac Biorach : 17 baskets, 400 in each and another 14 baskets later same year	MacKenzie 1911
1902	Total guillemot: 4800 (poor year), good year generally 6000	Wiglesworth 1903, 55
Puffin eggs		
early C18	54 creels, 600 in each, from 'one rock'	MacLeod 1756-75
Unspecified eggs		
1697	One expedition: 29 baskets, 400-800 in each	Martin, 1716, 293
1697	60 visitors given 16,000 eggs in 21 days	Martin 1753, 10

Table 17 gives such figures as can be found in the literature for numbers of birds and eggs taken. Clearly some of these cannot be taken seriously: Martin's figure of 22,600 for an annual harvest of gannets would result in serious depletion of the population at present levels for instance, and all the figures for numbers of eggs in baskets are suspect: the maximum total population of guillemots recorded on all the Soay Sound stacks is 2680 individuals in 1959 (Tasker et al 1988, 25) and Stac Biorach could scarcely hold more than it does now, so the maximum number of eggs that could be taken from it is likely to be less than 1,000. 400 guillemots eggs would weigh about 95 pounds, not an easy burden to manouevre carefully. 54 creels, each containing 600 puffin eggs, would require the raiding of 32,400 puffin burrows or over half the recent population of Dun, and the contents of one creel would weigh about 85 pounds. Nineteenth century figures may be more accurate but latterly they represent harvesting by a declining population.

By 1902 (Wiglesworth 1903, 59, 63) puffins were taken only for food and for sale; the birds were increasing in numbers and damaging pasture. The people said that manx shearwaters were less numerous because the puffins had driven them out.

Other birds

Some birds other than those taken for food or feathers were harried. The falcons noted by early authors (Monro 1961, 78; Martin 1753, 26, 55–6) were probably of economic importance; they were likely to have been peregrine falcons, highly prized for hunting. Martin watched two young men raid a nest and bring the birds back. The last entries in the MacLeod accounts relating to falconry date to 1706 (Grant 1981, 630), when MacLeod's falconer and his men were sent south from Skye with hawks. Some birds were regarded as competitors and treated accordingly. The nest of a white-tailed sea eagle was destroyed by fire (Connell 1887, 125) and black-back gulls were tortured (MacAulay 1764, 158; Elwes 1869, 36).

Effects of Tourism

The earliest record of a demonstration of fowling is that of MacAulay (1764, 184–5), who found the potential danger shocking. Visitors often came at times when cliff fowling was not 'in season' and the demonstrations became displays of skill, usually at Bearraidh na h-Eige (the Gap), the nearest convenient place to give a display that was impressive and on the smooth vertical cliff avoided disturbing the fulmar before the young were at their best (Seton 1878, 198–200).

Latterly, eggs and birds were collected for sale, particularly once the steamer services started in the late 1870s; visitors bought 'pretty' eggs as souvenirs. This was an expanding market, with dealers placing orders for unlimited numbers of eggs from species rare elsewhere, such as the fulmar, Leach's fork tailed petrel and the local wren (Wiglesworth 1903, 21). Some felt that the last two were endangered by extensive collecting. In the spring on a visit to Boreray as many eggs as possible were collected for blowing and selling to visitors (Ross 1890, 5, 53, 90), some being sent away by post. Most eggs were sold at 1d each, but those of manx shearwaters fetched 1/- (Elliott 1895a, 133, 1895b 286). In 1902 eggs of the following were taken for sale: raven, hooded crow, peregrine falcon, shag, gannet, eider duck, great black backed gull, guillemot, puffin, storm and Leach's petrels – the last in several hundreds (Wiglesworth 1903, 43–68).

Stac Biorach

When men climbed Stac Dona (now Stac Biorach) the leader of this extraordinarily difficult climb earned four extra birds above his normal share (Martin 1753, 20). MacAulay indicates that this stac was climbed annually although the eggs harvested were not essential. By the nineteenth century, this rock was not always harvested: Atkinson (1831 f 45–9) learned that it was four years since it had been raided, but two young men, Roderick MacDonald and John MacDonald, climbed it for the reward of all the tobacco he and his friends could muster, and took a large number of guillemots from the top. It had not been climbed again by 1838 (MacLean 1838, 12). Barrington (1913, 195–202) is the only person other than a St Kildan known to have climbed this rock, which he did under the leadership of Donald MacDonald and Donald MacQueen in June 1883. In 1886 Connell (1887, 78) recorded that few men could now manage it and that one who had been up 'lately' said he would never go again. In 1896 Kearton (1897, 124) learned that 'a few years ago' two men had climbed it; Heathcote (1900a, 142) said that two men went up in 1898 or 9 but it was 7 or 8 years since the previous ascent, and in 1902 there were five men alive who had climbed it, three of whom were too elderly to attempt it again (Wiglesworth 1903, 23).

Fowling accidents

Moray (1678, 928–9) suggests that accidents were not unusual. Both he and Martin (1716, 294) record one exceptional incident when a man setting snares caught his big toe in one and fell, hanging head down on one of the lower cliffs all night before being rescued. MacAulay (1764, 183–4) heard of a man who fell the full length of a cow-hide rope in 1759; his companion braced himself and was able to keep his station.

MacCulloch (1819, 30), Atkinson (1831, f33) and MacKenzie (1911, 23–26) agree that accidents while fowling were rare; Margaret MacLeod, aged 67 in 1843, knew of eleven in the previous sixty years, but the eleven names do not correspond exactly to the accounts MacKenzie gives of some accidents, nor to the circumstantial details given with the texts of some of the laments he recorded. Table 18 shows such information as is available; more detail is given about some of these incidents below.

Euphemia MacCrimmon's father and grandfather fell into the sea when the rock against which the younger man was bracing his foot gave way. A father lowered his son to a guillemot ledge on Dun; while catching birds, the son untied the rope to allow him to reach further, and fell into the sea. A woman checking snares set for fulmar in spring lost her footing and fell into the sea. Murdoch Gillies and his daughter (not listed in table) went to a ledge to wait overnight for guillemots and were never seen again. Neil MacDonald fell into the sea while going to collect a cache of birds during the August fulmar harvest. One lad fell from a cliff while trying to catch a falcon (Atkinson 1831, f 44). MacLean (1838, 12) tells of a sad incident in which a young man fell to a grassy ledge; though he survived, all the ropes the community had were not long enough to reach him and on the third day he died.

Elwes (1869, 33) speaks of young men being too keen to trust in their own skill and to work without ropes; three lives had been lost in this way 'in the

Table 18
Deaths while Fowling, or by Falling from Rock

1783–1843	Paul Finlay; Christian MacCrimmon and two of family; Murdoch Morrison and son John; John MacCrimmon; Neil MacDonald; Donald Gillies and two sons Finlay and Alexander
	(some of these may be the same as those listed below)
1783 or later	Donald MacCrimmon and ? MacKinnon (father-in-law)
c.1825–1830	Two sons of Alastair Gillies and another?
1830	20.7 Alastair Gillies, 62
1845	18.8 Donald MacDonald, c.25
1862	1.5 Ewen MacKinnon, 27
1866	4.6 John Gillies, 18
1888	22.12 John Gillies, 79 (possibly fishing? fell by Oiseval)
1906	2.10 Norman Gillies, 13 (fishing from Rubha Cholla)
1916	17.8 John MacDonald, 31 and Ewen Gillies, 34

Sources: Carmichael 1941, 106–7; Lawson pers. comm.; MacKenzie 1911, 23–26; MacLachlan 2.10.1906; Morgan 1862, 188: (5 deaths in 35 years previous to 1860)

last few years'. In 1866 John Gillies, when out on Oiseval to collect turf with his sister, on impulse went to get a puffin and fell (Wiglesworth 1903, 24; MacLachlan 14.3.1908). In 1892 a young girl watching men collect eggs on Dun miraculously survived when the wind blew her over a cliff; she fell onto an earth slope, her head in a puffin burrow, so that her shoulders took the force of her fall (Kearton 1897, 126).

Two accounts have been repeated by various authors. The first (MacLean 1838, 13) tells of the father and two sons who were all down a cliff; seeing that a sharp stone had cut the rope they realised it would support only one person; the sons prevailed upon their father to go first and he reached the top, to see his sons fall when the rope parted. The second account (Wilson 1842, 53–4) is of the higher of two men on one rope, who saw the rope fraying above him and concluded it would support only one man, so he cut the rope beneath himself and was hauled to safety just before it parted. MacKenzie, who must have known of these incidents if they happened, does not relate either of them.

MacKenzie speaks of the fear and sorrow occasioned by fowling accidents and Carmichael (1941, 106–7) noted that people felt particularly bitter when rough seas prevented their recovering a body. A number of the recorded songs are laments for people lost in this way; they illustrate the grief at the loss of a spouse or relative and often the main supporter of a family.

The Gannet 'Sentinel'

The accounts of catching gannets at night almost arouse suspicions that the St Kildans were spinning yarns for their visitors. Martin (1753, 29) says:

The Solan Geese have always some of their number keeping centry in the night, and if they are surprized, as it often happens, all the flock are taken one after another; but if the centinel be awake at the approach of the creeping fowlers, and hear a noise, it cries softly, Grog, grog, at which the flock move not; but if the centinel sees or hears the fowler approaching, he cries quickly, Bir, Bir, which should seem to import danger, since immediately after, the whole tribe take wing, leaving the fowler alone on the rock.

MacAulay (1764, 141–2) was told that the 'sentinel' story was not true, but that the fowlers could indeed tell from the birds' tone whether they were alarmed or not, and would only proceed when they cried *Grog, Grog.* When they had killed one, its neighbours began to mourn over it, and were so distracted that it was easy to kill them. Buchanan (1793, 124–5) heard a more confused and fantastic tale:

The fowler, with a white towel about his breast,…gently moves along on his hands and feet…the goose takes the fowler for one of the straggling geese coming into the camp, and suffers him to advance. Then the fowler very gently tickles one of his legs, which he lifts and places on the palm of his hand; he then as gently tickles the other, which in like manner is lifted and placed on the hand. He then…moves the centinel near the first sleeping goose

…which woke up and started fighting the sentinel, beginning a general dispute which occupied all the birds who fell easy prey to the fowlers. The sentinel story was still current in the twentieth century (SSS SA 1961/21) and was even repeated by zoologists such as Elliott (1895a, 134) and Kearton (1897, 92).

Fishing and the exploitation of sea mammals

In the late sixteenth century (Anon 1595) the St Kildans fished from the rocks but made no special effort to catch any quantity, although fish were plentiful in the seas around them. Martin (1753, 19) confirms this and names the fish: cod, ling, mackerel, conger, turbot, herring, 'braziers' and saith or lythe (Martin's 'graylords' and 'podloes' are either pollack or saith: both are also known as coalfish). Although there were plans to put up a fishing station on the island in the late eighteenth century (pp 93, 98), these came to nought, and in the early nineteenth century MacCulloch (1824, 184) and MacDonald (1823, 13) are agreed that the St Kildans did not fish, and MacKenzie (1911) does not mention it. In 1860 Otter (RHASS papers) pointed out that the lack of a good landing place and a secure anchorage for a boat was a deterrent to fishing, but he tried to encourage it, and 6,000 hooks were provided in that year. In 1873 long lines were requested (Smith 1879, 26) and in subsequent years men often went fishing overnight (Sands 1877a, 42; Connell 1887, 60–62) though the evenings available were limited by attendance at prayer meetings, as well as the weather.

Fish was not a popular dish (p 173; Sands 1877a, 39; Kearton 1897, 70). When fishing as a contribution to the rent the catch was divided equally among all the families but when fishing for food it was divided equally among the crew, and anyone fishing from the rocks might keep his catch (Ross 1890, 43–44). In the late 1890s there were several requests for boats for fishing (p 272). From at least 1874 salt fish contributed to the rent, the estate providing the salt (Sands 1877a, 42) but the quantity preserved varied considerably from year to year (figure 45).

In the mid sixteenth century preserved seals formed part of the rent (Monro 1961, 78). Moray (1678, 928) describes the danger of hunting seals in a geo on Soay. There is no record of later hunting.

While there is no record of any sort of whaling by the St Kildans, they used carcasses that came their way. Murray (20–25.8.1886) helped the men to tow a 28 foot whale from the Dun for the sake of its blubber. Kearton (1897, 45–6) was told that it was seen floating past and was towed into the bay, but the blubber melted in the sun's heat and the people were able to save only 150 gallons of oil. The jaw-bone seen in one of his photographs may have belonged to this whale. A scoop was made from the mandible of a large Pilot whale (p 170).

Between 1904 and 1928 there was a whaling station in West Loch Tarbert, Harris. The catchers sometimes left carcasses anchored in Village Bay to be towed back to Harris, a tantalising sight for people who valued the oil they represented. The whalers were very helpful in conveying post, and occasionally passengers (p 277).

13
Customs and Beliefs; Stories and Songs

In the late seventeenth and eighteenth centuries a diversity of customs and traditions enriched the lives of the St Kildans; during the nineteenth century many of these were eroded or lost through the disapproval of the church: 'they neither dance, nor sing, nor play games' (Heathcote 1900a 194).

Customs and Beliefs

Martin (1753, 62) refers to a game, probably a form of shinty, involving 'short clubs and balls of wood' which was played with enthusiasm on the beach, for prizes such as eggs, birds, hooks or tobacco. The people were also expert swimmers. MacDonald and MacKinnon (1982, 463–377) record the playing of shinty on the beach in Eigg at New Year.

The festivals of Christmas, New Year, Easter, Michaelmas (September 29), St Brendan (May 16) and St Columba (June 9) were kept (Martin 1753 44, 48; 1716, 287; Buchan 1727, 32; MacAulay 1764, 78, 81–2). Christmas and New Year's day were occasions for feasting, drinking, singing and dancing; Easter was observed with more solemnity. On St Columba's and St Brendan's days all the milk was given to the Steward in a 'treat'; in the mid eighteenth century he distributed it equally to all the people. At Michaelmas there were races on the ponies from the shore to the houses, every one taking a turn, riding with no saddle or bridle, only halters. A large triangular loaf was made, which was to be eaten within the day, shared by all the household. The custom of horse racing and the baking of the strùan or St Michael's cake, together with feasting and dancing, took place elsewhere in the Western Isles (Carmichael 1928, I 198–209). By 1758 this special cake was no longer made on St Kilda, and by 1799 (Campbell 1799, f35) the only holy days observed were Christmas, Good Friday, and Michaelmas, when the islanders fasted rather than feasting. The St Kildans continued to keep the 'old style' or Julian calendar until late in the nineteenth century; although Connell (1887, 72) noted that 'all the festivals are no more'. Murray (10.1.1887) accompanied the men in January to Soay to catch sheep for a New Year feast. The MacLachlans held school treats on New Year's day (MacLachlan 1.1.1907, 1.1.1908, 21.1.1909).

On the eastern slope of Mullach Geal is an area which was regarded as special in several ways (p 52; MacAulay 1764, 86–90). There was a little green plain there, called 'Liani-nin-ore' (*Lèana nan Ortha*) or 'Plain of Spells', where formerly the cattle were sained with salt, water and fire whenever they were moved from one grazing area to another. Here also is *Tigh an Triar* (House of the three or Trinity: Mathieson 1928, 127). Below this was another area, fertile in appearance, which the St Kildans obstinately refused to cultivate, on the grounds that it was sacred to a divinity whose name was forgotten, and that to till it was to invite disaster. Nearby was *Clach a' Bhainne* or the milking stone, where they used to pour milk for the *gruagach* or 'brownie' on Sundays, or, according to Mathieson (1928, 126) after the first spring milking, when they heard the fairies beneath rattling their spoons. Milk was offered to a *gruagach* in many other townships in the Western Isles (Martin 1716, 110; Carmichael 1928, II 306–7).

Another stone with unusual properties was the *Clach an eòlais*, a large stone not far from the burial ground. Anyone who stood on it on the first day of the quarter could foresee all that was to happen during that quarter (Sands 1977a, 81).

Some had the 'second sight' without seeking it. Martin (1753, 67) noted that only Roderick the Imposter (p 87) and a woman claimed to have it; within living memory a group of men on Soay had 'seen' the body of one of themselves floating in the sea shortly before his death by drowning. One of Roderick's descendants was the 'last pretender' to possession of this faculty in 1758 (MacAulay 1764, 240). However, Barbara MacPherson, widow of the missionary Alexander MacLeod (p 248), found that the people of St Kilda commonly had a presage of their own deaths; some months before the event, a person found he was accompanied by his own 'double' which mimicked his actions. One man tested it, by wearing straw rope garters instead of his usual ones, and the image appeared similarly attired (MacLeod 1763, 8).

In 1797 Clarke (1824, 277) was introduced to two men with the 'sight', one of whom sometimes saw other people clad in a winding sheet, before their deaths. MacKenzie (MacLean 1838, 22) was told by two men that they had each seen on separate occasions, a corpse being carried by a group of people; both visions foretold deaths.

Various manifestations of second sight, usually foretelling a death, have been related in the past in the Highlands and Islands (for instance: Martin 1716, 300–334; MacLeod 1763); they still occur and are not uncommon.

Occasionally there was an omen of an event, rather than a foresight; the cuckoo, an uncommon visitor, was regarded on St Kilda as foretelling the death of MacLeod or his Steward, or the arrival of an eminent stranger, and before 1697 a cuckoo had appeared before the deaths of the two last MacLeods (1664, 1693) and the two last Stewards (?, 1685), and before the arrival of several strangers (Martin 1753, 26). This belief survived: the cuckoo was seen before Norman MacLeod's death in 1895 (Kearton 1897, 128) and had not visited the island again by 1899 (Heathcote 1900a, 81) but in 1927 Cockburn heard one and neither MacLeod nor MacKenzie died (MacGregor 1931, 168); perhaps it was in honour of Seton Gordon's visit in June.

Stray herons, which lately have been recorded every year (Harris and Murray 1978, 14) were believed to be witches from Stornoway (Kearton 1897, 128).

MacKenzie (1911, 6) refers to a semi-transparent stone, valued both on St Kilda and in other parts of the Highlands. It could be obtained by boiling a raven's eggs and returning them to the nest. The raven would get a '*clach aotaig*' (*clach éiteig*) to try to revive the eggs, and it could be taken from the nest. Possibly the stone found in the 'Amazon's House' was such an amulet (p 64).

Martin (1753, 15) heard several traditions concerning the *Banaghaisgeach* (Female Warrior: 'Amazon'). In Gleann Mór was her house or dairy, within which there were places for her to lay her helmet and sword. She was reputed to have enjoyed hunting, and in her day the area between St Kilda and Harris was dry land, where she hunted deer. Unfortunately Martin would 'trouble his reader with no more' of the traditions about the 'Amazon', and all are now lost.

A custom in which Martin (1753, 61) was invited to take part was proof of a youth's eligibility for marriage. This test of balance took place on the 'lintel' of the natural 'doorway' on the west side of Ruaival. The young man stood 'on his left foot, having one half of it over the rock, he then draws the right foot towards the left, and in this posture bowing, puts both his fists further out to the right foot' and thus became 'worthy the finest woman in the world'. MacLennan (1925, 193, 350) gives the phrase *troigh is dòrn gulbann*: 'a foot and a fist from the toe' for this action. MacAulay (1764) makes no mention of this rite at all; it had been abandoned by 1799 (Campbell 1799, f 31). Martin refers to the stone as the 'Mistress-stone'. By the late nineteenth century the location was confused; Ross (1884, 84) refers to Stac Biorach as the 'Lover's or Mistress Stone' and Heathcote (1900a, 145) was shown a stone on the ridge near Claigeann Mór as the site. Martin only gives the name in English; possibly the name has some connection with a story told by Sands, identifying the lintel as a petrified maiden (see below).

Atkinson (1838, 219) noted in 1831 that the men assembled at a house slightly larger than the others; here they sat on the wall head and between them organised community affairs such as apportioning fowling rocks and settling disputes. Without mentioning the word, he compared it with Parliament, but Milner (1848, 2057) refers to their 'annual Parliament' though Sands (1877, 33) implies that he first named the assembly 'Parliament'. According to him, it was an almost daily meeting and was conducted in loud voices. Sometimes a minor matter was discussed at great length, but decisions could also be made swiftly (Ross 1890, 48–50).

Traditional tales

Campbell (1799, f 84) describes a gathering where stories were told; MacDonald (nd) says they were told at carding parties. The story of the burning of the people in a church has been recorded in Gaelic on tape (SSS SA 1952/132, SA 1961/19), but the other stories given here are known only in English texts. There are two main written sources of traditional stories gathered before the evacuation in 1930: a letter from Anne Kennedy, niece of the catechist, in 1862 (Kennedy and Thomas 1874, 702–11), and a book by Sands (1877a, 102–6), who spent a winter on the island in 1876/77.

Anne Kennedy was given her stories by Euphemia MacCrimmon, the oldest woman on St Kilda at eighty years; Carmichael (1928, 380–1) said she had

Table 19
Parallels for some St Kildan Stories

Place	Persons involved (if known)	Reference
Severing the hand/lighting fire to gain possession of land		
North Rona	Ness/Sutherland men	Thomas 1878, 556
Sutherland	MacKay/anonymous chief	Temperley et al. 1978, 173–4
Lismore	S Moluag/S Mahac or S Columba	Campbell 1885, 321–6
Ulster	MacDonnell/De Burgh	Day 1986, 92-3
Burning people in Church/Cave		
Toe Head	MacLeod/MacGhittich	Grant 1959, 64–6
Eigg Cave	MacLeod/MacDonald	Robertson 1898, 196–9; Grant 1959, 135-6, MacKinnon and MacDonald 1974, 141–2
Trumpan Church	MacDonald/MacLeod	Grant 1959, 137–9; MacLeod nd, 140–1
Kilnave Islay	MacDonald/MacLean	Clark & Fraser 1992, 110–7
Kilchrist, Urray	MacDonald/MacKenzie	MacDonald 1889, 11–35
St Duthus, Tain	?/MacKays	Douglas 1790, 394
Fairy Dairymaid with Milk		
Berneray, Harris		Dix & Paterson 1975, 132–5
Shawbost, Lewis		MacPhail 1897, 380
Achadh na ghirt, probably Glenshiel		Kennedy & Thomas 1874, 707
Changeling		
Benbecula		Carmichael 1954, 254–269
Upper Bornish, South Uist		Carmichael 1954, 254–269
Sollas North Uist		Swire 1966, 97–8
Eigg		Robertson 1898, 206

some beautiful songs. Sands must have heard tales from many different people. Table 19 gives parallels for some of the stories.

Severing the hand to gain possession of the island
First recorded by Morrison (1975 286–7), early in the nineteenth century.

St Kilda was claimed by both the MacDonalds of Sleat and the MacLeods of Dunvegan and Harris. It was agreed that the argument should be settled by a boat race: two boats the same size were to be built by the same person and allocated by casting lots. The two were to start at the same time and whoever arrived first and lit a fire was to be regarded as owner. MacLeod was ashore first and lit a fire and thus the islands came into the hands of the MacLeods. There is another version of this story in which the islands would go to whoever touched land first, after a similar race. Again the MacLeods won, but by a trick, as the MacDonald boat was to the fore when they neared the island, but one of the MacLeod crew cut off his hand and flung it ashore, so that a MacLeod hand first touched land (MacLeod nd 166).

MacCrimmon confuses this with the historical raid of Coll MacDonald or MacGilleaspuig in 1615 (pp 84–5); according to her, Colla Ciotach and his brother Gillespuig Og were racing for St Kilda: it was Coll who cut off his hand and threw it ashore at the point called Gob Cholla. This neatly explains Coll's nickname 'Ciotach' (left handed), and the two brothers may just be Coll himself, personified in different versions of his name.

The story occurs in several other places and is often associated with the MacDonalds (D A MacDonald, School of Scottish Studies pers comm). The hand appears in heraldic devices. St Moluag's sacrifice of a single finger is an interesting variant.

The Burning of the Population in the Church
(MacLean 1838, 20–21)

Several hundred years ago, two men from Lewis, Duigan and Fearchar mòr visited St Kilda. On a certain day the two went up to the top of Aois-mheall: they were no sooner up than down they came in a flurry, crying that the Sassenachs were coming, and, in the same breath, imploring the poor simple natives, who believed them implicitly, to betake themselves to the chapel…The inhabitants were no sooner in the chapel than the Lewis-men secured the door – set fire to the fabric, and burned every [one] living in the island except one young woman who happened to be absent. This woman, smelling that all was not right, concealed herself in a cave on the south side of the bay, preserving life for several months by stealing during [the] night from the ruffians' store. The Land stewart's Birlin was seen at the set time making towards the island; the

231

two men hurried to the beach to meet him and tell him a made-up tale; by this time the solitary woman made her appearance – the men were astonished – the secret was disclosed; – the stewart gave his verdict, namely, that Duigan and Fearchar mòr be both left upon Stac-an-ármin where they could get nothing but raw birds. Upon reaching Stac-an-ármin, Fearchar mòr said to Duigan, "Do not forget your flint and steel." On hearing this the stewart seized the fire-raisers, which when Fearchar mòr saw he gave a desperate leap into the fathomless main and was seen no more! Duigan was left on So'a, where he built a wall, to protect him from the north wind, which bears his name to this day, as also the cave in which he spent the remainder of his sorry existence.

MacCrimmon adds that Dugan and Fearchar were gathering heather which they used to set fire to the church. When the Steward left, he took the woman away and St Kilda was left uninhabited. Another version was recorded by John MacInnes from Norman MacQueen (MacInnes and MacQueen 1961, 215–219) in 1961, and his uncle, Donald MacQueen, had a similar version; both have variations from, and additions to MacLean's version. Both agree that the two men used to go to the Flannan Isles to steal sheep. The girl who escaped was nearly discovered one day when the two men smelt her fire; she covered the pot with her clothes to smother the smoke. The MacQueens agree that the girl hid in a cave, while MacCrimmon said that she hid in a 'teampull' on Ruaival, which Thomas identifies as St Brendan's – there is a cave in the cliff very close to St Brendan's called *Uamh Cailleach Bheag Ruaival*; a name which probably commemorates this event. According to Norman MacQueen, Dugan was 'there [Soay] alive for years: he used to eat the sheep and the birds. His ribs are there still; I myself have handled the ribs.'

MacGregor (1931, 128) relates a story of two St Kildans who rowed to the Flannan Isles in a day, (a distance of some fifty miles), took about a dozen sheep, and rowed back the next day. Probably this was an element which had become separated from the Dugan and Fearchar story.

The story of a group of people being burnt in a church or cave, occurs in several places (table 19). Not all of these incidents are historically attested, but the stories together show that the burning of people in a place of refuge, usually a church, occurs several times in Highland traditional history, particularly within the MacLeod areas; some of these incidents include the element of a single person escaping.

If this story was transplanted to St Kilda and given local detail after the smallpox epidemic, when new people may have brought their own stories with them, that would explain why Martin, Buchan and even MacAulay, do not mention it. Thus it was possibly established in local tradition in the later eighteenth century.

The Killing of the Son of the King of Norway

Effie MacCrimmon told this story:

> *A son of the king of Lochlin was wrecked on a rock a little west of St Kilda. He came ashore in a small boat, and while he was drinking out of a water-brook a little west of the present church, those who were then the inhabitants of St Kilda came on him and caught him by the back of the neck, and held his head down in the brook until he was drowned. The rock on which he was wrecked is called* Sgeir mac Righ Lochlain *or Rock of the Son of the King of Lochlan (Norway or Scandinavia), until this day.*

Sgeir Mac Righ Lochlainn is a small rock to the south of Soay. It is not known why the people killed this unfortunate castaway.

Thomas says that 'it would take many a page to relate all that is said to have happened in the isles to a son of a king of Lochlain; but in every place he appears to have come off "second best"'.

The Cave of the Irishman

A more fortunate castaway was an Irishman, who was crossing an inlet with a keg of whisky to visit friends one Christmas morning. He was storm driven to St Kilda, where he was rescued from a cave at the foot of cliffs. Almost a year passed before an opportunity arose for him to return home (Wilson 1842, 67).

Calum Mór's House (pp 147–8)

This building was said to have been built by one man in a single day (Kearton 1897, 82). MacGregor (1931, 128) states that it was a return for the help of a friend who plucked his sheep along with the rest when a group of men went to Boreray for that purpose. When they came back, they found the house ready for occupation. Possibly Calum is to be identified with the man left on Hirte when eighteen men were storm-stayed on Boreray (Carmichael 1941, 112–3).

The First MacDonald on St Kilda, and Refreshment from a Fairy Woman

Effie MacCrimmon related a story including several elements:

> *The first MacDonald who came to St Kilda was with his brother on the shore [of Uist?], gathering seaweed; he struck his brother on the head, and he thought he had killed him. He fled to St Kilda and had a family there. He had a son named Donald. Donald and another man, named John MacQueen, were going up to Oiseval, the most eastern hill, to hunt sheep. As they were passing a little green hillock they heard churning in the hill. John MacQueen cried, 'Ho! wife, give me a drink.' A woman in a green robe came out and offered him a drink [of*

233

milk]; but although he had asked for it, he would not take it. She then offered it to Donald, and he said he would take it with God's blessing, and drank it off. They then went to their hunting, when John MacQueen fell over a precipice and was killed; and it was thought he met his fate for having refused the drink. Donald MacDonald lived in St Kilda till he was an old man. He then went to Harris, where he was seized with the smallpox, and died there, about 133 years ago.

His clothes were brought back, and this started the smallpox epidemic of 1727 (pp 88–90). If this were true, then Donald MacDonald, and possibly his father too, would have been alive when Martin visited, and would be among those described as first or second generation immigrants. If the accident or murder took place in Uist, as Thomas suggests, that would be consistent with the claim of one of the St Kilda families to be related to Clanranald (p 130).

MacKenzie (MacLean 1838, 22) also had the story of the fairy refreshment, but in his version the men's names are not recorded. The one who refused the milk was told by the woman that he would not survive long for mocking her, and indeed he died in his house that night. According to MacCrimmon and Sands, when new houses were being built in the late 1830s, this very hillock was cut into to make a level space for foundations, and an ancient structure similar to the Amazon's house was found.

Other examples of this story are very similar, apart from the one from Shawbost, where a solitary woman was offered refreshment: the donor reassured her by invoking the curse of barrenness upon herself if it should do the recipient any harm.

This story is one example of the delicate relationship between humans and fairies, and the penalty paid for upsetting the latter.

As the basic story is clearly widespread, it may, if such an incident did not actually occur on St Kilda, have been transplanted. It is very like the Berneray version and could well have come with immigrants from the Sound of Harris, and been given local detail. This may be true also of other stories involving fairies, recorded by Sands.

"The Gift of the Gab"

One day a St Kilda woman was sitting alone in a hut, rocking her child in a cradle, when two strange women, dressed in green, entered the door, and, by some magical power, deprived her of the power of speech, so that she could not call to her neighbours; but she heard one of the women say to the other, 'This child, I see, has drunk of the milk of the cow that ate the mothan, and we can do nothing for him except give him the talent for language.' When the child grew into a man, it is related that he possessed an extraordinary fluency, could compose a rhyme on any subject at the shortest notice, and would talk more than any six men on the island – a questionable gift for his neighbours. His mother died in Harris when the grandfathers of old men were living.

The *mothan* was used in a variety of charms and if eaten by a cow protected not only the animal but also those who drank her milk, and her calf (Carmichael 1928, II 329–330; 1941, 132–3).

"A changeling"

It was in the harvest time, when a couple went into a croft in front of the village to pull their corn. The woman carried an infant, and before beginning her work she walked up to a hillock to lay her child upon it. The man looked alarmed, and earnestly entreated her not to lay the infant in that place. 'Mind your own business,' said she. 'Take your own way, then, as you always do,' he answered. In a short time she went to take the child off the hillock again, when her husband beseeched her, for the love of God, not to remove the child for a little. Happening to be in a more compliant temper, she did as she was asked; and it was a fortunate thing for her, because the man being gifted with the second sight, had seen the fairies come out of the hillock, take away the child, and leave an ugly goggle-eyed brat of their own in its place.

This is another example of a hillock in the village area being associated with fairies.

The story of the changeling child is a common and widespread one. The *mothan* and charms or spells could be used to prevent such an occurrence in some circumstances. Carmichael (1954, 254–269) gives several examples of incidents in the Hebrides where these precautions had been forgotten, and subterfuge was necessary to beguile the fairies into replacing the human child and reclaiming their own.

"A Water Bull"

One day a man who came down from the lag, *or hollow at the back of the village, with a burden of peats on his back, saw a door open in the side of a small conical hill. With great presence of mind he whipped out his knife, and stuck it in the ground at the foot of the door, and as he gazed, lo! a spotted bull came out and dropped a cow. This cow in course of time produced a calf which had no ears.*

There is a story about a man who shot a tarbh uisge, *or water-bull, with a bow and arrow, in a lake on the top of* Sgal.

J F Campbell (1890, xci) remarks that 'there are numerous lakes where the water-bulls are supposed to exist, and their progeny are supposed to be easily known by their short ears. When the water-bull appears in a story he is generally represented as friendly to man.' Fairy cattle and water bulls were widespread in the Hebrides, though probably no other water bull has ever inhabited such a small body of water as that on Mullach Sgar, where a pool sometimes lies in winter.

A more alarming tale concerned a beast on Boreray:

"The Devil in the Shape of a Bull"

Long, long ago, a party of St Kildians happened to be in the island of Boreray, and were living in the Taigh an Stallir, or the Hermit's House, and being short of provisions, one of them expressed the wish that they had the fattest ox in Clanranald's herd, when, on the instant, the lowing of an ox was heard outside. 'There,' said one of the party, 'now your wish has been granted; go out and kill him.' The man was too frightened to go out, but next morning the marks of cloven hoofs were to be seen in the mud outside.

It is not clear from the story that the beast was identified with the devil by the St Kildans, but perhaps Sands gathered this from his informant.

"The Well of Youth"

Once on a time an old fellow, in going up Connagher with a sheep on his back, observed a well which he had never seen or heard of before. The water looked like cream, and was so tempting, that he knelt down and took a hearty drink. To his surprise all the infirmities of age immediately left him, and all the vigour and activity of youth returned. He laid down the sheep to mark the spot, and ran down the hill to tell his neighbours. But when he came up again neither sheep nor well were to be found, nor has anyone been able to find the [Tobar na h-oìge] to this day. Some say that if he had left a small bit of iron at the well – a brog with a tacket in it would have done quite well – the fairies would have been unable to take back their gift.

The Soay Giant and the Petrified Maiden

On the summit [of Ruaival] a great number of huge blocks of trap have been piled up…One of the blocks rests like a lintel on two others…Whilst a girl was engaged snaring puffins on the cliffs about a mile from this spot, a strange man suddenly jumped to her from the island of Soa, another mile or so distant, and the prints of his heels are still to be seen in the place where he alighted. The girl was so frightened that she leapt to this mount; but fell petrified on the awkward place in which she now lies.

Songs

In the seventeenth century the St Kildans were fond of music, song and dancing. The only instrument they had was the jew's harp, though visitors sometimes brought pipes or a violin. Some had a talent for composition, their subjects being mainly love songs, and laments for relatives, extolling their courage, abilities, and affection for their family. The women sang while harvesting, working at the quern, spinning or waulking cloth; the men sang while rowing (Martin 1753, 38, 47, 57, 63; Martin 1716, 294; MacAulay 1764, 216–8). This general enjoyment of music continued into the early nineteenth century (Brougham 1871, I 101; Campbell 1799, f 52–6).

In the 1830s MacKenzie (1911, 4) encouraged the people to tell their stories and sing, during the winter evenings. His collection of songs, mostly laments, is the largest single surviving group. In 1865 Carmichael (1941, 106) and Euphemia MacCrimmon aroused strong disapproval by recalling and recording songs and poems 'for the people of St Kilda have now discarded songs and music, dancing, folklore, and the stories of the foolish past'. Although a few more songs were recorded subsequently, generally the people did not sing secular songs (Ross 1890, 36; MacDonald 1988, 140–1).

Campbell (1799, f 83) participated in a cheerful gathering, mainly of women, one evening, where songs were sung, tales told, and there was dancing to a sung accompaniment (probably *port a beul*). By 1842 (Wilson 1842, 24) dancing was apparently regarded as frivolous and was abandoned.

Nearly forty songs and verses composed on St Kilda have been recorded, some of them only in English paraphrases. They are important in being almost the only expressions of their own feelings by the St Kildans themselves. Table 20 shows a list with dates of publication. This shows that two thirds of the songs were collected before 1843, and that two of them exist in several versions.

The songs fall into four groups: numerous elegies, several love songs, several religious songs, and a small miscellaneous group; a few of those known only in English are probably considerably different from the Gaelic songs on which they are based.

Of the elegies, one commemorating the death of a youth on Soay is recorded from nine sources. The authorship is uncertain. Three early versions which are almost identical (MacDiarmid, Stewart, Campbell) give it as a lament of a young widow for her husband, but others (*Scots Magazine*, MacLean, and, much later, Connell) give it as the lament of a widowed mother for her son; and three early versions (*Scots Magazine*, MacKenzie) give the name of the lad as Iver. Several lines which do not occur in other versions have been omitted from the following:

Table 20
List of Songs and Sources

* These songs have music recorded.
E English text only

	MacDiarmid c.1770	Gillies 1786	Johnson (1788) 1853	Campbell 1799	Scots Magazine 1802/18	Stewarts 1804	Campbell 1818	MacKenzie 1830s (1906)	MacLean 1838	Dun 1848	Carmichael 1860s	D.R.M. 1876	Stewart 1877	MacKenzie 1880	Connell 1887	MacDonalds 1911
Elegies																
'Sann thall ann an Sòa	x	-	-	E	E	x	x	x	x	-	-	x	-	-	x	-
Elegy by Christian Campbell	-	-	-	-	E	-	-	-	-	-	-	-	-	-	-	-
Lament for John of t. yellow hair	-	-	-	-	E	-	-	-	-	-	-	-	-	-	-	-
Ach a Righ	-	-	-	-	-	-	-	x	-	-	-	-	-	-	-	-
Bheir mi toiseachd so thuiridh	-	-	-	-	-	-	-	x	-	-	-	-	-	-	-	-
'S goirt a dh'fhairich mi bhliadhn	-	-	-	-	-	-	-	x	-	-	-	-	-	-	-	-
'S tric mi 'g amharc gach là	-	-	-	-	-	-	-	x	-	-	-	-	-	-	-	-
Cha'n e uisge nan gleannta	-	-	-	-	-	-	-	x	-	-	-	-	-	-	-	-
'S tric mi amharc, 's gur cruaidh	-	-	-	-	-	-	-	x	-	-	-	-	-	-	-	-
'Nuair dh'fhalbh uait an todha	-	-	-	-	-	-	-	x	-	-	-	-	-	-	-	-
'S mi gun suigeart's mi gun sòlas	-	-	-	-	-	-	-	x	-	-	-	-	-	-	-	-
'S gur mise tha gu dubhach	-	-	-	-	-	-	-	x	-	-	-	-	-	-	-	-
Gur mise tha fo ghruaim	-	-	-	-	-	-	-	x	-	-	-	-	-	-	x	-
'Sann Di h-aoine roimh'n Domhnach	-	-	-	-	-	-	-	x	-	-	-	-	-	-	-	-
'S mor a briseadh a dh'eirich	-	-	-	-	-	-	-	x	-	-	-	-	-	-	-	-
Is olc leam mar thachair	-	-	-	-	-	-	-	x	-	-	-	-	-	-	-	-
Bithidh mo bhrathair air thus	-	-	-	-	-	-	-	x	-	-	-	-	-	-	-	-
Gur a mise tha air mo chlisgeadh	-	-	-	-	-	-	-	x	-	-	-	-	-	-	-	-
Tha mo cheist a Leodach	-	-	-	-	-	-	-	x	-	-	-	-	-	-	-	-
Cha b'e Sgioba na faiche	-	-	-	-	-	-	-	-	-	-	x	-	-	-	-	-
'Sann an caolas an lionaidh	-	-	-	-	-	-	-	-	-	-	-	-	-	-	x	-
Love Songs																
Tha Fleasgach anns a'bhaile so*	-	x	-	-	-	-	-	-	-	-	x	-	-	-	-	-
St Kilda Song*	-	-	E	-	-	-	-	-	-	-	-	-	-	-	-	-
Love song by Marion Gillies*	-	-	-	-	E	x	-	-	-	-	x	-	-	x	-	x
Iorram Hirteach	-	-	-	-	-	-	-	-	-	-	x	-	-	-	-	-
Oran Luathaidh Iortach	-	-	-	-	-	-	-	-	-	-	x	-	-	-	-	-
Oran Luaidh Iortach	-	-	-	-	-	-	-	-	-	-	x	-	-	-	-	-
The St Kilda maid's song	-	-	-	-	-	-	-	-	-	-	-	-	-	-	E	-
Religious Poems																
Bha sgeula air fhoillseachadh	-	-	-	-	-	-	-	x	-	-	-	-	-	-	-	-
Ochoin a Thi nach foir thu mi	-	-	-	-	-	-	-	x	-	-	-	-	-	-	-	-
Dia na gile, Dia na greine	-	-	-	-	-	-	-	-	-	-	x	-	-	-	-	-
Various subjects																
Nuallan na Calluinn	-	-	-	-	-	-	-	x	-	-	-	-	-	-	-	-
Eala bhi	-	-	-	-	-	-	-	-	-	-	-	x	-	-	-	-
Na Fir Chrodha	-	-	-	-	-	-	-	-	-	-	-	x	-	-	-	-
Oran Irteach*	-	-	-	-	-	x	-	-	-	-	-	-	-	-	-	-
Tobair nam Buadh (MacIain 1886)	-	-	-	-	-	-	-	-	-	-	-	-	-	-	x	-

MacDiarmid *c.*1770: Thomson 1992; Scots Mag 1802/1818: Leydon & Campbell 1802, Viator 1818
Carmichael 1860s: (1928, 1941, 1954); Melodies: Atkinson 1831, f 73; MacDonald 1895, Appendix 24, 30

Last Summer a-twelve-month left me sad and forlorn – the scramble for eggs caus'd all my woe and distress. In the Island of Soay, I left my dear love – I left the youth who was firm, who strengthen'd my weakness, and gather'd my sheep from the hill. In the cave that is narrow, thou wert left, my love, and mournful I stay behind.

The waves buffet thy body; thy limbs they tear and destroy. Curst be the cliff where thy feet lost their hold …I lost my sweet Iver: Ah! me, he'll never return.

My share of the eggs I shall never receive; the strong and alive will have them – for thou my son art gone! My share of the fowls now fly in the air – up to the clouds they ascend; there they sport and they flutter; but I am sad and forlorn! Thy mother's best blessings attend thy dear ghost – In the world everlasting may thy rest be serene. Thou wouldst not harrass nor distress; thou wouldst not come home with a lie.

The elegy recorded by Campbell (1799) in English is derived from this one but much of it is almost certainly Campbell's invention.

Another example was composed by Christian Campbell, for her husband:
Alas! I am sad: sorrow overwhelms me; my strength fails; I cannot climb the higher grounds. I have lost my delight! my mind is oppress'd; my spirit is heavy, and my pipes are not in tune. I knew thee well at a distance – thy cheeks were blooming; thy beautiful locks in curling ringlets hung.

Alas! that I was not near thee, when the knot loosen'd and thy hold gave way – I would fly with a rope to thy aid. Tho' my joints were lengthen'd, I would strive to relieve you; I would strive to relieve you unless my body would fail. Though not tall from earth, I delight to see thee – I would love thee more than a tacksman, though no cattle were counted for thee. Though distress'd by hunger, I fear'd not thy return with the night, no angry reproachful words flow'd from thy lips to my harm.

Though not tall in thy stature, thou wert handsome and lovely. Well could I know thee alone collecting the fuel for fire: – Alas! lonely and mournful at home, I weep and lament my fate. I am not single in sorrow – many women are afflicted with me.

Could I get them to purchase, you would not want linen or clothes – for beneath the sun I saw none I could compare with my love, and for him I would like to provide.…When fatigued with the toil of the day, I retire alone to my bed. Ah! wet is my pillow; in copious floods my tears of sorrow fall. But 'tis god who afflicts me – beneath his rod of affliction I groan.

Other earlier or contemporary elegies composed elsewhere sometimes contain similar formulas such as two by John MacCodrum (c.1693–1779):

'There is a load on me and a stitch torturing me with pain…Thou wert not insignificant to see on the sward' (Elegy for Alexander MacDonald of Balranald) and 'I have nothing in return, now that my support has forsaken me, but dullness of hearing and of sight and of vigour' (Elegy to Sir James MacDonald of Sleat) (MacCodrum and Matheson 1938, 84–9, 150–9) and and one by Mary MacLeod (Màiri nighean Alasdair Ruaidh c.1614–post 1705) 'This is a sore tale for the wife thou hast left' (Elegy for Iain Garbh Macleod of Raasay) (MacLeod and Watson 1934, 26–31).

All but one of the love songs are by women. One well known one was composed by Marion Gillies, celebrating her affection for Robert Campbell who visited in 1799 (p 104). His account suggests a brief flirtation rather then a long term commitment, though Seton (1878, 55) states that he returned in 1800 but the islanders were alarmed by guns on his vessel and hid. Marion had been betrothed (or, possibly, married) to John or Angus Gillies, but according to the song, determined to forsake him for Campbell of Islay.

> I love the youth whose locks are brown; great is the love I bear to him. I gave him a kiss in the evening; ah! how he then embraced me. Happy indeed was our meeting, though revilers make free with our fame. Is it wonderful that I should rejoice? Good cause have I to be gay since first the youth beheld me, – since the day he gave me his heart, and promised his faithful love. His ribbands stream on my shoulders, – they brightly encircle my head, and bind in ringlets my hair…I detest them who hearken; – I hate all who listen and tell. They delight to defame, – scandal is for ever their theme…Were I blest with the power of writing, I would soon send to —— a letter, to tell my love of my state, and inform him how every tongue speaks to his undoing and mine…With thee I would fly through the world. When shall I hear from my love, – when will he rush to my arms? Though I had for my portion all the riches possessed by the wealthy son of Bernera, I could yield it all for thee, and be happy, – I would yield it, my dear, to live with thee in a desart, where no step could approach us, and no voice of man could be heard.
>
> Though I delight to be merry, I will henceforth shun the young men. He who has wooed and won me; to him I will be faithful. I will not join in their follies, – no more rejoice in their sports. Angus descended from the tribe of Gillies. Angus of the dark brown locks, once I was thought to be thine, nor did I spurn at thy suit. But he, my beloved, came from his Isle; I will listen no more to thy voice.

Another song takes the form of an exuberant conversation between Euphemia MacCrimmon's parents before their marriage, so this must have been composed in the late 1760s or 1770/1. Extracts follow:

He: *Away bent spade, away straight spade,*
          Away each goat and sheep and lamb;
      Up my rope, up my snare, -
          I have heard the gannet upon the sea!

      Thanks to the being, the gannets are come,
      Yes, and the big birds along with them;
          Dark dusky maid, a cow in the fold!
      A brown cow, a brown cow, a brown cow beloved,
      A brown cow, my dear one, that would milk the milk for thee

She: *Thou art my handsome joy, thou art my sweetheart,*
      Thou gavest me first the honied fulmar!
          Dark dusky maid, etc.

He: *Thou art my turtle-dove, thou art my mavis,*
      Thou art my melodious harp in the sweet morning.
          Dark dusky maid, etc.

She: *Thou art my treasure, my lovely one, my huntsman,*
      Yesterday thou gavest me the gannet and the auk.
          Dark dusky maid, etc.

Two of the religious poems were composed during MacKenzie's revival in the early 1840s. One is by Neil Ferguson:

      Alas, oh Lord, won't you help me
      From my thoughts to an awakening
      Before the time comes when I die
      When there won't be time for repentance

The other, by Finlay MacQueen, describes the nativity and the spread of the gospel to foreign lands and to St Kilda. A shorter poem is in a similar vein:

      God of the moon, God of the sun,
      God of the globe, God of the stars,
      God of the waters, the land, and the skies,
      Who ordained to us the King of promise.

It was Mary fair who went upon her knee,
It was the King of life who went upon her lap,
Darkness and tears were set behind,
And the star of guidance went up early.
Illumed the land, illumed the world,
Illumed doldrum and current,
Grief was laid and joy was raised,
Music was set up with harp and pedal-harp.

In the 'miscellaneous' group, the 'New Year's Day' incantation is very similar to those recorded in Barra (Carmichael 1928, I 150–1) South Uist (Shaw 1955 24) Benbecula (Carmichel 1928, I 152–5; 1928, II 376) and Lewis (MacLean 1982, 362–5). This version from Benbecula is almost identical:

Now since we came to the country
To renew to you the Hogmanay,
Time will not allow us to explain,
It has been since the age of our fathers.
Ascending the wall of the house,
Descending at the door,
My carol to say modestly,
As becomes me at the Hogmanay.
The Hogmanay skin is in my pocket,
Great the fume that will come from that;
No one who shall inhale its odour,
But shall be for ever from it healthy.
The house-man will get it in his grasp,
He will put its point in the fire;
He will go sunwise round the children,
And very specially round the goodwife
The wife will get it, she it is who deserves it,
The hand to distribute the Hogmanay.
…
Since drought has come upon the land,
And that we do not expect rarity
A little of the substance of the summer,
Would we desire with the bread.
If that we are not to have it,
If thou mayest, do not detain us.

Another song was apparently composed at a time when there was a dearth of birds on St Kilda, though there is no clear reference to it in the song. There are references to fowling:

> *The killers of the solan goose –*
> *Much fair fame is theirs to tell of.*
>
> …
>
> *Thou wouldst bring the razor-bill*
> *From the ledges of the Dunan,*
> *And didst thou but get practice*
> *Thou wouldst harry the fulmar.*

One song refers to Saint John's Wort, valued as a charm against witchcraft, the evil eye, second sight and death; and with the positive property of ensuring peace in the home and fruitfulness of stock and crops. It is only effective when found accidentally (Carmichael 1928, II 96–7)

> *Saint John's wort, Saint John's wort,*
> *My envy whosoever has thee,*
> *I will pluck thee with my right hand,*
> *I will pluck thee with my left hand,*
> *Whoso findeth thee in the cattle fold,*
> *Shall never be without kine.*

Very little music has been recorded: there are tunes to accompany five songs, and one for which no words are known.

Wells

Within historic times in Scotland, some wells were and still are believed to have curative properties, often for specific ailments, and small gifts of pins, rags, pebbles and coins might be left by them (Walker 1883, 155). Three wells on St Kilda had special properties, and a fourth, Tobar Childa Chalda, near the village, was in daily use. It was the subject of a strange couplet known to Watson (1926, 98) during his childhood in Easter Ross in the late nineteenth century:

'*Tobar Childa Challda, allt Chamshroin a lobhair*'

an old St Kildan had a different version:

'*Tobar ghildeir chaldair, allt chamar nan ladhar*'

Martin (1753, 16) refers to the Well of Youth, in a place of difficult access on the north east side of the bay; his description locates it on Oiseval, whereas Sands' story locates it on Conachair and indicates that it was a magic well which appeared only once.

243

The well at St Brendan's, now a small pool, was used to summon a fair wind for sailing to Harris: each man 'stood astride the water, and when the last man so stood the wind immediately changed into the desired direction' (Mathieson 1928a 125).

The best known of all the wells was *Tobar nam Buadh*: Well of the Virtues or of the Excellent Qualities. Martin (1753, 16) implies that Harris people went to use it; possibly they travelled as part of the Steward's crew, and they found it effective against 'windy-cholics, gravel, and head-aches'. MacAulay (1764, 94) mentions a Harris man who went specifically in hopes of curing a disease from which he had been suffering for some time. He says it was supposed to cure deafness and nervous diseases. Nearby was an altar where offerings were laid: shells, pebbles, rags, pins or nails, and, rarely, copper coins of low value. A poem about Tobar nam Buadh was probably written by Rev Dr John MacDonald, the 'Apostle of the North' in the 1820s (p 248). When Rev John MacKay went to St Kilda to celebrate communion in 1925 (SG 3.9.1925), Lachlan MacDonald was his guide to Tobar nam Buadh (pers comm).

14

Religion, Education and Health

Apart from the ownership of the island and arrangements for paying rent, organised and long term contact with the mainland was, until the twentieth century, almost entirely in the hands of those concerned with the spiritual welfare of the islanders and with their education. A resident nurse was provided by the Government from 1914.

Religion: Ministers and the Church

A list of clergy resident on St Kilda is given in table 21, and details of their families are given in figures 80 and 81, with references.

In the late sixteenth century (Anon 1595) the islanders supported an old priest or clerk who guided them in the keeping of holy days. There is said to have been a 'priest' present in 1615 who was so ignorant that he could not teach the people the Lord's Prayer, the Creed, or the Ten Commandments (Buchan 1727, 36–7). If it is true that an elderly cleric was stationed there, he is unlikely to have been an ordained priest, as sixteenth century accounts (Boece 1527; Anon 1595; Monro 1961, 78) are agreed that a priest went in midsummer to baptise any children who had been born since his last visit. He also celebrated marriages as requested, and administered the sacraments, using his discretion. Monro implies that the visit was not invariably annual, saying that if the priest did not go, the people baptised their own children. He also says that they were 'scant learnit in ony religion', so any cleric based there in his day was not very diligent.

By 1673 the Reformation had affected the island; according to Moray (1678, 929) marriages were solemnised by the ground officer, and when children were fifteen or sixteen they went with the steward to Harris to be baptised there, which suggests that the people no longer had the privilege of a regular visit from any sort of clergyman. MacAulay (1764, 271–2) knew of this practice and was told that Iain Mór Macleod (d. 1649) was sponsor at the baptisms of an old man and his son, and on the same occasion several marriages contracted on St Kilda were declared legal. They were 'much given to keeping of Holy-days; having a number of little Chappels, where

245

sometimes they watch whole nights, making merry together with their offerings.'

In 1697 John Campbell, the minister of Harris, who had been to St Kilda before, was accompanied by Martin Martin (1753, 43–7, 1716, 287) who recorded that the people believed in 'God the Father, the Son and Holy Ghost; in a future state of happiness and misery, and that all events, whether good or bad, are predetermined by God.' They had prayers in the morning and evening, and 'begin their labours always in the Name of God.' A brass crucifix kept in Christ's church was used in celebrating marriages and in making an end to disagreements. The people stopped work at noon on Saturday and on Sunday they assembled in the burial ground, Christ's Church being too small to hold everyone, to say the Lord's Prayer, the Creed and the Ten Commandments. They fasted on Fridays (Adv Ms 33.3.20).

Baptisms were performed by the Ground Officer or a neighbour, another neighbour and his wife acting as godparents, bringing the two families into a special relationship with each other. The officer might also perform marriages; with everyone assembled he conducted a ceremony finishing with the couple putting their hands on the crucifix and swearing fidelity. The marriages might be ratified by the minister when he came. Mr Campbell married fifteen couples in this way in June 1697. By 1799 the crucifix had been taken away (Campbell 1799, f 37).

Christmas, New Year's Day, Easter, St Columba's day, St Brendan's day and Michaelmas were kept as festivals. By the end of the eighteenth century these were reduced to a few days kept by fasting (p 227).

In 1704 when the General Assembly decided to send someone to St Kilda to instruct the people in religion, Alexander Buchan, an army veteran (1727, 39–44) offered his services. When church funds failed he was supported by the Society in Scotland for the Propagation of Christian Knowledge and was ordained in March 1710. By 1727 he felt that the islanders could be regarded as 'Reformed Christians ...; yea, and Presbyterians too', and had so endeared himself to the people that they would not allow him to leave, even briefly to attend to his affairs on the mainland. The decimation of his flock by smallpox in 1727 (pp 88–90) must have been a great blow to him, and may have contributed to his death early in 1729.

The following year Roderick MacLennan and his wife went to St Kilda. Lady Grange (Mackenzie, 1817, 339) wrote that the minister was 'a serious and devout man', and he spent what time he could spare visiting her; the sympathy of the MacLennans may well have been the reason for their removal in 1743, to Tongue.

In 1733 (Scott, 1928, 193–4) Alexander MacLeod, advocate, (figure 39) who had supported Buchan, gave to the SSPCK £333 6s 8d, the interest from which was to be used to support a clergyman on St Kilda, preference to be given to those whose name was MacLeod. In 1739 the Society increased the annual salary to £25.

Table 21
List of Ministers, Missionaries and Catechists

Year	Incumbent
1704–1729	Alexander Buchan (1640/5–1729)
1729–1743	Roderick MacLennan
1743–*c*.1758?	Alexander MacLeod (?–*c*.1758)
c.1758–*c*.1768	?
c.1768–11785	Angus MacLeod (MacDhonil Oig) (?–*c*.1785/88)
1788–1820	Lauchlan MacLeod left 1821 (1762–1832)
1820–1829	No resident clergyman
1829–1830	Peter Davidson (did not go to St Kilda) (1788–1875)
1830–1843	Neil MacKenzie (1795–1879)

1843 Islanders joined the Free Church

1843–1856	No resident clergyman
1856–1863	Duncan Kennedy, catechist
1863–1865	A Cameron
1865–1889	John MacKay
1889–1902	Angus Fiddes

1902 1900 Islanders joined United Free Church

1902–190n	Lachlan MacLean
190n–1906	John Fraser
1906–1909	Peter MacLachlan (1856–1921)
1909–1912?	Dugald MacLean (1858–1924)
1912?–1914	Calum MacArthur
1914–1919	Alexander MacKinnon
1919–1926	Donald Cameron (? –1950)
1926–1929	John MacLeod (1885–1964)
1929–1930	Dugald Munro

Sources: Cameron 1973; Clarke 1824, 267–8; Connell 1887, 143; Ewing 1914, II 235; MacAulay 1764, 241; MacDonald 1823, 28; MacLachlan 1906–9; Muir 1861, 214; 1885, 61; Scott 1923, 93; 1928, 100, 193–4; 1950, 689–90; School Log Book; Seton 1878, 209; Steel 1988, 103; NTS Archive.

Alexander MacLeod, a Skyeman educated at King's College, Aberdeen, took up the post of catechist in 1743. His son, Donald, later became proprietor of St Kilda (p 99). Alexander died before 1758, but there was a missionary present when MacAulay visited in that year, whom MacAulay (1764, 24) described as a man of sense, virtue and piety, though in poor health. The next incumbent recorded by Scott (1928, 194) is Donald MacLeod, a Skyeman educated at King's College Aberdeen, given as catechist in 1774, but other evidence suggests that one Angus MacLeod had been catechist from about 1768. As he was also known as 'MacDhonil Oig' some confusion may have arisen. Originally from Bracadale he studied law in Inverness and afterwards went as a farmer to South Uist. According to Buchanan (1793, 143) he 'failed in his circumstances'. In Uist he was appointed catechist in 1768, possibly to go to St Kilda, as Clarke (1824, 267–8) noted in 1797 that the 'present minister' had been there for ten years, and his father for sixteen. In 1785 he petitioned the Presbytery to consider his old age and ill health, and soon after the appointment of Lauchlan, his son, to replace him, he died.

Lauchlan was educated at a parish school in Skye, and ordained by the Presbytery of Skye in 1788. Clarke met the minister, his wife, three small children, and his mother. Buchanan (1793, 143) said that he was illiterate 'farther than his little knowledge of the English language'. Neither Brougham (1871, I 108) nor Campbell (1799, f9–11) found him very prepossessing, though Campbell was impressed by the service he held in his kitchen. His salary then was still £25 a year but by 1815 (MacCulloch 1819, 23–4, 1824, 17, 89) it had risen to £35. Lauchlan was away when MacCulloch called, but his wife received the visitors. After resigning in 1820, he left the island in April 1821. In 1827 he was on the superannuated list of the Society for the Support of Gaelic Schools (Ann. Rept 16 1827, 48–9).

In the 1820s the teacher, Alexander MacKenzie, held meetings on Sundays for reading and prayer, but Rev Dr John MacDonald (the Apostle of the North) found when he made several visits to St Kilda (1932, 88–100, 106–124, 135–147, 278–291) that the islanders' knowledge of Christianity was superficial. He endeavoured to convey to them the true meaning of the scriptures and encouraged them in the practical demonstration of their beliefs.

The chapels having fallen into disrepair in the eighteenth century, both services and school classes were held in the common barn. The house formerly occupied by the missionary was private property. Dr MacDonald toured the country, preaching in an effort to raise funds to pay for the building of a new church and manse. Building was in progress in 1827, and completed before 1830, when MacDonald made his last visit, accompanying Neil MacKenzie, the new minister, his wife and baby to St Kilda.

Figure 83. *Ministers' and Missionaries' families I*

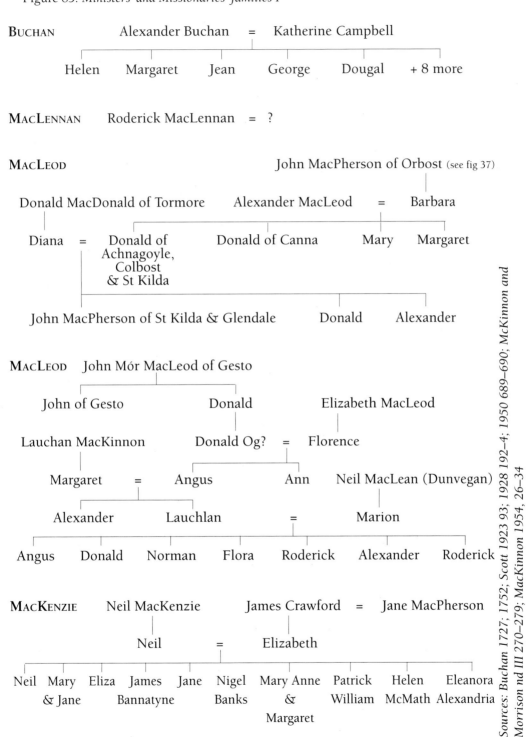

Sources: Buchan 1727; 1752; Scott 1923 93; 1928 192–4; 1950 689–690; McKinnon and Morrison nd III 270–279; MacKinnon 1954, 26–34

Figure 84. *Ministers' and Missionaries' families II*

MacKay   John MacKay = Catherine Ross   Isabella = William Munro

John   Margaret   Isabella Ross Munro = Neil MacDonald

MacLachlan   Archibald MacLachlan

John = Ann MacLean   John Scroggie = Mary Craig

Alexander   Donald   Peter   =   Alice

Flora   (Susan)

MacLean   John MacLean   =   Marion Sinclair

Dugald   =   Mary MacNiven

Donald   Willie   Elma

MacArthur Archie MacArthur = Flora Kennedy   Finlay Gillies = Catherine Gillies

Calum   =   Catherine

MacKinnon   Alexander MacKinnon   =   Mary Barr

Marion Finnie   Hugh

Cameron   Donald Cameron   =   Christina MacPhie

Donald   =   Mary Flora MacCorquodale

Mary   Christine

MacLeod   John MacLeod = Katie MacDonald[1]   Elizabeth Gamble[2]

Donald John   Alexander   Chrissie   Kenneth

Sources: Census records; NTS archives; MacLeod 1988; Cameron 1973

Despite MacDonald's visits, MacKenzie (1911, 29–38) felt that the spiritual health of the people was in a poor state, their understanding being still very imperfect. He began a programme of meetings both on Sundays and week days which were well attended, but not until 1838 was he satisfied that some were fit to be admitted as full members of the church. In that year a Kirk Session was constituted and communion first celebrated. Dr Dickson from Edinburgh and Dr MacLeod (Caraid nan Gaidheal) from Glasgow, together with other passengers from the 'Vulcan', were present. The SSPCK gave a communion cup, server and font to be used in the church, a pulpit was installed, and a Mr Ewing in Glasgow sent a hand bell to call the people to church. (MacLean 1838, 50; Connell 1887, 142–3).

In the winter of 1840/1 there was an extraordinary outbreak of religious fervour. Services were accompanied by public proclamations of unworthiness and repentance, groaning, weeping and occasionally fainting. In the summer this excitement died down, but occurred again over the winter of 1841/2. MacQueen (nd, 4–5) notes that little work was done during those years. MacKenzie at last felt that a proper appreciation of the scriptures had been truly instilled in the people, and that his work was now finished. When he left in 1843 or 1844, he had not only consolidated spiritual reform, but he had also been responsible for totally rebuilding and relocating the village, and reorganisation of the arable land holdings within a new enclosing dyke (p 105).

When a Free Church deputy visited St Kilda in 1846, he found that all the people wished to join the Free Church. At that time the proprietor would not allow the church to be used, and no one was appointed until 1859 when Duncan Kennedy went to the island as catechist. Two years after his departure John MacKay was sent as minister in 1865 (Ewing 1914, II 235).

Sands (1877a, 29, 115) described MacKay as 'a well meaning but feeble-minded, irresolute but domineering fanatic' and Connell (1887, 37–8, 54–5) agreed that he was under the influence of his servant, Ann MacDonald. MacDiarmid (1878, 241) described him as of 'kindly disposition, fair intelligence, but far from robust-looking, and apparently rather deficient in vigour and action', and Connell contrasted the energy of MacKenzie with the inertia of MacKay. He was not unchallenged: Donald Ferguson, a church elder, had apparently told him that if his sermons did not improve he would have to look for another job (Connell, 1887, 87). Murray (1.10.1887) commented that the sermons were 'poor feeding for the people or, rather, good food spoiled in the serving out. Ecclesiastically matters are asleep'. He found the minister and his servant kind but he was depressed by the dissension among the people, some of it caused by gossip from the manse. On Sundays MacKay held three long services, and on Wednesday evenings the elders held a prayer meeting. Rigid adherence to restrictions on any form of work on the Sabbath prevented the immediate unloading of much needed supplies when boats arrived late on a Saturday or on a Sunday (MacDiarmid 1878, 234; Connell 1887, 21). MacKay did not leave the island until he retired in 1889. In 1886 his salary was £80 annually (Connell 1887, 53).

His replacement was Angus Fiddes, a younger and more energetic man. He continued the three long services which occupied most of Sunday (Elliott 1895a, 119). Though the prevailing Sabbath gloom and silence observed by Sands had lifted and people would converse cheerfully to friends (Kearton 1897, 10–11), they were no less devout. Heathcote (1900, 80) believed them to be 'the most truly religious people' he had ever encountered. There was some serious disagreement between the islanders and Fiddes before he left in 1902 (Aberdeen Daily Journal 17.1.1903).

The missionaries of the twentieth century were younger men; most of them were married and some had young families; indeed in 1909 and 1918 there were births in the manse for the first time since MacKenzie's stay. Accounts by MacLachlan (1906–9), Cameron (1973) and MacLeod (1988) indicate that faith was tempered with tolerance and humour.

Figure 85. *Stevenson's plans for Church and Manse, 1827*

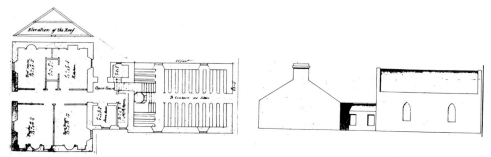

After Stevenson National Library of Scotland ms 5862.9

The Church and Manse

In 1826 plans were drawn up by Robert Stevenson (NLS Ms 5862.9, figure 85) for a new church and manse. These show similarities to Telford's plans (figure 86) for the churches and manses built in a number of places in the Highlands and Islands between 1823 and 1835. Those on St Kilda were a little more modest, and cheaper, being completed by 1830 for a cost of £600.

The church is a simple building 30' by 17'9" internally, with a high ceiling (figure 87). It was originally lit by four lancet windows, one of which was later converted into a door through to the school. It had plastered walls, bare

Figure 86. *Telford's plans for 'Parliamentary' Churches and Manses*

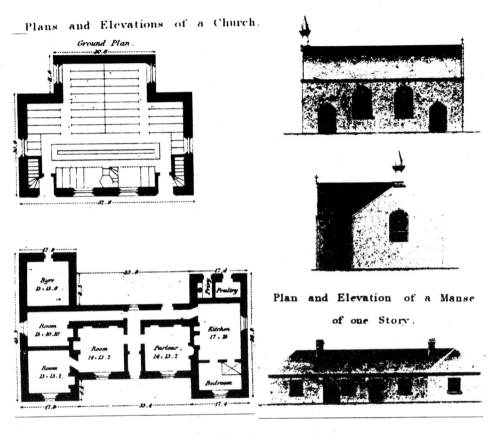

HIGHLAND CHURCH AND MANSES.

Plans and Elevations of a Church.

Plan and Elevation of a Manse of one Story.

Plans and Elevation of a Manse.

rafters, and a sloping earth floor. There was a door through to the manse opening onto the landing by the pulpit (MacDiarmid 1878, 240). By 1885 there was a central gangway of rough concrete and the walls were whitewashed (Connel 1887, 84). A stove sent 'recently' for the church was regarded as 'godless' by the minister's housekeeper and was never installed. In

1898 when the schoolroom was added, the church was refurbished: lined throughout with matchboarding, a level wooden floor inserted, and a carpet at the pulpit end (Heathcote 1900, 97). Possibly the minister's private entrance was removed at this time.

Figure 87. *Church, manse and schoolroom: plan and elevations*

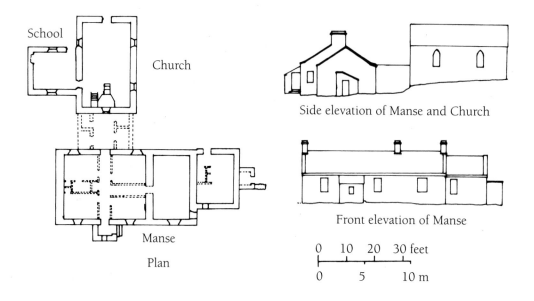

School

Church

Side elevation of Manse and Church

Front elevation of Manse

Manse

Plan

| 0 | 10 | 20 | 30 feet |

| 0 | 5 | | 10 m |

When the people left in 1930 the church had served the community for just one hundred years.

In MacKenzie's day the manse had four rooms, with outhouses. The walls were finished in plaster directly onto the masonry, and there was a damp problem, but the house was carpeted and furnished (Wilson 1842, 11). An extension was built in 1838 or 1839 (MacLean 1838, 46). These were probably the additions shown on Sharbau's plan of 1860 (figure 39) and in a photograph of 1886 (Wilson 1886, 6192): a porch, and a narrow block, probably outhouses, attached to the east gable. After MacKenzie left the building was empty for some time and by 1861 needed replastering and some new windows (Power 1983, 21.7.1861). Two men were working on both manse and church for two months in 1883, but in 1896 Fiddes felt that more work was necessary (MacKenzie ms). He installed the stove intended for the church (Ross 1890, 150). Part of the eastward extension was enlarged and converted into two extra rooms, probably in 1908 when contractors were working on the manse during the missionary's holiday (MacLachlan

11.6.1908; figure 81). It may have been then that the bathroom with flush toilet was installed, fed by water piped from the Minister's well (Atkinson 1949, 221; MoD plan 1969).

Communion plate and tokens

Five communion vessels used on St Kilda are now in the care of the National Trust for Scotland (figure 88).

Figure 88. *Communion vessels*

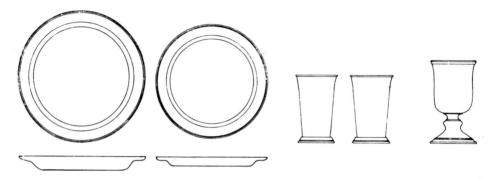

Communion tokens are the only mass produced items made specifically for use on St Kilda. Two types are known to have been produced, both for the Free Church of Scotland. These tokens (figure 89, overleaf) conform to the commonest type issued in the nineteenth century in both the Church of Scotland and the Free Church; they are of tin lead alloy and both bear the name of the congregation and the text 'This do in remembrance of me' (Luke xii 19 and 1 Cor. xi 24). Neither is dated, but they must have been produced after 1846. Inscriptions in Gaelic are exceptional: very few of the Highland and Island congregations in any of the churches had Gaelic tokens, other examples being Church of Scotland congregations at Aberdeen, Bernera (Harris) and Kintail, and Free Church congregations at Carloway, Tarbert (Harris) and Inverness (Kerr and Lockie 1942–3, 49–146; 1944–5, 26–80).

Figure 89. *Communion tokens*

Education

A list of teachers known to have worked on St Kilda is given in table 22.

There is no record of the St Kildans receiving any sort of formal education before 1704. Martin (1716, 63) notes in 1697 that 'writing was most astonishing to them; they cannot conceive how it is possible for any mortal to express the conceptions of his mind in such black characters upon white paper'. When he suggested that they could learn to read or write within two years, this was regarded as impossible.

However, within a few years Buchan (1727, 41–3, 49–52) had by his own account taught many of the people to read and write, though he sent some of his own children to schools in Glasgow and Edinburgh. In 1710 he was officially appointed teacher. His instructions included the following: he was to erect a school in which he was to teach the inhabitants, especially 'the younger sort'; in winter he was to teach in one session, but when the days were longer, in two, if the parents could spare them so long; he was to encourage any who came to him wanting to learn, and he was to go from house to house teaching and instructing in religion. Teaching was to include reading and writing in English.

Buchan's successor, Roderick MacLennan, was probably responsible for teaching Neil MacLeod, the Steward's son, during his summer visits. In 1773, MacLeod told Boswell and Johnson (1934, 388) that he had lived for some time in St Kilda, and there had first read Horace and Virgil.

Perhaps Buchan's best pupils perished in the smallpox epidemic; MacLennan's successors seem to have been less well educated and less diligent in teaching, for in 1758 MacAulay (1764, 219) found that all but three or four of the people were 'perfectly illiterate'.

In 1821 it was suggested to the Society for the Support of Gaelic Schools (GSR 1822, 36) that the island would be a suitable place for a school, there being 58 children between the ages of 5 and 16. Mr MacLellan, the tacksman, had undertaken to put up a building for the accommodation of both teacher and school, together with the provision of a patch of ground, grazing for cattle and sheep, and fuel supplies. Accordingly Alexander MacKenzie was sent out in June 1822. When Rev Dr John MacDonald and Mr MacLellan inspected the school in September they were impressed by the enthusiasm and progress of the pupils (GSR 12 1823, 37). By 1823 60 people were able to read the Bible (GSR 14 1824). School was held from 7 to 9 am, 12 to 1, and for two hours in the evening, presumably to avoid infringing too much on the working day (GSR 14 1825, 35). By June 1825 nine scholars had left, 'being able to read fluently'. In the previous winter MacKenzie had held a night school but in summer there was no mid day school as the scholars were

Table 22
List of Teachers

Year	Teacher
1704–1730	Alexander Buchan
1730–1822	
1822–30	Alexander MacKenzie
1830–43	Neil MacKenzie and D MacQueen, D MacKinnon
1843–56	Carmichael & MacEwen; M Ferguson, M MacQueen, N Ferguson
1856–63	Duncan Kennedy and his niece, Anne Kennedy
1863–84	No resident teacher (1872: Education Act)
1884–85	Kenneth Campbell
1885–86	Hugh MacCallum
1886–87	George Murray
1887–88	?
1888–89	Rae
1889–90	John Ross, MacFarlane
1890–1900	Angus Fiddes ?
1900–1	James MacKenzie
1901–2	Campbell (Mary C MacKenzie, summer 1902)
1902?–3	(Edith Findlay, summer 1903)
1903–4	MacDonald (Kathleen M Kennedy, summer 1904)
1904–5	R MacDonald (W Gollan, summer 1905)
1905–	?
1906–9	Peter and Alice MacLachlan
1909–12	Annie MacLean
1912–14	Calum MacArthur
1914–19	Mary MacKinnon
1919–26	Mary Cameron
1926–29	John MacLeod
1929–30	Dugald Munro

Sources: School Log Book; Logie 1889, 39; MacQueen nd; Ross 1889-90

herding cattle (GSR 15 1826, 30–1). By 1827 at least one person in every household could read the Bible (Kennedy 1932, 284). MacKenzie lived in the house 'lately used by the missionary' and taught in the barn, which was common property (MacDonald 1823, 8).

However, Neil MacKenzie (1911, 32) found that very few people could read; he taught reading, writing and arithmetic and by his own account long before he left in 1843 most people could read fluently and write in Gaelic. MacLean (1838, 39) saw a new one room school 9' by 8', with one window, in which MacKenzie taught, though Wilson (1842, 12) says he taught in the church. The schoolroom mentioned may have been the small building of which one end survives in the glebe wall, with a window space, and turf on the wall head suggesting a thatched roof (pp 104–5).

Despite all this instruction, when Otter drew up an agreement in 1860 whereby provisions were exchanged for work, the sixteen men who participated all put a cross by their name (RHASS papers). In 1859 MacRaild reported that Kennedy was doing his best and that the people could generally read the Gaelic Bible; in the early 1860s his neice, Anne Kennedy, was teaching, with a salary of £10 in 1863 (RHASS papers).

When the Education Act was passed in 1872, MacLeod negotiated with Harris Parish Council for exemption for St Kilda on the grounds that education was being supplied, and thus avoided paying school rates (SRO AF 57/04).

In 1884 the Ladies' Highland Association started sending teachers to St Kilda, generally young men who stayed for nine or ten months from one summer to the next. They taught in the church, or in winter, in the Factor's House, where they stayed. The role of teacher was gradually combined with that of minister or missionary, or their wives. Sometimes the work was shared: Peter MacLachlan did most of the teaching, his wife taking classes in sewing and singing. In the 1900s, other teachers came for a few weeks in the summer.

Though attendance generally was good, school work often took second place when help was required with unloading boats, agricultural work or fowling; on such occasions the school might be closed for lack of pupils (Murray 28.10.1886; 5.5.1887; MacLachlan 9.11.1907, School Log Book 1901–1930).

In the 1900s His Majesty's Inspectors of Schools made regular visits to St Kilda; some examples of comments from their reports follow: the junior classes should practice speaking English (1901); reading and arithmetic were slightly better than the previous year but written and spoken English required greater efforts (1906); special mention was made of the good use by pupils of the school's excellent library (1907); progress was rated as 'good to fair', even the weakest having a passable knowledge of reading, writing and arithmetic (1922); and knowledge of geography was good, but history and singing were poor (1927) (School Log Book).

A number of letters written by St Kildans, mostly by men, from the 1860s onwards survive (MacLeod Muniments, MacKenzie mss, RHASS papers). Though the punctuation and syntax are sometimes unconventional, probably because the correspondent was communicating in an unfamiliar language, the message is generally clear. In July, 1897, for instance, Finlay MacQueen wrote to Mr MacKenzie:

Dear Friend,

I hope you got a good passage, from our Island, and has arrived all safe at home. I am at present the same as when you saw me and all the family & the rest of the inhabitants now we got some of the turf, and the weather is fine, but today is not we were at Soa cutting the lambs and did good work. now as you ordered me I send you the tweeds to send to Mr Kearton you will get my name on the so I hope you will send them I must close with my fondest wishes to you

> *I remain yours*
> *loving friend*
> *Finlay MacQuien*

also I am going to send you the clock to be cleaned, she is not keeping the time I hope you will do this for me

A school exercise book used by Donald Gillies in 1930, when he was twelve years old, also survives (SRO GD 1/817/1). It contains exercises in spelling, grammar, dictation and composition, the last about different aspects of island life: 'A Rainy Day'; 'A Sail to Boreray'; 'A Trip to the Dune'; 'Sheep Shearing' and 'A Trip to Boreray'.

In 1898 a schoolroom was added to the church, a light high ceilinged room, timber lined, with a fireplace, an outside door and a door through into the church (Heathcote 1900, 92–6; figure 87).

Health

Two complaints are particularly associated with, though not peculiar to St Kilda: the 'boat cold' and the more serious infant tetanus. Both have been described by many authors: Gibson (1926, 50–62) and Collacott (1981, 224–7) summarise the evidence for the latter.

Martin (1716, 38–40) noted that the St Kildans 'were not infested with several diseases which are so predominant in the other parts of the world'. Like his contemporaries, he did not realise that lack of exposure to an infection was accompanied by a lack of resistance, and he found the existence of the 'boat cold' hard to credit, as did many later visitors. The 'boat cold' or *cnatan nan gall* (cold/cough of the strangers/foreigners) affected the whole population soon after the arrival of a boat at the island. MacAulay (1764, 200–209) observed it himself: on the third day after his arrival, some people had symptoms of a violent cold; within eight days all were affected, some having fever and headaches as well. Mrs MacLeod, widow of the missionary Alexander MacLeod, told him that she had been immune to it during her first three years on the island, but thereafter she succumbed with the rest. The people had pointed out to Martin that babies, who were affected as much as everyone else, would scarcely be capable of simulating the cold. Various explanations, none entirely satisfactory, were suggested by different authors, among them that the cold resulted from the exertion and wetting involved in helping the steward to land, or from the consumption of alcohol and change of routine accompanying his visit. The people themselves believed that they were infected by those who lodged with them.

Morgan (1862, 185) observed the whole population affected ten days after the visit of the 'Porcupine' in June, 1860. Ross (1884, 82) noted that the people could distinguish between colds associated with boats from different places, and that colds from Glasgow or Liverpool were not as severe as those from Harris. Seton (1878, 233) was the first to mention the parallel example of Tristan da Cunha. Later other examples were cited, such as Tahiti (Dixon 1886, 286), Wharekauri, New Zealand (Chudleigh 1886, 484), and the 'shore cough' which sailors often contracted after the isolation of a long sea voyage (Anon 1926, 81)

It is now generally recognised that communities which have not been exposed to an infection will have little or no resistance and may suffer severely when a new one is introduced. There is no reason to doubt accounts of the universal and virulent affects of *cnatan nan gall*.

A similar lack of resistance, probably combined with malnutrition, was responsible for the devastating effects of the smallpox epidemic in 1727. Small pox was serious enough in larger populations; on St Kilda only 30 of well over 100 people survived, 11 of these escaping infection altogether because they were on Boreray or Stack an Armin (p 88).

Martin (1716, 39) recorded one earlier case when a man was infected by two of the Steward's party who were not fully recovered from it, but MacAulay (1764, 197–9) declared that smallpox was unknown before the epidemic. In June, 1873, seventeen people, including all the children, were vaccinated against smallpox by Dr Webster of Dunvegan and the rest later in the year by Dr Murchison from Harris (Seton 1878, 235). One doctor who came to vaccinate was drunk (MacLeod 1953, 246) and by 1899 the people refused to allow their children to be vaccinated (Heathcote 1900a, 70–1).

MacKenzie (1904, 399) noted that 'when hooping cough, measles or scarlet fever visit the island, there are more than the average number of deaths', and Sands (1877a, 13) observed that the people had a great terror of infection and would avoid a visitor whom they suspected of having been in contact with 'fever'. Increased contact through the summer steamers and fishing boats in the winter was probably responsible for later epidemics, including typhus and whooping cough in 1892 (Dougall, 1892, 1388), influenza in 1901 (School Log Book), 1913 and 1914 (SRO AF 57/13, AF 57/17), mumps in 1920 (SRO AF 57/22), whooping cough in 1921 (Anon 1921, 416), pneumonia in 1924 (SG 2.10.1924), and influenza in 1926, when four elderly people died (SG 3.6.1926). Fiddes (MacKenzie ms) attributed an epidemic of 'fever' in autumn 1896 to the use of surface water in winter, when the cattle were within the head dyke.

Martin (1753, 38–42, 58; 1716, 284–5) says that the people suffered from 'fluxes, fevers, pleurisies and the spleen'. The 'spotted fever' and 'leprosy' have been considered above (p 128).

Both MacAulay (1764, 210) and MacDonald (1827, 26) observed that the adults were very healthy, and Clarke (1824, 273) Atkinson (1831, 31) and Sands (1877a, 24) all remark on their excellent teeth. However, MacKenzie (1904, 31) during his long stay noted dyspepsia, nervous disorders, 'spotted fever' and swelling and bowing of the limbs (possibly rickets). Two young women died of 'green sickness' (anaemia). Surgeon Scott (MacDiarmid 1878, 251) reported that rheumatism and dyspepsia were common, but skin disease was not; in 1884 and 1885 Acheson (MacNeill 1886, 8–9) found, in addition to the rheumatism and dyspepsia, anaemia and palpitation in children, and incipient scurvy. The lack of fruit and green vegetables in the diet caused some deficiency diseases; but considering the high consumption of flesh and eggs, anaemia is surprising.

Tuberculosis was unknown until a young man suffering from it returned home in 1928; he died, but Mary Gillies had contracted the disease: she died in July 1930 (SRO AF 57/26/27).

Mitchell (1865, 899–902) found no evidence of problems arising from marriage of close relatives; of fourteen couples in 1860, five were second cousins, and none closer. He did learn of one woman who was 'of weak mind', Kirsty MacLeod, who went to Harris in 1860 or 1861, and provided Carmichael (1928, II 379) with useful material. She is probably the same Kirsty Macleod who is listed in the Harris census of 1871 as an imbecile. Sands (1877a, 23–4, 135–6) refers to an old man who was an imbecile, generally harmless (Roderick Gillies) and Murray (5.3.1887) noted that Mrs Ann Gillies was partly deranged. John MacKinnon was listed as mentally deficient in 1930 (SRO AF 57/26). His name does not appear in the school register. His parents and two of his great grandparents were first cousins; two other great grandparents were first cousins once removed; one was sibling to Roderick Gillies and the other to Ann Gillies. Sands also listed several people with physical disabilities: a woman with a deformed foot, her daughter with a deformed chest, an old man (John MacDonald) blind from cataract and Donald MacQueen who had a rupture.

MacAulay (1764, 199–200) is the first to mention infant tetanus:

The St Kilda infants are peculiarly subject to an extraordinary kind of sickness: On the fourth, fifth or sixth night after their birth, many of them give up sucking; on the seventh, their gums are so clenched together, that it is impossible to get anything down their throats: Soon after this symptom appears, they are seized with convulsive fits, and after struggling against excessive torments, till their little strength is exhausted, die generally on the eighth day.

It is unlikely that Martin, with his interest in medicine, would have omitted to mention this if it occurred in his day, so probably the tetanus bacillus travelled to St Kilda in the early eighteenth century, possibly with people sent to augment the population after the smallpox, or perhaps carried by migrating birds.

Later visitors were more interested in the boat cold and the high infant mortality was not remarked again until 1822 (MacDonald 1827, 26). MacKenzie (1911, 13), who lost three of his own children in infancy, noted that no special clothing was provided for new born babies, who were wrapped in a piece of cloth for the first ten days of life, until, as Connel said later (1887, 110) they had proved their 'right to wear the clothing of a decent Christian baby'.

Many nineteenth century visitors wrote of this scourge and there was much speculation as to the cause. Some attributed it to the foetid air within the houses and initial feeding with melted butter and milk instead of breast feeding, but there was no improvement after new houses were built in 1860. The diet of the mothers was suggested, and the treatment of the umbilicus considered, though it was believed to be the same as elsewhere in the Western Isles. Mitchell (1865, 902) stated that the disease did not occur throughout the Long Island but was known in Uig and Barvas in Lewis, the Faeroe Islands and parts of Iceland; and Morgan (1862 179–183) cited the Westmann islands, Dublin Lying-in Hospital and the West Indies as parallels. More recently, Ferguson (1958, 140–146) has shown that in the second half of the nineteenth century the number of babies dying between 4 and 14 days after birth (not necessarily diagnosed as having tetanus) in most parts of rural Lewis, in Harris and South Uist was between 30 and 40 per 1000 live births, far lower than on St Kilda, but twice the rate on the east coast of Ross and Cromarty. On the other hand it occurred rarely or not at all on Foula and Fair Isle, where conditions were similar to those on St Kilda (Gibson, 1926, 54).

Between 1830 and 1891, of 160 baptisms and births recorded, 92 died within the first few weeks of life, many simply being recorded as '8 days', and most of these deaths were probably the result of tetanus. In some years no babies survived, the worst record being between 1866 and 1870 when all fourteen whose birth is recorded died (Lawson pers comm; figure 54). Morgan (1862 178) learned that of fourteen children born to Malcolm and Betty MacDonald, twelve had died of tetanus. In 1876 Sands (1877a, 12–13) attended the funeral of the infant Mary Gillies and saw two small boxes in the grave opened for her: her father, twice married, had lost eight children. Murray (12.1886) attending the burial of twelve day old Anne MacKinnon, likewise saw the coffins of her brothers when she was buried.

Some mothers tried to avoid the risk by going to Harris to have their babies. Four births are recorded in Harris between 1868 and 1875 (Lawson pers comm) and Sands (1877a, 71; Holohan, 1985, 52–3) met two women returning home in 1876 after spending the winter in Harris. Mary MacDonald's son Donald survived, but Marion MacQueen lost hers twelve days after his birth. Some of the women who spent months in Harris, which they found a poor place, probably stayed with Donald MacKinnon, who had left St Kilda before 1840, in Obbe. His daughter Janet practised as a midwife, going on to train in Glasgow in the 1880s. One of the women who went was Donald MacKinnon's sister-in-law and three others were married to his nephews (Lawson pers comm).

Gibson (1926, 50–62) suggests that tetanus was the result of mis-management of the umbilical cord. Two women he spoke to in the Western Isles had been accustomed to dressing the cord with a rag which had a hole burnt through it, and in Barvas this was often smeared with butter. He suggests that on St Kilda fulmar oil was substituted, and that the midwife would keep a supply, probably in the usual gannet's stomach, which she would replenish as necessary. Hanging in the house, this would provide an ideal cultural medium for the tetanus bacillus, and a source of infection for practically every baby. Whether Gibson was correct in his theory that 'the fulmar gull squirted its ruby jet across a page of medical history' can now only be a matter of opinion.

The midwife reigned supreme: some time before 1830 a group of men told Mrs MacDonald of Balranald that they could no longer have children because their midwife had died, and in the 1860s two girls offered the same explanation for not marrying to Captain Otter's pilot (Carmichael 1941, 107;

1928, II 166). The midwife whom Morgan (1862, 178) interviewed in 1860 must have been Betty MacDonald (Scott), who had been practising for thirty years, initially probably as a young apprentice. She was one of those lost on the 'Dargavel' in 1863 (p 269). It was Rachel, Donald Ferguson's wife (Collacott 1985, 182) with whom the first nurses sent to the island had to compete until she died in October 1891.

There were resident nurses in the 1880s and from 1914 (table 23).

In 1877 Emily MacLeod, sister of the proprietor, went to St Kilda and supervised the post natal care of Anne MacQueen who survived (MacLeod 1953, 245–7). She made several further visits, and offered to pay for one of the women to visit Skye to learn English and then train as a nurse in Glasgow, but none would leave the island. About 1879, she employed Mrs Anne McKinlay, a trained nurse aged 65, who despite her age stayed on the island for nine years, though by 1887 she was not in good health herself (Murray 12.4.1887). Neither she nor her immediate successors were popular and when Nurse Chisnhall left in 1892 she was not replaced. Fiddes' petition to Queen Victoria for the provision of a nurse in 1890 was unsuccessful, but he collected funds to pay the expenses of Nurse Chisnhall from the Glasgow Sick-poor and Private Nursing Association. Both she and Fiddes took advice from Professors Reid and Taylor in Glasgow as to the treatment of the babies. Between 1891 and 1892, of five births, one baby was still born, two died of tetanus (two of these three were not registered at all) and the only two whom the nurse was permitted to treat from the first survived. Fiddes himself continued postnatal treatment with scrupulous care after Nurse Chisnhall left, and was able to report in 1894 that the five babies born since her departure had all survived. No further cases of infant tetanus were recorded.

From 1914 a resident nurse was provided. Doctors who visited in an official capacity or as tourists were in demand. There were deaths which only rapid communication and transport could have avoided: in 1922 Donald Gillies died on Boreray, of appendicitis, and early in 1930 Mary Gillies was taken off by a fishery cruiser; she died in hospital.

According to Martin (1716, 284) fulmar oil and giben were used to relieve aches and pains, and these prized products were exported. Clarke (1824, 270) remarked on the 'large bunches of long bladders' full of fulmar oil, which was used for rheumatism, sprains and swellings as well as lighting. These local remedies were gradually superseded: the list of goods required for 1873 (MacKenzie mss) includes $4^{1}/_{2}$ lb Epsom salts and 9 pint bottles of castor oil. In 1903 the estate sent out 'medecine, plasters, pills and 26 bottles embrocation' (MM 2.652/19).

The St Kildans visited various hospitals. Payments (£5/2/6) were made by the MacLeod Estate to the Gesto Hospital for treatment of a St Kildan in 1887–8 (MM 2.630/10). Before 1890 Norman Gillies had apparently been to Glasgow Infirmary for a hip operation (Ross 1890, 153). In 1906 young Neil Gillies was in hospital in Glasgow but it was not possible to treat his leg (MacLachlan 21.8.1906). In 1908 young Norman MacQueen's leg was broken when his father was throwing bales of cloth down from the loft, and father and son went, with Norman's elder brother as interpreter, by trawler to Aberdeen, where Norman was left for several weeks (MacLachlan 25&31.5.1908). At the end of 1928 Neil Gillies died in hospital in Oban (SG 11.1.1929).

Table 23
List of Resident Nurses

Date	Nurse
1879/80?–88	Mrs Ann McKinlay
1888–1890	Mrs Urquhart
1890–1892	Nurse Chisnhall
1892–1914	No resident nurse
1914–19nn	Mrs M E McLennan
19nn–1923	Mrs J M MacKenzie
1923–1925	Nurse MacDougall
1925–1928	Nurse Littlejohn (ill early 1928, temporary replacement)
1928–1930	Nurse Williamina Barclay

Sources: Gibson 1926; Stornoway Gazette 30.8.1923; 25.6.1925; 7.6.1928; 1.6.1928; SRO AF 57/1

15
Communications

'The seais are stark and verie evill entering in ony of the saids Iles'. Thus wrote Dean Monro in 1549 (1961, 78). The sea about St Kilda is often 'evill', but there are periods of relative calm, and occasionally of glassy stillness.

How much traffic was there between St Kilda and the Hebrides or the mainland?

In the sixteenth century Monro says the Steward went once a year, taking a chaplain, and this is generally repeated in later accounts. By the late seventeenth century, it was customary for the Steward to take also a large following of poor people, probably mostly from Pabbay, and they were quartered with the islanders. There are a number of indications that contact between St Kilda and 'the Continent' was not always limited to the Steward's annual visit. Some of the islanders travelled to the Hebrides or beyond, and people other than the Steward visited them. The eighteenth century saw the beginning of an increase in such contacts, and by the late nineteenth century there was a flood of visitors. Informal postal arrangements through Dunvegan followed by the establishment of a post office in 1900 allowed the people to keep in touch with friends and relatives elsewhere, and for brief periods in the twentieth century rapid communication was possible without a vessel of some sort, during the times when wireless stations were in operation. However, until the end of the nineteenth century, the island was without planned communication with any other community for many months between autumn and spring, and the problem of winter communication was never satisfactorily resolved.

The people had at least one boat of their own almost continually throughout their recorded history, but there are few references to their making voyages to the Long Island. The distance may be considered a sufficient deterrent, but it is worth pointing out that for at least five hundred years it was considered reasonable for small groups of men to sail every year in late summer from Ness, Lewis, across forty miles of ocean to Sula Sgeir, a rock so small that it could not be seen when they set out (pp 300–2).

Boats

A boat is essential to make effective use of the grazing on Boreray and Soay, and to harvest birds from these islands and the stacs; without a boat, life on Hirte would be possible, but much poorer. References to numbers of boats, new boats and losses of boats are noted in table 24.

The St Kildans have usually had at least one boat of their own since Monro's time. In 1697 (Martin 1753, 49, 59–60) it was sixteen cubits long, and was

> very curiously divided into apartments proportionable to their lands and rocks; every individual has his space distinguished to a hair's breadth, which his neighbour cannot encroach so much as to lay an egg upon it.

Each partner provided a turf to cover the boat and protect it from the sun in summer. 'The cubit, or *lave keile* (*làmh choille*) is the distance from the elbow to the fingers' ends; this they only use in measuring their boats'. This is usually between 18 and 24 inches, giving an overall length of between 24' and 29'4". Martin does not mention the use of sails, but says (1716, 291) that the men were stout rowers. They did not use a compass, but steered by the sun, moon and stars, though they relied mostly on the course of groups of seabirds in flight. On one occasion they had been driven to Uist, where they had been kindly received, as they had themselves been hospitable when a group of Uist men were storm-driven to St Kilda.

Moray (1678, 927) describes their landing on Boreray:

> When they come near the rock, they turn the boat and set the side to the shore, two men, one at each end of the boat, with two long poles keeping it off, that the waves dash it not so violently against the rock, when it rises; at which time only the fellow, who is to land, makes his attempt. If he miss his landing place he falls into the sea; and the rest of the people hale him aboard ... when he safely lands, the rest of his fellows land one by one: except so many as they leave to attend their little boat, which ordinarly is of six oars.

When they had finished their work, they lowered any eggs or birds into the boat, and 'the ablest fellow is always left behind; who, having none to help him, must throw himself into the sea, and so recover the boat.' Moray also mentions their hunting seals in a narrow geo on Soay, generally with four men in the boat, a hazardous operation.

MacLeod (1756–75) recalls the usual method of getting a boat ashore and launching it:

> They always land and hawl up their boats upon a certain rock which has a sloping descent towards the sea. Their method of drawing on their boats is so peculiar that I shall endeavour to give some idea of it. The boats that belong to the Island and such as are sent thither have a hole made on purpose through

that end of the keel which is towards the stem: through this hole a rope is put before the boat bound for St. Kilda is launcht out to sea: there are also two ropes fixt to the stern on the outside, one of which goes along each side of the Boat, and when they are prepared to draw the Boat the ropes are thrown to the inhabitants on shore, who take hold of them and draw on the boat, for the water is so deep at the landing place that they cannot take hold of the boat itself untill it is got on dry ground: the ropes fixt to the stern are designed to keep it endways to them when it is in the water. When they launch out their boat the same method is used for security because the rock is so steep that when the people apply their force to the boat, it might slip out through their hands to sea before they had men or oars on board if some of 'em had not hold of the rope to stop its too rapid motion.

Martin (1716, 76) refers to a Harris man and his son who had spent a year on the island working on the boat. The boy was instrumental in exposing Roderick the Imposter, so this was before 1693 (p 87). Presumably this was not just routine maintenance, which might have been done during the Steward's extended stay, if the islanders could not manage it themselves. Any work requiring much new timber would involve importing wood.

An accident which Martin does not mention in 1698, but includes in his book of 1703 (1716, 286), may have taken place between those years. All the men had gone to Boreray in mid-March; the boat was left tied and the rope broke, the men being marooned until the end of May, when the Steward came out on his usual trip and rescued them. Possibly Martin (1716, 293) was referring to the same incident when he says 'some years ago' the boat was broken on the west side of Boreray and the men had to climb a cliff to safety. They may well have been without a boat for several years after that, as the rentals record in 1712 the cost of a boat bought for the people 'after their remarkable disaster in the island of Borera' (Morrison 1966, 332). A boat was in use just before the smallpox epidemic in 1727 as many of the survivors were those who had been stranded all winter on Boreray or on Stac an Armin. Possibly after that the boat was not properly looked after as in 1735 the rents were given up to buy another boat (Morrison 1968, 73).

By 1758 there was only one boat, and the St Kildans' way of keeping it safe from winter storms may have contributed to its decay, for MacAulay says (1764, 142, 266, 192–3) that they filled it up with earth and stones in a secure place, and he comments that 'the St Kilda boat is peculiarly subject to casualties' another of which occurred the year after his visit. On October 6th, 1759, nineteen men set out for Boreray; ten were landed, and when the weather blew up, the other nine sheltered in the boat for three days in the lee of a rock, till at last, in desperation, they steered for the beach, though the storm had not abated.

Table 24

Details of Boats: Numbers, New boats, Losses

1697	One only	Martin 1753, 59
1697–1703	'Some years ago' boat lost at Boreray, men stranded	Martin 1716, 286, 293
1712	New boat bought for £8.2.9	Morrison 1966, 332
1735	New boat bought for £7.4.6	Morrison 1968, 73
1740s	Use of 'boats' implies more than one	Macleod 1756–75 f 183
1758	One only	MacAulay 1764, 142
1759	Boat wrecked returning from Boreray, 10 marooned over winter. Held 19	MacAulay 1764, 192–3
1780s/90s	Several men drowned when boat returning from Boreray capsized at landing place [Same as above ?]	MacKenzie 1911, 24
C18th	'Many years' before 1842: boat lost Stac Lee, one survivor; another boat lost previously, marooned crew rescued by steward [Version of Boreray losses?]	MacGillivray 1842, 65
	18 men to Uist for seed corn, lost on return voyage. No date.	Carmichael 1941, 107
1797	Two boats	Clarke 1824, 266
1799	Three boats, sheltered over winter in boathouse; one held 16.	Campbell 1799, 11, 45
1804–10	Given two boats by proprietor	MacDonald 1811, 818
1815	Two boats, only one serviceable	MacCulloch 1819, 26
1822	Two boats	Kennedy 1932, 92
1831	One boat, 2–3 tons, 6 oars, sail. Held at least 16	Atkinson 1831 ts 32–3
1838	One boat implied. Held 11. People requested a new boat.	MacLean 1838, 39, 47
1841	One boat, held at least 19	Wilson 1842, 26
1847	Two boats, both usable, one held at least 14.	Milner 1848, 2058–9 '
1853	One boat, 8 oars, sail, held at least 19	MacKenzie 1921, 93
1860	Three boats, one large, two small. Large one destroyed by storm, October. Replacement bought in Uist: 5 tons, for £21.5.6 with gear, from Kelsall Fund	RHASS papers
1861	New 30' boat (Dargavel) built by Darroch and Espie, Glasgow, for £45.16.6 with gear, from Kelsall Fund through Otter	RHASS papers
1863	Dargavel lost in April with all hands: 7 men, 1 woman, on voyage to Harris	RHASS papers Seton 1878, 59–60
	New boat for £24.15.6 from Kelsall Fund through MacRaild	RHASS papers

1865	New small boat built by D MacDonald, Skye, for £8.0.0. from Kelsall Fund through MacRaild	RHASS papers MacDiarmid 1878, 254
1869	Two new boats and gear built by John McNeil, Colbost, for £50.0.0 from Kelsall Fund through MacDonald, Tormore	RHASS papers MacDiarmid 1878, 254
1875	New boat given by Young of Wemyss Bay	Sands 1877, 6
1876	New boat built in Ardrisaig given through Sands, lost in storm before 1883	Sands 1877, 64 Gillies 1884, 873
1877	Four boats, two almost new; rumour that Government giving another later in 1877	MacDiarmid 1878, 249
1882	New boat sent by Kelsall Fund	MacKay 1884, 868
1883	'Four or Five boats'	MacKay 1884, 868
1885	Old boat, previously noted unseaworthy, destroyed in storm, four excellent boats left, one large and nearly new	McNeill 1886, 6
pre 1886	'a few years ago' boat (gift) chopped into firewood, considered unsuitable	Connell 1887, 57
1886	Four boats, owned in common	Connell 1887, 61
1890	One 25' boat in good order, one boat repaired in Skye for £10.0.0 through Kelsall Fund; requesting new 21' boat	RHASS papers
1891	New 25' boat built by J McKenzie & Co, Leith, for £40.0.0 through Kelsall Fund; wrecked and sent Dunvegan for repair	RHASS papers
1892	New boat returned, request for another to be repaired	RHASS papers
1894	Only one boat used, two others rotting for want of care	Elliott 1895, 118
1896	Two boats damaged beyond repair in gale, including 1891 boat, one old boat left. Three groups men requested boats	MacKenzie mss.
1902/3	Request for payment of repair of boat given by Congested Districts Board	RHASS papers
1908	New 25' boat built by James G Marr, Leith, for £43.2.6 from Kelsall Fund	RHASS papers
1920s	Four boats shared by families *Finsbay* [MacDonalds & F Gillies] *Grosebay* [MacDonalds & JF Gillies] *Cruisgean* [Fergusons & Gillies] *Lochmaddy* [MacDonalds, F MacQueen & MacKinnons]	MacDonald 1988, 127

Three men were washed away; the other six got ashore, but the boat was broken. The men on Boreray were marooned until the Steward came in June in the following year. MacGillivray (1842, 65) may have a confused version of the Boreray incidents in his story of boats being wrecked on Stac Lee on two separate occasions.

Perhaps it is such an event which is remembered in a song (Carmichael 1941, 112–3; p 238), about a time when eighteen men were storm-stayed on Boreray for eighteen weeks, only one man, Calum, being left on Hirte. On another occasion (Carmichael 1941, 107) eighteen men went to Uist for seed corn after their own crops had been destroyed by a bad storm. They were all lost, with the boat, on the return voyage. There is no other record of this disaster, which must have taken place before 1830. Although Carmichael does not say so, this may have been the time when the boat, bound for Obbe Harris, was driven off course to Hougharry North Uist, some time in the early nineteenth century, this being the last time that a woollen sail was seen in the Western Isles (Carmichael, 1972, 124). At one time sails were normally made locally of wool, and Grant (1959, 360) notes the purchase of thirty yards of white plaiding for a sail for 'MacLeod's Birlinn' in 1706. As Carmichael points out, a wet woollen sail would be so heavy and awkward that it could be dangerous. It continued in use on St Kilda well into the nineteenth century, for in 1831 Atkinson (1831 f 33) noted the square woollen mainsail, which was 'curiously varied' and in 1838 MacLean (1838, 46) saw the sail

> Made up of 21 patches of varied sizes and shades, like what you would fancy Joseph's coat to have been, and of coarse plaiding, the contribution of 21 partners, in proportion to their share of land and rocks severally. The reefs are as varied as the sail, and of old garters or woollen ropes.

In 1815 MacCulloch (1819, 26) observed that only one of the two boats was serviceable,

> And their indifference to this kind of property and the accommodation it affords, is marked by their improvidently suffering the other to go to decay on the shore for want of a few trifling repairs. With the effective one they make a voyage once or twice in the year to the Long Island.

There they sold wool, feathers, cheese, and bought various goods. By 1831 the only boat was a heavy ship's boat of six oars. Atkinson (1831, 32–3) found the islanders very awkward oarsmen, but expert at landing and embarking: the procedure for landing was evidently the same as that described by Moray, but Atkinson adds that the first person ashore took a coil of rope, which was held taut between him and the boat, thus assisting others to land.

In 1838 the name of the boat was the 'Lair Dhonn' (Brown Mare) (MacLean 1838, 39, 42, 46–7). MacLean refers to the 'subtacksman's boat', so possibly there were two, one held in common, and one belonging to Donald MacKinnon, or perhaps MacLean was referring to his being 'in charge' of the communal boat.

From 1860 onwards, the islanders received a number of new boats, as table 24 shows, many of them paid for from the Kelsall Fund (figure 90). Sands (1877, 42, 64, 71) intended his boat, which was paid for by public contributions, to be suitable for the Atlantic. It was specially built by a man at Ardrishaig on Loch Fyne who had been to St Kilda and knew the seas there. MacDiarmid (1877, 22–5) felt that none of the four boats he saw were suitable for an independent voyage to the Western Isles, and suggested that the people should be given something larger, though he admitted that that would require a better landing place. Gordon Cumming (1883, 328, 337) records that in 1883 there was one boat larger than the rest, and that in April that year five men had sailed in her to Dunvegan to ask for assistance, being without meal or seed corn and potatoes.

Connell (1887, 57, 61) relates:

A few years back this singular people chopped up one of their boats into firewood. The boat was a gift from people in the South, and on the islanders being remonstrated with on the enormity of their conduct they coolly replied that the boat did not quite suit their purpose, and they had made up their mind to burn it, so that their kind friends in the South might have a chance of giving them a better one.

The four boats they had were unlikely to survive for long:

[They] are simply going to wreck in their hands, and one apparent reason is that they are common property. What is everybody's business is nobody's business, and so the boats are allowed to lie and rot uncared for on the beach.

This was not entirely true: a photograph of 1886 (GWW 6203 or 5) is titled 'Mending the Boat', but no doubt it was the reason why boats were sent to Dunvegan for repair in the 1890s.

In November 1896 Donald Ferguson (Ground Officer) wrote to MacKenzie to report that two of the boats were so badly damaged that they could not be used without repair, and that only 'the old white boat' remained in use. He said that some of the men were not willing to repair them and were asking for new boats, and there are letters written in that autumn asking for three boats, of 15'6" to 16' length, with four oars and a helm, each for three different groups of men, who intended to use them for fishing. There is evidence for some division in the community at the time, reflected in this scheme for separate ownership of boats by different groups. Apparently MacKenzie sent them the address of a boat builder (MacKenzie mss). It must have been about this time that a boat was presented to the people by the Congested Districts

Figure 90. *Invoice for boat built 1861*

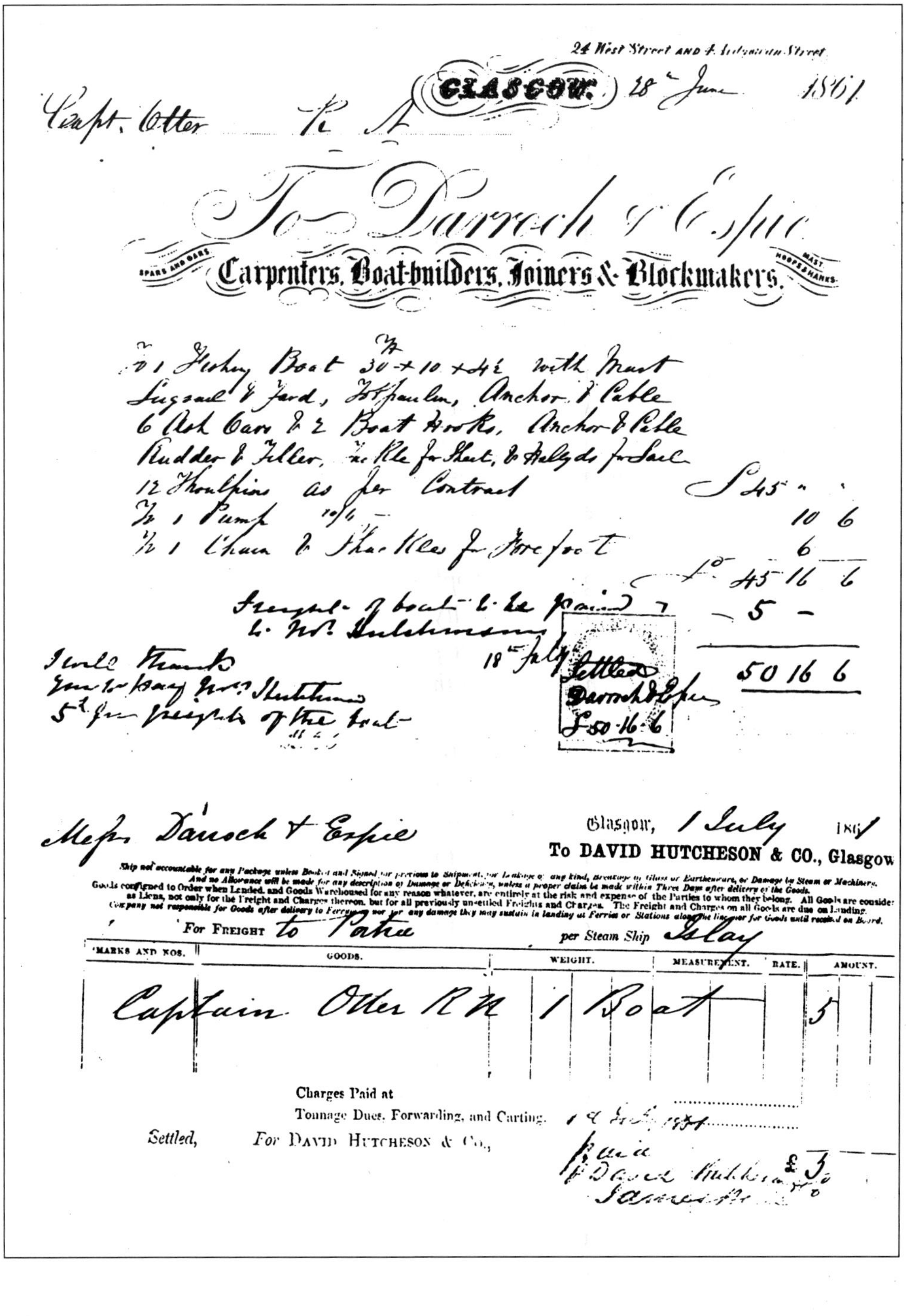

Board; this needed repair in 1902. By 1908 the boat held in common was worn out 'from tear and wear' and a new one built by Marr of Leith, was paid for by the Kelsall Fund (RHASS papers). MacGregor's photograph (SEA C15528) of the jetty in 1930 shows four boats drawn well up on the slip.

Kearton (1897, 123) says that the St Kildans followed the same method of landing on Boreray and Soay as described by early authors. This can be seen in photographs and sketches by Heathcote (1900, 120–9) and Pike's film (1908), which show that the methods of landing and embarking had not changed since Moray's time apart from the last man not jumping into the sea.

Although many authors record the skill of the St Kildans in landing and embarking, some report that they were indifferent seamen: Atkinson (1831, 48), who came from a major seaport, was not impressed by their boat handling:

> We had an opportunity of remarking on their miserable ignorance of naval tactics, which renders them the most awkward, timid sailors I ever met with: they pull six oars at a time; two men sitting on the same bench, but as their oars are inconceivably heavy and clumsy, and they ingeniously contrive never to dip two of them together, the progress of the boat is attended by a continued splash, except when the rowers are being relieved by their six companions, and then there is no cause to complain of unnecessary agitation of the water, for they gossip and chat and idle about, till you long to see them splashing again.

Connell (1887, 31–2) made the same point: 'It is painful to see the clumsiness with which they set to the task of getting the boat into the water and plying the oars. Evidently the St Kildians are not on good terms with the ocean'; but Ferguson (1885, 20) disagreed: 'I never before saw a boat handled with such rare pluck and skill: indeed, I never saw a boat venture out in such a sea'. It was so rough that the passengers of the 'Dunara Castle' were unable to land, but perhaps the anxiety of the people to collect provisions overcame their caution.

Landing Place

Many people commented on the lack of a good landing place or a sheltered area in which a boat could be anchored. Martin (1753, 9–13) mentions the 'Gallies Dock' where the Steward's boat was secured. This is not now identifiable. He also describes being carried ashore from the boat, which was brought up beside a rock called the Saddle, but kept off it with long poles. When the weather was suitable, a boat could be brought ashore up a gently sloping rock, probably the rock marked 'Lech' (Slab) on the mid-nineteenth century map. Martin and later authors agree that everyone helped to haul the boat up above tide level, though sometimes small boats required less community effort. Morgan (1861, 105, 110) describes how he and his companions were brought ashore in their small tender:

> As we approached, six or eight men came down to the rocky margin of the sea, to point out to us the best landing place. It is situated to the north of the harbour, and consists of a perfectly smooth shelf of rock sloping downwards towards the water, covered with short tangle, and very slippery...The St Kildeans walked fearlessly into the surf, and, catching the boat as she rose on a wave, carried her and ourselves out of reach of the spray.

When they left, they were relaunched in a similar fashion:

> They speedily hauled [the boat] a short way up the slippery ledge of the rock, set her high and dry on her keel, and persuaded us to "take our seats". In another moment they ran down with her towards the sea, and launched her with such an impetus as fairly carried us beyond the reach of the surf.

Hall Maxwell, after a conversation with John MacPherson MacLeod and Norman MacRaild, his factor, in November 1859, noted that among projects which would benefit the islanders would be the building of a slip or means of hauling up boats which would allow the people to use larger boats. Maxwell must have discussed this with Captain Otter, who took up the scheme with enthusiasm and in 1860 engaged men from Skye to blast large boulders and clear a small area of shore adjacent to the landing rock. He put up a breakwater and a crane to raise and lower the boats from higher ground, but this was partly destroyed in the hurricane of October 1860 (RHASS papers).

In 1877 MacDiarmid (1878, 250) recommended making a safe anchorage for a vessel, and there was some correspondence between Government departments. In 1883 Donald MacDonald (1884, 871) told the Napier Commission that a pier was needed. Two years later MacNeill (1886, 7) recommended that improvements should be made to the landing place and included different schemes in his report. The files were brought out again in 1898 when the Congested Districts Board asked about earlier plans, and in 1899 a lengthy corrrespondence took place over whether the supervisor superintending the building of a small jetty and boat slip might have an extra wages allowance for remoteness (SRO AF 57/5). Matthews and his companion (Matthews 1969, 78–9) spent the winter on the island. He found, like MacKenzie in the 1830s, that the men would not be given orders, but they would work willingly alongside him. By April 1901 (SRO AF 57/6) the jetty was proving useful though not finished. It was completed in 1902 (Wiglesworth 1903, 7–8).

Traffic

The Steward is known to have made an annual visit from at least the mid-sixteenth century, usually accompanied by a clergyman. Others, such as Coll MacDonald, and the troops searching for Prince Charles Edward Stuart, visited once for specific purposes. Fishermen working in the area would have found the island useful to replenish supplies, particularly water, and there are indications of international fishing round St Kilda and to the west in the seventeenth century, and evidence of efforts to encourage local fishing in the eighteenth century. Some people made landfalls unintentionally, perhaps storm driven such as the Icelandic bishop (p 71) and a hapless Irish reveller (p 233). Carmichael (1954, 294–5) recorded an incident which must have occurred early in the nineteenth century or before, when four men were storm driven from Uig in Lewis to St Kilda. Relatives, having searched locally, even as far as the Flannan Isles, sent to Duncan MacInnes in Benbecula, famous for augury; he 'saw' the men safe on St Kilda and foretold correctly that they would arrive home in March. Other unintending visitors had been wrecked. There are a number of records of shipwrecked sailors arriving at St Kilda, and many more must have gone unrecorded in early times. Some people went in connection with their work: from 1705 a succession of ministers, missionaries or catechists stayed on the island. They might occasionally be visited by colleagues. In the early and late nineteenth century school teachers were stationed on the island, and from the 1880s there was usually a nurse also. From the 1870s there were also visits by doctors, and various Government officials.

The first person known to have visited to satisfy his curiosity, and who afterwards wrote a lengthy account was Martin Martin, who published *A Late Voyage to St Kilda* in 1698. This book, together with his *Description of the Western Isles of Scotland* (1703), was reprinted several times and must have contributed to an increased interest in the island in the eighteenth century, which, in turn, encouraged more people to visit it and to record their observations and experiences. By the late nineteenth century, after the steamer services had begun in 1877, an ever increasing number of visitors was contributing to a large volume of literature. In 1885 McNeill (1886, 7) estimated that at least two hundred people had visited the island, and in 1902 Freer (1902, 391) noted that while recently only three people had visited Eriskay within two years, over three hundred had been to St Kilda in a fortnight. Many of these visitors have been noted here and their accounts have contributed to this work. The visitors included a number of naturalists, and the 1880s saw the first of many papers devoted exclusively to aspects of natural history (for instance: Seebohm 1884, Dixon 1885, Barrington 1886).

There are records of St Kildans visiting the Hebrides, and beyond, especially within this century. In the seventeenth century some islanders went to Skye for a formal baptism (p 245). Martin (1753, 41, 49, 63) recorded visits to Harris and Skye; the Ground Officer occasionally went to Skye with companions. One man had been taken to Glasgow, where he found many things strange to him (Martin 1716, 296–9). In the eighteenth century, Buchan (1727, 40) took two young men to Edinburgh in 1710. Smallpox broke out in 1727 after the clothes of a man who went to Harris were retrieved by his friends the following year.

In 1815 MacCulloch (1819, 26) found that the people went once or twice a year to the Long Island to buy and sell commodities; this is supported by MacQueen (nd, 1). Regular visits were made in the 1850s (MacKenzie 1921, 23). In April 1862 a boat bound for Harris was blown off course to Uist (Seton 1878, 59; RHASS papers), and on a similar voyage the following year it was lost with all hands.

Apparently the islanders rarely ventured so far in their own boats again: the last recorded instance was in 1883 (MacKay 1884, 864). In the 1870s some women went to Harris to have their babies (p 263). Once the steamer services started in the 1880s it was easier for the islanders to travel, and by the 1890s islanders were occasionally going to the mainland for hospital treatment (pp 264–5). In the twentieth century some visited Harris on whalers (MacLachlan 1906–9) and Rachel Gillies paid a brief visit to Fleetwood on a trawler in 1928 (Daily Mail 28.5.1928).

There was some emigration from the island from at least the late eighteenth century (p 131), and in the twentieth century other islanders visited their relatives and went to the mainland for holidays.

Although the records indicate that there might be periods of over a year when little national news reached the island, the Steward's visits and the St Kildans' own visits to the Hebrides provided opportunities for the exchange of local news and comparisons of lifestyles. As few of the islanders spoke anything but Gaelic until the late nineteenth century, conversation with other visitors was more limited. From the 1880s an influx of summer visitors, visiting fishing boats, and access to newspapers increased the information available.

Ewen Gillies shared his experiences of world travel on his return visits in 1873 and in the 1880s. On clear days the length of the Long Island can be seen from Hirte: the islanders must always have been aware of larger lands and communities on their horizon, and although their comprehension of these may have been limited by their own experience, it is clear from MacKenzie's account (1911, 28–29) that they were not as naive as some visitors believed.

Postal Service

Until the 1850s most of the few messages to and from St Kilda were between the minister or missionary, or the teacher, and their colleagues, and there is scarcely any record of these exchanges, which were probably conveyed by the Factor when he made his visit.

The history of the postal services has been studied in depth by MacKay (1963, 1978). After the emigration of some people to Australia in 1853, there was exchange of news between the people at home and relatives in the Antipodes. From 1873, when John MacKenzie, postmaster at Dunvegan, took over as Factor, mail was carried by him twice a year. There was no demand for change until in 1876 and 1877 Sands campaigned for a regular and more frequent postal service. A fortnightly service for Fair Isle started late in 1877 but ironically St Kilda was considered too isolated for officially organised communication. However, in 1878 the Post Office surveyor of the Scottish district reported that letters sometimes lay for months at Dunvegan or in Harris, and he suggested that two trips, in the spring and autumn, should be made, to supplement the factor's visits. A Post Office official, finding that mail had been received in April and June 1878, concluded that the Post Office could not afford to make special provision for a service which would carry no more than 120 letters a year.

In the 1880s and 1890s the steamer service increased to six trips, providing a regular summer service for mail. Letters for the island increased in number, and the outgoing mail was swelled by letters from tourists; in 1897 the figures were 208 and about 500 items respectively. At the same time mail in both directions was being carried by fishing boats from Aberdeen and Fleetwood. In 1899 John MacKenzie applied to the Post Office for the establishment of a sub-post office on St Kilda, and though the volume of mail was considered too small for such a measure, the sending of sealed mail bags to a place where there was no official to receive them was regarded as irregular, so in July 1900 Angus Fiddes was appointed sub-postmaster at a salary of £5 a year. A date stamp and a mail bag seal were sent out, and a room in the Factor's House became the post office. Here Fiddes sold stamps and the recently introduced postcards. The missionaries who succeeded him also took over the post office, until December 1906 when Peter MacLachlan resigned in favour of Neil Ferguson, son of the Ground Officer. He remained postmaster until the post office was closed at the evacuation in 1930.

There were attempts in 1903, 1906 and 1912 to arrange for a regular winter service by the lighthouse supply ship which called at the Flannan Isles, fifty miles away, but the Northern Lighthouse Board resolutely refused to commit their vessel to any extra expense or responsibility, particularly at a time when adverse weather conditions might disrupt their own essential schedule. Winter mails continued to be carried by trawlers from Fleetwood and Aberdeen, and the Post Office paid a nominal fee for this informal service, which was irregular, depending on the movements of fish and the goodwill of company owners and skippers.

In 1910 Neil Ferguson's salary was increased to £10 and he also received payments for ferrying mailbags between the trawlers and the jetty, and for house to house deliveries. In 1913 the post office was moved to a new purpose built corrugated iron shed beside Neil Ferguson's house, No 5.

During the war the islanders became accustomed to a regular and frequent service all the year round, but after the war the winter service reverted to the haphazard arrangements, mainly via Fleetwood. In the early 1920s this was satisfactory, but in 1928 and 1929 the system broke down and there was no contact with the island for over two months. This probably contributed to the death of Mary Gillies from tuberculosis in 1930.

It was clear that by now on humane grounds a more reliable and regular winter service was required, and in the early summer of 1930 it was decided that the Post Office and the Scottish Health Department would jointly pay for a monthly winter service by trawler at £15 per trip. Only one Fleetwood company was willing to undertake this, but it proved unnecessary, since the people left in August. News of the evacuation aroused considerable interest and one result was a number of letters and cards sent under cover to Neil Ferguson for dispatch by the last mail. With the assistance of Alasdair Alpin MacGregor 900 lb of mail was stamped on August 27th, the largest mail ever dispatched. By now, Neil's salary had risen to £15 4s 0d, with a bonus of £10 13s in 1926, when his payments for ferriage and delivery amounted to £8 19s 4d, so in the last few years he was receiving £30 or more for his postal duties.

The Post Office refused to re-open the St Kilda establishment after the evacuation, but up to 1939 private stamps were used to mark the mail of the summer visitors before it was posted in official boxes.

The Wireless

In May 1912, in response to a story that the St Kildans were starving, both the Government and the *Daily Mirror* went to their aid. The paper started a fund to provide a wireless station to guard against similar emergencies in future, and eventually this was set up in July 1913 (figure 88). Two 75' masts were put up near the Factor's House and the equipment installed in one of the rooms, the post office moving to new premises. There were initial maintenance problems, but over the winter of 1913–14 the station was in use.

Figure 91. *Wireless mast base, 1913*

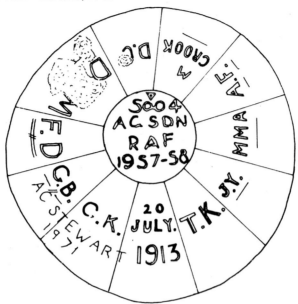

In the spring the *Daily Mirror* decided to dispose of it, and as no one was willing to take it over, it was closed down. However, in January 1915 it was re-opened by the Admiralty, who set up a War Signal Station which remained, with a small garrison, until February 1919. The wireless station was the cause of the only 'engagement' with the enemy involving St Kilda, when in May 1918 a submarine fired 72 shells in an attempt to destroy the station, which was put out of action for a while. No one was hurt, though considerable damage was done. At the end of the war the station was dismantled.

Mailboats

Lady Grange (pp 90–1) was the first person to send a form of mailboat: it is recorded (Buchanan 1793, 144) that she spent much time tying letters round pieces of cork with yarn and throwing them into the sea in the hope that they might be passed on to her friends in Edinburgh.

In 1876, John Sands, stranded on the island over the winter, had a similar idea (Sands 1877, 109–121). In December he made a miniature ship, and put a letter in her hold, hoping that she would be found in a place that had a post-office, so that his friends would have news of him, and the public be told that the island was short of food.

In January 1877 the situation became more urgent after a group of shipwrecked Austrian sailors arrived. Sands had made a second boat, and at the captain's request he added a letter to the Austrian Consul in Glasgow, and launched her when the wind was from the north-west, hoping it would carry her to Uist or some other place where there was a post office. She had a small sail, and "Open this" printed on the deck with a hot iron. They also sent off a life-buoy from the Austrian ship, with another bottle, and a sail attached.

The lifebuoy, sent on January 30th, reached Birsay in Orkney and was sent to Lloyd's agent in Stromness on February 8th, while the 'canoe' was sent on February 5th and was found at Poolewe on 27th by a Mr John MacKenzie, who posted the letters. Help came as a result of the lifeboat message, HMS 'Jackal' arriving on February 22nd. She took the sailors and Sands to Oban, and left some supplies.

The next record of mailboats being used is in September 1885, when three were sent after a storm had destroyed a boat and damaged some crops. Two of the boats reached Lewis and Harris within two weeks and assistance was sent. One of these boats is described as being about a yard long; two bottles, each containing a letter, were secured in a small hold by a hatch, and the boat had a sail and a piece of iron on the base. The words 'St Kilda – Please open' were cut into the wood (McNeill 1886).

Table 25, derived mainly from MacKay (1963, 54, 68) shows some details for those boats recorded as being sent before 1940. He notes that John MacRitchie of Barvas found mailboats in two successive years and requested some reward for passing them on to the Post Office; in February 1906 the G.P.O. authorised the payment of 2/6 to anyone finding a boat, but no records of such payments have survived. By 1896 mailboats appear, from Kearton's account (1897, 28–31), to have been used for ordinary communication rather than only in emergency: apparently two thirds of those sent were found and their contents sent on. Kearton illustrates one sent in March 1897 with a

Figure 92. *Examples of mailboats*

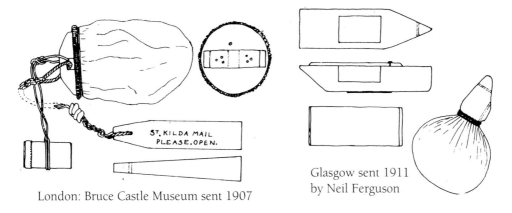

ST. KILDA MAIL PLEASE, OPEN.

London: Bruce Castle Museum sent 1907

Glasgow sent 1911 by Neil Ferguson

letter for him. It was sent by Neil Ferguson and is very similar to the one he sent to Messrs Gowans in February 1911, with a note saying all was well.

This and other surviving boats (figure 92) show that there were two types of boat: the boat shape with a hold cut for the receptacle for the letters, and the timber baulk with letters in a separate tin which was protected by a tight canvas binder. Both types of 'boat' were tied to a float, which was also of two different types. These examples show that the use of a sail was abandoned, though sometimes there was a flag attached to the float. Although many of these boats were found in the Hebrides, the inscriptions, usually 'St Kilda Mail Please Open', were apparently always in English rather than Gaelic.

John MacInnes recorded a conversation in 1961 with Donald MacQueen of No. 10 (1981–2, 446–450) about mailboats. He described the shaping of a boat with a hold, and making a float from a sheepskin, left in a tanning solution for a week and then stretched before being gathered round a wooden stopper which had a hole through it to blow up the float. The hole was caulked with a piece of rope. He and one of his brothers had made such a boat to send to a tourist from London; after reaching Shetland in two days it was duly sent on to the man who acknowledged receipt of it by conventional mail the following year. This must have been before 1909, when both Donald MacQueen's brothers who had survived infancy were drowned. Although some accounts refer to sheep bladders being used as floats, this description and all the floats in museums confirm that normally a sheepskin, rather than a frail bladder, was used.

From the end of the nineteenth century onwards a number of boats were probably sent for the amusement of tourists and to earn some money: Donald MacQueen gained £1 from his efforts, refusing a larger sum for a few hours' work.

Table 25
Mailboat Records

Sent	Found	Location	Sender
? 12 1876	? 9 1877	Sortlund, Verbacle, Norway	Sands
30 1 1877	8 2 1877	Birsay, Orkney	Sands
5 2 1877	27 2 1877	Poolewe, Ross-shire	Sands
? 9 1885	24 9 1885	Gallan head, Uig	A G Ferguson
16 9 1885	28 9 1885	Taransay, Harris	John MacKay
16 9 1885	? 10 1885	West Coast of Lewis	
28 2 1896	14 3 1896	Malvarg (Miavaig?) Lewis	
24 3 1897	31 3 1897	Vallay, North Uist	Finlay MacQueen
9 7 1898	3 12 1898	Knockintorran, North Uist	
3 7 1899	9 10 1899	Haugesund, Norway	Finlay MacQueen
16 1 1899	4 3 1899	Borve, Lewis	
8 1 1905	10 1 1905	Lower Barvas, Lewis	
20 4 1905	21 6 1905	Bigton, Dunrossness, Shetland.[1]	
? 1 1906	20 1 1906	Lower Barvas, Lewis	
8 12 1906		noted by MacLachlan	
? ? 1907	? ? 1907	? took a month;[2]	
pre 1909		Shetland in 2 days	Donald MacQueen
17 2 1911	20 2 1911	Veilish, North Uist[3]	Neil Ferguson
? 3 1912	? 3 1912	West Coast North Uist (5½) days	
19 1 1929	8 4 1929	Shetland	
25 8 1930	? 11 1930	N W Norway[4]	N Ferguson and A A MacGregor
27 8 1930	8 9 1930	Off west coast of North Uist	
12 8 1931	31 8 1931	Flodda Is. Grimsay, North Uist	
1 7 1934	? 11 1934	Extreme north coast Norway	
27 7 1938	24 8 1938	Offshore, Borve, Lewis	Neil Gillies

[1] Photo Shetland Museum, Lerwick

[2] Now in Bruce Castle Museum, London No. M 4705 Class 569

[3] Now in Glasgow Museums and Art Galleries No. A 679a

[4] Now in Dunvegan Castle

Other boats in Royal Museum of Scotland, Department of History and Applied Art, Edinburgh No. VGA 10, West Highland Museum, Fort William No. 1013, Corran Halls Museum, Oban No. 331, and Scarborough No. 138.39

16

Comparative Islands and Communities

There are many islands and communities similar to St Kilda, some more and some less remote. For reasons of space, only a few can be considered here. In general it is important to remember that islands, whether near to or far from other land, are easily approached by boats in suitable weather, but they may be isolated for long periods by bad weather and sea conditions, and often an artificial landing place makes a considerable difference to communication. Access is now much easier by aeroplane or helicopter, but this was scarcely relevant when St Kilda still had native inhabitants.

'It is curious…to reflect on the coldly scientific manner of our approach…the islanders remained little more than a peculiar element in the mammalian fauna. If we thought of them at all, it was as incidental curiosities which we might glimpse briefly on our way to more important fields of study. We were concerned chiefly with photographing them and recording them as curiosities' (Holdgate 1958).

The attitude of Holdgate and his colleagues soon changed when they met the 'curiosities' and friendships formed, but he speaks for many visitors to islands and 'different' communities all over the world. Holdgate was a member of an expedition visiting Tristan da Cunha. Rose Rogers (1926) wife of the missionary stationed there from 1922 to 1925, also wrote an account of the island.

Tristan da Cunha
Tristan da Cunha, the peak of a volcano in the middle of the south Atlantic, is 1,320 miles from the nearest inhabited land, St Helena. Only a small coastal plain is cultivable. Two smaller islands, Nightingale and Inaccessible, lie about twenty miles away (figure 93).

Tristan was colonised in the 1810s. The community grew rapidly, but with groups emigrating in the 1850s and 1889 to America and South Africa, the maximum population up to 1925 was 135, recorded in that year (figure 101). In 1885 fifteen men were lost at sea together with their boat.

The islanders grew potatoes and vegetables, and kept cattle, sheep, pigs and donkeys. In the nineteenth century they thrived, but in the twentieth continuous cropping and severe overgrazing took their toll; yields were poor, and the stock had a high mortality. A diet of potatoes, with some fish and occasionally mutton or beef, and seabirds and eggs in season, led to digestive troubles, and there were years of hunger. In the warm climate, and with little salt, birds and eggs did not keep long.

Figure 93. *Location and map of Tristan da Cunha*

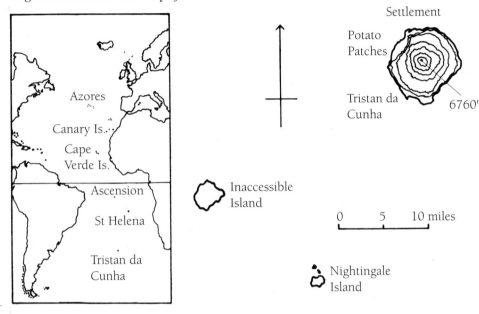

In the nineteenth century fresh provisions were traded with passing vessels for goods such flour and cloth, and the timber, canvas, nails and paint necessary to make the light canvas covered boats the islanders used for fishing and for visiting the other two islands. There they harvested eggs and seabirds, also available on Tristan itself, and culled the cattle and sheep pastured on Inaccessible. Precious driftwood was collected round all three islands. As shipping routes changed vessels called less frequently; with a scarcity of produce the islanders had less to exchange, but still needed materials for making and maintaining boats, and they acquired a reputation for begging and theft. Goods received in barter were divided equally among the families, regardless of the number in each family.

No mail was received between 1906 and the end of the first World War. In 1925 the islanders sent a petition to the Government requesting an annual mail service. While the Government had every sympathy with this request, they could only undertake to try to arrange a visit by one of His Majesty's ships every three or four years, and to take advantage of any other opportunity for communication that might arise. From 1851 to the 1930s there was a resident missionary/teacher at intervals. On several occasions the islanders were given the opportunity to be resettled in South Africa, but the majority refused and the community stayed.

In the second World War a Naval garrison was stationed on the island, and in 1949 the Tristan da Cunha Development Company established a crawfishery, with a canning factory on the island. This provided paid employment for many islanders, together with regular communication. Resident 'incomers' increased: an Administrator, nurse, clergyman, teacher, doctor, Agricultural officer, meteorologist, radio operator, Company manager and accountant were all accompanied by their families. A shop was opened. In 1956 there was no pier or jetty, boats being launched from the beach in suitable weather.

In October 1961 the whole populaton was evacuated to Britain after the volcano began to erupt. Despite reluctance on the part of the Government, the islanders finally returned home in 1963.

The history and lifestyle of Tristan da Cunha, for the century up to 1940, is strikingly similar to that of St Kilda in many respects, one of the major differences, apart from their geographical situation, being the Tristan islanders' enjoyment of music and dancing.

The Faeroe Islands

The following (in the 'ethnographic present') is based largely on Williamson's book, which records Faeroese life into the late 1940s. This and other accounts describe many cultural features common to the Faeroes and the Highlands and Islands generally, though some aspects, such as the fowling, occur in limited areas, and some are peculiar to the Faeroes (Jackson 1991, Williamson 1970, Nørrevang 1977).

The Faeroes are much larger and more remote than St Kilda, the eighteen main islands together having an area the same as that of Shetland, which, 200 miles distant, is the nearest land (figure 94). Of volcanic origin, the islands are characterised by steep slopes and cliffs, most of the land lying between 1,000 and 2,500 feet; only valley floors and small areas of coastal plain are sutiable for cultivation. Faeroe was first inhabited by Irish monks, but did not support a self perpetuating population until Norse colonists settled in the ninth century. The islands remained under Norwegian government until 1536 when Norway fell under the rule of Denmark. A measure of independence was gained in 1948.

Figure 94. *Location and map of Faroe Islands*

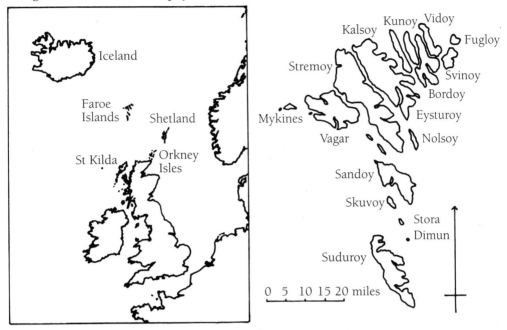

For centuries the islanders were supported largely by their own subsistence economy, growing barley, keeping cattle, sheep and geese, and exploiting the bird colonies and, locally, fish, seals and whales. Potatoes were introduced in the eighteenth century. In the sixteenth century the islands paid tax in wool, fish, barley, butter, whales, seals and seabirds, the first two being most important. In the eighteenth century besides imports of necessities such as hemp, iron, tar, glass, nails and leather, there were luxury items such as tea, sugar and tobacco.

The settlements are mainly villages close to arable ground which is surrounded by a dyke; beyond is the outfield, used for grazing. Rights in grazing, peat cutting and fowling sites are related to the proportion of infield owned. In many villages land is divided equally among a person's children; as a result, an individual may own many small and scattered patches. A few stones mark boundaries. The sloping ground is drained by a system of close-set parallel ditches which are recut regularly; potatoes are sometimes grown on 'lazy-beds'. Cultivation relies almost entirely on spades, rakes and an instrument used for breaking up clods. Dung, seaweed and offal are used as fertiliser. Barley is seldom grown now, but formerly a rotation of crops provided for a year growing barley followed by several fallow years when a haycrop was taken from the field. Barley was cut green and after drying in sheaves for a few days the ears were separated by hand, then dried on a bed of straw in a kiln very similar to those of the Hebrides, save that the floor of the drying platform was of poles with gaps between. Threshing and winnowing took place on the lower floor. Hand querns were used, but from the eighteenth century horizontal watermills were often used for milling.

A very large number of sheep is kept; in some islands sheep are owned individually, and in others the flock is owned in common by a village, people having shares according to their land holdings. Most of the sheep graze on the outfield, but some are brought into the infield in winter. In some areas sheep are lowered on ropes to inaccessible slopes or ledges to take advantage of precious grazing. The wool is plucked and various plants provide different dyes. For a few months in summer cattle are grazed on the outfield; sometimes a twice daily walk of several miles is necessary to milk them. In winter cattle are kept on hay in a byre. Ponies are used for transport, with panniers or small carts. Pony races take place on St Olaf's Day (July 29th).

The old houses had a stone cellar, used for storage and as a byre and workshop; the dwelling, above, was wooden, with a turf roof. Slatted timber outhouses have a similar function to cleitean; they allow the wind to pass between the laths and are used for drying mutton, storing crops, or even drying the washing. They are often sited on cliff tops or beside swift streams, which provided an air current. Wooden locks were used on the storehouses.

Peat is used for fuel, and when dry, the peats are stacked, sometimes with a loose stone wall around them, or put in a stone storehouse similar to a cleit; throughout the year regular trips to the moor are necessary to collect fuel for two or three days.

There is a heavy reliance on fishing and whaling for food, the driving, killing and division of groups of pilot whales being well organised since at least 1584.

There are large seabird colonies, mainly auks, petrels and gulls. Fulmar colonised the Faeroes in the mid nineteenth centry and now are numerous. There are also shags and small numbers of cormorants, and a gannet colony, in existence by 1500, contains up to 2,000 nest sites.

These birds are exploited by sophisticated fowling methods.

Puffins are taken in greatest numbers; in an average year, about 400,000 or 500,000 birds are taken. Fulmar may now be more important than guillemots, though young fulmar are no longer taken. Young shearwaters and young kittiwakes are taken, the kittiwakes being of minor importance except in poor years. Shags and cormorants, and in winter some gulls, are eaten. Up to about 1,000 young gannets are taken; formerly adult birds were also killed. Most of the birds are salted for the winter. Very large numbers of guillemot eggs and smaller quantities of puffin and kittiwake eggs are gathered, and preserved in a mixture of water, salt and peat ash.

Much of the fowling occurs on steep slopes, cliffs, and sea rocks, where ownership of sites is strictly controlled, but some takes place at sea, where fowling is free to all.

There is considerable reliance on the skilful use of the *fleyg* net, a triangular net supported by forked arms on a long pole, the butt end of which helps in manouevring on the cliffs, as in swinging out from an overhang, for instance. The birds are caught on the wing; on ledges, as they fly past; some sites on cliff edges are used when birds are blown in updraughts; birds are also caught from boats. For puffins, traditional sites for fleyging are strictly adhered to, as any change upsets the birds. Guillemots are fleyged on ledges or from boats. A stick with a hook on the end is used for taking puffins and young shearwaters from their burrows; the latter are also caught outside at night. The twentieth century saw the introduction from Iceland of the use of multiple nooses on boards floating in the sea, popular because not subject to land ownership regulations. At sea rafts of unfledged guillemots are herded by boats into inlets and many killed.

Cliff work is a well organised communal activity. Long ropes are used, and sometimes men are let down in stages to reach all possible areas; cliffs are also climbed from boats. Climbing up may be made easier using pins fixed in the rock, and, to get up a short shear face, a rope may be supported by a block on the end of a pole held at its base by several men. Ropes let down from cliff tops are wound round two stout pegs driven into the ground to help those at the top control them, and at the edge, the rope runs over a piece of wood or a running block, to avoid fraying. The man on the lower end is in a harness with bands around the waist and thighs, and loops around the shoulders; this helps him to stay upright and leaves the hands free. On the ledges men may remove the rope for easier movement, but there is great consciousness of safety; a man using a fleyg net on a narrow ledge may have a safety belt attached to a peg in the rock, for instance. Difficult gullies may be crossed using a pole and rope for support. Birds and eggs are carried in two bags slung at the fowler's side, and sometimes lowered into boats. On some difficult cliffs fowling may take days and the men stay in caves, or sheds built on the ledges.

The gannets, on rocks by Mykines island, were harvested twice, but the April hunt for adults has been given up. In autumn, fledging young are killed at night, the men being lowered down a cliff to the ledges, and in the early morning the birds are either thrown into the sea for collection by boat, or, if the weather is unsuitable, laboriously hauled up the cliff. Young birds are also taken on a stack during the day, when they are herded into the centre of the level summit. A second stack was raided formerly; a rope cast over it from the adjacent island allowed fowlers to ascend the stack from a boat.

The feathers, especially the soft feathers from auk breasts, are used for stuffing pillows and quilts, and exported.

Small but fat storm petrel chicks are sometimes taken and dried, and, with a wick threaded through them, used as candles.

The Faeroese are very careful to conserve the bird colonies; puffins are taken in burrows early in the season, when it is believed that a mate can be replaced; later, during the breeding season, any bird carrying fish is spared, and in some places puffins are encouraged to nest in new areas by making shallow artificial burrows with a special scoop.

Thus, recently major changes in fowling have occurred; the exploitaton of a new species: the fulmar; the cessation of part of the gannet hunt, and the introduction of floating multiple snares, for instance, all demonstrating that while some old techniques are used, fowling is not static. There are many similarities to the St Kildan fowling, and some differences. The Faeroese *fleyg* net takes the place of the noose on the rod, not used in Faeroe; there is no reference to the use of dogs, or of multiple snares on land; both these methods fail to discriminate between breeding and non-breeding birds. The St Kildans, less used to the sea, did not catch fledging birds on the water. The use of ropes and harnesses in Faeroe is more sophisticated than the climbing on St Kilda, and in Faeroese communities, where probably more able bodied men are available, more are involved. There is a hint that greater attention is paid to safety in Faeroe.

In the 1930s people in Faeroe and, later, Iceland, became ill after the fulmar harvest; in Faeroe, 32 people died. The disease was identified as psittacosis and as a result, in Faeroe the taking of young fulmar has been forbidden since 1936, and fulmar fowling has been illegal in Iceland since 1939. Fisher noted in 1952 that there was no sign of psittacosis in fulmar in Britain, and that this is most easily accounted for if Rasmussen's explanation is accepted. He suggested that the Faeroese birds were infected by sick parrots jettisoned from cargoes of diseased birds exported to Europe after an outbreak in Argentina in 1929. It was thus a matter of chance that British fulmar were not affected, and there remains a possibility of infection from Faeroese colonists (Fisher 1984 382–5).

Mingulay

At the south end of the Long Island, Mingulay is very similar in many respects to Hirte. The area at sea level is almost the same as that of Hirte, but the island is lower, rising to a maximum of 895' (figures 95, 96). A ridge of hills surrounds a broad eastward facing glen with a sandy beach at its foot: here was the settlement, just above the shore. On the south side of the hills another area of low lying ground was used for shielings. To the north, west and south the coast is rocky, with cliffs ranging from 100' to 700' high in the north and west coasts, while landing is possible in places on the east and south coasts.

There is no historical record of a gannetry anywhere in the Barra Isles, and the fulmar did not colonise these islands until early in the present century,

Figure 95. *Location map: comparative islands in the Western Isles*

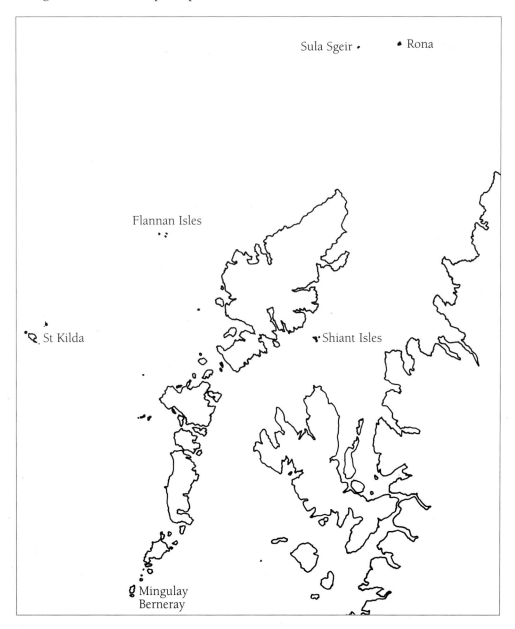

but auks are present in large colonies on both Mingulay and Berneray, the islands now supporting a total of about 22,000 guillemots, 20,000 razorbills, 11,000 puffins and, in addition, 7,000 kittiwakes (Cunningham 1983, 128–138).

The natural similarities between St Kilda and Mingulay makes this the best single island in the Western Isles for comparison with St Kilda. There is an interesting contrast in the amount of information available: records for the southern isles of Barra are scanty.

Figure 96. *Mingulay and Berneray: topography*

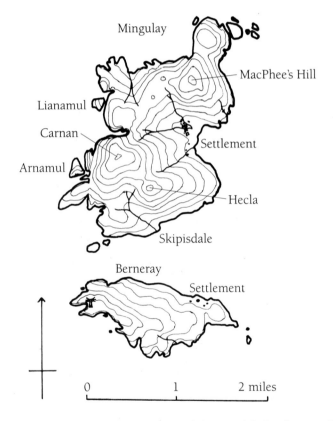

Since this work was written, Buxton (1995) has published a good detailed account of Mingulay and the other Bishop's Isles.

In 1549 (Monro 1961, 72) all these islands belonged to the Bishop of the Isles: Mingulay was inhabited and cultivated, good for fishing, and good corn. Sibbald (MacFarlane 1907, 177), at the end of the seventeenth century, found that all the islands produced crops and dairy products. The rent paid was half the annual crop, butter, cheese and anything else produced during the year.

Each island had an officer responsible for collecting these commodities. By then the islands belonged to MacNeil of Barra (Martin 1716, 94–99). Martin was confused about the identity of individual islands, but from his account it is clear that in both Mingulay and Berneray seabirds were caught and were preserved using the salty ash of seaweed, within a bag or package of cow hide. In Berneray, the people were diligent in manuring their arable land with dung, seaweed and sand, and were careful to avoid letting MacNeil or his Steward see the true quantity of fish they caught.

Martin's account of the climbing of Lianamul is very similar to his account of the climb of Stac Biorach; a group of men approached the rock in a boat; one man man landed, and, using a horse hair rope, helped the others ashore; then he led the climb. His only reward was a few more birds than the general share, and the prestige. Martin refers to the leader as 'Gingich', a term used by MacAulay (1764, 188–9) for the leader of rock climbs on Hirte.

The Steward of the Barra Isles took grain, butter, cheese and fish, and each family paid him an 'Omer' of barley. An 'inferior officer' – perhaps similar to the Ground Officer of Hirte – had a share of this produce. The MacNeil apparently ran a 'marriage bureau' for those of his tenants who were bereaved; he assigned second partners to them. He also replaced any cattle they lost and took into his own household elderly tenants who could no longer support themselves.

In 1793 (MacQueen 1793, 328–9) all the southern isles were regarded as difficult of access because of strong currents around them. A priest went twice annually, with additional visits if requested to administer extreme unction. The islands were good for crops and grazing, but grazing was precious: on Mingulay men climbed an adjacent stac to haul up wedders on a rope and so use the luxuriant grass on top. The large populations of seabirds on both Mingulay and Berneray were harvested for food and the feathers sold locally at 6d per lb. Nicolson (1840, 201–2) adds that eggs were harvested. Fowling was dangerous and two deaths had occurred in this way.

From the mid-nineteenth century the census returns show that Mingulay was supporting more people than St Kilda (figure 101). Muir (1885, 53–5, 255–260) visited Mingulay in 1866. He landed in the bay, where he saw the huddle of houses. The people lived by fishing, and growing potatoes, oats, rye and barley. Each crofter had two or three cows and at least one pony, supported by good grazing. There was plenty of peat from which to cut fuel. Muir, who had travelled extensively in the Highlands and Islands, observed that the people and their homes looked exceedingly poor. A school supported by the Ladies Highland Association had been held since 1850 in a building similar to the houses. The first teacher was surrounded on his arrival by the children, who wanted 'to see the school they had been told they were going to have. They thought he had it with him packed up in his trunk'. Carmichael visited Mingulay several times between 1865 and 1871, and recorded various aspects of life, including songs sung by the women while they were carding and spinning, and at a waulking (1941, 89; 1954, 61). Elwes (1869, 26–28) recorded that recently the sea had swept over an island in the Sound of Mingulay and washed all the sheep off it, though it had always been considered safe for grazing, and was, he reckoned, nearly 100' high. This may well have been Geirum Beag (89') or else Geirum Mór, the only other island in the Sound, with a grazing area on top entirely over 125'.

Elwes was told that in the late eighteenth century, puffins had increased considerably, and shearwaters deserted Mingulay almost entirely. Formerly a barrel of young shearwaters was part of the rent paid by each tenant. Both they and young kittiwakes were very highly esteemed. Elwes met an old man who had been one of the best fowlers in his day: probably Roderick MacNeill, who gave information to Carmichael and to Campbell of Islay when they were storm-stayed in 1871. He was then 92. According to Carmichael (1928a xxiv, 1928b 352) the quantities of shearwaters formerly paid for lands of different values varied from a quarter barrel to two barrels: he says 'probably not less than twenty barrels of these birds went to MacNeill yearly', all from Grianamul (probably Lianamul). The proprietor used to go to Mingulay for a month, two weeks each side of Lammas day, and the people were not allowed to go to the rocks till he left. By the 1870s fewer birds were killed. Carmichael adds that ropes were not used to climb on Mingulay, the people clambering among the rocks (1884, 456).

Harvie-Brown and Buckley (1888, lxxvii–lxxx), who visited in 1871 and 1887, also compared St Kilda with Mingulay, which they found

'Of fresher interest, and much more primitive than St Kilda, especially as regards the cottars' and crofters' houses. The picturesqueness of St Kilda bay and village will not for a moment compare with that of Mingulay. At present it grazes about 200 sheep, but could carry more. A score of these are grazed upon the summit of the Stack of Arnamull, and about five had on Lianamull. It also carries about a score of good-looking highland ponies, and some cattle. The ponies have only about a fortnight's work to do in each season carrying down the peat, cut high upon the hills. Lobster fishing is well prosecuted by the people of both Mingulay and Barray [Berneray].'

Some of the older peat hags were almost worked out, but new ones were being opened and there was no shortage of peat.

There had once been a rope bridge across to Lianamul, but now both Lianamul and Arnamul were climbed from a boat. Manx shearwaters had once inhabited the top of Lianamul, but had been replaced by puffins. Harvie Brown considered that the stac was the most densely packed guillemot station he had ever seen, with numerous very suitable ledges, 'along many of which two men could crawl abreast on hands and knees'. People also took eggs from the great cliff of Aoinaig, though not as often as formerly. Gordon (1937, 127) was told that in the nineteenth century guillemots and razorbills were caught with a noose on the end of a rod, and puffins taken from their burrows.

Freer (1903, 392–404) noted in 1898 that a well known as Columcille's well was regarded with especial reverence, and the water used as 'holy water'. The people crossed themselves with it when passing, and carried it in the prows of their boats. She considered the people to be 'exceptionally well-off and comfortable…So far are they from exploiting the stranger, as is the custon in St Kilda, that we had the greatest difficulty in persuading them to take payment even for laborious services, and to prevent them from robbing themselves to give us such necessaries as added greatly to our comfort.' Months might pass without a visit from a priest, but by 1898, a house with chapel above were under construction. MacGregor (1971, 144) states that this was never completely finished, and that the workmen were among the last inhabitants of the island. A school with adjoining schoolhouse was built, probably in the late nineteenth century.

Accounts vary as to which year most of the people left Mingulay, but there seems to have been a major move in 1907 or 1908, when a number of families squatted on Vatersay, which was then a farm. In 1909 the Congested Districts Board bought Vatersay and settled 58 families on it, including many from Mingulay, the last families leaving in 1911 (Murchison 1959, 313–40).

A number of people, including Freer, MacKinnon (1983, 5–6, 42–47) and MacGregor (1935, 230–7) have told the story of the depopulation of Mingulay by disease in the distant past, and its resettlement. Traditionally, MacNeil had noticed that for some time there had been no communication from Mingulay, and sent a boat to investigate. One man, MacPhee, landed, and found all the houses empty except one where the family lay dead, there being no-one to bury them. The boat crew, when they heard his news, refused to take him back in the boat, fearing infection, and MacPhee was abandoned. MacGregor was told that they threw him a smouldering peat before returning to Kismul. After some time a boat was sent to see how MacPhee was faring, and when he was found alive, MacNeil asked him if he would stay on the island. MacPhee chose companions to resettle the island. The old houses were burned and a village built on a new site.

There were fairies on Mingulay, and a waterhorse which lived in a bottomless well on MacPhee's Hill. At least one case of 'second sight' is recorded. (Carmichael 1954, 117, MacGregor 1949, 174–5).

The village on Mingulay is a cluster of buildings and small enclosed yards on either side of the main burn, snug against the ridge which divides the east facing glen into two (plate 44). Blown sand now encroaches on the eastern edge of the village. The drystone walls of the thirty-odd buildings are well preserved, though some details are obscured by sand and collapsed walling. Some are clearly not houses, but byres or stables, and at least three are almost certainly kiln-barns. The census returns indicate a maximum of 34 dwellings, most of which must have had two rooms each with at least one window. Most of the buildings in the village which are likely to be dwellings have the common pattern of a central doorway with a window on either side; almost all must have had hipped gables. There are indications of change before the people left; some houses have fireplaces in the gable ends; one has mortared chimneys and a mortared house has pointed gables with chimneys. The burial ground is at the heart of the village. Some distance upstream is a small horizontal water mill.

The gently sloping ground above the village is surrounded by a head dyke and divided into small areas (plate 45). There is evidence of a higher dyke enclosing a larger area.

Other buildings, high up in the east glen near Hecla, on the south side in Skipisdale (plate 46), and near Hecla Point, are less well preserved, but most show subrectangular or oval plans. These structures, which are on slight mounds of bright green turf, were probably shielings. Some have fold areas associated with them. They are well placed for keeping stock away from the main arable area. Their shape and pattern is not uniform, and they are not necessarily all contemporary. The lower part of Skipisdale and lower slopes of Hecla are covered by a system of large adjoining enclosures containing 'lazy beds'. When these were cultivated the amount of grazing would be considerably reduced, and it is unlikely that shielings would be contemporary with such widespread cultivation.

On the upper slopes of the hills there are areas of old peat cuttings. Associated with these are oval features, mostly low mounds surrounded by stones, but some are simply oval settings of stones. They are on dry sites, and many are well placed to take advantage of the drying effect of wind. These are almost certainly sites for peat stacks. Although most people in the Western Isles now take their peats home by lorry or trailer, this was not always the pattern, and peats were sometimes stacked where they were cut, and taken home daily by the sackful for immediate needs.

Thus life on Mingulay was very similar to life on St Kilda, though there was less reliance on seabirds and tweed on Mingulay, and probably more reliance on fishing. Contact with neighbouring islands was easier, though Mingulay could be isolated by bad weather for many weeks at a time (Carmichael 1940, 4). From 1833 the lighthouse boat calling regularly at Berneray provided an indirect means of communication. One of the greatest differences between the islands, reflected in the information now available about them, was the attention St Kilda received from visitors and from the Government. Mingulay had no steamer service, no local postal service, no resident nurse, and no resident priest. Visitors were rare. Twenty years before the St Kildans appealed for assistance in leaving their island, the people of Mingulay had more quietly gone elsewhere.

Shiant Isles

The Shiant Isles in the North Minch are four miles east of Park, Lewis, and twelve miles north of Trotternish, Skye (figures 95, 97). Garbh Eilean is about 1 mile long and ½ mile wide; it is triangular, rising from a rocky coast at sea level on the southwest side to nearly 500' at the north-east corner, most of the shore being steep crag or cliff. At the south-east corner a pebble bar joins Garbh Eilean to Eilean an Taighe lying to the south, about 1 mile long and up to ¼ mile wide, rising from a rocky shore at sea level on the west side to 400' on the east side which drops to the sea in cliffs. ½ mile to the east Eilean Mhuire is of uneven triangular shape, and consists of an undulating plateau 150' above sea level, rising to a maximum of 295'. There are large auk

Figure 97. *Shiant Isles: topography*

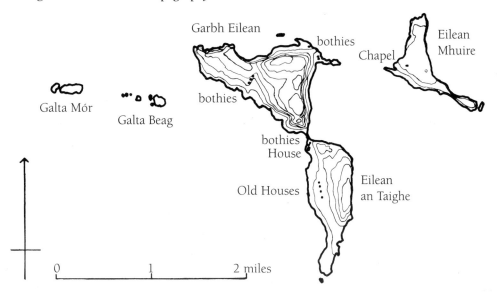

colonies: 8,000 guillemots, 3,500 razorbills, about 90,000 pairs of puffins, and in addition 1,170 pairs of kittiwakes (Cunningham 1983, 127–138).

On Eilean Mhuire are the remains of St Mary's chapel. A number of mounds in the vicinity may be associated with this or may be the remains of seasonal dwellings. Almost the whole island plateau is covered with old cultivation ridges. On Eilean an Taighe is the only house still habitable, and the ruins of several dwellings and outbuildings (plate 47). Extensive areas were cultivated. On Garbh Eilean there are the remains of several small buildings, probably shielings and fishermen's huts, and further areas of cultivation.

Monro (1961, 85) noted in 1549 that the islands were very good for growing corn, and for grazing and fishing. Martin (1716, 26–7) confirms that Eilean Mhuire and Eilean an Taighe were valued for growing crops and grazing, Garbh Eilean being used only for grazing.

Walker (1980, 25) gives the population in 1764 as 22, and O'Farrell (1852) noted that about 80 years before 1852 there had been five families on the Shiants. By 1797 there was only one family on the islands (Simson 1797, 276) and they continued to be occupied by a single family until about 1903; at least three different shepherds with their families lived there in succession, though there was a gap of about twenty years in the mid-nineteenth century when the islands were uninhabited. The Shiants continue to be valued for the grazing, the tenant visiting them at intervals during the year with assistants to attend to lambing, gathering and shearing.

Although there are large seabird colonies there are few references in the literature to fowling. Before 1797 the daughter of the shepherd had fallen to her death while collecting eggs; MacKenzie (1921, 71) was told in the mid-nineteenth century by people from Park that they went to the islands to take boatloads of puffins for eating and for their feathers. The birds were killed or stunned by lads lying on the slopes and hitting the puffins with a fishing rod as they flew past; the dead and stunned birds were collected at the bottom of the slope and loaded into boats. Families from Rhenigidale in Harris used to take puffins from the Shiants up to about 1910 (Angus Campbell pers comm).

North Rona

North Rona is 45 miles north-north-east of the Butt of Lewis (figures 95, 98). It is an irregular triangle about 1 mile long along its southern base, rising along the north-east edge to a ridge 260' high, with a rounded summit 355' high at the east end. The southern slope is gentle, but the north-eastern slope drops steeply in the central section to the isthmus of the low peninsula to the north. Most of the island is bordered by cliff, but landing is possible in calm weather on low sloping rocks on the northern peninsula and in places on the southern edge. There is no shelter for a long term anchorage. There are colonies of over 3,000 pairs of kittiwakes, 17,800 guillemots and 1,200 razorbills on the cliffs and 4,750 pairs of puffins on steep slopes, besides fulmars which colonised the island in the nineteenth century, and smaller petrels (Benn, Murray and Tasker 1989, 36). There are no land mammals other than domestic sheep; grey seals now breed on the island in the autumn.

On the south facing slope there are the remains of a settlement, consisting of a small chapel within an oval burial ground and three groups of dwellings with associated buildings, all surrounded by extensive cultivation strips and contained within a head dyke (plate 48). On Fianuis, the northern peninsula, there are several structures which may have been shielings, and traces of a complex pattern of dykes.

Nisbet and Gailey (1962, 111–115) suggest that the corbelled oratory within the burial ground, traditionally associated with Saint Ronan, was built in the seventh or eighth century AD, and that the adjoining nave was added in the twelfth century. The dwelling complexes may have their origins in mediaeval dwellings with subsequent alterations and additions.

Figure 98. *North Rona: topography*

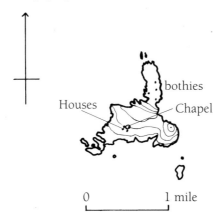

Monro (1961, 87–88) writing of 1549, notes that Rona was inhabited; barley was grown and there was good pasture for cattle and sheep. Rent was paid in good quality bere meal, cattle, sheep, dried mutton and dried seabirds. The inhabitants also took whales and large fish. Morrison (1907, 212) wrote in the late seventeenth century that the five tenants of Rona depended on seabirds to a great extent, catching them in gins and at night. He mentions oil from gannets, which must have been taken from Sula Sgeir, and this, together with Monro's reference to whales implies that a boat was available. MacKenzie

(1681–4) adds that sea bird feathers contributed to the rent and that there was no peat moss, the people relying on drift wood for fuel. There had been five families for generations and there was a limit of 30 persons imposed on the population; if it rose above that number, one or more had to emigrate to Ness. Daniel Morrison, minister of Barvas, held Rona as part of his glebe (Martin 1716, 19–25). He described three enclosures in the village in which each of the five tenants had a dwelling, barn and byre, with a porch on either side of the door. The houses were thatched with straw. In the 1680s rats had got ashore and a passing ship took the only bull; the rats consumed provisions and the cows ceased to give milk and the whole community perished from starvation.

Colonists sent out by Morrison, or their descendants, apparently suffered another calamity: all the men were drowned while seal hunting and their families returned to Ness (MacCulloch 1824, 312; Robson 1991, 174). In 1764 the population was 9 (Walker 1980, 25). In the 1790s the island was rented to the Murrays of North Dell, Ness. They kept a shepherd there and each year sent a boat to collect corn, butter, cheese, a few sheep, birds, feathers, and sometimes a cow (MacDonald 1797, 270–1). Wool was also sent off the island (MacCulloch 1824, 315). There was a succession of shepherds who stayed with their families for several years at a time until 1844. There have been no permanent inhabitants since 1844. The island continues to be used for grazing sheep and generally an annual visit is made to shear sheep and remove some of the stock (plate 49).

Sula Sgeir

Sula Sgeir is 11 miles to the west of Rona and 40 miles north of the Butt of Lewis (figures 95, 99). It is just over ½ mile long and at most 300 yards wide, and is surrounded by cliff or steep rocks. It rises to a maximum height of 230' at the southwest end. There are nesting on it about 9,000 pairs of gannets and 25,000 guillemots, together with increasing numbers of fulmars, about 1,000 kittiwakes, 800–900 razorbills and 500 pairs of puffins (Benn, Murray and Tasker 1989, 36).

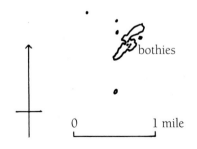

Figure 99. *Sula Sgeir: topography*

bothies

0   1 mile

Monro (1961, 88) refers in 1549 to men going from Ness at fledging time to stay for seven or eight days on the island to take birds and feathers; according to him and to Walker (1980, 48) eider down was obtained in significant quantities. There is no further reference to the harvesting of birds until 1797 when MacDonald (1797, 270–1) recorded that the boat going to fetch produce from Rona called at Sula Sgeir for birds and feathers, and that 'for a few years back' men had gone from Ness in an open six-oared boat to collect birds, some landing while others tended the boat.

According to MacDonald (1978, 190) the tenant who rented Rona and Sula Sgeir early in the nineteenth century assumed the right to harvest birds from the rock, and gannet 'poachers' were in trouble in 1811 and 1821. The collecting of birds and feathers by the tacksman continued until the latter part of the nineteenth century (MacCulloch 1819, 205; Muir 1885 98–9). By the end of the century one or more groups of men were going annually from Ness. In 1850 an Ordnance Survey officer described the bothies in which the hunters stayed for up to three weeks and noted that one building known as the Teampull was reserved for prayer on the Sabbath (Carbery, 1850). Swinburne (1885, 51–67) was told that men from Ness spent seven or eight days in early September killing young gannets which were salted for the winter. No other birds would be available in any number in the late summer.

More details are given in an account of 1912 (*Highland News* 7.9.1912). In that year ten men left Ness on August 13th, taking provisions and fuel in their boat which they hauled up onto the rock. Some birds were readily accessible but most were on ledges and the fowlers were lowered down the cliff face and took the birds using a noose on the end of a rod. Once a number had been collected they were hauled to the top of the cliff in a bundle. Normally 1,000 or 1,500 birds was considered a reasonable total catch but in that year the fowlers took 2,200. Their return was delayed for eleven days by bad weather and they were absent for four weeks. The feathers were used locally and sold in the south, and oil extracted from the birds was used as a tonic for stock and in carding wool. Each man could expect £4 or £5 as a share of the bird sales. In 1915 the birds sold at a shilling each.

Apart from the war years and other occasional gaps, the hunt has continued to this day (Beatty 1992; Harman in prep.). A group of about ten men, taking fuel and provisions, including fresh water, stay in the bothies on the rock, generally for two to three weeks. For about ten years after 1945 several boats went with smaller parties. There have been a number of changes since 1912. The crew make use of tinned food and bottled gas, besides taking more traditional supplies. Light mattresses are used instead of straw, and polythene sheeting and artificial textile provide better wind and waterproofing of the bothies than was possible formerly. After the second World War a battery operated radio provided contact with Ness and more recently radios and personal stereo sets provide entertainment. From the 1950s the crew have been landed from a boat and left on the rock, the date for collecting them being agreed by radio; the days of hauling the boat up the rock have gone. There have been innovations in the fowling equipment: besides the snares on rods, pincers worked by a spring, like long-handled pruners, are also used to catch birds; a wire cable or 'Blondin' is used to transport sacks of birds from higher ground to the processing areas; blow lamps are used to complete the singeing after plucking, and a wooden chute is constructed annually above the landing rock to facilitate hauling gear up the rock and sliding gear and the salted gugas down at the end of the trip. The work remains very similar: the birds are collected from the ledges; they are killed and the heads cut off. Groups are taken to the top of the cliff and then transported to the processing area near the bothies. Here the birds are plucked and singed, then gutted, the oily offal being used to feed the fire. Then the tails and wings are removed, and the carcass split down the back with a knife and the rib cage removed. Finally they are salted and stacked on two stone bases beside the chute site, ready to leave the island.

Each hunter receives a share of about 100 birds; the rest are sold on the return to Ness (plate 51). In 1992 they were rationed to 2 per person and cost £6 each. In the 1950s the numbers taken increased to about 4,000 in some years but are now limited to 2,000 by licence from Scottish Natural Heritage. The Protection of Birds Act 1954 would have made the guga hunt illegal but from 1955 it was permitted under 'The Wild Birds (Gannets on Sula Sgeir) Order' and similar provisions have been made in subsequent Acts.

Flannan Isles

The Flannan Isles or Seven Hunters lie twenty miles west and slightly north of the nearest land, Gallan Head in Uig, Lewis (figures 95, 100). There are three groups of islands and rocks. All the islands rise precipitously to over 125', and have flat or gently sloping summits. The only evidence of occupation is on the two largest, Eilean Mór, which is just under $1/2$ by $1/4$ mile, and Eilean Taighe, which is $1/2$ mile long but 300 yards wide at most. The islands support large colonies of auks: 10,000 guillemots, 3,500 razorbills and 3,600 pairs of puffins, together with nearly 2,000 pairs of Kittiwakes (Cunningham 1983, 127–138).

On Eilean Mór there are a small chapel and two ruined bothies (plate 51), and a lighthouse completed in 1899. On Eilean Taighe there is a ruined bothy. There has been no detailed study of the older structures other than those of Muir (1861, 178–82: 1885, 60) and Thomas (1870, 162). The chapel is very small, but broadly comparable with some Irish mediaeval buildings. The bothies show some similarities to the cells on Skellig Michael; it possible that they are early Christian buildings and have been re-used extensively.

Monro (1961, 80–1) makes no mention of the chapel or of fowling, but says that the islands were 'holy' and supported wild sheep put there beyond living memory in 1549. MacLeod of Lewis sent men to hunt the sheep with dogs. In the late seventeenth century Morrison (1907, 211–2) and Martin (1716, 15–19) refer to a chapel used by St Flannan. Men went in the summer to take sheep and also birds, taking great quantities of birds, eggs, feathers and down. They worked in pairs to kill the birds, one hitting them with a rod as they flew past while his partner collected them as they fell. Various rituals, regarded as extremely important, were observed by the fowlers, including making a circuit of the chapel on their knees while praying, both when they arrived and every morning and evening during their stay.

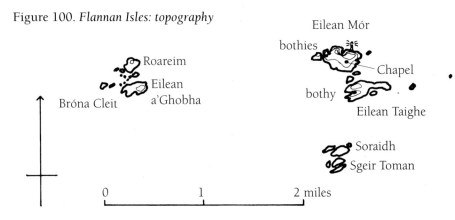

Figure 100. *Flannan Isles: topography*

Fowling continued to be important well into the nineteenth century, the islands being well known also for fattening sheep, which fetched a very good price (Walker 1980, 34, 42, 48; Monro 1792, 282; MacCulloch 1819, 198–9; Hayes 1852). By the mid-twentieth century the grazing was the most important aspect, and sheep no longer bred there but were taken out annually and exchanged for the previous year's group which were well fattened. Despite the effort involved it was worth putting even 3 sheep on Roareim and 3 on Sgeir Toman; Eilean Mór grazed about 25. The men who went to exchange the sheep took the opportunity to gather a few sacksfull of puffins, guillemots and shags (Stewart 1933, 49–53; Atkinson 1949, 160–176; Gunn 1949, 250–273). The late grazing tenant had not visited the islands for about twenty years and there are no longer any sheep on the Flannan Isles.

Deserted Islands

Mingulay and the four Lewis islands and island groups are particularly good examples of many Hebridean islands with similarities to Hirte and adjacent islands. Moisley (1966, 44–68) has noted the desertion of other Hebridean islands which once held thriving populations, such as Taransay, Pabbay, Boreray (Uist) and the Monach Isles, and since then Scarp has been abandoned. Some offshore islands are now even abandoned as grazing islands, such as the Flannans and Mealasta island, Lewis. The occupation and evacuation of St Kilda are thus part of an historic trend for the establishment of diffuse largely self-sufficient settlements followed by a retreat to a smaller number of the larger islands and a greater reliance on communication and trade with the mainland. Elsewhere, small remote communities such as those on Foula, Fair Isle and Tristan da Cunha have survived.

Figure 101. *Population figures: St Kilda, Mingulay , Berneray, Tristan da Cunha*

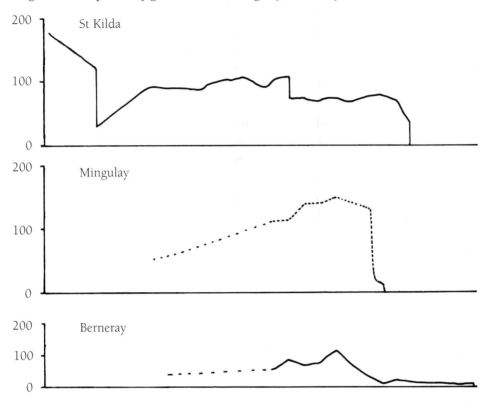

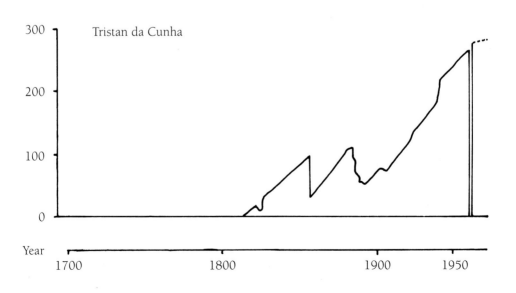

17

In Conclusion

People are intrigued by extremities: the expressions 'Land's End to John o'Groats', and 'Bho Hirt gu Peirt' [from Hirte to Perth] convey something of the aura which these places have. St Kilda was referred to even in 1527 as 'the last and outmaist isle', and in the 1930s as the island on the 'Edge of the World'. Of the small isolated Scottish islands, only St Kilda combines the features of distance, wealth and variety of natural life, and a comparatively well documented human population with a poignant end to their residence on the island. This has led to an extraordinary number of visitors who have left an extensive literature about all aspects of St Kilda. I have followed a well-trodden path, but in this work have added some aspects hitherto neglected and expanded others.

I have tried to bring together as much evidence as possible for the prehistoric and mediaeval periods of the islands' history, in the context of that of the Long Island, and, without trespassing on the present excavation programme, have been able to provide more detail than has been available before. In considering the historic period, I have been able to clarify events in the later eighteenth and early nineteenth centuries, besides adding much detail for the later nineteenth and twentieth century. Here the MacLeod Muniments and the papers in the care of the Royal Highland and Agricultural Society of Scotland were particularly useful.

Hitherto those writing about St Kilda have tended to consider the islands in isolation, often reflecting their perception of them as remote. It is true that they are separated from the Long Island by forty miles of sea or more, but the sea, though often regarded as an obstacle and so a divisive feature, is a highway for those accustomed to travelling by boat, and in the past has been a cohesive factor for the west coast of Scotland and for the north east Atlantic.

Comparisons with other islands show that St Kilda is not unique in the sense that there are other islands and archipelagos which have or are supporting human populations in similar circumstances, and beyond the Hebrides some of these places have attracted visitors and generated literature to a similar degree. Thus the islands should be seen as part of a larger community, in many respects sharing the lifestyle of their neighbours. Fowling was practised wherever there were large seabird colonies; St Kilda was only peculiar in the extent of its dependence on fowling and the range of species involved. Some of the detailed information available for St Kilda can be used, with caution, to augment knowledge of the Long Island.

In the 1830s Rev. Neil MacKenzie observed of the St Kildans: 'in all their work there is a terrible lack of thoroughness which their favourite phrase "it will do" exactly expresses'. I have tried to avoid emulating the St Kildans in this though I fear that those with a detailed knowledge of a particular field may find this account superficial in some respects.

Some aspects of St Kildan history and culture have been covered very fully by others; for instance: Bill Lawson (1981 and 1993) has published work on the families of St Kilda; Steel (1988) has considered events leading up to the evacuation and the evacuation itself in considerable detail; MacKay (1963 and 1978) has made a very full assessment of the postal and wireless services to the island; while Coates (1990) published his book on place names while this work was in progress.

In trying to present a balanced view of the history and culture I have summarised some of the detailed work carried out by others, and have also included summaries of some of my own work which I intend to present in more detail elsewhere, particularly the work on the buildings, a consideration of the maps of the islands, the customs, stories and songs, and an account of visitors to the island. Although I have found answers to a number of questions, more have been raised through this work.

There is, perhaps, a tendency to think of the culture of the St Kildans as static; of successive generations living through an annual cycle of agriculture and fowling reaching back into 'time immemorial' with little change until the nineteenth century. The records for the last three centuries of the community's life show that it was subject to frequent changes such as the years of tyranny by Roderick the Imposter; survival of the smallpox by a few followed by large scale immigration; tyranny of the Steward in the later eighteenth century; re-organisation of the village and land holding in the 1830s, a religious upheaval in the 1840s; large scale emigration in 1852, and then increasing contact with visitors and reliance on imported goods. Finally there came the last response to accumulated pressures arising from change: leaving familiar surroundings and a way of life for ever.

The earlier history of the west coast of Scotland is subject to political, religious and climatic changes which would no doubt have been felt on St Kilda as elsewhere. We can only surmise, as MacAulay did, that similar changes occurred beyond recorded history from one source or another. While any early St Kildans probably practised agriculture and fowling, the social organisation of the historic community cannot be projected backwards in time.

Descriptions and pictures of life on St Kilda in recent historic times fail to evoke two aspects of life obvious to the contemporary visitor: smell and sound. The stench of rotting bird entrails no longer hangs over the village, nor the peat reek, the smell of cattle dung, drying fish, wet tweed or the scent of new-mown hay. To the constant sounds of the sea, the wind and sheep the modern visitor should add, for instance, cattle lowing, dogs barking, and the sounds of a community at work and at play - the clack of the loom, babies crying, children laughing, pony hooves drumming on the turf, and people singing, in love, in praise, and in lamentation.

Bibliography

If authors are known to have visited the islands before 1940, the date(s) of visit(s) are given in [**bold**] in brackets immediately after the author's name. In some cases these are significantly different from the date of publication.

Abbreviations:

AF   Agriculture and Fisheries Department of Scottish Office
Adv. ms.   Advocates manuscript (held in National Library of Scotland)
DNB   Dictionary of National Biography
GSR   Gaelic School Report(s)
NLS   National Library of Scotland
NMRS   National Monuments Record of Scotland
NTS   National Trust for Scotland
OSA   Old Statistical Account
PP   Parliamentary Paper
PRO   Public Record Office
PSAS   Proceedings of the Society of Antiquaries of Scotland
RCAHMS   Royal Commission on the Ancient and Historical Monuments of Scotland
RMS   Register of the Great Seal of Scotland
SEA   Scottish Ethnological Archive
SG   Stornoway Gazette
SRO   Scottish Record Office
SSS   School of Scottish Studies

Acland, Anne 1981 *A Devon Family: The Story of the Aclands* Chichester: Phillimore and Co.
Admiralty 1865 *Chart 2474 Hebrides or Western Isles from Barra Head to Scarpa Island* and subsequent editions
1911 *Chart 1144 Plans in the Hebrides* and subsequent editions
1934 *West Coast of Scotland Pilot* London 8th edition
Anderson, James M 1884 Evidence to the Napier Commission pp 3157–9
Anderson, Joseph 1885 *Notice of a bronze Cauldron found with several small kegs of butter in a moss...Skye* in *PSAS* 19 1884–5, pp 309–15
Anonymous 1595 *The Description of the Isles of Scotland* (probably 1577–95) printed as appendix to Skene, W F *Celtic Scotland* 1880 vol 3 pp 428–440
*c.*1594 *A Short Description of the Western Isles of Scotland, lying in the Deucalidon Sea, being above 300. Also the Iles of Orknay and Schetland or Hethland* printed as part of *Certain Matters concerning the Realme of Scotland composed together*, London. 2nd edition by Simon Stafford 1603. Also as an addition to Monipennie's *Scots Chronicles* 1612, reprint in *Miscellanea Scotica* 1818, Vol I pp 175–191 Glasgow: John Wylie and Co
1751 *A Voyage to Scotland, the Orkneys and the Western Isles of Scotland* London: C Corbet
1846 The Story of Lady Grange. In *Chambers Edinburgh Journal* 114 March 7 pp 145–148
1921 Rarity of second attacks of Whooping Cough Epidemic. In *British Medical Journal* II p 416
1926 St Kilda. In *British Medical Journal* II p 80–1
Arnet, H ed. year *Extracts from the records of the Burgh of Edinburgh 1701–1718*

Arrowsmith, Aaron 1809 *Memoir relative to the construction of the Map of Scotland* published by him in 1807 London

Atkinson, George Clayton [**1831**] 1831 *A few Weeks' Ramble among the Hebrides in the Summer of 1831* Ms account, typescript copy in NTS Archive. pp refer to typescript
1838 An Account of an Expedition to St Kilda in 1831. In *Trans. Nat. Hist. Soc. Northumberland, Durham and Newcastle* II pp 215–225, map Pl III

Atkinson, Robert L [**1938–1953**] 1949 *Island Going* London: Collins. Photographs in School of Scottish Studies collection: reference prefixed S

Baillie, Lady, of Polkemmet [**1874**] 1875 A Short Visit to St Kilda by a Lady: 1874. In *Church of Scotland Missionary Record* Jan. 1875 pp 254–257

Baldwin, John 1974 Seabird Fowling in Scotland and Faroe. In *Folk Life* 12 pp 60–103

Barrington, Richard M. [**1880s**] 1886 Note on the Flora of St Kilda. In *Journal of Botany* 24 pp 213–6
1913 Ascent of Stack na Biorrach, St Kilda. In *Alpine Journal* 27 pp 195–202

Barron, J 1912 *The Northern Institution and its Leading Members 1825–1835* Inverness: Inverness Courier

Beare, T Hudson 1908 Notes on the Coleoptera from St Kilda. In *Annals of Scottish Nat Hist* 17 pp 30–5

Beatty, John 1992 *Sula: The Seabird Hunters of Lewis* London: Michael Joseph

Benn, Stuart, Murray, Stuart, and Tasker, Mark 1989 *The Birds of North Rona and Sula Sgeir* Peterborough: Nature Conservancy Council

Black, Ronald 1974 Colla Ciotach. In *Transactions of the Gaelic Society of Inverness* 48 1972–4 pp 201–243

Blankenhorn, V S 1979 From the Farthest Hebrides (Review article). In *The Scottish Review* 16 pp 53–5

Boece, Hector 1527 *Scotorum Regni Descriptio f xiiii:* part of: *Scotorum Historiae Prima Gentis Origine cum aliarum et rerum et gentium illustratione non vulgari* Paris another edition 1574, (f 8)

Brougham, Lord [**1799**] 1799 letter to Robert Lundie NLS Ms 1675
1871 *Memoirs of the Life and Times of Lord Brougham written by himself* I London and Edinburgh

Buchan, Alexander [**1704–1729**] 1727 *A Description of St Kilda* Edinburgh: Lumisden and Robertson reprinted with substantial alterations by Miss Buchan, 1752

Buchanan, George 1762 *The History of Scotland* Edinburgh

Buchanan, John Lane 1793 *Travels in the Western Hebrides from 1782 to 1790* London: GGJ and J Robinson, J Debrett

Buchanan, Margaret 1983 *St Kilda: A Photographic Album* Edinburgh: William Blackwood
Buchanan, Margaret (editor) 1995 *St Kilda The Continuing Story of the Islands* Glasgow and Edinburgh: Glasgow Museums and H.M.S.O.

Burt 1754 *Letters from a Gentleman in the North of Scotland* London: S Birt 2 vols

Buxton, Ben 1995 *Mingulay An Island and Its People* Edinburgh: Birlinn

Cameron, Mary [**1919–1926**] 1969 Our Childhood on St Kilda. In *Scots Magazine* March 1969 pp 565–571
1973 *Childhood Days on St Kilda* Gairloch

Campbell, Alexander 1818 *Albyn's Anthology* Edinburgh: Oliver and Boyd

Campbell, Archibald 1885 *Records of Argyll* Edinburgh: William Blackwood and Sons

Campbell, John Francis 1890 *Popular Tales of the West Highlands* 2nd edition 4 vols. Paisley: Alex. Gardner

Campbell, John Lorne 1984 *Canna* Oxford: Oxford University Press

Campbell, R N 1974 *St Kilda and its Sheep* in Jewell et al. 1974 *Island Survivors* pp 8–35

Campbell, Robert [1799] 1799 *An Account of the Island of St Kilda and Neighbouring Islands, Visited August 1799* NLS Ms 3051
1809 Map of the Islands of St Kilda, Borrera, etc, taken Aug 1799 in Arrowsmith 1809, p 20 and plate opposite

Campbell, Robert 1945 Obituary: John Mathieson FRSE FRSGS. In *Scottish Geographical Magazine* 61 p 71

Carbery 1850 Account of Sula Sgeir. In *Ordnance Survey Name Book for Ness, Lewis*, copy in NMRS

Carmichael, Alexander [1865] 1928–1971 *Carmina Gadelica* Vols. I (1928a), II (1928b), IV (1941), V (1954) and VI (1971) Edinburgh and London: Oliver and Boyd

Carruthers, R [1834] 1843 *The Highland Notebook; or sketches and anecdotes* Edinburgh: A and C Black

Celoria, Francis 1966 *Report on a preliminary Survey of the Archaeology of St Kilda* University of Keele Typescript report in NTS Archive

Chambers, William 1874 The Story of Lady Grange. In *Chambers Journal* 551 July 14 1874 pp 449–452

Chudleigh, R Augustine 1886 The Strangers' Cold. In *British Medical Journal* Sept 4 p 484

Clark, Gilbert and Fraser, I A 1990 *The Battle of Traigh Ghruinneart* In *Tocher* 44 pp 110–7

Clarke, Edward Daniel [1797] 1824 *The Life and remains of Edward Daniel Clarke* ed. William Otter London

Clegg, E J 1977 Population Changes in St Kilda During the 19th and 20th centuries. In *Journ. Biosoc. Science* 9 pp 293–307
1982 Further Studies on the Population of St Kilda: Coefficients of Inbreeding and a Partial Pedigree. In *Proc of the Indian Statistical Institute Golden Jubilee International Conference on Human Genetics and Adaptation* 1 ed KC Malhotra and A Basu pp 9–14
1984 Some Factors Associated with Island Depopulation and the Example of St Kilda. In *Northern Scotland* 6 pp 3–11

Coates, Richard 1988 *Notes on the Past of the Gaelic Dialect of St Kilda* Brighton: University of Sussex Cognitive Science Research Reports 81
1990 *The Place-names of St Kilda* Lampeter: Edwin Mellen Press

Cockburn, A M [1927–8] 1934 The Geology of St Kilda. In *Trans Royal Soc Edin* 35 part 2 no.21 pp 511–547

Collacott, R A 1981 Neonatal Tetanus in St Kilda. In *Scottish Medical Journal* 26 pp 224–7

Connell, Robert [1886] 1887 *St Kilda and the St Kildians* London and Glasgow: Thomas D Morison

Cottam, B 1973 *St Kilda Archaeological Survey I,* typescript
1974 *St Kilda Archaeological Survey II* typescript copies of both in NTS Archive
1979 Archaeology. In *A St Kilda Handbook* ed. Small, Alan Edinburgh: National Trust for Scotland

Cramp, Stanley et al. 1977, 1985 *Handbook of the Birds of Europe, the Middle East, and North Africa: the Birds of the Western Palearctic* 7 vols Oxford: Oxford University Press Vol 1 1977, Vol 4 1985

Crawford, Iain A 1971–1981 *Excavations at Coileagan an Udail North Uist* Interim reports, privately produced
1977 A Corbelled Bronze-Age Burial Chamber and Beaker...Evidence from the Rosinish Machair, Benbecula. In *PSAS* 108 1976–7 pp 94–107
1986 *The West Highlands and Islands: A View of 50 centuries* Cambridge: The Great Auk Press

Cumming, C F Gordon 1883 *In the Hebrides* London: Chatto and Windus

Cunningham, W A J 1983 *Birds of the Outer Hebrides* Perth: Melven Press

D.R.M. 1876 Cumha Hirteach *An Gaidheal* 5 p 54

Darling, Frank Fraser 1941 *Island Years* London: George Bell & Son
1947 *Natural History in the Highlands and Islands* London: Collins

Davidson, J 1969 *Notes made after visiting St Kilda in connection with second edition of OS map* Ms in NMRS

Davison, C 1924 *A History of British Earthquakes* Cambridge: Cambridge University Press

Day, Catharina 1986 *Ireland* London: Cadogan Books

Dix and Paterson, I 1975 *Tocher* 20 pp 132–5

Dixon, Charles 1885 The Ornithology of St Kilda. In *Ibis* 3 pp 69–97, 358–362

Dixon, Harold G 1886 The Strangers' Cold. In *British Medical Journal* p 286

Douglas, George 1790 Parish of Tain OSA 1791–9 ed John Sinclair III pp 389–398

Dougall, John 1892 Epidemic on St Kilda Island. In *British Medical Journal* p 1388

Dryden, James 1930 St Kilda's Floating Mail. In *Gibbons Stamp Monthly* Dec. 1930

Duckworth, C L D and Langmuir, G E 1950 *West Highland Steamers* London: Richard Tilling

Dun, Finlay 1848 *Orain na h-Albain* Edinburgh: Wood and Co

Dunlop, Jean 1978 *The British Fisheries Society 1786–1893* Edinburgh: John Donald

Dwelly, Edward 1920 *The Illustrated Gaelic-English Dictionary*

Earwood, Caroline 1991 Two Early Historic Bog Butter Containers. In *PSAS* 121 pp 231–240

Elliot, J Steele [**1894**] 1895a St Kilda and the St Kildans. In *Journal Birmingham Nat Hist and Phil Soc.* 1 pp 113–135
1895b Observations on the Fauna of St Kilda. In *The Zoologist* 19 pp 281–286

Elwes, Henry John 1869 The Bird Stations of the Outer Hebrides. In *Ibis* 5 pp 20–37

Elwes, J 1912 Notes on the primitive breeds of Sheep in Scotland. In *Scottish Naturalist* x 1912 pp 25–29

Emery, F V 1958 The Geography of Robert Gordon 1580–1661 and Sir Robert Sibbald 1641–1722. In *Scottish Geographical Magazine* 74 pp 3–12

Emery, Norman 1987–1991 Excavations on St Kilda. Interim reports in *St Kilda Mail* 11 1987 pp 6–8; 12 1988 pp 9–10; 13 1989 pp 16–17; 14 1990 pp 19–21; 15 1991 pp 18–19

Emery, Norman and Morrison, Alex 1995 The Archaeology of St Kilda in Buchanan, Meg (ed) *St Kilda the Continuing Story of the Islands*

Erskine, William 1798 letter to Mrs Lundie NLS Ms 1675

Evans, W 1906 Some Invertebrata, including Oxodes borealis from St Kilda. In *Annals of Scottish Nat Hist* 15 pp 93–8

Ewing, William 1914 *Annals of the Free Church of Scotland* Edinburgh: T T Clark 2 volumes

Farmer, David Hugh 1978 *The Oxford Dictionary of Saints* Oxford: Oxford University Press

Fenton, A and Hendry, C 1984 Wooden Tumbler Locks in Scotland and Beyond. In *Review of Scottish Culture* 1 pp 11–28

Ferguson, M. 1885 *Rambles in Skye, with a sketch of a trip to St Kilda* Irvine

Ferguson, T 1958 Infantile Tetanus in some Western Isles in the Second half of the Nineteenth Century. In *Scottish Medical Journal* 3 pp 140–146

Fergusson, Donald A, MacDonald, Angus John and London, Jean F G 1978 *From the Farthest Hebrides* Toronto: MacMillan

Ferreira, REC, Gwynne, D, Milner, C and Dale, J 1974 St Kilda: Vegetation 1:10,000 map as endpaper to Jewell et al 1974 *Island Survivors*

Fisher, James 1951 *Portraits of Islands* London
1952 *The Fulmar* London: Collins

Forbes, Robert 1895 *The Lyon in Mourning* ed. Henry Paton Edinburgh: Scottish History Society

Fordun, John of 1871, 1872 *Chronica Gentis Scotorum* ed W F Skene Edinburgh: Edmonston and

Douglas vol 1 1871, vol 2 1872

Fraser, I 1978 *Placenames* Tocher 28 pp 258–9

Freer, Ada Goodrich 1903 *Outer Isles* Westminster: Constable and Co.

Gaelic School Reports: *Annual Reports of the Society for the Support of Gaelic Schools*: 11, 1822; 12, 1823; 13, 1824; 14, 1825; 15, 1826

Gardner, Michael 1986 Population in decline: St Kilda 1856–1891. In *Local Population Studies* 36 pp 27–35

Gauld, W W 1989 In the Lee of Rockall. In *Northern Studies* 26 pp 43–55

Gibson, George 1928 The Tragedy of St Kilda. In *Caledonian Medical Journal* April 1928 pp 50–62

Gillies, A 1884 E*vidence to Napier Commission* PP pp 873–5

Gillies, Donald [**1918–1930**] 1930 *School Exercise Book* SRO GD 1/817/1

Gillies, Donald John [**1901–1924**] 1988 Autobiographical notes in: Quine, D A *St Kilda Portraits* Ambleside pp 39–51

Gillies, John (ed.) 1786 *A Collection of Ancient and Modern Gaelic Poems and Songs transmitted from gentlemen in the Highland of Scotland, etc* Perth

Gillies, Neil [**1896–1930**] 1988 Autobiographical notes in: Quine, D A *St Kilda Portraits* Ambleside pp 37–39

Gordon, Seton 1937 *Afoot in Wild Places* London: Cassell and Co

Grant, I F 1959 *The MacLeods: The History of a Clan* London: Faber and Faber

Grimshaw, Percy H 1907 On the Diptera of St Kilda. In *Annals of Scottish Nat Hist* 16 pp 150–8

Gunn, Neil 1949 *Highland Pack* London; Faber and Faber

Gwynne, D and Milner, C 1974 The Plant Communities. In Jewell et al. 1974 *Island Survivors* pp 36–70

Hamilton, J D 1963 The freshwater fauna of Hirta, St Kilda. In *The Glasgow Naturalist* 18 pp 233–241

Hamp, Eric P 1991 A Few St Kilda Toponyms and Forms. In *Nomina* 14 1990–1 pp 73–6

Harding, D W and Armit, I 1988 note on Loch na Berie in *Discovery and Excavation in Scotland* Edinburgh: Council for Scottish Archaeology

Harding, R R 1966 The Major Ultrabasic and Basic Intrusions of St Kilda, Outer Hebrides. In *Trans. Roy. Soc. Edinburgh* 17 1965–6 pp 419–444
1966 The Mullach Sgar Complex, St Kilda, Outer Hebrides. In *Scottish Journal of Geology* 2 2 165

Harding, R R, Merriman, R J and Nancarrow, P H A 1984 *St Kilda: An Illustrated Account of the Geology* British Geological Survey HMSO

Harman, Mary 1977 An Incised Cross on Hirt, Harris. In *PSAS* 108 1976–7 pp 254–8
in prep. detailed survey of history and cultural remains of Lewis offshore islands

Harris, M P 1984 *The Puffin* Calton: T and A D Poyser

Harris, Michael P and Murray, Stuart 1978 *Birds of St Kilda* Cambridge: Institute of Terrestrial Ecology Natural Environment Research Council

Harrisson, H and Moy-Thomas, J A 1933 The Mice of St Kilda. In *Journal of Animal Ecology* 2 pp 109–115

Harvie-Brown, John Alexander and Buckley, Thomas Edward [**1887**] 1888 *A Vertebrate Fauna of the Outer Hebrides* Edinburgh

Hay, G D 1978 Scottish Wooden Tumbler Locks. In *Post Mediaeval Archaeology* 12 pp 125–7

Hayes, Michael 1852 Account of North Rona In *Ordnance Survey Name Book for Ness, Lewis*, copy in NMRS

Heathcote, Evelyn [**1898–99**] 1900 A Night in an Ocean Cave. In *Wide World Magazine* Aug 1900 pp 91–96
1901 A Summer Sojourn in St Kilda. In *Good Words* XLII 1901 pp 460–467

Heathcote, John Norman [**1898–99**] 1900a *St Kilda* London: Longmans, Green and Co.
1900b On the Map of St Kilda. In *Geographical Journal* XV London 1900 pp 142–144 and map

Heron, Robert 1794 *General View of the Natural Circumstances of the Hebrides* Edinburgh: John Paterson

Holbourn, Ian B 1938 *The Isle of Foula* Lerwick: Johnson and Greig

Holdgate, Martin 1958 *Mountains in the Sea* London: MacMillan and Co.

Holohan, Ann Maclean 1985 St Kilda: Childbirth and the Women of Main Street. In *Scottish Medical Journal* 30 pp 50–53
1986 St Kilda: Emigrants and Disease. In *Scottish Medical Journal* 31 pp 46–49

Hornung, M 1974 The Soils of Hirta. In Jewell et al. 1974 *Island Survivors* pp 70–87

Innes, Hammond 1962 *Atlantic Fury* London: Collins (Novel)

Jackson, Anthony 1991 *The Faeroes: The Faraway Islands* London: Robert Hale

Jewell, Peter A, Milner, C and Boyd, John Morton 1974 *Island Survivors* London: Athlone Press

Johnson, James 1853 *The Scots Musical Museum* ed. William Stenhouse and David Laing 4 vols, Edinburgh: William Blackwood and Sons (First Edition 1787–1803)

Johnson, Samuel and Boswell, James 1930 *Journey to the Western Islands of Scotland and Journal of a Tour to the Hebrides with Samuel Johnson, LL.D.* London: Oxford University Press

Kearton, Richard with illustrations by Cherry Kearton [**1896**] 1897 *With Nature and a Camera* London: Cassell and Co.
1899 Strange life of Lone St Kilda. In *Wide World Magazine* II 1898–9 pp 69–77

Kennedy, Anne and Thomas, F W L [*c.***1857–1862**] 1874 Letter from St Kilda with notes by F W L Thomas. In *PSAS* 10 1872–4 pp 702–711

Kennedy, John 1932 *The Apostle of the North; the Life and Labours of the Rev. Dr. J MacDonald* Inverness: Northern Counties Newspaper and Printing and Publishing Co.

Kerr, R and Lockie, J R 1943 Communion Tokens of the Church of Scotland in the Nineteenth and Twentieth Centuries. In *PSAS* 77 pp 49–146
1945 Communion Tokens of the Free Church of Scotland. In *PSAS* 79 pp 26–80

Kissling, Werner 1943 Character and Purpose of the Hebridean Blackhouse. In *Journal of the Royal Anthropological Institute* LXXIII 1943 pp 75–100

Knox, John 1787 *A Tour through the Highlands of Scotland and the Hebride Isles in 1786* London

Laing, D 1876 Mrs Erskine, Lady Grange in the Island of St Kilda. In *PSAS* XI pp 596–608
1878 Lady Grange in Edinburgh. In *PSAS* 12 pp 312–314

Lamb, H H 1982 *Climate, History and the Modern World* London: Methuen

Lawson, W M 1981 Families of St Kilda. In *St Kilda Mail* 5 pp 38–43
1993 *St Kilda and Its Church* Northton: Bill Lawson Publications
1993 *Croft History: Isle of St Kilda* Northton: Bill Lawson Publications

Leslie, John 1888 *The Historie of Scotland (1596)* trans. by James Dalrymple London and Edinburgh: Blackwood 1888

Leydon, John and Campbell, Alexander 1802 St Kilda Elegies. In *Scots Mag* December 1802 pp 976–7

Lind, James and Stewart, CP 1953 *Lind's Treatise on Scurvy* ed C P Stewart, D Guthrie, Edinburgh: University Press

Logie, D W [**1889**] 1889 *An Account of a trip from Stirling to St Kilda in S.S. Hebridean of Glasgow 12–17 Aug. 1889* Stirling

Low, Frank [**1929**] 1929 Film: Scottish Film Archive 940

MacAdam, W I 1882 On the results of a chemical investigation into the composition of the *Bog Butters* and of *Adipocere* and the *Mineral Resins*. In *PSAS* 16 1881–2 pp 204–223
1889 Notes on the Analysis of Additional Samples of Bog Butter found in different parts of Scotland. In *PSAS* 23 1888–9 pp 433–4

MacAulay, Kenneth [1758] 1764 *The History of St Kilda* London: Becket and de Hondt

MacCallum, H [1885] 1907 St Kilda. In *Caledonian Medical Journal* VII pp 18–24

MacCodrum, John and Matheson, W 1938 *The Songs of John MacCodrum* Edinburgh: Scottish Gaelic Texts Society

MacCulloch, John [1815] 1819 *A Description of the Western Isles of Scotland* London: Hurst, Robinson and Co. vol II and map vol III p 75
1824 *The Highlands and Western Isles of Scotland* London Vol III

MacDiarmid, John [1877] 1878 *St Kilda and its Inhabitants*. In Trans Highland and Agricultural Soc. Scotland X 1878 pp 232–254

MacDonald, Aidan 1973 Annat in Scotland: A Provisional Review. In *Scottish Studies* 17 pp 135–146

MacDonald, Angus John and MacDonald, Archibald 1911 *The MacDonald Collection of Gaelic Poetry* Inverness: Northern Counties Newspaper and Printing and Publishing Co Ltd

MacDonald, A and MacDonald, A 1904 *The Clan Donald* Inverness: Northern Counties Publishing Co Ltd 3 vols.

MacDonald, C R 1886 St Kilda: Its Inhabitants and the Diseases peculiar to them. In *British Medical Journal* II 1886 pp 160–163

MacDonald, D A and MacKinnon, Hugh 1982 Shinty in Eigg. In *Tocher* 36/7 1981–2 pp 365–377

MacDonald, Donald 1797 Parish of Barvas In OSA 1791–9 ed. John Sinclair XIX pp 263–273

MacDonald, Donald 1884 Evidence to the Napier Commission pp 870–3

MacDonald, Donald 1978 *Lewis: A History of the Island* Edinburgh: Gordon Wright

MacDonald, Finlay J 1982 *Crowdie and Cream* London: MacDonald and Co
1983 *Crotal and White* London: MacDonald and Co
1985 *The Corncrake and the Lysander* London: MacDonald and Co

MacDonald, J 1811 *General View of the Agriculture of the Hebrides* Edinburgh

MacDonald, John [1820s] 1823 Journal and report of a Visit to the island of St Kilda appendix to SSPCK Sermon preached by Rev. W A Thomson, June 6 1822
1827 Journal appended to Gaelic School Report 16 1827
and see Kennedy 1924

MacDonald, Keith Norman (ed) 1895 *The Gesto Collection of Highland Music* Glasgow: Alexander MacLaren and Sons

MacDonald, Kenneth 1889 A Modern Raid in Glengarry and Glenmorriston. In *Transactions of the Gaelic Society of Inverness* XV 1888–9 pp 11–35

MacDonald, Lachlan [1906–1930] 1988 Autobiographical notes in Quine, D A *St Kilda Portraits* Ambleside pp 115–147

MacDonald, Reginald Henry 1962 *Notes on the Kingsburgh Family* Pittsburgh, Pennsylvania

MacFarlane, Walter 1908 *Geographical Collections* Edinburgh 3 vols.

MacGregor, Alastair Alpin [1930] 1931 *A Last Voyage to St Kilda* London: Cassell and Co
1931 The Folklore of St Kilda. In *Scottish Field* October pp 128–9; November pp 168–9
1935 *Summer Days Among the Western Isles* Edinburgh: Chambers
1949 *The Western Isles* London: Robert Hale
1969 *The Farthest Hebrides* London: Michael Joseph
1969 St Kilda's Mailboats. In *Country Life* Oct. 2
1971 *Islands by the Score* London: Michael Joseph

MacGregor, D R 1957 St Kilda Village map privately produced for National Trust for Scotland
1960 The Island of St Kilda – a survey of its character and occupance. In *Scottish Studies* 4 1960 pp 1–48

MacGillivray, J [1840] 1842 Account of the Island of St Kilda, chiefly with reference to its natural history. In *Edinburgh New Philosophical Journal* 32 1842 pp 47–70

MacIain 1886 Note *Celtic Magazine* 11 1885–6 pp 124–6

MacInnes, John 1899 *The Brave Sons of Skye* Edinburgh: Norman MacLeod

MacInnes, John and MacQueen, Donald [1886–1920s] 1961 tape recordings School of Scottish Studies Archive nos SA 1961/20, SA 1961/21

MacInnes, John and MacQueen, Donald 1982 St Kilda Mail. In *Tocher* 36–7 1981–2 pp 446–450

MacInnes, John and MacQueen, Norman [1903–1925] 1961 tape recordings School of Scottish Studies Archive SA 1961/18, SA 1961/19
1961 A Folktale from St Kilda. In *Scottish Studies* 5 1961 pp 215–219

MacIntosh, C Fraser 1897 *Antiquarian Notes* Inverness

MacIver, Evander 1905 *Memoirs of a Highland Gentleman* Edinburgh: Constable

MacKay, James A 1963 *St Kilda, Its Posts and Communications* Edinburgh: Scottish Postmark Group

MacKay, John 1884 Evidence to the Napier Commission pp 864–870

MacKay, W R 1985 Early St Kilda – A Reconsideration. In *West Highland Notes and Queries* 26 pp 13–19, 27 pp 17–21

MacKenzie, Alexander 1881 *History of the MacDonalds* Inverness: A and W MacKenzie

MacKenzie, Alexander Downie and MacKinnon, Alister Downie 1883 *The Family of MacKinnon* London: Edward Stanford

MacKenzie, Sir George of Tarbat 1681–4 *An Account of Hirta and Rona* published in MacFarlane, W 1908 Vol 3 p 28

MacKenzie, Sir George Steuart of Coul [1800] map in Wilson, James, 1842
1817 An Account of the Misfortunes of Mrs Erskine of Grange, commonly known as Lady Grange. In *Edinburgh Magazine* 1 pp 333–9 (published under Gael)

MacKenzie, Hector Rose 1885–6 St Kilda. In *Celtic Magazine* 11 pp 9–16, 62–69, 121–126

MacKenzie, John T [1873–1890s] 1884 Statement to the Napier Commission Appendix XII pp 38–41

MacKenzie, Lachlan 1793 Parish of Lochcarron OSA 1791–9 ed John Sinclair XIII pp 551–561

MacKenzie, Mary [1853] 1921 Account of visit in MacKenzie, Osgood Hanbury 1921 *A Hundred Years in the Highlands* London: Edward Arnold

MacKenzie, Murdoch 1798 letter NLS Adv ms. 21.1.5.f 224

MacKenzie, Neil [1829–1843] 1904 Antiquities and Old Customs of St Kilda, compiled from notes by the Rev. Neil MacKenzie ed. J B MacKenzie. In *PSAS* 38 1904 pp 397–402
1911 Episode in the Life of the Rev. Neil MacKenzie, at St Kilda from 1829 to 1843 ed. J B MacKenzie Privately printed
1906 Bardachd Irteach. In *Celtic Review* – 2 pp 328–342

MacKenzie, Osgood Hanbury [1853] 1921 *A Hundred Years in the Highlands* London: Edward Arnold

MacKenzie, William Cook 1905 Notes on the Pigmies Isle, at the Butt of Lewis. In *PSAS* 39 pp 248–258
1905 *The Lady of Hirta* (Novel)

MacKenzie, William 1880 Leaves from my Celtic Portfolio. In *Trans Gaelic Soc Inverness* 9 1879–80 pp 19–74

MacKenzie papers 1872–1897 letters sent to J T MacKenzie, factor, in NTS Archive

MacKinnon, Donald 1954 The MacPhersons of Skye. In *Scottish Genealogist* 1, 2–3 pp 26–34

MacKinnon, Donald and Morrison, Alick nd–1974 The MacLeods: *The Genealogy of a Clan* five volumes: Vol 1 nd, Vol 2 nd (this volume exists in two different editions, neither of which is dated, though there are substantial differences in the order of pagination. One has 131 pages, the other has 129 pages; the former has been used in this work), Vol 3 nd Vol 4 1974 by Morrison only

MacKinnon, Hugh and MacDonald, D A 1974 The Eigg Cave Massacre. In *Scottish Traditional Tales* Edinburgh: School of Scottish Studies pp 141–2

MacKinnon, Nan 1983 various tales In *Tocher* 38 pp 3–11, 42–47

MacLachlan, Alice [**1906–9**] 1906–9 Diaries typescript copy in NTS Archive

MacLaren, A 1974 A Norse House on Drimore machair, South Uist. In *Glasgow Archaeological Journal* 3 pp 9–18

MacLean, Calum I and Gillies, Donald [**1891–1930**] 1952 tape recording School of Scottish Studies Archive SA 1952/132/3

MacLean, Calum I and Gillies, Kate [**1895–1930**] 1952 tape recording School of Scottish Studies Archive SA 1952/132/4

MacLean, Charles 1977 *Island on the Edge of the World* Edinburgh: Canongate

MacLean, Finlay, MacDonald, Donald and Paterson, Ian 1982 Duan na Calluinn. In *Tocher* 36–7 1981–2 pp 362–5

MacLean, Lachlan [**1838**] 1838 *Sketches on the island of St Kilda* Glasgow: McPhun

MacLennan, Malcolm 1925 *Gaelic Dictionary* Edinburgh: John Grant

MacLeod, Alexander 1988 Biographical notes on John MacLeod in Quine, D A *St Kilda Portraits* Ambleside pp 198–213

MacLeod, Brenda 1953 Aunt Emily goes to St Kilda. In *Countryman* Summer 1953 pp 245–7

MacLeod, Donald 1814 Notices on the present State of St Kilda. In *Scots Magazine* Dec. 1814 pp 912–913

MacLeod, Iain N 1980 Meirlich Dhun Bheagan. In *Gairm* 111–112 pp 257–9

MacLeod, John 1792 Parish of Harris OSA 1791–9 ed John Sinclair XIII pp 342–392

MacLeod, John 1910 *Reminiscences* Elgin: Moray and Nairn Newspaper Co Ltd

MacLeod, Mary and Watson, J Carmichael 1934 *Gaelic Songs of Mary MacLeod* Glasgow: Blackie and Son

MacLeod Muniments: Papers held at Dunvegan Castle: references from list compiled by National Register of Archives of Scotland

MacLeod, Neil ? *c.*1756–1775 letter NLS Adv ms. 21.1.5 ff 183–5

MacLeod, Roderick Charles 1938 *The Book of Dunvegan* vols I and II Aberdeen: Third Spalding Club
nd *The MacLeods: Their History and Traditions* Edinburgh

MacLeod, Rory 1615 Letter to Lord Binning In *The Book of Dunvegan* ed. R C MacLeod Vol 2 1938 pp 53–55

MacLeod, William (Theophilus Insulanus) 1763 *A Treatise on the Second Sight, Dreams and Apparitions* Edinburgh: Ruddimans, Auld and Co.

MacPhail, M 1897 Folklore from the Hebrides. In *Folklore* 8 pp 380–6

MacQueen, Edward 1793 Parish of Barray OSA 1791–9 ed John Sinclair XIII pp 326–342

MacQueen, Kelman nd Memoirs of his Ancestors typescript in NTS Archive. Now published as *St Kilda Heritage* ed. Kelman and Ewen G McQueen 1995 Edinburgh: Scottish Genealogy Society.

McNeill, Malcolm 1886 Report on the Alleged Destitution PP 57

McVean, D N 1961 Flora and Vegetation of the Islands of St Kilda and North Rona in 1958. In

Journal of Ecology 49 1961 pp 39–54

Martin, Martin [**1697**] 1697 Several Observations on the North Islands of Scotland. In *Philosophical Transactions of the Royal Society* 19 1697 pp 727–729
1753 *A Voyage to St Kilda* 4th edition London: Brown and Davis (first edition 1698)
1716 *A Description of the Western Isles of Scotland* London: Bell, Varnam and Osborn, Taylor, Baker and Warner (first edition 1703)

Matheson, William 1952 Mary MacLeod: Her family connections; her forgotten songs. In *Transactions of the Gaelic Society of Inverness* 41 1951–2 pp 11–25

Matthews, A E H 1969 Sappers at St Kilda – 1900. In *Sapper* May pp 78–9

Mathieson, John [**1927**] 1928 Antiquities of the St Kilda group of Islands. In *PSAS* 62 1927–28 pp 123–132
1928 Map of St Kilda or Hirta Ordnance Survey
and Cockburn, A M, Gladstone, J and Gordon, S. 1928 St Kilda. In *Scottish Geographical Magazine* 44 1928 pp 65–90
and Cockburn A M 1929 St Kilda In *Trans. Edinburgh Geological Society* 12 1929 pp 287–288
1930 The Evacuation of St Kilda. In *Scottish Geographical Magazine* 46 1930 pp nn
1930 Lone St Kilda. In *Scottish Motor Traction Magazine* Aug. 1930 pp nn

Megaw, B R S 1969 The Date of Pont's Survey and its Background. In *Scottish Studies* 13 pp 71–4

Megaw, J V S and Simpson, D D A 1961 A Short Cist Burial on North Uist. In *PSAS* 94 1960–61 pp 63–78

Milner, C and Gwynne, D 1974 The Soay Sheep and Their Food Supply. In Jewell et al. 1974 *Island Survivors* pp 273–325

Milner, W M E [**1847**] 1848 Some Account of the people of St Kilda, and of the Birds in the Outer Hebrides. In *The Zoologist* 6 1848 pp 2054–2062

Mitchell, Arthur 1865 Consanguineous marriages on St Kilda. In *Edinburgh Medical Journal* 10 April 1865 pp 899–904
1901 List of Some Accounts of Visits to St Kilda 1549–1900. In *PSAS* 35 pp 440–2
1902 The Prehistory of the Scottish Area. In *PSAS* 36 1901–2, pp 11–65

Mitchell, W R 1990 *St Kilda: A Voyage to the Edge of the World* Oban: Oban Times

Moir, D G, Young, A, Bartholomew J C, Simpson D C and Smith, R L 1973 *The Early Maps of Scotland to 1850* Edinburgh: Royal Scottish Geographical Society

Moisley, H A 1966 The Deserted Hebrides *Scottish Studies* 10 1966 pp 44–68

Monro, Donald 1961 *Description of the Western Isles of Scotland* ed R W Munro Edinburgh: Oliver and Boyd

Monro, Hugh 1792 Parish of Uig OSA 1791–9 ed John Sinclair XIX pp 280–288

Moray, Robert 1678 A Description of the Island of Hirta In *Philosophical Transactions of the Royal Society of London* 12 1678 pp 927–929

Morgan, John E [**1860**] 1861 The Falcon among the Fulmars; or six hours in St Kilda. In *MacMillan's Magazine* June 1861 pp 104–111
1862 The Diseases of St Kilda In *British and Foreign Medico–Chirurgical Review* 29 1862 pp 176–191

Morrison, Alick 1974 *The MacLeods – the Genealogy of a Clan* Vol IV
1966 The Contullich Papers. In *Transactions of the Gaelic Society of Inverness* 44 pp 310–348
1968 The Harris Estate Papers. In *Transactions of the Gaelic Society of Inverness* 45 pp 33–97
1969 The Island of Pabbay. In *Clan MacLeod Magazine* 6 pp 17–23

Morrison, Donald 1975 *The Morrison Manuscript* ed N MacDonald and Alec Morrison

Morrison, John 1907 Description of the Lews in MacFarlane, Walter *Geographical Collections* 2

Muir, Thomas Smyth [**1858**] 1858 *St Kilda, a Fragment of Travel by Unda* Edinburgh

1861 *Characteristics of Old Church Architecture* Edinburgh

1885 *Ecclesiological Notes on Some of the islands of Scotland* Edinburgh

Muir, T S and Thomas, F W L [**1858, 1860**] 1860 Notice of a Beehive House in the Island of St Kilda In *PSAS* 3 1857–60, 225–232

Munch, Peter A 1971 *Crisis in Utopia* London: Longman and Co.

Munro, Jean and Munro R W 1986 *Acts of the Lords of the Isles 1336–1493* Edinburgh: Scottish History Society

Munro, R W 1979 *Scottish Lighthouses* Stornoway: Thule Press

1982 Hirta or Harris? *West Highland Notes and Queries* 18, Oct 1982 pp 16–19

1982 Earthquake Shocks *West Highland Notes and Queries* 18, Oct 1982 p 27

Murchison, T M 1959 Deserted Hebridean Isles: Notes and Traditions *Transactions of the Gaelic Society of Inverness* 42 1953–1959 pp 283–344

Murray, A ? 1735 A Politicall Whim concerning St Kilda one of the Western Isles of Scotland written in the year 1735 NLS Adv.ms 29.1.1. vii ff 169–72

Murray, George [**1886–7**] 1887 Diary typescript extracts in NTS Archive

Murray, George Augustus Frederick John (Duke of Atholl) [**1860**] 1860 letter 6.6.1860 Atholl Archive Box 58 Bundle 30 Document 10

Murray, S and Wanless, S 1986 The Status of the Gannet in Scotland 1984–85 *Scottish Birds* 14 pp 74–85

Napier Commission 1884 Highland Crofters: Report of Her Majesty's Commissioners of Enquiry into the Condition of the Crofters and Cottars in the Highlands and Islands of Scotland Parliamentary Accounts and Papers 34

Nicol, Thomas 1931 *By Mountain, Moor and Loch to the Dream Isles of the West* Stirling

Nicolson, John 1937 John Sands. In *Shetland Times* 3.7.1937

Nicolson 1840 Parish of Barra in New Statistical Account Edinburgh 1845

Nisbet, Helen C and Gailey, R A 1962 A Survey of the Antiquities of North Rona In *Archaeological Journal* 117 pp 88–115

Nørrevang, Arne 1977 *Fuglefangsten på Faeroerne* Copenhagen: Rhodos

O'Dell, A C and Walton, K 1962 *The Highlands and Islands of Scotland* London and Edinburgh: Thomas Nelson and Sons

O'Farrell 1852 Account of the Flannan Isles In *Ordnance Survey Name Book for Uig, Lewis*, copy in NMRS

Ordnance Survey 1970 Maps: Scale 1:10560 (6 inches to 1 mile): *Sheet NA 00 SE; Parts of sheets NA 10 NW, NE, SW and SE; Parts of sheets NF 09 NE and NF 19 NW*

1973 Map: Scale 1:25,000 (Pathfinder) *Sheet 1373 St Kilda NA 00/10 and NF 09/19*

Pennie, Iain D 1958 Early Medecine in the Highlands and Islands. In *Scottish Medical Journal* 3 1958 pp 398–408

1964 Scottish Ornithologists: 1 Sir Robert Sibbald In *Scottish Birds* 3 pp 159–167

1966 Scottish Ornithologists: 2 Martin Martin In *Scottish Birds* 4 pp 64–73

Pike, Oliver G 1908 Film Scottish Film Archive 988

c.1917 Film Scottish Film Archive 978

Pickard–Cambridge, O 1905 Spiders of St Kilda In *Annals of Scottish Nat Hist* 14 pp 220–3

Pomfret A A 1931 The Evacuation of St Kilda In *Journal of the Royal Naval Medical Service* 17 1931

Poore, M E D and Robertson, V C 1949 The Vegetation of St Kilda in 1948 In *Journal of Ecology* 37 July 1949, 82-99

Powell, L F 1940 The History of St Kilda In *Review of English Studies* 16, pp 44–53

Powell, Michael 1990 *Edge of the World* London: Faber and Faber

Power, William A 1983 *The Log of the Olivia* Richmond

Quine, David A 1982 *St Kilda Revisited* Frome: Dowland Press

Quine, David A 1988 *St Kilda Portraits* Ambleside: Quine

Quine, David A 1991 Australian MacQueens – Links with St Kilda In *St Kilda Mail* 15, pp 4–9

Rees, Sian E 1979 Stone Ard points from Orkney and Shetland. In *Tools and Tillage* III 4 249–254

Register of the Great Seal of Scotland 1912 Vol 1 (1306–1424); 1892 Vol 7 (1603–1620)

Richards, Eric 1992 The decline of St Kilda: Demography, Economy and Emigration. In *Scottish Economic and Social History* 12 pp 55–73

Robertson, Anne S 1983 Roman Coins found in Scotland 1971–82 In *PSAS* 113 pp 405–485

Robertson, C M 1899 Topography and Traditions of Eigg In *Transactions of the Gaelic Society of Inverness* 22 1897–8 pp 193–210

Robson, Michael 1991 *Rona: The Distant Island* Stornoway: Acair

Rogers, Rose Anne 1926 *The Lonely Island* London: Allen and Unwin

Romilly Allen, J 1880 Notes on Wooden Tumbler Locks In *PSAS* 14 1879–80 pp 149–162

Ross, Alexander [1883] 1884 A Visit to the Island of St Kilda In *Trans Inverness Scientific Soc. and Field Club* 3 pp 72–91
    1895 Scottish Home Industries

Ross, John [1889–90] 1890 St Kilda as it now is manuscript account in NTS Archive

Roy, Archie 1970 *All Evil Shed Away* London: John Long (Novel)

Royal Commission on the Ancient and Historical Monuments of Scotland 1984 *Argyll* Vol 5

Royal Highland and Agricultural Society of Scotland Papers: collection of letters, receipts, etc relating to Kelsall Fund

Rutherford, I 1946 *At the Tiller* London: Blackie & Son

Ryder, Michael 1974 Some Wool Cloth from St Kilda In *Scottish Studies* 18 pp 133–135

Sands, John [1875–1877] 1877a *Out of the world; or, Life in St Kilda* Edinburgh: MacLachlan and Stewart
    1877b Life in St Kilda *Chambers' Journal* 1877 pp 284–287, 312–316, 331–334
    1878 Notes on the Antiquities of the Island of St Kilda In *PSAS* 12 1876–8 pp 186–192

School Log Book 1901–1930 Ms volume in Western Isles Library, Stornoway

School of Scottish Studies, University of Edinburgh Photographic Archive

Scott, Hew 1923–50 *Fasti Ecclesiae Scoticanae* Edinburgh: Oliver and Boyd Vol 4 1923, Vol 6 1926, Vol 7 1928, Vol 8 1950

Scott, W R 1914 *Report to the Board of Agriculture on Home Industries in the Highlands and Islands* Parliamentary Paper

Scottish Ethnological Archive, Royal Museum of Scotland Photograph collection

Seebohm, Henry 1884 On a new Species of British Wren In *Zoologist* 8 pp 333–5

Seton, George [1877] 1878 *St Kilda Past and Present* Edinburgh: Wm. Blackwood and Sons

Seton–Watson, R W 1931 The Strange Story of Lady Grange In *History* 16 pp 12–24

Seymour, W A 1980 *A History of the Ordnance Survey* Folkestone: Wm Dawson and Sons

Shand, Alexander Innes 1897 *The Lady Grange* London: Smith, Elder and Co. (Novel)

Sharbau, H [1860] 1860 *Plan of St Kilda Village* Society of Antiquaries of Scotland Mss collection 158. copy SRO (RHP 6778)

Shaw, Margaret Fay 1955 *Folk Songs and Folk Lore from South Uist* Aberdeen: Aberdeen University Press
    1993 *From the Alleghenies to the Hebrides* Edinburgh: Canongate

Shepherd, I A G and Tuckwell, A N 1977 Traces of Beaker-period cultivation at Rosinish Benbecula In *PSAS* 108 1976–7 pp 108–113

Shepherd, I A G 1975 Rosinish, Benbecula In *Discovery and Excavation in Scotland* eds M E C Steward and C M Lythe Edinburgh: Council for British Archaeology Scottish Regional Group p 50

Simson, Alexander 1797 Parish of Lochs OSA 1791–9 ed John Sinclair XIX pp 274–9

Skene, William F 1880 *A History of Celtic Scotland* Edinburgh: David Douglas 3 vols

Small, Alan ed. 1979 *St Kilda Handbook* Edinburgh: National Trust for Scotland

Smith, Beverley 1984 Birds in Orcadian Prehistory in Booth, C, Cuthbert M, and Reynolds, *The Birds of Orkney* Stromness: The Orkney Press

Smith, R Angus [1873] 1875 A Visit to St Kilda in 1873 *Good Words* pp 141–144, 264–269
1879 *A Visit to St Kilda in the Nyanza* Glasgow: Robert MacLehose

Society of Antiquaries of Scotland: Notes of Donations and Purchases for the Museum (now the Royal Scottish Museum) in: *PSAS* 3 1857–1860 p 212; *PSAS* 12 1876–1878 p 185; *PSAS* 27 1892–1893 p 244; *PSAS* 31 1896–1897 pp 153–5; *PSAS* 46 1911–1912 p 373; *PSAS* 51 1916–1917 p 12; *PSAS* 60 1925–1926 p 245; *PSAS* 62 1927–1928 p 134; *PSAS* 64 1929–1930 p 245; *PSAS* 65 1930–1931 pp 14, 298; *PSAS* 76 1941–1942 p 133; *PSAS* 91 1957–1958 p 203; *PSAS* 99 1966–1967 p 267; *PSAS* 101 1968–1969 p 296; *PSAS* 103 1970–1971 p 245; *PSAS* 110 1978–1980 p 536

Spackman, R A 1982 *Soldiers on St Kilda* Uist: Uist Community Press

Steel, Tom 1965 *The Life and Death of St Kilda* Edinburgh: The National Trust for Scotland
1988 *The Life and Death of St Kilda* revised edition Glasgow: Fontana/Collins

Steer, K A and Bannerman, J W M 1977 *Late Mediaeval Monumental Sculpture in the West Highlands* Edinburgh: RCAHMS

Stell, Geoffrey P and Harman, Mary 1988 *Buildings of St Kilda* Edinburgh: RCAHMS

Stewart, Alexander 1877 The St Kilda Maids' Song In *Gael* 6, April 1877 p 125

Stewart, Alexander, and Stewart, Donald 1804 *A Choice Collection of the Works of the Highland Bards* Edinburgh: T Stewart

Stewart, Malcolm 1931 *Bibliography of St Kilda* In *St Kilda Papers* Oxford: Oxford University Press
1933 *Ronay* Oxford: University Press
1938 Natural History notes on Scottish Islands In *Scottish Naturalist* pp 107–114

Stone, Jeffrey 1989 *The Pont Manuscript Maps of Scotland: Sixteenth Century origin of a Blaeu Atlas* Tring

Svensson, Roland 1955 *Lonely Isles* Stockholm

Swinburne, J 1885 Notes on the Islands of Sula Sgeir and North Rona In *Proc Royal Physical Society Edinburgh* 8 pp 51–67

Swire, Otta F 1966 *The Outer Hebrides and their Legends* Edinburgh: Oliver and Boyd

Tasker, Mark L, Moore, Peter R and Schofield, Richard A 1988 The Seabirds of St Kilda In *Scottish Birds* 15 pp 21–29

Tasker, Mark L, 1995 Bird and Marine Life in Buchanan, Meg (ed) *St Kilda the Continuing Story of the Islands*

Taylor, A B 1961 Early Maps of Scotland In *Scottish Geographical Magazine* 77 pp 37–43
1967 The Norsemen on St Kilda In *Saga Book of the Viking Society* 17 1967 pp 106–114
1969 The Name 'St Kilda' In *Scottish Studies* 13 1969 pp 145–158

Temperley, Alan and pupils of Farr Secondary School 1978 *Tales of the North Coast* London Research Publishing Co.

Thomas, Frederick W L [1860] 1860 Notice of Beehive Houses in Harris and Lewis In *PSAS* 3 1860–62 pp 127–144

1862 Notice of a Beehive House in the island of St Kilda In *PSAS* 3 1860–62 pp 225–232

1868 On the Primitive Dwellings and Hypogea of the Outer Hebrides In *PSAS* 7 1866–68 pp 153–195

1878 Traditions of the Morrisons: Hereditary Judges of Lewis In *PSAS* 12 1876–78 pp 503–556

Thomson, Derick S 1978 Subterfuges of a Sennachie. In *Glasgow Herald* 14.12.1978 p 8

1993 *The MacDiarmid Ms Anthology* Edinburgh: Scottish Gaelic Texts Society

Trollope, Anthony [1878] 1878 *How the 'Mastiffs' went to Iceland* London: Virtue and Co.

Turner, G A 1895 The Successful Preventive Treatment of the Scourge of St Kilda (tetanus neonatorum) with some considerations regarding the management of the cord in the new born infant In *Glasgow Medical Journal* 43 March 1895 pp 161–174

Turrill, W B 1927 The Flora of St Kilda In *Rep Bot Exch Club Br Isles* 8 428–444B

'Viator' 1818 St Kilda Poetry In *Scots Magazine* March 1818 pp 241–2

Wager, L R 1953 Extent of Glaciation in the Island of St Kilda In *Geol Mag* 90 177–80

Walker, John 1980 *Report on the Hebrides* ed Margaret M MacKay Edinburgh: John Donald

Walker, J Russell 1883 "Holy Wells" in Scotland In *PSAS* 17 1882–3 pp 152–210

Waterston, James 1905 Notes on the Mice and Birds of St Kilda In *Annals of Scottish Nat Hist* 14 pp 199–202

1906 On some Scottish Siphonaptera In *Annals of Scottish Nat Hist* 15 pp 211–214

Watson, W J 1904 *Place names of Ross and Cromarty* Inverness: Northern Counties Printing and Publishing Co Ltd.

1926 *The History of the Celtic Place Names of Scotland* Edinburgh

Weir, Tom 1958 Beathe ur air seain Eilean. In *Gairm* 3 pp 271–273

1969 Two men on the Stacs. In *Scots Mag* Dec 1969 pp 260–265

Wiglesworth, J [1902] 1903 *St Kilda and its Birds* Liverpool

Williamson, Kenneth 1958a Ancient St Kilda. In *Scottish Field* March 1958 pp 46–49

1958b Life on St Kilda. In *Scots Mag* Oct. 1958 pp

and Boyd, John Morton 1960 *St Kilda Summer* London: Hutchinson and Co

and Boyd, John Morton 1963 *A Mosaic of Islands*

1970 *The Atlantic Islands* London: Routledge and Kegan Paul

Williamson, Robert [1615] 1615 Statement taken 13.5.1615 in *Calendar of State Papers of Ireland 1615–1625* ed Charles W Russell and John P Prendergast 1880 London: Longman and Co. pp 57–59

Wilson, George Washington 1886 Photographs (taken by N Macleod)

Wilson, James [1841] 1842 *A Voyage round the Coasts of Scotland and the Isles* Edinburgh II pp 1–113

1842 Additional Notice Regarding St Kilda. In *Edinburgh New Philosophical Journal* 32 pp 178–180

Appendix 1

Tables of equivalents for Scots, Imperial and Metric measures and Scots, old Sterling and Decimal currency systems

Measures of Length

St Kilda: *Lamh choille* or cubit is distance between elbow and fingertips (Martin 1753, 49) – usually between 18 and 24 inches (45.7 cm – 60.9 cm)

St Kilda yard = 4 feet = 122 cm

(Scots Ell = 37.2 ins = 94.5 cm; English Ell = 45 ins = 114.4 cm)

Imperial			Metric equivalent	
Inch			0.0254 m	(2.54 cm)
12 inches	=	.1 foot	0.3048 m	(30.48 cm)
3 feet	=	1 yard	0.9144 m	(91.44 cm)
1,760 yards	=	1 mile	1609 m	(1.609 km)

Measures of Weight

St Kilda stone = 24 lb = 10.9 kg

Imperial			Metric equivalent
Ounce (oz)			0.0283 kg
16 oz	=	1 pound (lb)	0.4536 kg
14 lb	=	1 stone (st)	6.3503 kg
2 st	=	1 hundredweight (cwt)	50.802 kg

Measures of Capacity

St Kilda *Amir* = nearly 2 pecks
St Kilda *Maile* = 10 pecks (Martin 1753, 48-9) [? *màla* : bag, sack]
Scots *omer* = 2 pecks in Invernessshire (NSA XIV 1845, 211)

For barley, oats, malt

Scots	Imperial	Metric equivalent
1 peck	2.912 gallons	13.24 litres
4 pecks = 1 firlot	11.65 gallons	52.96 litres
4 firlots = 1 boll	46.6 gallons	211.84 litres

(*Scottish National Dictionary* X 1976, 316-7)

Imperial	Metric equivalent
8 pints = 1 gallon	4.546 litres
2 galls = 1 peck	9.09 litres
4 pecks = 1 bushel	36.37 litres

Boll: a boll of oats, barley or potatoes contains *c.* 6 imperial bushels; a boll of meal weighs *c.*140 lb; there is much local variation. (*Scottish National Dictionary* II 1941, 203)

Currency Systems

In 1707 the following prevailed; although Scots currency was abolished by the Act of Union in that year it continued in use for some time

	Scots	Sterling equivalent	Decimal equivalent
	1 penny (d)	$^1/_{12}$ penny	0.035 p.
2 pennies	= 1 bodle	$^1/_6$ penny	0.07 p.
4 d or 2 bodles	= 1 plack	$^1/_3$ penny	0.14 p.
12 d or 2 bawbees	= 1 shilling	penny (d)	0.42 p.
20 shillings	= 1 pound	1 s 8 d	8.3 p.
13 shillings 4 pence	= 1 merk	1 s 1$^1/_3$ d	5.5 p.

By the end of the eighteenth century Scots currency had been abandoned. Decimal currency was introduced in February 1971.

Sterling currency	Decimal equivalent
1 penny (d)	0.42 p.
12 d = 1 shilling	5 p.
20 s = 1 pound (£)	1 pound (£)
usually expressed as £0 0s. 0d. or £0/0/0 or £0.0.0	£0.00
NB 1 guinea = 21 shillings	£1.05

Appendix 2 List of Place Names

List of Place names from original sources: some late nineteenth century and twentieth century sources which were clearly repetitive and contained few names have been omitted.

The main list of names is taken from the maps by the Ordnance Survey (1970) and Mathieson (1928). There are minor variations in spelling, and these are noted, Mathieson's version being given in [ ]. He included on his map an inset showing the village area at a larger scale, and on this he gives names which are omitted from the 1970 map for reasons of space. In the list these are followed by [Mathieson 1928].

Each name is followed by a suggested meaning and derivation; unless otherwise stated, derivations are based on Dwelly's Gaelic English dictionary, and W J Watson's *Place names of Ross and Cromarty* (1904). G: Gaelic; ON: Old Norse.

For those with no knowledge of Gaelic it should be explained that in Gaelic all nouns are either masculine or femenine, and the definite article, nouns and adjectives decline: the form of the word changes according to gender, whether it is in the singular or plural, and how it is being used; thus Gleann Mòr (masculine) is simply 'Glen Large'; while Abhainn Mhòr (feminine) is 'Stream Large', and Abhainn a' Ghlinne Mhòir is 'Stream of Glen Large', Ghlinne Mhòir being the possessive form of Gleann Mòr. Dwelly's dictionary and any good Gaelic grammar will give guidance concerning these changes.

The list is arranged by island: Hirte, Dun, Soay and its stacks, Boreray and its stacks; within each island the names are given in alphabetical order, ignoring the definite article (Am, An, A', An t-, Na, Na h', Nam, Nan). Names which are related are cross-referenced: for instance Abhainn a' Ghlinne Mhòir is derived in part from Gleann Mòr.

At the end of the main list there is another list of 'lost' names; these are names which are found in the early literature but are not on the two recent maps. Any which can reasonably be equated with names on those recent maps are given as a cross reference with the appropriate name in the main list, and this is noted in the list of 'lost' names. Some of the remainder can be located reasonably accurately and these are given in a separate map (Fig 21).

Names Associated with Hirte

Hirte ?Hirtir (Prest's saga early C13); Hert (Reg.Sig.Mag. 1.1.1372/3); Heryce/Hyrte (Reg.Sig.Mag. 9.1.1372/3); Hirth (Fordun 1380); Hirtha (Boece 1527); Hirta/Hirt (Monro 1549); Irt (Anon 1577-95); Hirta (Anon 1594); Hirta (Reg.Sig.Mag. 7.3.1610); Zirta (MacLeod 1615); Art (Williamson 1615); Hirta (Moray 1678, 927); Hirt (local)/Hirta (Martin 1697); Hirta from Irish Ier, = West (Martin 1703); Hirt/Hirta (Adv ms 33.3.20); Hirta (Adv Ms 15.1.1); Hirta (Buchan 1727); Hirt/Hirta (MacAulay 1764); Herta (Buchanan 1793); Uirt/Huirt (MacKenzie [1830-43] 1911) not recorded here from literature after 1830.

Hirte was also called 'the Country' when the people were at sea, as they didn't like to mention the name (Adv ms 33.3.20).

St Kilda St. Kilda/St Kilder (Martin 1697); St Kilda/St Kilder – from Kilder, who lived here, and from him the large well Tonbir Kilda has also its name (Martin 1703); St Kilda/Saint KildarY (Adv ms 33.3.20); Saint Kilda (Buchan 1727); St Gilda (MacDonald 1746); St Kilda (?Macleod 1746 Adv Ms 21.1.5); St. Kilda (MacAulay 1764); St Kilda (Buchanan 1793); St Kilda (Clarke 1794); St Kilda (Campbell 1799); St Kilda (?Campbell 1799) (Stopped recording after 1800).

Abhainn Alltan Stream of Brooks (*abhainn* G: river, stream; *allt* G: mountain stream, rill, brook)

Abhainn bheag *see* **An t-Sruthan, Abhainn Mhór**

Abhainn a' Ghlinne Mhóir River of the Big Glen (*abhainn* G: river, stream; Gleann Mór), The

Glen R. (Martin 1697, map), The Glen River (MacAulay 1764), Glen Burn (Ross 1889), Glen River (Heathcote 1900) *see* **Gleann Mór**

Abhainn Gleisgil [Gleshgil Matheson 1928] Shining Stream in the Gully (*abhainn* G: river, stream; *glise* Norweg: to shine; *gil* ON: a ravine with a stream at the bottom. Taylor 1967, 142)

Abhainn Ilishgil [Matheson 1928] The Deep Stream of the Spring (*abhainn* G: river, stream; *íla* ON: spring; *gill* ON: a ravine with a stream at the bottom. Taylor 1967, 141; or possibly Deep Stream of Rage or Evil [ilskugil] Coates 1990, 109)

Abhainn Mhór Big River (*abhainn* G: river, stream; *mór* G: large, great), Avon More (Anon pre 1840), Abhain mhòr (MacLean 1838), Amhuinn Mhor (Ross 1889), Abhain Mor (Heathcote 1900 map), Amhum mhor – could be mis-typed (MacLachlan 1906-9) [contrast with the Abhainn Bheag or An t-Sruthan to the east]

Abhainn Riasg [Matheson 1928] Stream of the marshes or moors (*abhainn* G: river, stream; *riasg* G: moor, marsh, sedge, peat moss)

Abhainn Ruaival Stream of Ruaival (*abhainn* G: river, stream; and Ruaival) *see* **Ruaival**

Aird Uachdarachd Upper Promontory (*airde* G: height, promontory; *uachdarachd* G: state of being higher, superior)

Airigh Mhór/Amazon's House Big Shieling (*airidh* G: shieling, summer pasture; *mór* G: large, great) **Tigh na Banaghaisgeach /Airidh na Banaghaisgeach** House or Shieling of the Female Warrior or Heroine (*taigh* G: house; *bana-ghaisgeach* G: heroine, female warrior) (Warrior's House Campbell 1799), Areyvore (Anon pre 1840), 'Giantess' House' (MacKenzie [1830-43] 1911), Tigh na Banaghaisgeach /Airidh na Banaghaisgeach (Kennedy [1862] 1874), Airidh Mhòr (Sands 1878), Airidh mhòr (Steele Elliott 1895) *see* Gleann Mór and (pp 74–77)

Baghan Little Bay (*bághan* G: little harbour, creek; or *baghan* G: stomach) [but seems to be applied to a small rock]

Bearraidh na h-Eige Precipice of the Edge (*bearraidh* G: precipice; *eag* G: notch, gap) (Cameron 1973) *see* The Gap

Beul na Geo Mouth of the Cleft (*beul* G: mouth, opening; *gjá* ON: cleft)

Am Blaid The Mouth – perhaps the mouth of the glen – the way over to Gleann Mór (*blad* G: mouth, wide mouth). Col (Ross 1889) probably refers to this.

Na Bodha Sine [Matheson 1928] Nipple Rocks (*bodha* G: rock over which the waves break; *sine* G: teat, nipple)

Bradastac Steep Stack (*bratti* ON: steep; *stakkr* ON: stack. Taylor 1967, 141), Bragstack (Anon pre 1840), Brata Stac (Heathcote 1900 map) *see* Geo Bhradastac

Am Broig The Shoe or Hoof (*bròg* G: shoe, hoof) *see* Geo a' Bhroige

Calum Mór House Big Malcolm's House (*Calum* G: Malcolm; *mór* G: large, great) The Strong Man's House (Kearton 1897) (p 233)

Cambir Crest or Ridge (*kambr* ON: crest or ridge. Taylor 1967, 141) Camper (MacAulay 1764 but he says p 28: 'a rivulet runs through [Glen Mor] and discharges itself into the sea, near the small creek they call Camper, or crooked landing place, where the people make a shift to put in, if under an unavoidable necessity of making so desperate an experiment, or if the sea be quite smooth' so he appears to have understood it to be a different feature from that now called Cambir). Camber – Thomas: from Norse *Kambr*, a crest or ridge (Seton 1878) Camber (Murray 1886) Cambargh (Heathcote 1900 map) Cambergh (MacLachlan 1906-9) *see* Geo Chaimbir

Caolas an Duin Kyles of Dun/Straits of Dun (*caolas* G: strait, ferry; and Dun) *see* Dun: Caolas an Duin

326

Carn Mór Great Cairn or Pile of Rocks (*càrn* G: cairn, heap or pile of stones; *mór* G: large, great) Carnmhor (Murray 1886), Cairn Mor (Heathcote 1900 map)

Clash na Bearnaich Fissured Gutter (*clais* G: furrow, hollow, gutter; *beárnach* G: notched, abounding in fissures)

Claigeann Mór Big Nob (*claigionn* G: skull, commonly applied to a knob shaped hill; *mór* G: large, great) Craig Mor (Heathcote 1900 map)

Claigeann an Tigh Faire Nob of the Watch House (*claigionn* G: skull, commonly applied to a knob shaped hill; *taigh* G: house; *faire* G: guard, watch) Tigh an fhir faireadh [the Watchman's House] (MacKenzie [1830-43] 1911)

Na Cleitean The Cliffs (*klettr* ON: cliff, rock) The Cleit (Heathcote 1900 map)

Cnoc a'Bheannaichta Hillock of the Blessed (*cnoc* G: hill, knoll; *beannaichte* G: blessed, holy, happy) (p 52)

Cnoc na Gaoithe Knoll of the Wind (*cnoc* G: hill, knoll; *gaoth* G: wind)

Cnoc Sgar O.S. 1970 probably a mistake for Loch Sgar Matheson 1928 Bare Knoll (*cnoc* G: hill, knoll; *skalli* ON: bald head, bare hill top. Taylor 1967, 141)

Conachair possibly Roarer, from the noise of the winds roaring up or down its slopes (*cona-ghaothach* G: tempest, raging gale; or *conghair* G: uproar, clamour, tumult – as MacLean 1838, 43 suggests) Conagir/Conagor (Martin 1697) Conagir (Adv ms 33.3.20) Conagra (MacAulay 1764) Congara (Buchanan 1793) Conagra (?Campbell 1799) Conochan (MacCulloch 1819) Congar (MacDonald 1822) Conichan (Stevenson 1826) Conichar/Conachar (Atkinson 1831) Conagar (Anon pre 1840) Conachan (MacGillivray 1842) Connagher (Wilson 1842) Conaker (Milner 1848) Conagra (Muir 1861) Mullach Onachail (MacDiarmid 1877) Connagher (Sands 1878) Conagher/Conna-ghàir (Seton 1878) Conacher/Conagher/Connagher (Murray 1886) Conachar (Ross 1889) Conacher/Mullach Conacher (Steele Elliott 1895) Conagher (Kearton 1897) Connacher (Heathcote 1900 and map) Conacher (MacLachlan 1906-9) Conachir (Admiralty 1909) and Glacan Chonachair
Not far from Geo-nam-plaideachan 'is a bare and high rock, called Con'-ghàir, which being as it were a fissure from the highest mountain, and from the gàir or boiling noise the sea makes here unceasingly, gives it its name, Con'-ghàir (also noted as Conna-ghàir). (MacLean 1838, 43) This sounds as though he was applying the name to a stack adjacent to the Conachair cliff – possibly he was between Bradastac and the main island though this is really below Mullach Mór – but it is west of Geo nam Plaidean, and that seems to be the direction in which they were travelling, as they landed in 'Dickson's Bay' (Loch Hirta).

Creagan Breac Speckled Small Crag (*creag* G: crag, rock, cliff; *breac* G: spotted, speckled)

Creagan Dubh Black or Dark Small Crag (*creag* G: crag, rock; *dubh* G: black, dark)

Na h-Eagan The Ridges (*egg* ON: edge, ridge)

The Gap only in English on O.S. 1970 and Matheson 1928. Probably **Bearraidh na h-Eige** Precipice of the Edge (*bearraidh* G: precipice; *egg* ON: edge, ridge) Berenahake/Beren-na-hake (MacLachlan 1906-9) Lookout Gap (Admiralty 1909) *see* Bearraidh na h-Eige

An Gearraidh [Matheson 1928] The Park, or The Grazing (*gearraidh* G: enclosed grazing, or grazing and arable, between the crofts and the open moor – *gardr* ON: enclosure) contrast with An Gearraidh Ard

Gearraidh Ard [An Gearraidh Ard Matheson 1928] The High Park (*gearraidh* G: enclosed grazing, or grazing and arable, between the crofts and the open moor – *gardr* ON: enclosure; *àrd* G: high) contrast with An Gearraidh

Geo na h-Airde Cleft of the Promontory (*gjà* ON: cleft; *airde* G: height, promontory) Geó-na-h-àirde: the creek of the eminence (MacLean 1838) *see* Gob na h-Airde

Geo na Bà Glaise Cleft of the grey Cow (*gjà* ON: cleft; *bó* G: cow; *glas* G: grey, pale, sallow) Uamh na ba glas [Cave of the grey cow] (Heathcote 1900 map)

Geo Bhradastac Cleft of the Steep Stack (*gjà* ON: cleft and Bradastac) *see* Bradastac

Geo a'Bhroige Shoe cleft (*gjà* ON: cleft; *bròg* G: shoe, hoof) *see* Am Broig

Geo Brababy Cleft? (*gjà* ON: cleft; and possibly connected with *breabail* G gurgling noise, or *prabair* G: worthless fellow; or *pràpadh* G: tangling, disordering) Compare with Geodha Bratabili in Ness, Lewis: bilidh possibly connected with *hlid* N: steep slope (Iain Fraser pers comm 1991)

Geo na Capuill Cleft of the mare/horse (*gjà* ON: cleft; *capull* G: mare, sometimes horse)

Geo Chaimbir Cleft of the Cambir (*gjà* ON: cleft; and Cambir) *see* Cambir

Geo Chalum McMhuirich [Geo Chalum M'Mhurich Matheson 1928] Malcolm Murchison's Cleft, or Cleft of Malcolm, Murdo's son (*gjà* ON: cleft; *Calum* G: Malcolm; McMhuirich G: Murchison or *mac Mhuirich* G: son of Murdo)

Geo Chruadalian ? Dangerous Cleft (*gjà* ON: cleft; *cruadal, cruadalachd* G: hardship, danger, difficulty) but possibly the same as Uamh Cruaidh [Hard or difficult cave] (Heathcote 1900 map) which is in the same location

Geo Chrùbaidh [Geo Chrubi Matheson 1928] Cleft of the Bending or crouching (*gjà* ON: cleft; *cróbadh* G: bending, crouch, crinkle)

Geo Chille Brianan Cleft of Brendan's Church (*gjà* ON: cleft; *cill* G: cell, church and Brianan) *see* names of Chapels or Churches at end of Hirte section

Geo Creag an Arpaid Cleft ? (*gjà* ON: cleft; and ?) possibly from **Creag an Airgiod**, Rock of the Silver, an unlocated name – see end of list or Cleft of the Crag of the Great Black-backed Gull (*creag* G: crag, rock, cliff; *farspag* G: Great Black-backed Gull Coates 1990, 90)

Geo na Eaige possibly for Geo na h-eige, Cleft of the Edge/Ridge (*gjà* ON: cleft; *egg* ON edge, ridge) *see* The Gap

Geo an Eireanach Cleft of the Irishman (*gjà* ON: cleft; *Eireannach* G: Irishman) Damph-an-Eiranich (Wilson 1842) Irishman's Cave (Heathcote 1900 map) so called because 'An Irishman was crossing an inlet of his own green isle, with a keg of whisky to make merry with his father and other friends one Christmas morning, but being carried out to sea by a squall, he was driven he knew not where, till he found himself at the mouth of a cave in St Kilda. He was descried by the natives from the cliffs, who at first entertained a superstitious fear of an individual who they thought must either have dropped from the clouds, or risen from the sea, but so soon as they perceived his boat, they lowered their ropes, and drew him up when he was almost gone from want. He remained with them for about a year, before an opportunity occurred of his being conveyed to his own country.' (Wilson 1842, 67).

Geo Gharran Buidhe Cleft of the tawny horse (*gjà* ON: cleft; *gearran* G: horse, gelding; *buidhe* G: yellow)

Geodha Glann Neill [Geo d'ha Glann Neill Matheson 1928] The MacNeils' Cleft (*gjà* ON: cleft; *clann* G: clan, descendants; *Neill* G: Neil)

Geo na Lashulaich Cleft ? (*gjà* ON: cleft; possibly connected with *lasail* G: fiery, inflammable)

Geo Leibli Cleft ? (*gjà* ON: cleft; *bli* may be from *hlid* N: steep slope Iain Fraser pers comm 1991)

Geo na Mol Cleft of the Shingle (*gjà* ON: cleft; *mol* G: shingle, shingly beach)

Geo Mór [Matheson 1928] Big Cleft (*gjà* ON: cleft; *mór* G: large, great)

Geo na Muirbhuaile Bream Cleft (*gjà* ON: cleft; and *muirbhuale* G: bream Matheson 1928) The two bream occurring most commonly in the area are black or red sea bream.

Geo Oscar Cleft of the Leap, Cleft of the Ruinous Fall, Cleft of the Champion (*gjà* ON: cleft; *oscar* G: leap, ruinous fall, champion)

Geo nan Plaidean Cleft of the Blankets (*gjà* ON: cleft; *plaide* G: blanket, plaid) "Geó-nam-plaideachan: the creek of the blankets…where the natives lie the whole night in narrow cliffs, with blankets to cover them from the sea spray, watching the arrival of the Fulmer in the morning" (MacLean 1838, 42)

Geo nan Ròn Cleft of the Seals (*gjà* ON: cleft; *ròn* G: seal) Uamh na Ron [Seal Cave] (Heathcote 1900 and map)

Geo Rubha Mhuirich [Geo Rudha Mhuirich Matheson 1928] Cleft of Murdo's Point (*gjà* ON: cleft; *rudha* G: point of land, promontory; *Muireach* G: Murdo) *see* Rubha Mhuirich

Geo an t-Samh Cleft of the Sorrel/Surge/Stink (*gjà* ON: cleft; *samh* G: common sorrel, surge of waves, stink) or Cleft of the Open Sea (*haf* Scand: open sea as suggested by Fraser (Coates 1990, 87))

Geo na Seanaig Cleft of the little old woman (*gjà* ON: cleft; and *seanag* G: little old one [feminine])

Geo nan Sgarbh Cleft of the Cormorants (*gjà* ON: cleft; *skarfa* ON: cormorant)

Geo Sgeir Chaise Cleft of the steeper rock (*gjà* ON: cleft; *sker* ON: skerry, rock; *caise* G: more or most steep)

Geo na Stacan Cleft of the Little Stac (*gjà* ON: cleft; *stakkr* ON: stack)

Giasgeir Skerry of the Geo or Cleft (*gjà* ON: cleft; *sker* ON: skerry, rock. Taylor 1967, 143) noted as Lasgol by Heathcote (1900)

Glacan Chonachair Conachair Gulleys (*glac* G: hollow valley, defile and Conachair) *see* Conachair

Glacan Mór The Big Gulleys (*glac* G: hollow valley, defile; *mór* G: large, great)

Glacan Oiseval Oiseval Gulleys (*glac* G: hollow valley, defile and Oiseval) *see* Oiseval

Gleann Mór Big Glen (*gleann* G: valley, dell; *mór* G: large, great) Gleann na Bana-ghaisgeach The Glen of the Female Warrior (*gleann* G: valley, dell; *bana-ghaisgeach* G: heroine, female warrior) The Female Warrior's Glen (Martin 1697) Glen of the Female Warrior (Adv ms 33.3.20) Female Warrior's Glen (MacAulay 1764) Glen na Bannagashich? (Anon pre 1840) North Glen (MacKenzie [1830-43] 1911) Female Warrior's Glen (Muir 1861) Glen Mòr (MacDiarmid 1877) Glen Mór (Sands 1878) Glen Mòr or the Amazon's Glen (Seton 1878) Glen Mhor (Ross 1889) The Glen (Heathcote 1900 map) The Glen/Female Warrior's Glen (MacLachlan 1906-9) contrast with Glean Beag for An Lag bho'n Tuath and see Airidh Mhór and (pp 74–77)

Gob na h-Airde Point of the Promontory (*gob* G: beak, mouth, point; *airde* G: height, promontory) Runahardveg? (Anon pre 1840) Cop a'sairde (Admiralty 1865) Cop a's airde (Heathcote 1900 map) *see* Geo na h-Airde

Gob Chathaill Point of ? the Wailer (*gob* G: beak, mouth, point; and perhaps *caothaill* G: referring to the cries from the manx shearwater colony on Carn Mór) or Chair Point (*cathair* G: chair Coates 1990, 96) Possibly the same as Gob Cailleach (Heathcote 1900)

Lag Aitimir Hollow ? (*lag* G: hollow, pit, dell and ?)

An Lag bho'n Tuath The Northward Hollow (*lag* G: hollow, pit, dell; *bho* G: from; *tuath* G: north) Glen Beag (Ross 1889)

Laimhrig nan Gall Landing place of the Strangers (*laimhrig* G: landing place; *gall* G: lowlander, stranger, foreigner) probably the same as Bid a Ghaul (Ross 1889) and Landing Place of the Englishmen (Heathcote 1900 and map) which are in the same location

Leac Mhina Stac Mina Stac Slab (*leac* G: flag, slab, flat stone; and Mina Stac) *see* Mina Stac

Leacan an Eitheir Slabs of the Boat (*leac* G: flag, slab, flat stone; *eathar* G: vessel, boat)

Leacan an t-Sluic Mhóir Slabs of the Big Cavern (*leac* G: flag, slab, flat stone; *sloc* G: pit, hollow, cavity, hole; *mór* G: large, great) probably referring to the adjacent 'tunnel', a vast natural arch

Leathad a 'Ghlinne Broad Slope of the Glen (*leathad* G: hill side, slope, broad slope and *gleann* G: valley – from Gleann Mór)

Leathad na Guiltichean Broad slope of ? (*leathad* G: hill side, slope, broad slope and ?)

Leathad a'Sgithoil Chaoil Broad Slope ? of the Narrow Bothy (*leathad* G: hill side, slope, broad slope; ?*sgithiol* G: shieling hut; *caol* G: small, slender, thin, narrow, though sgithiol is masculine so the form of the article is wrong)

Loch a' Ghlinne or Glen Bay (*loch* G: lake, arm of the sea; *gleann* G: valley, dell) Loch a Gleana (Anon pre 1840) Mcleod's Bay (named by MacLean and friends in 1838 in commemoration of Dr MacLeod's visit (MacLean 1838, 43) McLeod's Bay (MacGillivray 1842) West Bay/ MacLeod's Bay (Wilson 1842) Glen Bay (MacLachlan 1906-9) Bagh a Glinne (Admiralty 1909) *see* Gleann Mór

Loch Hirta or Village bay (*loch* G: lake, arm of the sea and Hirte) Dickson's bay (MacLean 1838) Dickson's Bay (MacGillivray 1842) East or Village Bay/Dickson's Bay (Wilson 1842) Village Bay (Admiralty 1865) Village Bay (Kearton 1897) Village Bay (Heathcote 1900 and map) The Bay/ The Loch (MacLachlan 1906-9)

Loch Sgar [Matheson 1928] (*loch* G: lake, arm of the sea; *skalli* ON: bare hill top) probably for Loch or pool on Mullach Sgar; associated with a water bull (p 303) *see* Mullach Sgar

Lover's Stone equated with the Mistress' Stone equated with Stac Biorrach by (Connell 1887) Lover's Stone placed at a new site (Heathcote 1900 and map) Lover's Stone [almost certainly Heathcote site] (MacLachlan 1906-9) (pp 297-8)

Mina Stac Lesser Stack (*minni* ON: lesser; *stakkr* ON: stack. Taylor 1967, 141) or Mouth or Opening Stack (mynastakkr Coates 1990, 99) Minastack (Anon pre 1840) Miana Stac (Admiralty 1865) Mian-a-Stac/Miana Stac (Heathcote 1900 and map) *see* Leac Mina Stac

Mol Carn na Liana Shingle of the Heap of Rocks of the Plain (*mol* G: shingle, shingly beach; *càrn* G: cairn, heap or pile of stone; *lian* G: plain, field)

Mol Ghiasgar Shingle of the Skerry of the Cleft (*mol* G: shingle, shingly beach; *gjà* ON: cleft; *sker* ON: skerry, rock, as in Taylor 1967, 143)

Mullach Bi Pillar Summit (*mullach* G: top, summit, hill; *bìgh* G: pillar, post) Mullach Bith/ Mullach Bich (Heathcote 1900 and map)

Mullach Geal White Summit (*mullach* G: top, summit, hill; *geal* G: white) Mulach-geall (MacAulay 1764) Mullach-geal from *mullach*, top, and *geal*, white (MacLean 1838, 3) Druim Geal (MacDiarmid 1877) Mullach-geal (Seton 1878) Mullách-geal (Connell 1887) (Mullach) Geal (Steele Elliott 1895) Mulloch Geal (Admiralty 1909)

Mullach Mór Big Summit (*mullach* G: top, summit, hill; *mór* G: large, great) Mullach Mor (MacKenzie [1830-43] 1911) Mulloch More (Wilson 1842) Mulach Mor (Ross 1889) Mullach Mor (Heathcote 1900 and map)

Mullach Sgar Bare Summit (*mullach* G: top, summit, hill; *skalli* ON: bald head. Taylor 1967 141) Mullach-scail from *mullach*, top, and *scail*, bald (MacLean 1838, 3) Mullach Skaill (MacDiarmid 1877) Sgal/Sgar (Sands 1878) Mullách scail – bald top (Seton 1878) Scal (Murray 1886) Scal (Ross 1889) Mullach-Scail (Steele Elliott 1895) Mullach Sgail (Heathcote 1900 map) Mullach Sgail (MacLachlan 1906-9) Mullach Sgall (Admiralty 1909)

Na Mullichean Mór The Big Summits (*mullach* G: top, summit, hill; *mór* G: large, great)

Oiseval Eastern Hill (*eystra-fjall* ON: eastern hill. Taylor 1967 141) Oterveaul (Martin 1697) Ostrivaill (MacAulay 1764) Orwall/Orwall-hill (Kennedy 1822) Aoismheal (MacKenzie [1830-43] 1911) Aois-mheall from *aois*, age and *meall*, a conical hill (MacLean 1838, 3) Oiseval (Kennedy [1862] 1874) = Austr-fell East hill {Norse} (Thomas 1874) Mullach Oshival (MacDiarmid 1877) Oswald or Osimhal (Sands 1878) Mullách-osterveaul/Mullách-Oshival (Seton 1878) Osevall (Murray 1886) Oshvall (Ross 1889) Oshival (Steele Elliott 1895) Oisaval/Mullách Oshival (Kearton 1897) Oiseval/Oisaval (Heathcote 1900 and map) Oshaval/Oshavale (MacLachlan 1906-9) Oisirbhal (Admiralty 1909)

Poll a'Choire Cauldron Pool (*poll* G: hole, pool; *coire* G: cauldron, kettle, vat)

Ruaival Red Hill (*rauda-fjall* ON: red hill. Taylor 1967 140) Ruaimhail/Ruaimhaill (MacAulay 1764) Ruaveil (Ruadh-mheall) (Kennedy 1822) Rueval? (Anon pre 1840) Rua'-mheall from *ruadh* , roy, or madder colour, and *mheall*, a conical hill (MacLean 1838, 3) Ruaival (Kennedy [1862] 1874) Ruaidh Bhail (Sands 1878) Ruival (Murray 1886) Ruaval Point (Connell 1887) Ruaidhbhal (Ros 1889) Ruadhval/Ruadval (Heathcote 1900 and map) Ruadval (MacLachlan 1906-9) Ruibhal (Admiralty 1909)

Rubha Challa or Point of Coll [Rudh Challa Matheson 1928] (*rudha* G: point of land, promontory and Coll) Ruchell (Anon pre 1840) Rudhen Cholla/Rudha-cholla (MacLean 1838) Point of Coll (Heathcote 1900 map) Point of Coll (MacLachlan 1906-9) almost certainly the same as Gob Cholla (Kennedy [1862] 1874) *see* also Tobar Cholla (unlocated)

Rubha Ghill [Rudh Ghill Matheson 1928] Stream Point (*rudha* G: point of land, promontory; *gil* ON: ravine with a stream at the bottom) or White Point if *ghile* G whiter Coates 1990, 101, though Coates suggests yellow, but this is not the usual meaning of geal or Point of the Wager or Bet (*geall* G: promise, pledge, wager Iain Fraser pers comm 1991)

Rubha Mhuirich Murdo's Point [Rudha Mhuirich Matheson 1928] (*rudha* G: point of land, promontory; *Muireach* G: Murdo)

Rubha an Uisge Point of the Water/Wave/Rain (*rudha* G: point of land, promontory; *uisge* G: water, wave, rain) Ruenuiskey (Anon pre 1840) Rudha an Uisg (Admiralty 1909)

Sgeir na Caraidh Skerry of the ? fish trap (*sker* ON: skerry, rock; *caraidh* G: mound thrown across over a river or estuary to catch fish)

Sgeir Dhomhnuill [Sgeir Dhomhuill Matheson 1928] Donald's Skerry (*sker* ON: skerry, rock; *Domhnall* G: Donald)

Sgeir Mhór Big Skerry (*sker* ON: skerry, rock; *mór* G: large, great) [below Carn Mór] Sgurr Mor (Admiralty 1865) Sgurr Mor (Heathcote 1900 map)

Sgeir Mhór Big Skerry (*sker* ON: skerry, rock; *mór* G: large, great) [at end of Kyles of Dun]

Sgeir nan Sgarbh Rock of the Cormorants (*sker* ON: skerry, rock; *skarfa* ON: cormorants) Skernaskarar (Anon pre 1840) Skart Rock (Heathcote 1900 map)

Sgeir Thormoid [Matheson 1928] Norman's Skerry (*sker* ON: skerry, rock; *Tormoid* G: Norman)

An t-Sruthan [Matheson 1928] The Burn or The Rivulet (*sruthan* G: streamlet, brook, rivulet) [almost certainly the same as 'Abhain bheag', the 'little stream', probably the one flowing from Tobar Childa; as opposed to the Abhainn Mhór] (MacLean 1838)

Stac a' Langa Long Stack or Stack of the Guillemot (*stakkr* ON: stack; *langa* ON: long or possibly *langach* G: guillemot – it supports a fairly large colony of guillemots) (Gaelic) Stacklanga (Anon pre 1840) Stac Lang (MacLachlan 1906-9)

Tarn [in Gleann Mór]

Tarn [between Mullach Mór and Conachair] Though no longer distinguishable on the ground, this may well be the site of Poll na Ban-tighearna [The Lady's Pool] (Sands 1878) where Lady

Grange's peats were cut. (pp 51, 90–91, 166)

Souterrain Taigh an t-sithiche/Tigh fo Talamh [Fairy's House or House Under the Ground] (Sands 1878) Tigh na Sithich (Ross 1889) The Fairy's House (MacLachlan 1906-9) (*taigh* G: house; *sìthiche* G: fairy, elf; *fo* G: under; *talamh* G: earth)

Tigh an Triar House of the Three: perhaps of the Trinity (*taigh* G: house; *triùir* G: three persons) (p 228)

Tobar nam Buaidh Well of Excellent Qualities (*tobar* G: well, spring; *buadh* G: virtue, excellence, qualifications) Tou-bir-nim-beuy (Martin 1697) Well of Qualities or Virtues (Adv ms 33.3.20) Tobirnimbuadh or spring of diverse virtues (MacAulay 1764) Tobernimbriadth (Well of many virtues) (?Campbell 1799) Tober-nam-buy (MacCulloch 1824) Well of virtues (Atkinson 1831) Tobar-nam-buaidh (Well of Virtues) (Mackenzie [1930-43] 1911) Tobar-nam-buadh (MacLean 1838) Tobir na slainnte (MacGillivray 1842; probably T n B but not located) Tobirnimbuadh : Tobar-iomadaiche-buadhan, The well of many virtues (Muir 1861) Tobar nam buaidh (Sands 1878) Tobar-nam-buaidh (Connell 1887) Tobar nam Buaidh (Ross 1889) Well of Virtues (Heathcote 1900 map) Tobar Nam buadh – Well of Virtues (MacLachlan 1906-9)

Tobar Childa [Matheson 1928] Well Cold Well (*tobar* G: well, spring; *kelda kalda* ON: cold well. Taylor 1967, 141) St Kilder's Well/Kilder's Well (Martin 1697) Tonbir-Kilda (Martin 1703) Tober Childa Chalda (MacAulay 1764) Tober Childa Chalda (Muir 1861) (p 243)

Tobar a'Chleirich [Matheson 1928] The Clergyman's Well (*tobar* G: well, spring; *clèireach* G: clerk, clergyman, writer) Toberi Clerich (MacAulay 1764)

Tobar na Cille [Tobar na Gille Matheson 1928] Well of the Church (*tobar* G: well, spring; *cill* G: cell, church)

Tobar Gille Cille [Matheson 1928] Well of the Servant of the Church (*tobar* G: well, spring; *gille* G: lad, boy, man-servant; *cill* G: cell, church)

Tobar Chonastan [Matheson 1928] Well ? (*tobar* G: well, spring and ?)

Tobar a Mhinisteir [Matheson 1928] The Minister's Well (*tobar* G: well, spring; *ministear* G: clergyman, minister, servant)

An Torc The Boar (*torc* G: boar, hog) Sgurr Tor (Heathcote 1900 map)

Tot a Chombaiste Knoll of the ? compass (*tobhta* G: little knoll, turf; *combaiste* G: compass, circle)

Uamh Cailleach Bheag Ruaival Little Old Woman's Cave, Ruaival (*uaimh* G: cave, den; *cailleach* G: woman, old woman, spinster; *beag* G: little, short, small; and Ruaival)

Names Associated with Dun

Dun Fort or Fastness (*dùn* G: hill, fortified house or hill, castle, fastness; sometimes with *fir-bholg* G: the ancient Irish) Down (Martin 1697) Dun-fir-Volg (applied to fort) (Martin 1703) the Down (Adv ms 33.3.20) Dun-Fir-Bholg (MacAulay 1764) Dunfir Volg (Buchanan 1793) Dun fir Bhorg (Campbell 1799) Dunfir Bhorg (?Campbell 1799) Dune (MacCulloch 1819) Doun/ Down (Atkinson 1831) a fort called Dun-fir-bholg from *dun*, a fort, *fir*, men and *bolg*, a quiver (MacLean 1838, 3) Dune (Anon pre 1840 also marks Old Fort) Dun/Dun Island (MacKenzie [1830-43] 1911) Dun (Wilson 1842) Dun (Milner 1848) Dun (Kennedy [1862] 1874) Dun (Admiralty 1865) Dun (MacDiarmid 1877) The Dun (Sands 1878) The Dune (Seton 1878) The Dun (Murray 1886) Dun (Ross 1889) Dune/Doon/the Doon (Steele Elliott 1895) the Doon (Kearton 1897) Dun/Dùn Heathcote 1900 and map) The Dùn/The Dùn/The Dune (MacLachlan 1906-9) Dun (Admiralty 1909).

Caolas an Duin Kyles or Straits of Dun (*caolas* G: strait, ferry; and Dun) Caolas between Dun and the mainland (Murray 1886) Caolas-an-Dun -Dun Strait (Connell 1887) Caolis an Dun

(Ross 1889) Dûn Passage (Heathcote 1900)

A' Bhì The Pillar (*bigh* G: pillar, post)

Bioda Mór Big Peak (*bioda* G: pointed top, hill top; *mór* G: large, great) Biodag More (Admiralty 1909)

A' Chlaisir ?The Cleft (from *clais* G: furrow, gutter, streak, groove)

Cul Cleite Back of the Cliff or Rock (*cul* G: back; *klettr* ON: cliff, rock)

An Fhaing The Fold or The Obstacle or The Raven or The Prison (*fang* G: sheep fold, difficulty, raven, prison)

Geo Ghiasgeir Cleft of the Skerry of the Geo or Cleft (*gjá* ON: cleft; and *gjá* ON: cleft; *sker* ON: skerry, rock. Taylor 1967 143)

Geo na Ruideig Cleft of the Kittiwake (*gjá* ON: cleft; *ruideag* G: kittiwake)

Giumachsgor Lobster skerry (*giomach* G: lobster; *sgòr* G: concealed rock jutting into the sea; steep precipitous height on another hill.)

Gob an Dùin Point of Dun (*gob* G: beak, mouth, point; and Dun) Gob an Dun (Murray 1886) Gob an Dun (Admiralty 1909) *see* Dun

Gob na Muce Pig's Snout (*gob* G: beak, mouth, point; *muc* G: sow, pig)

Hamalan Anvil Rock? (*hamarr* ON: hammer shaped rock, or crag sticking out like an anvil) or Little Islet (G diminutive of *holmr* N: islet Coates 1990, 80-81)

Na Sgarain The Fissures (*sgar* G: fissure in wood, seam or joint as in boat)

Seilg Geo Geo of Seals (*sela-gjá* ON: geo of seals. Taylor 1967, 143)

Sgeir Cul an Rubha [Sgeir Cul and Rudha Matheson 1928] Skerry at the back of the Point (*sker* ON: skerry, rock; *cul* G: back; *rudha* G: point of land, promontory)

Natural Arch **Toll saDuin** [Hole of Dun] (Admiralty 1909) (*toll* G: hole, hollow, and Dun)

Levenish ? Grey Island (*li ath* G: grey; *innis* G: island Coates 1990, 62) or Grey Cape (*nes* ON: ness, cape) Levinis (Martin 1697) Livinish (MacAulay 1764) Lavinish (Campbell 1799) Lavinish (?Campbell 1799) Levenish (MacCulloch 1819) Levenish (Stevenson 1826) (Labelled and referred to as Sulisker by Atkinson 1831) Levenish (Anon pre 1840) Levenish (MacGillivray 1842) Levenish (Milner 1848) Levenish (Admiralty 1865) Levenish (Seton 1878) Levenish (Ross 1889) Levenish (Steele Elliott 1895) Rock Lavenish (Kearton 1897) Stac/Levenish/Levenish (Heathcote 1900 and map) Levenish (MacLachlan 1906-9)

Na Bodhan The Skerries (*bodha* G: rock over which the waves break)

Names Associated with Soay

Soay Sheep Island (*saudr* ON: sheep; *ey* ON island) Soa (Moray 1678, 927) Soa (Adv Ms 15.1.1) Soa (Martin 1697) Soa (Adv ms 33.3.20) Soay (?MacLeod 1746 Adv ms 21.1.5) Soay/Soa (MacAulay 1764) Soay (Buchanan 1793) Soay (Campbell 1799) Soa (?Campbell 1799) Soa (MacCulloch 1819) Soay (MacDonald 1822) Soa (Stevenson 1826) Soa (Atkinson 1831) So'a from south and a for an island (MacLean 1838, 3) Soa I. (Anon pre 1840) Soay (MacKenzie [1830-43] 1911) Soay (MacGillivray 1842) Soa (Wilson 1842) Soa (Milner 1848) Soa (Muir 1861) Soay (Kennedy [1862] 1874) Soay (Admiralty 1865) for Sanda-ay Sheep or Wether island {Norse} (Thomas 1874) Soa (MacDiarmid 1877) Soa (Sands 1878) Soa (Seton 1878) Soa (Murray 1886) Soa (Connell 1887) Soa (Ross 1889) Soa (Steele Elliott 1895) Soa (Kearton 1897) Soay (Heathcote 1900 and map) Soay (MacLachlan 1906-9)

The Altar Altar (Heathcote 1900 map)

An Airde The Promontory (*airde* G: height, promontory)

Bearraidh na Creige Chaise Precipice of the Steepest Cliff (*bearraidh* G: precipice; *creag* G: crag, rock, cliff; *caise* G: more or most steep)

A' Chala The Hussy? or The Shore – possibly to indicate a landing place (*caile* G: hussy, strumpet; *caladh* G: harbour, port, shore though it is given the wrong gender)

Cnoc Glas Grey Hill (*cnoc* G: hill, knoll; *glas* G: grey, pale, sallow)

Creagan Cliffs (*creag* G: crag, rock, cliff)

Geo Phursan Pursan's Cleft (*gjá* ON: cleft; and Pursan) *see* Phursan a' Chaim and Gob Phursan

Geo nan Ròn Cleft of the Seals (*gjá* ON: cleft; *rón* G: seal) [possibly the narrow geo where seals were hunted (p 225)]

Geo Ruadh Red Cleft (*gjá* ON: cleft; *ruadh* G: red, ruddy)

Glamisgeo Noisy Cleft or less likely, Glámr's Cleft (*glam* ON: noise; *gjá* ON: cleft; or *Glamr* ON personal name, rather rare. Taylor 1967, 142) or Jaws of a Vice Chasm (*klambsgjá* Coates 1990, 157)

Gob na h-Airde Point of the Promontory (*gob* G: beak, mouth, point; *airde* G: height, promontory)

Gob a' Ghaill Point of the Stranger (*gob* G: beak, mouth, point; *Gall* G: lowlander, stranger, foreigner) Cop na Bheurla [Point of the Englishman] (Heathcote 1900 map)

Gob Phursan Pursan's Point (*gob* G: beak, mouth, point; and Pursan) *see* Phursan a' Chaim and Geo Phursan

Laimhrig Adinet ? Landing Place (*laimhrig* G: landing place and possibly *dionaid* G: secure place [dion aite] possibly secure for birds Iain Fraser pers comm 1991)

Laimhrig na Sròine Landing Place of the Neb (*laimhrig* G: landing place; *sròn* G: nose, promontory)

Lianish Ness of the Slope ? (*hlìdar-nes* ON: ness of the slope. Taylor 1967, 142) or possibly Grey Ness (*liath* G: grey. Coates 1990, 160)

Mol Shoay Beach of Soay (*mol* G: shingle, shingly beach; and Soay)

Poll Adinet Pool ? (*poll* G: hole, pool; and possibly *dionaid* G: secure place [dion aite] possibly secure for birds. Iain Fraser pers comm 1991)

Pursan a'Chaim ? of the Fraud or Deceit (? and *cam* G: fraud, deceit; possibly connected with *peursa* G: signal pole. Iain Fraser pers comm. 1991) *see* Geo Phursan and Gob Phursan

Scarpalin Sharp Rock or Sharp Slope (*skarpr* ON: sharp; *hlein* ON: projecting rock, or *lein* O.Norweg: slope, or *hlidin*: slope. Taylor 1967 142)

Tigh Dugan Dugan's Home (*taigh* G: house; and Dugan) Dugan's Cave (Kearton 1897) [the outlaw] (pp 231-232)

Tobar Ruadh Red Well (*tobar* G: well, spring; *ruadh* G: red, ruddy) [There is a trickle of water with iron staining here]

Am Plastair ? Smooth Stack or ? The Splashed One (*bladh* G: smooth; *stakkr* ON: stack or connected with *plais* G: splash) Plaste (MacAulay 1764) Plaste (Campbell 1799) Plasta (?Campbell 1799) Plasta (Wilson 1842) Plasta (Seton 1878) probably same as Blath Stac (Heathcote 1900 map)

Sgeir Mac Righ Lochlainn Skerry of the Son of the King of Norway (*sker* ON: skerry, rock; *mac* G: son; *righ* G: king; *Lochlann* G: Scandinavia) Sgeir Mac Righ Lochlain (Kennedy [1862] 1874) Sgurr MacRigh Lochlin/Sgurr Mac Righ Lochlain (Heathcote 1900 and map)

Stac Biorach Pointed Stack (*stakkr* ON: stack; *biorach* G: sharp pointed) Stacki-birach/Stack-Birach/Stakbirah (MacAulay 1764) Stack Birah (?Campbell 1799) Stack Bioroch and 'the

Thumb rock' (Atkinson 1831) Stackbirrach (Anon pre 1840) Stacca-biorrach i.e. the pointed rock (MacLean 1838, 3) Stachbiorrach (MacKenzie [1830-43] 1911) (Stack) Biorach (Wilson 1842) Stack Biorrach (Seton 1878) Stack Beeruck (Steele Elliott 1895) Stack Biorrach (Kearton 1897) Stac na Biorrach/Stac na Biorrah (Heathcote 1900 and map)

Stac Dona Bad or Evil Stack (*stakkr* ON: stack; *dona* G: evil, bad, dangerous) Stacka Donna (Moray 1678, 927) Stacka Donna (Adv Ms 15.1.1) Stackdonn/Stakdon (Martin 1697 text and map) Stacka donna/Stackdon (Adv ms 33.3.20) Stacki-don /Stakdon (MacAulay 1764) Stack-don (Campbell 1799 also marks The Thumb) Stack Donne (?Campbell 1799) Stack Donna (Atkinson 1831) Stackdonna (Anon pre 1840) Stack Donadh (Wilson 1842) Stack Donadh (Seton 1878) Stac Dona (Heathcote 1900 map)

Soay Stac (*stakkr* ON: stack; and Soay) Soa Stack (Atkinson 1831) Soastack (Anon pre 1840) Stack Soa (Wilson 1842) Stack Soa (Seton 1878) Soay Stac (Admiralty 1865) Soay Stac (Heathcote 1900 map)

Boreray Fort Island (*Borg* ON: a fort; *ey* ON: an island) Burribaugh (Williamson 1615) Burra (Moray 1678, 927) Burra (Adv ms 15.1.1) Borera (Martin 1697) Borera/Boreray/Borreray (Martin 1703) Burra (Adv ms 33.3.20) Boreray (?MacLeod 1746 Adv Ms 21.1.5) Boreray/Bocra (MacAulay 1764) Boreray (Buchanan 1793) Borera (Clarke 1794) Borrira (?Campbell 1799) Borera (MacCulloch 1819) Boreray (MacDonald 1822) Borera (Stevenson 1826) Borera/Borrera (Atkinson 1831) Borreray (Anon pre 1840) Boreray/Borrera (MacKenzie [1830-43] 1911) Borera (MacLean 1838) Borreray (MacGillivray 1842) Borrera (Wilson 1842) Borrera (Milner 1848) Boreray (Kennedy [1862] 1874) Boreray (Admiralty 1865) Boreray (Sands 1878) Borrera (Seton 1878) Boreray (Murray 1886) Boreray (Connell 1887) Boreray (Ross 1889) Borrera (Steele Elliott 1895) Boreray (1897) Boreray (Heathcote 1900 and map) Borrera/Borera (MacLachlan 1906-8)

Clagan na Rósgachan [Clagan na Ruskochan Mathieson 1928] Nob of the fleeces? (*claigionn* G: skull, commonly applied to a knob shaped hill; and *rùsgadh* G: peeling, fleecing, fleece) (Iain Fraser pers comm 1991)

Clais na Runaich Hollow of the Inclination or Desire? (*clais* G: furrow, hollow, gutter; *rùnaich* G: wish, desire, resolve, purpose) or possibly Hollow of the Mackerel (*reannach* G: mackerel. Iain Fraser pers comm 1991)

Cleitean McPhaidein MacFadyen's Cleits (*cleit* G: shed; *MacPhaidein* G: MacFadyen)

Clesgor Rift of the Cliff (*klifs-sgor* ON: rift of the cliff; Taylor 1967, 144) Clesgoth (Heathcote 1900 map)

Coinneag Bay of a Woman? (possibly *konu* ON of a woman; *vik* ON: bay. Taylor 1967, 144) or possibly Frothy Bay (*cuinneag* G: milk pail; as suggested by MacLeod (Quine 1982, 45))

Creagan Fharspeig Crag of the Great Black-backed Gull (*creag* G: crag, rock, cliff; *farspag* G: great black-backed gull)

Creagan na Rubhaig Bana Cliffs of the Pale or Waste Rope ? (*creag* G: crag, rock, cliff; *rubhag* G: thong of hemp or flax; *bàn* G: white, pale, waste) or Cliffs of the Little White Point (diminutive of *rubha* G: point. Iain Fraser pers comm 1991)

Gearrgeo [Geargo Mathieson 1928] Short Cleft (*geàrr* G: short; *gjá* ON: cleft)

Geo an Araich Cleft of the Lookout or Cleft of the Tether or Cleft of the Stranger or Cleft of the Apparition (*gjá* ON: cleft; *àrach* G: watchman, grazier or *àrach* G: tie, band, restraint; or *atharrach* G stranger, alien; or *arrach* G: apparition, spectre, runt)

Geo an Fheachdaire Warrior's Cleft (*gjá* ON: cleft; *feachdaire* G: warrior)

Geo na Leachan Móire Cleft of the Big Slabs (if nan leacan móra: *gjá* ON: cleft; *leac* G: flag, slab, flat stone; *mór* G: large, great)

Geo Sgarbhstac Cormorants' Stack Cleft (*gjá* ON: cleft; and Sgarbhstac) *see* Sgarbhstac

Geo Shunadal Sunadal Cleft (*gjá* ON: cleft; and Sunadal) *see* Sunadal

Geo na Tarnanach Cleft of the Thunder (*gjá* ON: cleft; *tàirneanach* G: thunder, thundering noise)

Gob Scapanish Point of the Point of Caves (*gob* G: beak, mouth, point; *skalp-eid* ON: sword sheath, something hollowed; *nes* ON: ness, cape. Taylor 1967, 143) or possibly Point of Sharp Headland (*skarpnes* N: sharp headland Coates 1990, 73)

Laimhil ? (possibly connected with: *làmh* G: hand, arm; or *laibh* G: clay, mire, dirt)

Mullach an Eilean Summit of the Island (*mullach* G: top, summit, hill; *eilean* G: island, isle)

Mullach an Tuamail Summit abounding in Hollows or Bumps (*mullach* G: top, summit, hill; *tuamail, tuamach* G: abounding in graves, tombs, cavities, or mounds)

Na Roàchan obscure (possibly connected with *rothach* G: wheeled; Iain Fraser pers comm 1991)

Rubha Bhrengadal [Rudha Bhrengadal Mathieson 1928] Point of Brengadal (*rudha* G: point of land, promontory; *bringudal* ON dale of the breast. Taylor 1967, 144)

An t-Sail The Heel or The Sea? (*sail* G: heel; or *sàl* G: sea)

Sgarbhstac Cormorants' Stack (*skarfa* ON: cormorant; *stakkr* ON: stack) Scarastac (Admiralty 1865) Scarastac (Heathcote 1900 map)

Sunadal ? dale (? and *dalr* ON: dale. Taylor 1967, 144) Sunadail (Heathcote 1900 map) Coates rejects Sun Valley (*sunnudalr*) and suggests Vertigo Slope from *sundl* Icelandic: vertigo and *hallr* ON: slope

Tigh Stallar Stallar's House: ? Steward's House or Smuggling House (*taigh* G: house; *stallari* ON: king's marshal or similar officer: Taylor 1967, 132; or from *taigh stail* G: a distillery or smuggling bothy and therefore a secret, hidden house) or House of the Overhanging Rock or Crag (Stalla G: overhanging rock, lofty precipice) Taigh Stallir Stallir-House (Martin 1697) Stallir's house (Adv ms 33.3.20) Staller, or the man of the rocks (MacAulay 1764) Stal house (Atkinson 1831) Tigh a Stalair: bed spaces called: Rastalla, Ralighe, Beran, Shimidaran, Leaba nan Con, or the dog's bed, Leaba an tealich, or the Fireside bed; Bar Righ was the name of the door (Kennedy [1862] 1874) Taigh an Stallir (Sands 1878) Staller's Ho. (Heathcote 1900 map)

Rastalla Stallar's Mound or Fort (*rath* G: fortress, artificial mound or barrow, and Stallar)

Ralighe ? (? connected with *laighe* G: lying, reclining Coates 1990, 77)

Beran Cranny (*beàrn* G: fissure, crevice Coates 1990, 77)

Shimidaran obscure

Leaba nan Con The Dogs' Bed (*leabaidh* G: bed, couch; *cù* G: dog)

Leaba an tealich The Fireside Bed (*leabaidh* G: bed, couch; *teallach* G: hearth, fireplace)

Bar Righ Top of the Bothy (*bàrr* G: top; *righe* G: sheiling, bothy)

Udraclete Outer Cliff (*útarr* ON: outer; *klettr* ON: cliff, rock)

Stac an Armuinn The Warrior's Stack or The Hero's Stack (*stakkr* ON: stack; *àrmunn* G: hero, warrior, brave man) or possibly Steward's Stack (*ármadr* ON: steward (MacLennan 1979, Coates 1990, 63) Stack-Narmin/Armin (Martin 1697 text and map) Stack N'armin (Martin 1703) Stack na Armin (Adv ms 33.3.20) Stack-in-Armin/Armin (MacAulay 1764) Stack narmin (Campbell 1799) Stack Narmen (?Campbell 1799) Stack an armin (MacCulloch 1819) Stackanarmin/Stack-an-armin (Atkinson 1831) Stac-an-armin (MacLean 1838) Stackinarmin (Anon pre 1840) Stack-an-armin (MacKenzie [1830-43] 1911) Stack Narmin (MacGillivray 1842) Stack Narnin (Wilson 1842) Stacharumil (Kennedy [1862] 1874) Stac and Armin (Admiralty 1865) Stack-an-Armin (Seton 1878) Stack Armin (Sands 1878) Stack Anarmu (Murray 1886) Stack 'n Armin (Ross 1889) Stack-an-Armin (Steele Elliott 1895) Stac an Armin (Heathcote 1900 and map) Stack an Armine (MacLachlan 1906-9)

Am Biran The Spike (*bioran* G: stick, staff, sharp pointed thing)

Rubha Bhriste [Rudh Bhriste Mathieson 1928] Broken Point (*rudha* G: point of land, promontory; *briste* G: broken)

Stac Lee ? Sea Stack or Water Stack or Grey Stack (*stakkr* ON: stack; *lì* G: colour, hue, water, the sea; *liath* G: grey) Stack-Ly/Stakley (Martin 1697 text and map) Lij/Stakley (MacAulay 1764) Stack-ley (Campbell 1799) Stac Lii (MacCulloch 1819) Lee Rock (MacDonald 1822) Stack Lea (Atkinson 1831) Leey (Anon pre 1840) Stacklia (MacKenzie [1830-43] 1911) Stac-lia, the hoary rock (MacLean 1838, 3) Stack Ly (MacGillivray 1842) Stack Leath/Stack Ly (Wilson 1842) Stac Lii (Admiralty 1865) Stack Lii – (Leathad) (Seton 1878) Stack Lee (Murray 1886) Stack Ly (Ross 1889) Stack Li (Steele Elliott 1895) Stack Lee (Kearton 1897) Stac Lii (Heathcote 1900 and map)

Geo Lee Sea Cleft or Water Cleft or Grey Cleft (or Cleft of Stac Lee) (*gjá* ON: cleft; *lì* G: colour, hue, water, sea; *liath* G: grey)

Rubha Langa [Rudh Langa Mathieson 1928] Long Point or Point of the Guillemot (*rudha* G: point of land, promontory; *langa* ON: long or possibly *langach* G: guillemot)

Unlocated Names

Names of Chapels or Churches

St Brianan (Martin 1697) St Brianns (Adv ms 33.3.20) Brendan's temple – in gaelic Brianan (MacAulay 1764) St Brianan (Clarke 1794) St Brianan's (MacDonald 1822) Kilbrinan (Anon pre 1840) church dedicated to 'Brenan' (MacKenzie [1830-43] 1911) St Brimmin (Wilson 1842) St Brendan (Muir 1861) Brendan (Sands 1878)

Christ's Chapel Christ Chapel/Christ's Chappel/Christ Church (Martin 1697) Christ's Church (Adv ms 33.3.20) Christ's church (MacAulay 1764) Christ's Church (?Campbell 1799) Christ's Church (MacDonald 1822) church dedicated to Mary (MacKenzie [1830-43] 1911) Cill-chriosd (MacLean 1838) St Mary (Wilson 1842: info probably from MacKenzie) Christ Church (Muir 1861) Teampull na Trionaid (Kennedy [1862] 1874) Christ (Sands 1878)

St Columba (Martin 1697) St Columbs (Adv ms 33.3.20) Columbcille (MacAulay 1764) St Columba (Muir 1861) Columba (Sands 1878)

St Peters (Adv ms 33.3.20)

St Johns (Adv ms 33.3.20)

St Clemens (Adv ms 33.3.20)

Names of Fields

Multus Agris (Martin 1697); Multum agria (MacAulay 1764) Tilled earth or barren earth (*mold* ON: earth-mould; *akri* ON: tilled ground; *magr* ON: barren. Taylor 1967, 128)

Multa Terra (Martin 1716); Multum taurus (MacAulay 1764) Dry earth or Turf soil (*mold* ON earth-mould; *purr* ON: dry. Taylor 1967, 128; and *torv* Faroese: turf: Coates 1990, 151)

Multum favere or Multum fodere (MacAulay 1764) Fair earth (*mold* ON: earth mould; *fagr* ON: fair: Taylor 1967, 128)

Queen o Scot (MacAulay 1764) Enclosure at…possibly the hollow or nook (*kvín á* ON: enclosure at; Taylor 1967, 128; *skot* Icelandic: nook or *skúti* Faroese: sheltered hollow: Coates 1990, 152)

Land dotteros or the Doctor's ground (MacAulay 1764) Possibly Daughter's land or Land of the Rent or Rift (*land* ON: land; *dóttir* ON daughter: Taylor 1967, 128 or *dottur*: rent, tear: Coates 1990, 149)

Lan-phalin or Paul's division (MacAulay 1764) Possibly Paul's land, or slumped land (*land* ON: land; *dóttir* ON: daughter: Taylor 1967, 129 or *dottur*: rent, tear: Coates 1990, 149) Possibly implies an enclosure (*lann* G: enclosure, especially a religious one; Iain Fraser pers comm 1991)

Other Names not on Mathieson's Map

Hirte

Baradh nan Glacha (Ross 1889) Ridge of the Gulleys (bàrr G: top; glac G: hollow, valley, defile

Clach a' bhainne (Mathieson 1928 b) The Milk Stone (clach G: stone; bainne G: milk) (p 228)

Clach an eòlas (Sands 1878) Stone of Knowledge (clach G: stone; eòlas G: knowledge) (p 228)

Conirdan Conirdan (Martin 1697)

Cop Caillach (Heathcote 1900 map) Point of the Old Woman (*gob* G: beak, mouth, point; *cailleach* G: woman, old woman, spinster) *see* Gob Chathaill

Creag-an-airgid from *creag*, a rock, an, prep. airgiod, silver – the sheep-silver or mica (MacLean 1838, 3) Craiganarrogitch: silver craig (Wilson 1842, 67)

gnocan sithichean 'green mounds looked upon as the abodes of fairies scattered in arable land' (MacKenzie [1830-43] 1911) Fairy Hillocks (*cnoc* G: hill, knoll; *sithiche* G: fairy, elf)

(Landing place) Lech (Anon pre 1840) Slab (*leac* G: flag, slab, flat stone) The Saddle (Landing rock, village bay) (Adv ms 33.3.20) (MacAulay 1764)

Lasgol (Heathcote 1900 map) obscure: refers to Giasgeir

Leathadmor (Heathcote 1900 map) Big Broad Slope (*leathad* G: hill side, slope, broad slope; *mór* G: large, great)

Liani-nin-ore (plain of spells) (MacAulay 1764) (*lian* G: plain, field; *or* G: prayer, petition, incantation)

The Mistress Stone The Mistress Stone (Martin 1697) Lover's Stone (Morgan 1861) Mistress' Stone – also referred to as Lover's Stone and equated by Connell with Stac Biorrach (Connell 1887) Lover's Stone (Kearton 1897) p 229)

Oshval Point (Ross 1889)

Pollnaneug? (Anon pre 1840) Pool of Death or Pool of the Spectres (*poll* G: hole, pool; *eug* G: death, ghost, spectre) or Pool of the Notch (*poll* G: hole, pool; *eag* G:nick, notch, gap; Iain Fraser pers comm 1991)

Poll na Ban-tighearna (Sands 1878) The Lady's Pool (*poll* G: hole, pool; *baintighearna* G: lady, gentlewoman) (pp 51, 90–91, 166)

Rathad nan Each – a pass at the Cambir (MacGregor 1931) Track of the Horses or Path of the Horses (*rathad* G: road, way, path; *each* G: horse)

Stronabec? (Anon pre 1840) Small Point (*sròn* G: nose, promontory; *beag* G: little, short, small)

Tobar-Cholla (MacLean 1838) Tobar Cholla (Kennedy [1862] 1874) Coll's Well (*tobar* G: well, spring; and Coll) see Rudha Cholla and (pp 231)

Well of youth Well of Youth (Martin 1697) Well of youth (Atkinson 1831) Tobir na h'oige (MacGillivray 1842) Tobair na h'-oige (Sands 1878) (*tobar* G: well, spring; *òige* G: youth) (p 236)

Uamh Baidh (Heathcote 1900 map) Cave of the Bay (*uaimh* G: cave, den; *bàgh* G: bay, harbour)

Uamh Cruaidh (Heathcote 1900 map) Difficult Cave (possibly the same as Geo Chruadalian] (*uaimh* G: cave, den; *cruaidh* G: hard, difficult, distressing)

Dun

Sean Tigh (Sands 1878) Old House (*sean* G: old, aged, ancient; *taigh* G: house)

Sgòr (Connell 1887) Rock (*sgòr* G: concealed rock jutting into the sea, steep slope on another hill)

Soay

Laidh (Heathcote 1900 map)

Blath Stac (Heathcote 1900 map) for Am Plastair

Boreray

Boreray Caolas Sound of Boreray (Kennedy [1862] 1874)